RSL
Oct 1976

A HISTORY OF MAGIC,
WITCHCRAFT AND OCCULTISM

W. B. CROW

Dr. W. B. Crow was born near London in 1895. He served in the Army, Royal Naval Airforce and Royal Navy during the First World War, after which he lectured H.M. Forces. Dr. Crow is a Dip.Sci. and a Ph.D. of the University of London and a M.Sc. of both London and Wales Universities. He also has degrees and doctorates from foreign universities. He has lectured in biology as Head of the Department and Senior Lecturer in several technical colleges since 1919. He has published works on medical, psychological and occult subjects, and is a Fellow of various medical, scientific and occult societies.

W. B. CROW

A HISTORY OF
MAGIC, WITCHCRAFT
AND OCCULTISM

First published in Great Britain in 1968 by
The Aquarian Press
Copyright © W. B. Crow, 1968
First Abacus edition 1972
Reprinted October 1973

ISBN 0 349 10640 1

*Printed in Great Britain by Hazell Watson & Viney Ltd
Aylesbury, Bucks*

CONTENTS

AUTHOR'S NOTE

The reader will find that names of historical personages, especially
Oriental and Ancient Egyptian ones, are given generally as they
have long appeared in English literature. I am fully aware that
more modern renderings have been proposed for many of them.

W. B. CROW

Woodford Green,
Essex.
May, 1968

INTRODUCTION

Scope of this Work. The present publication is entitled *a* history, and not *the* history of magic, witchcraft and occultism. The reader, we hope, will not expect to find herein a complete record of these subjects. To deal with them all fully would require several volumes. The task of covering the whole field in detail could have been reduced in one of two ways, *viz.* either by confining our studies to a particular country or to a particular period, on the one hand, or by selecting what appear to us as the outstanding features of the subject in all countries and periods, in other words to make a summary of the whole field. We have chosen to do the latter, partly because it does not appear to have been attempted before, partly because of our great interest in this manner of treatment. Our account also involves some attempt to correlate magic and cognate phenomena with many other human activities, as well as showing the inter-relationship of the various occult fields.

Magic and History. A story is told of a professor of history who resigned his post because he had come to the conclusion that history consists largely of lies. If history were merely the record of events one might exclude much that is not literally true, particularly in dealing with such a subject as magic. But there are the careful records of events, and there are also myths, legends and fairy-tales. We have tried to distinguish the two, but it is not at all easy. We have however included some of the mythological material, because we consider it to represent a poetical expression of important truths, making it clear, however, to the reader, where possible, the difference between an actual event as ascertained by historical research on the one hand and the well-known mythic tradition on the other. After all it is important to know, not only what happened, but also what people thought happened. In many cases it is quite impossible, at the present time, to tell in terms of physical events, exactly what took place. We have to be content with records.

Belief in Magic. This work may be read by many who do not

believe in magic, and it would lead us away from our topic, into philosophy, were we to present any apology for the belief. It is however, difficult, if not impossible, to take an impartial view of this subject. The phenomena are too widespread to be dismissed as delusion and fraud. Some of the events have been imitated by conjurors, but this does not mean that they have all been produced by trickery. And in this connection a protest must be raised against these self-avowed tricksters calling themselves magicians, or referring to their art as magic. The latter is far too serious a matter to be treated lightly, and it is doubtful whether a disbelief in magic, whether caused by demons or in some other way, is consonant with acceptance of the Catholic Faith.

What is magic? The word *magic* comes to us, through Latin and Greek, from a Persian word meaning the work of the priests or wise men. Such activity was and is done for the benefit of mankind. But the word has altered its significance, and is now usually applied to acts of a selfish or even harmful kind. Many authors distinguish such as *black magic.* The latter, however, is very frequently a parody or perversion of the work done by priests. Thus the *black mass* was a horrible parody and perversion of the holy sacrifice of the mass, the Eucharist, the chief of the seven sacraments of the Catholic Church. It is quite impossible to deal with magic, without mentioning the faith and practice of religion, with which it is connected throughout the greater part of history, and against which it so often stands in opposition.

Both *hierurgy* the work of priests, and black magic its opposite, use the principle of analogy. In the latter, however, its use is often crude and ineffective, as in that type of activity known as *sympathetic magic.* The latter is well exemplified in those well-known cases wherein, when it was desired to do harm to an individual, a wax image of that individual was made, and injuries were inflicted on the image. It was thought that the image, particularly if linked to the original by baptism or other ceremonial, was "in sympathy" with the individual, and a psychic link was forged.

Magic also makes use of imaginary or real phenomena, such as clairvoyance or telepathy, the nature of which, in recent years, has become the subject of psychic research.

Theories of Magic (1). Magic consists of primitive science. Astrology was primitive astronomy, and alchemy was primitive chemistry, and so on with the other occult arts or sciences. These gradually threw off their superstitious features and became subject to the rules of inductive science laid down by Francis Bacon.

It is true that astronomy and astrology were formerly closely associated, as were alchemy and chemistry. But the occult subject in each case was based on analogy—in astrology the analogy of the planetary positions with earthly affairs, in alchemy the relation of chemical transformations with psychological events. It is these occult aspects which have been thrown off by modern science, and that they are superstitions is a minority opinion, although widely spread at the present day among western people who have not had the opportunity of acquaintance with other cultures, especially those of the past.

(2) Magic is due to *hypnotism* or *suggestion*. In many cases we can bring magic into connection with so-called hypnotic phenomena, or can see its similarity with effects of suggestion. But as no satisfactory theory has ever been put forward to explain either suggestion or hypnotism this is merely translating one unknown into terms of another.

(3) Another theory of black magic or rather of witchcraft which has become widespread in recent years is that it represents the pagan element repressed by Christianity, rather in the same way that dreams are believed by Freudian psychologists to express repressed wishes. The absurdity of this theory should be obvious to all, since black magic and witchcraft were well known and detested for thousands of years among the pagan Greeks and Romans, not to mention still older civilisations.

What is Witchcraft? The identification of the witch-cult with that of the pagan goddess Diana was put forward by the Italian G. Tartarotti in 1749 on the basis of certain allusions in mediaeval literature of witchcraft, especially an account by Reginò (10th century). It has been upheld by certain English authors. The matter will be discussed later.

Witchcraft was rather a perversion of religion, a form of black magic, carried out by people, often, but by no means always, in a humble station in life, and having, as we would now say, an inferiority complex. It was not a question of upholding a different religion to the prevailing, but a deliberate perverting of this religion, a sort of turning it upside down. In most cases they made, or imagined they made, some sort of compact with a devil, and went about deliberately in the pursuit of mischief. However further details will appear in the body of this work.

What is Occultism? The word *occult* means hidden. Under the general term *occultism* we group a number of subjects that are not taught today in schools, colleges or universities. They include theosophy, anthroposophy, the kabalah, the gnosis, Rosicrucianism, the study of the Yi-King and the Tarot, alchemy, astrology, spiritualism, some forms of dream-interpretation, rhabdomancy (divining-rod phenomena), radiesthesia (pendulum phenomena), prophecy, divination, oracles, evocation of spirits, lycanthropy (transformation of human beings into animals), vampirism, demonology, sorcery, numerology, yoga, physiognomy, cheirognomy, phrenology and graphology. There are also occult aspects of certain other subjects, e.g. heraldry. These subjects are occult, simply because they are, in fact, hidden from the majority. It was not always so. Astrology, for instance, was taught, with astronomy in the universities until about 1800. Many of the earlier professors of this subject issued annual predictions, rather on the lines of present day Old Moore's Almanac, but much more dignified, and taken more seriously by the educated public. It would be better to call these subjects *arcane sciences* to signify that they are secret rather than unknown. They are, in fact, studied carefully by a few, but today the number of people who take them seriously is a small but not inappreciable minority.

In conclusion, acknowledgements and thanks are due to the following:

Those members of public bodies who have been kind enough to aid my researches:

The Librarian, Zoological Society of London,
The Librarian and the General Secretary of the Theosophical Society in England,
The Research Secretary, Society of Psychical Research,
The Secretary, British Israel World Federation.

Those relatives and friends who have answered queries, commented on the manuscript or read the proofs.

CHAPTER I

THE CAVE MEN

Ape-Men and Men. All the human beings living in the world today belong to a single species (*Homo sapiens* Linnaeus). That means all existing races can interbreed freely. This species, according to the view of modern biologists, has existed very roughly for about half a million years. During the greater part of that time, during the *Pleistocene,* the period of the great ice ages in the Northern hemisphere, which corresponds with the great cultural period known as the Old Stone Age (*Palaeolithic*), there existed on the face of this earth several other species which we can call *ape-men.* Without going into details which interest the biologists, we can say there were many different kinds, that some were spread over the whole of the Old World, and that, although of varied characteristics, they were all, on the whole, more like men than are the existing anthropoid apes (chimpanzee, orang-utan, gorilla and gibbon). Unlike apes they walked more or less erect.

Some of these ape-men used fire, and in fact it seems possible that fire was used by extinct man-like apes (*Australopithecus*), in Africa. These differed very little from the anthropoid apes of today, although in some respects they were more human.

Giants and Ogres. The most primitive ape-men, as distinct from man-like apes, have been found in Java. The earliest was discovered long ago (Dubois, 1892) and is the famous *Pithecanthropus.* Nearly as primitive are the remains found near Pekin (*Sinanthropus*) and these belonged to a species that certainly knew how to use fire, as remains of hearths are associated.[1] Two other types: *Gigantopithecus* of China and *Meganthropus* of Java are known from teeth, and if these were in proportion they were truly of enormous size. In fact the former is estimated to have been twice as large as a large gorilla.[2]

[1] W. E. Le Gros Clarke: *History of the Primates,* 2nd Ed., Brit. Mus., London, 1950.
[2] F. Weidenreich: *Apes, Giants and Man,* Chicago, 1946. Two lower jaw-bones of *Gigantopithecus* have recently been discovered.

In Europe, and probably of later date, and certainly contemporary with existing man, are more human-like species, the most abundant belonging to so-called Neanderthal man (*Palaeanthropus neanderthalensis*). This creature was no larger than man, but had a brain in which the sense-centres were more prominent than those connected with thought, when compared with the existing species. It was a powerful muscular creature, with stooping posture and lumbering gait. There are indications that it fought with mankind, used well fashioned flint weapons, axes and knives, threw balls of flint from slings, fastened points of bone to spears and darts, scraped skins for rough clothing, buried the dead with weapons and ornaments, even painted them with ochre, and had some sort of cult in which a bear was sacrificed. It was associated with a culture known as *Mousterian*. It probably had a somewhat limited kind of language. Neanderthal man exactly fulfils the rôle ascribed to ogres in fairy tales. The stories of Jack the Giant-killer would seem to come very near to the literal truth.

Both early true man and Neanderthal man lived in caves, although the former no doubt learned to build huts at an early stage. Both lived by hunting, and with the aid of fire were enabled to live near the margin of the ice-cap during the Ice Age. They followed the mammoth, the reindeer, the wild horse and the bison.

Cro-Magnon Race. The first true men at present known are described as belonging to the Cro-Magnon race and their remains are found chiefly in Western Europe. They were very fine specimens of humanity, to judge from the bones and associated artifacts. Broca long ago reported that their skull-content considerably exceeds that of modern European man. The average height of the men was six feet one and a half inches (more than six inches above the modern British average). They had broad shoulders, and arms short as compared with the legs (just the reverse of the apes), with thin nose, prominent cheek-bones, and chin massive (apes have no chin, although their jaws may be heavy).

There is no doubt that the *Aurignacean* culture was that of the Cro-Magnon race. They appear to have dressed in skins, although necklets and even mantles of shells may have been worn on ceremonial occasions. They had complex sacrificial rituals, highly developed arts, advanced knowledge of human anatomy and of zoology[3]

[3] Thus in their paintings it is possible to distinguish two species of bear and three races of horses.

acquired in hunting, idols of goddesses compared by Osborn with the work of modern cubists, the head-dresses of some of the god-desses being comparable, according to Breuil, with those of ancient Egypt. Their art, according to Spence, was far superior to that of the early ancient Egyptian.

The Aurignacean culture was more or less replaced in Europe by the Solutrean from the East. The Solutrean in its turn was super-seded by the Magdalenian, which seems to have been an efflor-escence of the Aurignacean, which it undoubtedly resembles.

The Magdalenians were of Cro-Magnon race. Their art compares with the best of Egypt and Babylon. According to Osborn they lived in a highly differentiated society in which each man worked in a particular profession or trade. There were priests, médicine-men, chieftains, hunters of big game, fishermen, flint-workers, dressers of hides, makers of clothing and footwear, makers of orna-ments, engravers, sculptors in wood, bone, ivory and stone, and artists with colour and brush.

Cult of the Caves. The Magdalenians lived either in natural caves that did not extend very far into the rock, or at the mouths of much more extensive ones. In warm weather they may have used huts. They sometimes made paintings on rock faces, and occasion-ally in their homes. But it is only in the recesses, deep in the rock, far from the entrance, that their art reaches its highest expression. These cave paintings are not represented in Britain, as Solutreans and Magdalenians never invaded this country. But they are numerous in France and Spain where thousands of examples have now been recorded. At first no one would believe that such art was the work of the Old Stone Age, until a cave was discovered, which was blocked up with undisturbed rubbish containing artifacts which were undoubtedly palaeolithic.

The difficulty of access to these caves has been graphically described by G. R. Levy[4] with the aid of diagrams. At Montespan she tells us, it requires three hours to reach the pictures.

The Cave-Pictures. The paintings include (i) inanimate designs, (ii) human figures, and (iii) animals. The last are by far the most numerous and conspicuous. They are mostly very well done and, for a reason that will appear later, sometimes painted over several times.

The animals include the lion, brown bear, cave bear, reindeer.

[4] *The Gate of Horn,* London, 1948.

bison, ibex, chamois, boar, horse, rhinoceros, mammoth and possibly the elephant. Some give anatomical details correctly, showing the heart and the muscles. Some are shown in traps, or wounded, with weapons attached, or surrounded with stones. These paintings are supposed to have aided, by sympathetic magic, the killing of such animals. Less frequently male and female animals are shown together; these are supposed to aid, in a similar way, the multiplication of the animals.

The human beings are mostly represented in what appears to be an attitude of worship, and are sometimes masked. This humble attitude has been connected with the belief of primitives that no animal ought to be killed unless its soul be willing; when a species is decimated permission to kill is withdrawn by the group-soul of the species or race.

The Magdalenians, then, lived at the mouths of caves and resorted to the obscurity of the depths for magical purposes, viz. to ensure success in hunting, and at times to increase the fertility of certain species. There is some evidence that ritual dances were carried out : masked dancers are sometimes shown on the carved implements. By the way, the carvings on the weapons and ritual-objects are very similar to those on the walls of the caves.

The Great Mother. We have heard much from psychoanalysts and other depth-psychologists about the important psychological rôle of the mother, both for the individual and the race. Whilst there is no evidence for a matriarchy among Old Stone Age people we find that they made statuettes or small images of the female figure. These are remarkable because the head was almost or completely featureless, the legs and arms poorly developed, without hands or feet, or almost so, whilst the breast, hips, abdomen and buttocks are enormously exaggerated. The head was usually inclined forwards, and there was little or no clothing. These are supposed to represent the great mother goddess, which later appeared as Isis among the Egyptians and as Diana of the Ephesians. Some of the best known figures have been ascribed to Venus, but this is obviously incorrect. The emphasis is on maternity and the erotic element is nil.

Fate of the Cave Men. The period of the Magdalenians was the latter part of the last glaciation. They disappeared about 10,000 years ago, although still represented to some extent by the Eskimo, who retain some of their physical features, and certain cultural similarities (semi-domestication of the reindeer, harpooning of fish).

After the retreat of the ice European man did not suddenly pass into the *Neolithic* (to be described in our next chapter). There were several thousand years (8000 to 2500 B.C.) of which nothing at all was known until quite recently. This period is termed *Mesolithic*.

CHAPTER II

STARS AND SACRIFICES

A New Kind of Life. The *Neolithic* period (New Stone Age) did not begin in north-west Europe until about 2500 B.C. In Egypt and Mesopotamia its onset was much earlier. Perhaps in Egypt mankind passed directly from the Old Stone Age to the Bronze Age. Already in 6000 B.C. and possibly in 8000 B.C. all the inventions of the Neolithic were represented in Egypt, perhaps with additional features not found elsewhere. H. G. Wells[1] placed the beginning of the New Stone Age between as early as 12,000 B.C. to 20,000 B.C. In north-west Europe the Neolithic continued until 1800 B.C. when copper came into use.

The distinctive features of the Neolithic culture were agriculture, domestication of animals, pottery, polishing of flints, basket-work and textiles, mud-daub huts, tombs which were long burrows or cairns, the calendar and the sacrifice of the god-king in ritual drama. Whether the sacrifice was originally an actual one or not may be disputed. If it was not it degenerated into a real sacrifice among certain peoples.

Origin of the Constellations. Our knowledge of Neolithic cultures is much more complete than that of Palaeolithic. All over the world, and particularly among the natives of America, these cultures are still in existence, modified in externals it is true, but still with basic religious tendencies. It is therefore with some confidence that we can state that the sun, moon, planets, stars and star-groups are closely associated by them with both their mythology and the rituals of their religion.

The *fixed stars* which, of course are only apparently fixed in position as contrasted with the planets, are so numerous that it is necessary to group them in some way. Even today they are grouped in *constellations* which are arbitrary figures, mostly derived from the ancient world, with only minor alterations during the course of centuries. Most of these are labelled on our celestial globes with

[1] *A Short History of the World,* Middlesex, 1922.

names derived from Greek mythology, but with very little altera-
tion the same figures are found to be used in the ancient astronomy
of Egypt, India, Persia, Phoenicia, Chaldaea and Accadia as determined from their archaeological remains. Among the Chinese and
Tibetans other symbols were in use, but there are analogies. Most
of these cultures also had the twenty-seven or twenty-eight mansions
of the moon (which of course overlie the zodiacal constellations).
They were and are particularly used in the astrology of India,
Persia and Arabia. The Arabic system uses them almost
exclusively.

The majority of constellations in present-day use, then, are very
old. Forty-eight of them are catalogued by Ptolemy in his *Catalogue*,
A.D. 137, where he gives the latitude and longtitude of 1,022 fixed
stars. But a similar list of constellations without the star positions
was given by Aratus[2] in his *Phenomena* said to have been published[3] about 270 B.C. but containing information of much earlier
date.

In the far East, in Japan, China and Tibet a different set of
symbols was being crystallised. The twelve corresponding to the
zodiacal are: rat, ox, tiger, hare, dragon, snake, horse, sheep,
monkey, cock, dog, boar. Of these only the second is similar in
oriental and occidental lists. But the different symbols had a somewhat similar meaning in East and West.

The Zodiac. The zodiacal constellations are not the same as the
zodiac. The latter is the path through which the sun, moon and
planets appear to move. The sun takes one year and the moon takes
twenty-eight days to complete this circuit. The planets take other
periods. The zodiac is not now used in astronomy, but is of much
importance in astrology. The zodiac is divided in twelve equal
divisions called *signs*.[4] It is unfortunate that these signs are named
after the twelve zodiacal constellations, with which they once coincided. Owing to the movement known as the *precession of the
Equinox* the zodiac is gradually shifting backwards through the
constellations. The point of the spring equinox, with which the
zodiac begins (0° Aries) is now in the constellation Pisces. The

[2] Aratus makes the *Pleiades* a separate constellation from the Bull, he also
lacks *Equuleus*, otherwise he agrees with Ptolemy, and both make forty-
eight in all, probably for symbolic reasons. See R. Brown: *The Phainomena
or Heavenly Display of Aratos*, London, 1885.

[3] E. W. Maunder: *The Astronomy of the Bible*, 3rd edition, London, 1909.

[4] The names of the signs are given later, see page 181.

zodiacal signs coincided with the constellations at about the time of Christ. Authorities are not agreed about the date; some make it up to 200 years later or earlier. Astrology as we know it in the West today can scarcely be earlier than the date of this coincidence, but it must be remembered that even today there are several distinct systems of astrology.

CHAPTER III

WITCH-DOCTORS AND MEDICINE-MEN

Animism. This term is derived from the word *anima*, the soul, and has been used in philosophy for the belief in souls and in anthropology, following E. B. Tylor[1] for the belief, ascribed by this school of thought to primitive man, that men have souls or spirits, that spirits of animals, plants and what we term inanimate objects exist, such spirits being contacted by man in dreams and visions. It is further thought by many animists that the spirits can and do leave the body, and that magic is wrought by their means.

The spirits include the souls of the dead, and various nature spirits and gods. Of course, in a wide sense, the word *animism* would cover all the higher religions, but it is only applied to those people who have no definite idea of a Supreme Being, and although they are still sometimes called primitives, it is now recognised that this is to some extent because they are not understood by European investigators.

After this theory of animism had been established other anthropologists, notably Marett[2] and Preuss,[3] discovered amongst these peoples a concept which they thought might be even more primitive than that of the soul, *viz.* a mysterious magical force or power, believed to exist in certain individuals, and responsible for many remarkable and wondrous happenings. This is called *mana* from a Melanesian word, but the same idea is expressed by *wakan* (Sioux) and *orenda* (Iroquois) among the natives of America. It is not surprising that psychoanalysts have taken cognizance of this belief, have shown its relation to hypnotism, and have attempted to relate it to their clinical findings. In particular the work of Roheim[4] is most detailed in this respect.

Mana or its equivalent is supposed to be possessed (i) by the dead,

[1] *Anthropology*, new ed. Lond., 1892; *Primitive Culture*, 4th ed., 2 vols., Lond., 1903.

[2] R. R. Marett: Pre-animistic Religion, *Folk-Lore*, 1900, and *The Theshold of Religion*, 1909.

[3] K. Th. Preuss: Urspruung der Religion und Kunst, *Globus* lxxxvi, 1904.

[4] G. Roheim: *Animism, Magic and the Divine King*, London, 1930.

and their earthly remains, (ii) by those who can communicate with the departed, by means of certain stones and other objects, such as the *chirungas* of the Australians, (iii) by priests and medicine-men, (iv) by chiefs and (v) by members of certain secret societies. It enables priests to communicate with the gods, and to control spirits. It makes the houses and property of priests and chiefs taboo. It enables the sorcerer or witch to cause disease or other troubles by supernatural means, but it also enables the good medicine-man to cure illness and remove evils. It gives chiefs and kings[5] their right to rule. It gives initiates of secret societies certain powers and privileges.

The medicine-man, like the modern spirit medium, could communicate with the dead, and bring messages from them. Like the medieval necromancer he claimed, however, power to control the spirits of the dead, and even other entities. Disease, it was thought, in the animistic view of the world, was due to the soul leaving the body, and its replacement by another entity. Efforts were made by the medicine man to bring the soul back, and to remove the entity in possession. Emphasis was sometimes placed on one of these processes rather than the other, but both are implied. Medicines capable of driving out the evil entity possess *mana*, but probably only in the hands of a medicine-man. That, at least, is so in Fiji, as recorded by Roheim.[6] The healing process, however, is more often effected by massage, cauterisation, scarification, puncture, trephining, bleeding, cupping and most frequently of all sucking.[7] After preliminary practices, sometimes an elaborate ritual, and a long bout of sucking, the operator sometimes triumphantly displays some sort of object, which is said to contain the spirit that is the cause of the trouble. The removed objects may be quartz crystals (Australia), needles and bits of wood (Borneo), pebbles, chicken's claws, feathers, bones and sticks (Africa) and even worms or snakes (S. America).

The medicine-man always had a *magic wand*. This was always consecrated, sometimes with very terrible ceremonies.[8] The chief often had a *sceptre*. Wands and sceptres were often very beautiful

---

[5] To kings also is ascribed healing power, hence *royal touch* which survived until relatively recent times; for the special powers of kings in magic, see Roheim, *loc. cit.*

[6] *loc. cit.*

[7] This, of course, gives the psychoanalysts a lot to talk about, see Roheim, *loc. cit.*

[8] See Roheim, *loc. cit.*, p. 128, where the murder of a child is described with revolting details, designed, it is thought, to place the spirit of the victim in the wand. But such cruelty is probably very rare.

objects. In Polynesia it was often the ivory of the narwhal, a creature of the whale family in which the male has a single very long tooth. In America and Polynesia head-dresses of horns and feathers were used, the kinds denoting rank. The dresses were the skins of sheep, American buffalo, deer and other animals, decorated with horns, claws, porcupine quills and feathers of creatures taken in the chase. In Polynesia beautiful robes of tapa-cloth are worn; this was and is obtained from the bark of a tree of the mulberry family. Feathered robes were worn by the chiefs and kings of Tahiti and Hawaii. The feathers were obtained from three birds of the Hawaiian honey-sucker family. One kind was of red plumage, another yellow, the latter being regarded as superior. But the King of Hawaii possessed a robe the tippet of which was exclusively of orange feathers, and these were obtained from another bird, which only had a few feathers of this colour, in two tufts near the wings. The sole remaining example of such a cloak is preserved in the Bernice Pauahi Bishop Museum at Honolulu.[9] S. Sitwell tells[10] us it was formed during nine successive reigns.

The smoking of tobacco is believed to have originated among the natives of America, and was a ceremony practised by the medicine-men. The *calumet* or tobacco-pipe was a ritual object of importance, and its use was surrounded by a number of taboos. Eventually this object became very decorative, and was sometimes presented to visitors as a mark of high honour ("pipe of peace"), but the original use was largely connected with healing, by way of complex rituals.

Fetishism. This flourishes in many parts of Africa, particularly in the Congo. The name was introduced[11] into the study of comparative religion in 1760 when Portuguese traders from West Africa reported that the natives paid a certain kind of devotion to relatively insignificant material objects, usually prepared or manufactured in some way, and which were called by the Portuguese name *feitiço,* derived from the Latin *factitius* meaning fabricated, This referred to small cut stones, shells and other articles such as we now term *amulets.* Anthropologists studying the region adopted the name, but found they had to extend it, since the same attitude is taken up to articles that are not manufactured. Possibly what the originator of the term had in mind was not *manufacture,* but *making magic.* Psychiatrists finally took over the word to indicate

9 *Handbook to the Ethnographical Collections,* Brit. Mus., 1925, p. 167.
10 De Brosses: *Du Culte des Dieux fétiches,* 1760.
11 S. Sitwell: *Primitive Scenes and Festivals,* London, 1942.

a perversion in which sexual excitement is caused by some trivial object, usually an article of clothing.

It is the anthropological usage that is of most interest here, and we need not discuss whether it has any connection with the psychiatric. Most Africans have an idea of a Supreme God, and of other spirits, but in those regions where fetishism prevails there seems to be a strong sense of veneration in each individual for a particular object which he regards as his *fetish*, and which is accepted by the community as such. The fetish is purchased from, or is given by, a *witch-doctor*. The fetish protects the individual in every way, not by itself, of course, for it is only a trivial object, but because of the spiritual or psychological power put into it. This power must be constantly renewed and in the lower Congo this is regularly done by sacrifices. An animal such as a goat or fowl is killed, and its blood is shed on the fetish. A pig does not seem to be used, as this animal is regarded as unclean (*cf.* Jews, Moslems). The sacrifice must be made at the proper hour and on the appropriate day. Sometimes the fetish has to be taken back to the witch-doctor, if it is not doing its work, which is to keep its owner well and happy. The witch-doctor has various ways of treating refractory fetishes.

The natives of Africa do not use the term fetish, but have several other names, the best known of which is *ju-ju*. They regard fetishes as medicine, using that term for the cure, not only of disease, but of all other evils. The fetish may consist of a single flint, a fossil or any stone of curious shape. It may be made by carving a figure, often human, but sometimes grotesque. It may be decorated in many ways. Sometimes nails are driven in, usually for a particular purpose. Sometimes the fetish is, or contains, a receptacle for a medicine. Very many substances are used for the latter purpose, often in powdered form : roots, leaves, flowers, fruits and seeds of herbs, shrubs and trees; the barks, woods and resins of trees, the roots, leaves and stems of climbing plants, the hairs, claws and teeth of certain animals, the feathers of birds, the heads of snakes, lizards, turtles, frogs and fish, bones of many sorts, various viscera of animals, notably hearts, brains and livers, gall and dung, also salt and many mineral powders. Parts of the pig are never used, nor those of the male human subject. Human milk occurs occasionally.

The fetish, unlike an idol, is a personal possession, and is only of use to its owner, like the Catholic rosary.

African Witchcraft. To thorough-going believers in fetishism, all evils : worry, sorrow, disease, even death are caused by bewitchment involving some individual, some spirit and some fetish. The world would be happy but for evil spirits and those wicked people who act as their agents.

Although the same power is supposed to be used for good and evil, it must not be imagined that the main work of the witch-doctor is causing trouble. On the contrary their chief employment is the removal of the numerous ills that afflict the community.

Voodoo. Haiti is a country occupying the western third of a large island of the West Indies, in the rest of which lies the Dominican Republic. Unlike that of the latter, the population is negro, many, however, with a mixture of white blood. Their ancestors were originally transported from West Africa. Although now and for a large part of its history independent, Haiti was at one time under French rule, and a French dialect, known as Creole, is widespread. Under French influence a large proportion of the population were converted to Catholicism. However, some of them amalgamated certain features of their African religion with Catholic practices and the resulting system, known as Voodoo, although now illegal and discredited, has been a cause of conflict with white settlers.

Various derivations have been given for the word *Voodoo*, but there is no doubt that it is merely a word from one of the dialects spoken in Dahomey, denoting the moral and religious life of the race that speak that particular dialect.[12]

As to Voodoo most revolting rites have been ascribed, it may be worth while to point out that W. B. Seabrook, who is very well acquainted with it from much personal experience[13] actually defends it as a religion. There is a good deal of bloodshed however, but it is fair to mention that it in no way involves intentional blasphemy, and that the presence of the Crucifix is far from being dishonoured as in rites of devil-worship and the Black Mass to be described later. It seems that Jesus, Mary and a number of Christian saints have been mingled with the African pantheon, and their images are found together with those of clearly African origin. There is a hierarchy of priests, at any rate two ranks corresponding with ordinary priest and bishop, but they also have priestesses, who apparently perform some rather different functions from those of

[12] For details and reference see W. B. Seabrook : *The Magic Island*, London, 1929, p. 276. This book contains a very full account of Voodoo and cognate subjects.

[13] *Loc. cit.*

the priests, including ritual dances. There are a number of minor ceremonies including the baptism of drums, comparable with the so-called baptism of bells in the Catholic religion. But the main act of the religion is the sacrifice of animals : fowls, doves, turkeys, goats and, on some important occasions, bulls. The pig is never used. The original sacrifice was no doubt human. Seabrook[14] describes one important ceremony when, after a number of small animals had been sacrificed, a girl was brought in, clothed only in a shift. She began to lament and a goat was placed beside her. Finally the goat was killed, by a sudden stroke to its neck, the girl fainted, and both the goat's body and the unconscious girl were carried out.

Another phenomenon, described by this author, is the sudden possession of one of the natives. A poor member of the community falls into a trance, is vested and regarded as a god. He proceeds to an altar, where he consumes certain sacrificial foods and drinks, and then makes a number of prophetic pronouncements, after the congregation have sung the appropriate hymns. Finally he reverts into sleep, and becomes an ordinary man again.

Zombies. Another phenomenon associated loosely with the Voodoo cult is the existence of the famous *zombies.* These work in the plantations, and carry out simple uninteresting duties. They show no signs of intelligence or feeling, they are undoubtedly in a coma-tose state. They are said to be dead persons, revitalised to some extent soon after death, and utilised in this peculiar way. Because natives of Haiti believe in this possibility, they often watch the graves of their newly buried dead for several days, until decay has advanced, for they hold that until this happens they can be dug up and made into zombies. In the criminal code of the Republic of Haiti, reference is made to the possibility of throwing a person into a prolonged lethargic coma, and to persons buried in this state. Seabrook[15] thinks the explanation is connected with this.

Shamanism. A group of remarkable phenomena, akin to animism, but presenting special features, so that another name is justified, is found in Siberia among the natives, such as the Tunguses, Ostyaks and Samoyedes, whilst a very similar system was formerly met with among the Eskimo, and there are other similarities among many of

14 *Loc. cit.*
15 *Loc. cit.,* p. 103.

the native red races of North America. In its typical form this system is called *Shamanism*, and we will attempt to outline its distinctive features.

Some of these tribes have an exogamic clan organisation, in others any clan development is weak. But they all acknowledge a special class in the community. A member of this special group may be male or female, and is termed a *shaman*. The word is of Tungus origin, and has come to us through Russia. A shaman finds it easy to pass into a state of communion with the spirit world, but unlike any spirit medium he has a remarkable control over spirits, many of which are attached to him, and serve to do his will.

Divination. Nearly all peoples have methods of divination, and these methods are exceedingly diverse. All the great religions condemn fortune-telling, and forbid any divination which suggests to the individual that his free-will is incapable of influencing what is about to happen. But apart from this it is admitted that the tendencies and inclinations may be pre-determined, so that divination is not always classed among the black arts, although much depends on the way it is done. It is nearly always dangerous.

Divination is effected in two ways *viz.* (i) by direct vision, as when a seer, in a dream or trance, or by gazing in a crystal, has a mental picture of something that may happen in the future or a feeling or impulsion of some sort, (ii) by analogy, as when a chance arrangement of certain symbolic objects, such as numbered or pictured cards laid out on a table, or tea-leaves inside a tea-cup represent a certain psychological situation, or a particular set of tendencies and events, that can be interpreted if one knows the rules applying to that particular form of symbolism. This section deals only with the second kind of divination.

In classical Rome a special order of soothsayers called *haruspices*[16] existed, for the purpose of divination from the sacrificial beasts. They observed the animal before its immolation, inspected the entrails, particularly the liver, after it had been sacrificed, they also noted the way in which the flames consumed it, and the quality of the incense, wine, meal and water accompanying the flesh. The haruspices were established by Romulus, therefore, near the time of the foundation of the city. They were trained from more ancient schools, and we now know that the *extispicium* or *haruspication*, as it was called, existed among the Etruscans, Greeks, Chaldeans and

16 Sing. *haruspex.*

Egyptians in still earlier times. A clay model of a liver,[17] with more than a dozen parts distinguished is almost certainly connected with this·practice, and is believed to have belonged to a Babylonian Temple School *circa* 2000 B.C.

Divination was also made from observation of parts of the human body,[18] from movements and positions assumed in ritualistic dances, and even from laughter. The dead human body was everywhere particularly favoured in black magic and witchcraft all over the world. We even meet with the use of parts of the body for the healing of disease.

The symbolic use of all kinds of artificial objects in divination is also universal. Simple dots made on the ground or on paper may serve, as in *geomancy*. Flat rods thrown down, with different markings on the two sides are the basis of a number of systems, including that embodied in the *Yi-King* of the Chinese. This may derive from the throwing down of arrows. Axes, swords, daggers and other weapons were used in the same way. All were thrown on the ground and their positions in relation to one another and to the cardinal points were noted. Keys, cups, rings and other objects were used. Foods of various kinds, especially wine were examined in various ways. The residues or dregs were sometimes inspected, after the manner of our present day superstitious divination by means of tea-leaves or coffee-grounds. Dice were thrown, cards were laid out, the *Tarot* pack in later times acquiring a high reputation for this purpose.

The casting of lots (*sortilege*) is a kind of divination. Names were pricked at random. A passage in a book, opened by chance, was unconsciously picked out, and was supposed to have a meaning. For this purpose the Bible and the works of Homer and Virgil were preferred.

Geomancy. This form of divination, quite simple in principle, but capable also of application to the whole cosmos, has been practised in Africa from early times, and related to astrology.[19]

In using this art in its most simple form one writes down sixteen lines of dots at random. Adding up each line we find either an even or an odd number of dots. If even we write down two dots,

[17] J. G. de Lint: *Atlas of the History of Medicine, I. Anatomy,* ed. C. Singer, London, 1926. Somewhat similar figures are given in E. A. Wallis Budge: *Amulets and Superstitions,* London, 1930.

[18] As most of this developed much later it is dealt with in another part of this book.

[19] J. A. Abayomi Cole: *Astrological Geomancy in Africa,* London, 1898.

if odd only one. Each *geomantic figure* consists of four rows of dots, consequently there are $2^4 = 16$ figures in all. The sixteen lines of figures give us four figures, one above the other.

Feng-shui. In the Taoist religion[20] of China there are special practitioners who select the sites for dwellings for the living and of graves for the dead. Their art is called *feng-shui* which means *wind-water*, because the spirits of these elements are supposed to be put into harmony with mankind by these practices. Bodies have often been kept unburied for a long time, owing to difficulties in finding a suitable place, by which we mean one where spiritual influences will allow the dead person to rest in peace. Even removal of a coffin from a grave and its reburial elsewhere has sometimes occurred. The making of roads and bridges, canals, wells and mines was formerly determined by feng-shui practitioners, and probably still is in some places. Mines and quarries have been known to be closed, when complaints that their presence caused bad harvests were alleged. Sometimes a tree was planted, or a tower built at a particular spot, determined by the art, and good fortune for the surrounding community was ensured.

[20] The Taoist religion is not really distinct from Confucianism; before the revolution the former regulated the spiritual affairs of China, the latter the temporal, see R. Guénon: *Autorité Spirituelle et pouvoir Temporel,* 2nd ed., Paris, 1947.

CHAPTER IV

THE DANCE OF THE GIANTS

Cyclopean Architecture. Neolithic (New Stone Age) men commenced building with large stones, unhewn, and fitted together
without.mortar or anything of that kind. In the later portion of
the New Stone Age and the early Bronze Age which succeeded it
this kind of architecture reached a high development. These rude
stone monuments are among the most remarkable structures ever
seen in the world (i) because considerable ingenuity must have been
used in hauling them to the place where they were used and erect-
ing them, (ii) because such gigantic stones were used, instead of a
number of small ones, *e.g.* one block in the temple of Hagiar Kim
at Malta measures 21 × 9 × 9 feet and one at Baalbec in the
Lebanon 62 × 20 × 15 feet, reported to be the largest single piece of
rock used in construction anywhere,[1] (iii) because to erect them a
vast and well-organised body of labourers must have been available,
involving many thousands of individuals working under unified
command, for long periods, (iv) because it is difficult to see how
such giant stones could have been quarried, and if they were not,
how they could have occurred in such large numbers in suitable
shapes, at suitable places for use.

Seven main structural types[2] of these cyclopean buildings exist,
and we enumerate them in order of complexity, beginning with the
more simple, which we have already mentioned :

(i) *Menhirs* or isolated megaliths 3 to 30 feet high, somewhat
numerous and common in certain areas.

(ii) *Trilithons* composed of two vertical stones, with a third horizontal one across the top.

(iii) *Dolmens* in which several stones stood vertically around a
central space, and a large horizontal stone covered the top.

---

[1] The largest stones of the pyramids of Egypt, which are a later development than the Cyclopean, are not more than 18 feet in any direction, and
they are only exceptional blocks, used for strengthening, whereas in the
Cyclopean nearly all the blocks are of gigantic size.

[2] The classification used is that of T. E. Peet : *Rough Stone Monuments
and their Builders,* London and New York, 1912, and appears to be more
accurate than that of some authors.

(iv) *Alignments* or rows of small or medium menhirs, arranged in series on some definite pattern.

(v) *Corridor Tombs* or rows of trilithons in line with one another, sometimes with side passages at right angles.

(vi) *Cromlechs* or rows of menhirs in a circle, ellipse or more rarely in a square, with horizontal stones along the top in some instances, as seen at Stonehenge.

(vii) *Megalithic Temples* of more complicated shape, probably relatively late, like some of the remarkable constructions in Sardinia, Malta and Gozo. These megaliths are associated in many places with tombs hewn in solid rock, and with the long burrows and cairns already mentioned. The inside of the burrow in some cases contains a megalithic structure identical with the corridor tomb mentioned above, in fact some of these, now exposed, may formerly have been inside a burrow, *i.e.* covered with earth.

A Widespread Cult. The distribution of the megaliths is as remarkable as their nature. They are frequent in the British Isles, being remarkably abundant in Wales. They are numerous in France, especially in Brittany, and both *menhir* and *dolmens* are Breton words. Innumerable examples occur in Spain and Portugal. They are common in Sweden, Denmark and North Germany. They are rarer in Holland and Belgium, and only two examples are known in Switzerland. In the Mediterranean they occur in Corsica, Sardinia, Malta, Gozo, Pantellaria, Lampedusa and to some extent in Sicily, but not in the rest of Italy. There are a few in the Balkans, but not in Greece.[3] They occur in the Caucasus and the Crimea, but not throughout Russia. They extend along the north coast of Africa, from Tripoli to Morocco, but not much in Egypt, where they seem to be replaced by the pyramids, but several have been found in the Soudan. In Asia they occur in Transjordania, Syria, Persia, India, Korea and Japan, and have spread into Alaska and even the islands of the Pacific.

In Mexico and Peru they seem, as in Egypt, to be replaced by a pyramid-cult, to be described later.[4] They are absent from most of Africa, from much of northern and central Europe and from large areas of northern Asia.

In Melanesia, especially on the islands of the New Hebrides there

[3] In Greece it was probably represented by, or grades over to, the Mycenean and in Crete by the Cretan.
[4] We are largely indebted to T. E. Peet, *loc. cit.* for the above mentioned facts, but have also consulted more recent authorities.

are not only a number of megaliths, but some are still being erected from time to time and a stone age cult[5] is, or was until quite recently, well developed, with sacraments or mysteries, closely resembling the early European, centring around a mother goddess and her son, who represents the higher aspirations of the people. There is also a pig-sacrifice. This sort of cult was formerly in vogue elsewhere, and Egypt, Crete, Greece and Rome were much influenced by it.[6] Images of the Mother Goddess, somewhat grotesque in our eyes,[7] have been recovered from the megalithic temples of Malta, together with both male and female figures of Sumerian and Cretan aspect.[8] But other animals than the pig were usually sacrificed, either the bull or sheep, or sometimes only plant products.

Primitively the unhewn stones of the megalithic structures bear little or no carving, but gradually incisions of various kinds were made, ending up with symbolic patterns, again merging with the early artistic-religious figures of the Mediterranean area.

It is certain that a large number of the megalithic structures have been taken down and broken up or used for building.

Some of the megalithic structures show a definite orientation and like almost all ancient monuments were connected with a kind of primitive astrology.

Giants and Wizards. No doubt, because of the size of the stones, they have been associated with giants, and because of the difficulties of putting them up, with magic.

Early British writers said that Merlin the wizard, afterwards famous at the court of King Arthur, brought over the stones[9] of Stonehenge from Ireland, by magical art and the aid of fifteen thousand men, and set them up in their present position, in memory of a number of famous warriors who had been slain by Saxon invaders. They were called *the Dance of the Giants* and stood in Killaraus, a mountain in Ireland, in the reign of Aurelius Ambrosius of Britain. They were originally brought by giants to Ireland from Africa. They were evidently looked upon as some sort of national palladium. The large number of men who went over to Ireland had

5 See especially J. Layard: *Stone Men of Malekula,* Vao, 1942, and for further references G. S. Levy: *The Gate of Horn,* London, 1948.

6 Levy: *loc. cit.*

7 Very like those obese figures described earlier.

8 See figures in Levy: *loc. cit.*

9 The legend is given as recounted by Geoffrey of Monmouth in his *Histories of the Kings of Britain,* trans. London. The original was written in the 12th century.

to fight for them, and when they came to possess them were quite unable to take them down, until Merlin came to the rescue with his own engines.

In France many of the megaliths were associated with Gargantua, a giant long familiar in French folk-lore before Rabelais made him the hero of his farcical romances.

A three-chambered corridor tomb in Berkshire is called the *cave of Wayland the Smith*. This alludes to a ghostly or mysterious farrier who was supposed to shoe horses in a magical manner, and manufacture wonderful swords and armour. He was known as Wieland in Germany, Völund in Scandinavia, and clearly corresponds with the classical Vulcan.

Another idea relating to megaliths was that they were connected with the Druids. This was upheld as a serious theory in the 18th century by W. Stukeley, the antiquary and W. Blake, the poet.

Temples of the Sun. There is little doubt that megaliths were connected with burial of important personages, and were associated with some sort of worship, probably with solar or planetary symbolism.

Stonehenge, on Salisbury Plain in Wiltshire, originally consisted of two concentric circles, with a mound of earth, still visible, all round. There is an altar stone and, in line with it some distance away, along an avenue bordered with earth, an upright stone known as the Friar's heel. Along this line the sun rises approximately at the summer solstice. When the structure was erected the orientation was supposed to have been exact.

There are a number of other cromlechs in Britain, some fairly complex. They are most common in Cornwall, but one in Somerset consists of a great circle and two smaller. Dolmens are common in Wales, Cornwall and Devon, but rarer in the rest of Britain.

Avebury in Wiltshire is the most extensive area of megaliths in this country. There are extensive earthworks, and Silbury Hill near by is believed to be an artificial mound. At Avebury there is a circle of about a hundred stones, within this two pairs of concentric circles. In the northern pair there is a sort of altar in the middle, a horizontal stone on three supports; in the southern pair a single menhir in the middle. A long avenue, fringed with alignments leads up to the whole arrangement. The avenue is not straight but serpentine in shape, which led Stukeley to associate it with Druidical serpent worship.

In Brittany there are many megalithic remains, the largest at the village of Carnac, where there are five alignments of very numerous stones, nearly 600, the largest 67 feet long, and several dolmens, mostly crowning cairns. Even so the numbers are believed to be enormously reduced today, as it has been estimated that there were originally some 15,000 stones in the alignments alone.[10]

In Malta and Gozo the megalithic temples are more like buildings as we know them, the giant stones in some cases forming a rough wall. There is also a wall of cyclopean stones at Tarragona in Spain.

Such structures lead over to other forms of architecture, which, whilst more closely resembling conventional forms to be described later, are really megalithic in the sense that giant blocks were used, although often carved and hewn.

The most remarkable of these are represented in the ruins of Tiahuanaco near Lake Titicaca, an enormous expanse of water, over 100 miles long, high up in the Andes mountains, in Bolivia. These ruins, which cover nearly an acre, are believed to belong to a culture preceding that of the Incas. Huge monoliths have been found here, presumably built into a large temple; there is no mortar, but there are some traces of bronze clamps being used to hold them together. The region is dreary and deserted nowadays.

On the east coast of Ponapé, one of the Caroline Islands in the north-west Pacific, lies a town called Nan-Matal, which has been called the Venice of the Pacific. For it lies on a number of islands, over fifty in number, separated by canals. Each island is artificial and has been constructed of huge prismatic blocks of basalt, laid in parallel layers alternately at right angles. Local tradition ascribes the construction to the magic power of two princes of an ancient race resembling the Greek Titans, with the assistance of spirits. Other cyclopean work is found on the island of Lele.

On Easter Island, an isolated outpost in the eastern Pacific, about 2,000 miles from the coast of South America, there are over 550 gigantic images[11] of crude, grim physiognomy, 3 to 70 feet in height. The race responsible for them was destroyed about 600 years ago by invaders of Maori affinity.

Finally we see the use of megalithic structures, now no longer crude, but carefully worked, in the great temples of Egypt. The work is different, and much more careful; nevertheless there are

10 Peet: *loc. cit.*
11 A few have been removed; one stands outside the British Museum, Bloomsbury, London; it is marked on the back with the *crux ansata* or Egyptian cross.

marked resemblances in shape, *e.g.* the entrances at the temple of Karnac show the form of the trilithon very clearly. And they made colossal statues. But these people, great adepts in magic as they were supposed to be, deserve a separate chapter.

The Stone of Destiny. The more complex megalithic structures, such as the temples at Malta have been associated by Sir Arthur Evans[12] with the use in worship of the *baetyl.* The latter was probably a tree in its original form; later it was an upright pillar of wood or stone. In fact the putting up of menhirs may originally have been suggested by these baetyls, and when cromlechs[13] were constructed there was a vertical sacred stone in the middle, or in the niche formed by a trilithon. Moreover there is an altar stone, or two stones, one vertical, one horizontal, in many of the megalithic temples, and altars have been consecrated from the earliest times, by anointing them with oil. Moreover priests and kings have been consecrated with oil, and have, in some instances, been elevated on an altar-like structure as part of the ceremony of their inauguration or coronation.

Although the story of the British coronation stone, or Stone of Destiny, is only a legend, we believe it embodies a valuable psychic link between the Holy Land, Ireland, Scotland and England. The stone is a block of steel-blue sandstone, veined red, $22 \times 13 \times 11$ inches, placed beneath the Coronation Chair, used for enthroning the British Sovereign at the Coronation.

This stone is said to be the one set up by Jacob, anointed by him with oil, and called by him the house (meaning the abode) of God.[14] In the days of the Hebrew kings it is said to have been in the Temple at Jerusalem, and the kings of Judah crowned on or beside it. In the 4th century B.C. the prophet Jeremiah, with the daughter of the last king of Judah and a princely scribe, left Palestine and travelled by way of Egypt and Spain to Ireland, taking the stone with them. Old Irish records record the arrival of the prophet, who received the name of Ollamh Fodhla, together with the princess and princely scribe. The party were well received, and the princess married Eochaid, the high-king of Ireland. Thereafter the high-kings were always crowned, for centuries, on the stone.

[12] Quoted by Peet: *loc. cit.,* p. 105.

[13] Menhirs and cromlechs were, curiously enough, sometimes constructed of wood; the remains of an artificial prehistoric circle of tree-trunks appropriately named Woodhenge, not far from Avebury, was discovered from the air.

[14] *Genesis* xxviii, 16–22.

Jeremiah is said to have also introduced the harp of David, which still figures on the British royal coat of arms and flag. His tomb is still shown on an island in Loch Erne.

About A.D. 502 Fergus, brother of the Irish king led an expedition of Scots against the Picts, in the country now called Scotland. He was successful and was allowed to be crowned, as king of Scotland, on the stone. Thereafter it was kept at Scone in Scotland, and thirty-four successive Scottish kings were crowned on it. In A.D. 1296 Edward I of England removed the stone to Westminster and had the present Coronation Chair made for it. Successive English kings were crowned on it and finally from the Union the joint sovereigns of the two realms.

A similar consecrated stone was used in the English coronation right back to Anglo-Saxon times, and is still to be seen at Kingston-on-Thames, from which this place gets its name. Another known as the *Königstuhl* was long preserved in a building at the junction of the Rhine and the Lähn, and on it the Holy Roman Emperors were enthroned. The *Mora Stone* at Upsala was used in the election of the kings of Sweden until the beginning of the 16th century. A *ducal stone* is recorded in Carinthia. Among the ancient kings of Munster one dynasty were inaugurated on a large stone, another under a sacred tree. The kings of Denmark were crowned within a stone circle, no doubt on or near the central stone. The same is recorded of King Arthur and other British kings. In the Bible there are references to kings being made near a pillar or tree.[15] In ancient Egypt a stone appears beneath the throne of the Pharaoh.

The title of *stone* was originally a divine title, and applied to priests and kings as representatives of the Godhead. Christ was called the *chief corner-stone*. When He called Peter a *rock* or in more correct translation, a *stone*, He was passing on one of His own titles, to His representative.

Stones from Heaven. That mineral bodies fall from the sky is a fact. When they reach the ground they are called *meteorites*. They are often rich in metal, principally iron. That objects appearing in this way should be regarded as of religious or magical significance is not surprising.

The most highly reverenced stone in the world was probably a meteorite. It is the *Hajaru'l-aswad* or *black stone* built into the south-east corner of the *Ka'bah*, the cubical building standing in

---

[15] *Judges* ix, 6, King James version says *pillar*, Vulgate *oak*; see also II *Chronicles* xxiii, 13, King James version.

the middle of the square which forms the large mosque at Mecca in Arabia. It is the centre of Moslem worship and each year large numbers of pilgrims assemble there. Towards it Moslems turn in prayer five times daily. The stone itself is oval in shape and appears to have been broken and cemented together. It is about 7 inches long and is set in a ring of cement, outside of which is a circular band of silver, formerly gilt. The ka'bah has been rebuilt several times. It was in existence before the time of the prophet Mohammed, whose family the Quraish were hereditary keepers of the sacred structure. It was rebuilt during the lifetime of the prophet, and during rebuilding a dispute arose as to who should put the black stone in place. It was agreed that Mohammed should decide, so he placed the stone on his cloak, and bade the contending parties all hold the edge of the cloak, thereby holding it and then hauling it into position guided by the prophet's hand. The stone was supposed to have been given by Gabriel to Ishmael.

The word *palladium*, meaning any venerated object believed to have a protective function over a community, is derived from the original name of a statue of Pallas Athene, possessed by the city of Troy, and which was said to have been carried away by the Greeks. Conflicting accounts of it are given by classical authors, but most of them state that it originally fell from heaven.

At Rome a sacred shield called *Ancile* was believed to protect the fate of the Roman people. It was fabled to have fallen from heaven, during the reign of Numa, who ordered eleven other objects of the same size and shape to be manufactured, and then appointed a college of twelve priests to look after the twelve shields, in the temple of Vesta. They were carried in procession round the city every March 1st.

The temple of Diana at Ephesus, one of the seven wonders of the world, was also said to possess a stone or image that had fallen from heaven.

The preference for meteorites in connection with the megalithic cult may explain the curious myth that the worship of stones was first introduced by Uranus, the god of the sky.

Heliolithic Culture. This is the name given by certain anthropologists[16] to a complex of customs which spread over a wide section of

[16] Notably Elliot Smith and Rivers; it is associated with Smith's diffusionist theory, according to which this culture diffused over the world from Egypt, a view largely discredited; nevertheless the features mentioned below do seem to be associated with one another, and do seem to represent one of the phases of human development.

the world and which developed out of the neolithic and the mega-lithic. In its more specialised form it is dealt with in the next two chapters. It was best developed in Egypt, from which some believe it spread elsewhere.

The heliolithic culture comprised the following features :

(i) The construction of great mounds, represented by the barrows of Britain, on the one hand, and the carefully constructed pyramids of Egypt and Mexico on the other; such mounds had both an astronomical and a funereal purpose.

(ii) The construction of megalithic calendar circles, *i.e.* cromlechs connected with astronomical phenomena in Britain, orientated temples in Egypt, Mexico and Peru.

(iii) Mummification of the Dead.

(iv) Tattooing of the Living.

(v) Circumcision.

(vi) The practice of massage.

(vii) *La Couvade*, the custom of sending the father to bed at the birth of his child.

(viii) The use of the *Swastika* as a magical religious symbol.

(ix) The search for gold,[17] and the use of gold for making objects of a magical significance.

(x) The use of certain shells as *life-givers*, or *elixirs of life*, especially the cowrie.

(xi) A dual political organisation, the country being divided into two kingdoms, as was ancient Egypt, under two crowns, as we shall see in the next chapter; this was symbolised in many ways in the rituals, as by a pot with two spouts, a figure with two heads, etc..

(xii) The existence of various classes of the community, and particularly the emergence of the class of *hereditary* warrior leaders. They or their representatives alone were allowed to wear a dagger or sword.

As far as we can ascertain these practices follow the distribution of the megaliths, or did in late neolithic and early bronze age times, assuming that the peculiar features of ancient Egypt and the old native cultures of Mexico and Peru are to be included with them, a problem we will now proceed to examine.

[17] Gold was probably the first metal to be used by mankind, and from its original significance as clearly magical, we can trace the origin of alchemy.

CHAPTER V

˙THE PYRAMIDS OF EGYPT

Egyptian Chronology. The recorded history of ancient Egypt extends over an immense period. During all this time certain customs remained more or less unchanged, and even the national organisation remained stable, except for a few revolutions. It begins with the first dynasty, now dated about 3300 B.C., and only ends with the death of Caesarion in 30 B.C. The last named was the son of Cleopatra VII and Julius Caesar. He was proclaimed king of Egypt, Cyprus and Coelesyria at the age of thirteen, and five years later he was killed (it is said) by the orders of Augustus, the Roman Emperor. Thereafter Egypt became a Roman Province. Even then the Roman Emperor took over some of the customs of the Egyptian ruler.[1] The latter was always termed *Pharaoh* and was as much high priest as king.

Already in the first dynasty, at the beginning of the historical period, the magical religious cult of the ancient Egyptians was highly developed, and the country was well organised socially, depending economically on the cultivation of the Nile Valley. Great attention was given to the embalming and burial of the dead, much of the ceremonial connected therewith having the magical object of helping the deceased in the next world, when it was hoped he or she would be united with the chief god, later called Osiris. The life of the living was full of magical acts. There was no distinction between industry and magic. Medicine was associated with astrology, metallurgy with alchemy. The *Book of the Dead* (more correctly the *Book of the Coming forth by Day*) exists in the several recensions of Heliopolis, Thebes and Sais, and numerous isolated chapters were inscribed on the walls of tombs, on pyramids, on sarcophagi and mummy wrappings. There are in all about two hundred chapters, written at different times, but all the basic

---

[1] Egyptian religion persisted under the Roman Emperors, inscriptions show the latter were regarded as pharaohs. This went on until the Coptic Christian conversion in the 3rd century A.D. The Coptic religion contains many features of the ancient Egyptian, even to the present day.

material being early. Thus buried with the deceased, they were believed to aid in the journey to the next world.[2]

Only two revolutions disturbed the tranquillity of the first twenty-six dynasties. After this the Persians came in for the twenty-seventh (Cambyses, Darius I, Xerxes, Artaxerxes and Darius II), and again for the thirty-first (Ochus, Darius III). Macedonians took over in the thirty-second (Alexander I, the Great, Philip Aridaeus, Alexander II). The last and thirty-third dynasty, sixteen in number, were all called Ptolemy, and were of Macedonian and Greek extraction.

As regards the first two revolutions the first was between the 14th and 17th when dynasties of *Shepherd Kings* or *Hyksos* took over the throne. They are said to have come from Assyria, and to have included the Pharaoh in whose reign Joseph was sold into Egypt. They were eventually driven out into Palestine, where they became the chiefs or lords of the Philistines.[3] They very largely adopted Egyptians customs whilst in Egypt but appear to have had gods of their own.[4]

The other disturbance took place in the middle of the eighteenth dynasty, when Amenhetep IV ascended the throne. He reigned 1380–1362 B.C. and tried to alter the established religion in many ways. He declared the sun-god Aten to be the only one, and attempted to transfer the veneration of the people for numerous images to the adoration of the sun's disc. He called himself Akh-en-Aten, meaning devoted to Aten. At his death the movement collapsed.[5]

Red and White Crowns. Throughout historic times the whole of Egypt was highly organised under the priesthood, who were the learned class, and ruled the country by means we would today regard as magical. As in many other countries, and as in China to quite recent times, the ruler was supposed to control the elements. In Egypt the pharaoh controlled the Nile, and therefore the welfare

[2] A Christianised version of the Book of the Dead has been discovered in Ethiopia. Even in the Russian Church printed prayers were sometimes buried with the dead. There is also a Buddhist Book of the Dead in Tibet.

[3] E. C. Brewer: *The Reader's Handbook*, New Ed., London, 1898.

[4] *Introductory Guide to the Egyptian Collections*, Brit. Mus., London, 1930.

[5] According to H. Spencer Lewis: *Rosicrucian Questions and Answers*, San Jose, California, 1929, this movement was the beginning of the Rosicrucians; it is noteworthy that the latter appeared in Europe at a time when the established Church was being challenged by the reformers in a somewhat similar manner.

of every member of the community. There were two great divisions
of the kingdom, but for most of this time they were closely united.
They were the land of the North or Lower Egypt, corresponding
with what the Greeks called the Delta, an extensive area around
the mouth of the Nile, and the land of the South or Upper Egypt,
a long strip along the river, extending to Ethiopia. The former was
ruled over by the god Horus, the latter by the god Set. The pharaoh
therefore was crowned with a double crown, one part shaped like a
mitre, but without the cleft, coloured white, representing the South,
and the other forming a sort of deep rim around the preceding,
raised up in front into the form of a cobra, and red in colour,
symbolising the North. Double plumes, partly with the same significance, projected on either side.

The Mummy. The practice of mummification is not confined to the
Egyptians. We find it began with the heliolithic culture, with which,
however, the Egyptian was included. It certainly developed to its
highest degree of art among the ancient Egyptians, but it is mentioned in the Old Testament, the embalming of Jacob occupying
forty days.[6] The practice spread over the world, even to America,[7]
but nowhere had it such a long history. It began soon after the
beginning of the Dynastic Period and continued even among the
Coptic Christians, for it does not come to an end until about the
4th century A.D.

At one time it was applied to the whole population of Egypt, rich
and poor alike, and even to the sacred animals. For the bodies of
rams, bulls, cats, ichneumons, shrews, apes, hawks, ibises and croco-
diles were mummified like human beings, often being carefully
bandaged. The immense numbers of such mummies can be judged
from an act of vandalism that took place in 1890 when a large
burial of mummified cats was discovered and the bodies sold as
manure, twenty-eight tons being brought to Liverpool.

We may also call attention to the *shabti* or *ushabti* figures which
were supposed to play a part in magic concerned with the next
world. In the early dynasties a small figure presumably representing
the deceased was placed in the tomb, and later this was super-
seded by a figure which represented a slave. Under the eighteenth
dynasty and later, it is clear from the inscriptions on these objects
that they were intended, in the event of the deceased being condemned to work in the fields of the Underworld, to do the work for

[6] *Genesis*, L, 2, 3.
[7] See next chapter.

the deceased. In some cases the ushabti bears an agricultural implement. Priests and nobles, and especially kings, had large numbers
of such ushabti figures buried with them.

Another curious custom, which began in the sixth dynasty, is the
burying of the viscera separately in four jars. They were associated
with certain gods or goddesses, later on with the gods of the four
directions. The jars at first had human heads modelled on them
but after the eighteenth dynasty they bore the heads of the appropriate gods, *viz.* (i) that in the South, which contained the stomach
and large intestines, had a human head, that of Amset or Meshta,[8]
(ii) in the North, contained the small intestines, it had the head of
a baboon, belonging to Hapi, (iii) in the East, contained the heart
and lungs, it figured the head of a jackal, that of Tuamutef, and
(iv) in the West, contained liver and gall-bladder, it had the head
of a hawk, denoting Khebsenuf. These jars went out of use in the
twenty-sixth dynasty. The viscera themselves were sometimes preserved by mummification.

Pyramids and their Meaning. Although the living houses of the
ancient Egyptians, and even their palaces, have been almost completely destroyed, many of their tombs remain. This is because the
people believed the house of the dead to be more important than
the house of the living, and seemed to think that, in a certain
sense, the deceased would live in the next world in safety, as long
as his tomb was maintained in this. One even gains the impression
that these tombs were designed to last for ever. They were, however,
designed so that the body could remain undisturbed therein, until
the soul returned to the body.[9] The largest tombs naturally belonged to the pharaohs and their relatives.

In spite of attempts to give the dead a permanent resting place
many of the tombs show evidence of damage by despoilers. Some of
the largest, which are most difficult to destroy, are still preserved,
although generally much damaged. These are the pyramids. About
100 are now known, some only from scanty remains, but there are
still other smaller buildings or traces of them, which were undoubtedly more numerous, and which surround these large monuments. They are the tombs of persons of lesser importance, and are
often like pyramids in form, but may be made of brick. The mum-

[8] There are many variations in the English spelling of the god-names
and king-names.
[9] Sir Banister Fletcher: *A History of Architecture on the Comparative
Method*, 16th edition, New York and London, 1954.

mies of the poorer class were crowded together in vast numbers in common crypts.

The pre-dynastic Egyptians did not build pyramids. Even in the archaic period (first and second dynasties) they were probably small and few, if developed at all. In these ages even the body of the king was buried in a *mastaba* or house of brick, with compartments for the body, and for various possessions.

The first pyramid of which we have any detailed knowledge is the *step-pyramid* at Sakkara, for the second king of the third dynasty, named Zoser. The Egyptians had a tradition that it was designed by Imhetep or Imhotep, vizier to that king, who was architect, physician, astrologer and magician, and who was afterwards deified as the god of medicine. This pyramid had a base, not quite square, about 400 feet along each side, and with sides arranged in four steps, the last being the flat top.

Another huge pyramid is at Dashur, with a base of 620 feet square. It is called "the bent pyramid" for the top part is sloped more obtusely than the lower part.

Most of the others are of a true pyramidal shape, or rather were so, when their outer coverings were in place. The three most famous are at Giza, near Cairo. Two of these are among the largest and all were constructed by pharaohs of the fourth dynasty. They were constructed for Cheops, Chephren and Mycerinos, the smallest of the three belonging to the latter. The largest is that of Cheops. The Greek historian Herodotus was the first to mention these three pharaohs in reference to the three pyramids at Giza, but the ownership of the various pyramids has been ascertained by the careful work of Egyptologists over more than a century. The second largest in Egypt is not at Giza, but at Dashur and has a base 719 feet square. It was probably built for Snefru. However, that of Chephren at Giza is almost as large, being 708 feet square. All these had relatively narrow spaces inside, and usually but not always the king was buried within.[10]

The great pyramid is 756 feet square at the base, and is bulkier than any other building in the world, although one or two cathedral spires exceed it in height. The apex, however, has been removed, down to a distance of 31 feet. When complete it was 481 feet high and a few inches. This vertical height, if taken as the radius of a circle, then the circumference of the latter, it is reckoned, would equal the sum of the length of the four sides. It is accurately orientated, the sides being exactly north, south, east and west, to

[10] Where he was not the monument is of the nature of a *cenotaph*.

within a very small fraction of a degree. Some of the stones of which it is constructed are very large, but they are very accurately hewn and fitted together. The name of Cheops, in Egyptian, is painted in red paint on the roof of the largest cavity (called the King's Chamber) inside. In this chamber there is a sarcophagus or coffer of red granite. The cubical capacity of this is four quarters, showing that the British measure of capacity, known from early times as the quarter, is derived from a measure known to the ancient Egyptians.[11]

The Great Pyramid is said to be situated at the exact centre of the land surface of the earth. The entrance passage points towards the north pole, and is said to be directed to exactly that point in the sky at which the pole star, then α *Draconis*, was placed when the pyramid was built. This point, first raised by Herschel, has been much debated in connection with the alleged date.

Pyramids were built as late as the twelfth dynasty and even recorded for the eighteenth, but after that they went out of fashion. More than 800 years later they were revived on a small scale in the extreme south, as pyramid tombs, the pyramidal part of which was generally rather tall in proportion. The habit spread north, one of the southerners having conquered the whole country about 270 B.C. and the pyramid habit began again, but they were small, and eventually deteriorated into brick structures about A.D. 200.

In the period when pyramids were not built the kings or pharaohs were often buried secretly in tombs excavated in the sides of mountains. It is supposed that this was done to thwart tomb-robbers. The famous Valley of the Kings near Thebes is one of the localities containing a number of these royal sepulchres of the eighteenth, nineteenth and twentieth dynasties.

In Ptolemaic and Roman times vast caves just outside Alexandria became burial places. Originally natural in origin, excavated by underground waters in the limestone rock, they were enlarged by human activity, and at first used as shelters in time of war and even as dwellings. They were described by Strabo, and came to consist of seven great chambers with a broad central passage. In the Middle Ages they were regarded as one of the wonders of the world.

[11] For numerical relations, both of the coffer and the pyramids, to measures of the solar system, see *The Canon*, London, 1897. This work was published anonymously, but a copy in my possession is inscribed "From William Stirling, the author." It is well known that C. Piazzi Smyth, astronomer-royal for Scotland in the last century, and a number of other authors, believe the measurements of the Great Pyramid are related to prophecy. The literature on this is extensive.

Before leaving the tombs it may be noted that the labyrinthine passages therein have been interpreted as representing the soul's wanderings rather than being due to the fear of sacrilegious intrusions. If so they are probably comparable with the long passages to the cave temples of Palaeolithic man.

The tombs, especially the pyramids, are, in the most general sense, comparable to altars. Offerings were made on, at or near them.

Monuments of Egypt. The temples of Egypt were among the finest and largest the world has ever seen, the ruins of some of them remain, but a great many deteriorated badly, and were damaged by vandalism during the last century, and to a lesser extent in the preceding periods of Moslem rule. There were also many gigantic statues. Lack of space for dealing with this makes it imperative to confine our remarks to two examples out of some thousands.

The *sphinx* is a colossal stone image in the sand, not far from the pyramids of Giza. It is 150 feet long, and 70 feet high, the body being recumbent. It was painted bright red, traces of the colour still being visible. This shows on some pieces of the uraeus crest and beard in the British Museum. It has been cleared of sand and repaired several times, once at least by the pharaoh Thutmosis IV (1425–1408 B.C., eighteenth dynasty) who placed an inscription on a stele before it, and that is still in place. He ascribed it to Cheops, but later writers said the face was that of Chephren. F. Lenormant,[12] however, mentions an inscription of the fourth dynasty (probably about 2900–2750 B.C.) which says that the sphinx had been found by chance at that time, buried beneath the sand, as if it had been forgotten for many generations. The image appears to represent a lion with a masculine human head, being the god Harmachis, a form of Horus. Such images are not uncommon in Egypt and appear to be less complex than the Greek conception of the sphinx. There is a small temple between the paws of the sphinx.

The other giant monuments, of which a pair remain, to which we wish to refer, are much later. They are two colossal seated statues at Thebes, not far from the west bank of the Nile. Both represent Amenhetep III (about 1412–1376 B.C., eighteenth dynasty). On their pedestals they are 65 feet high and during the inundation of the Nile they are surrounded by water. Each was originally constructed of a single stone, but the northern one was broken, probably by an

[12] *Introduction à l'Histoire d'Orient,* 1838.

earthquake, about the time of Christ. Thereafter peculiar sounds were made by the wind passing through the broken part. It was then regarded as an oracle, the sounds being referred to by several classical authors. It is even suspected that a priest delivered messages from a cavity in the stone; a space still exists in which a man could conceal himself.

CHAPTER VI

THE PYRAMIDS OF THE NEW WORLD

American Chronology. Here we are concerned with the natives of America, and particularly their condition before the coming of the white man. Columbus[1] reached the mainland of the continent in 1498.

The natives mostly belong to a distinctive physical type, with a reddish brown skin, dark straight hair, somewhat more allied to Mongols than to Caucasians or Negroes, but with sharp noses, quite unlike the most familiar members of the Mongolian race, such as we meet in Tibet, China, Indo-China and Japan.

No remains of early palaeolithic man have been found in the American continent. Mankind entered the New World at a relatively late date. The first arrivals, apart from Eskimos,[2] are estimated[3] to have entered the continent between 13,000 and 18,000 B.C. They are generally considered to have come in through the Behring Strait, which then may have been crossed by a land bridge. Writers on the occult, however, believe that they came from Atlantis, a fabulous continent in the Atlantic Ocean, of which the West Indies are supposed to represent the last surviving remains.[4] They spread all over both North and South America, and reached Patagonia, where human remains, estimated 3,000 to 5,400 years old have been found.[5]

The great majority of these peoples, for they no doubt came in several waves, had reached the neolithic, and probably the heliolithic stages. The fact that many were hunters over most of these continents does not detract from that. They would not be able to cultivate, except in places suitable for cultivation. If they had come through Siberia they would have passed through a large region un-

---

[1] Columbus was not the first European to discover America. It was visited by Norsemen in the 10th and 11th centuries, and there were probably other early contacts.

[2] See Chapter I.

[3] J. Collier: *Indians of the Americas*, reprinted New York, 1956 (first edition, 1947).

[4] Lewis Spence: *The Problem of Atlantis*, revised edition, London, 1925.

[5] Collier: *loc. cit.*

suitable for cultivation and the same applies to much of the
American continent. As a matter of fact over forty plants were
cultivated by the natives at the time of the arrival of the first white
men, some twenty of these intensively, and one, the maize, is the
most completely modified of all cereals, being the only one that cannot live at all without the hand of man. Since the arrival of the
whites no additions to the list of cultivated plants were made,
except possibly guayule.[6] The list itself includes such important
things as potato, manioc (source of tapioca), pineapples, avocado,
artichoke, peanut, strawberry, lima beans, kidney beans, squash,
pumpkin, chocolate, india-rubber, quinine, cocaine, tobacco, maté
(for maté tea), maple (for sugar), pecans, brazil-nuts and sar-
saparilla.[7]

Now the magic of the redskins is, over much of the continent,
very similar to what we have described in our discussion of Shamanism,[8] and in some places involves Totemism. But in three areas
it developed into a complex civilisation, even more extraordinary,
in many respects, than that of ancient Egypt, although it apparently
lasted a much shorter time. These began about 1000 B.C.[9] The early
history of these areas has not yet been reconstructed by archaeologists. But we know something of these peoples from their remaining
pottery, sculpture, architecture and mural paintings, and particularly
in Mexico, from some few writings and paintings that have survived on strips of deerskin and tree bark paper.

The areas of settled cultivation and city-life are as follows:
(i) in Mexico, in the region of what is now the state of Mexico with
its capital Mexico City; the first people who have a definite
(although fragmentary) history here are the Toltecs, who flourished
circa A.D. 550 to A.D. 950,[10] and they were followed by the Aztecs,
whose powerful empire was destroyed by the Spaniards under
Cortes 1519 to 1521. (ii) in Central America, in what are now the
most southern states of the Mexican republic: Chiapas and those
forming the peninsula of Yucatan, together with the adjacent
republics of Guatemala and Honduras; in this region flourished
the civilisation of the Mayas, regarded as the most highly developed
of all three; it reached a very advanced stage of elaboration about

6 Collier: *loc. cit.*
7 Further details in Collier *loc. cit.*
8 See Chapter III.
9 According to H. G. Wells: *A Short History of the World*, Middlesex,
1922, new ed. 1946, reprinted 1949.
10 According to a footnote to the foreword in the 1950 reprint of G. C.
Vaillant: *The Aztecs of Mexico*, first published in the U.S.A., 1944.

the first century of the Christian era, reached its climax *circa* A.D.[11] 700–800 and persisted until it was modified by intrusions from the north (Mexico) in the 11th and 12th centuries; thereafter it revived somewhat and was still in existence although rather degenerate at the time of the Spanish conquest in 1517 and 1523 under Cortes and Montejedo.

(iii) in Peru, Bolivia, Ecuador, Northern Chili and Northern Argentina flourished the Empire of the Incas, which reached its zenith 100 years before the conquest of Peru by Pizarro in 1532 to 1535; it was founded only about 300 years before that time, but replaced earlier civilisations about which much less is known; they include those responsible for the remarkable buildings at Tianhuaco, already described.[12]

Each of these cultures was quite distinct, and the last never had any communication with the first two. Archaeologists have studied them in considerable detail and distinguish various subdivisions of each. They all show some features which have been described as heliolithic; like the Egyptians the chief remains are of religious buildings, most of the homes of the people, having been flimsy, have perished. Their art is represented largely by carvings, sculptures and paintings and is extraordinarily grotesque, embodying animal figures of highly conventional patterns, particularly birds and serpents, often very elaborate, and with no close parallel in the Old World. Each region is of course distinctive but all are peculiar in the respects mentioned. H. G. Wells[13] remarks that many Maya inscriptions resemble certain elaborate drawings made by lunatics in European asylums and links this with the fact that all these peoples were dominated by the magico-religious shedding of blood, and the offering of human sacrifice.[14] No writings were made, apparently, among the Incas of Peru, but records were kept by means of the *quipu*. Many examples of the latter remain. Each is different, and consists of a cord, to which a number of coloured knotted strings are attached. Colour, form and number of knots and positions gave the clue to the meaning.

All these peoples put much stress on the rhythms or periodicity of nature and its numerical description. They had a complicated calendar which was regulated by the priesthood. Everything was

[11] According to H. G. Wells; more recent opinions may make it somewhat earlier.

[12] See Chapter IV.

[13] *Loc. cit.*, he says the nearest parallel in the Old World is found in certain archaic Indian carvings.

[14] See later in this chapter.

determined by astrology, which was not so much a matter of individual horoscopes, although there is evidence that these existed, but a science that regulated all political action. There is also evidence that the priests communicated with the dead. All their religion was designed to keep the world rhythms going.

Magical History. It was thought in Mexico that the sun was extinguished after a period, and that there was a danger of this happening at the end of each period of fifty-two years, called a *sheaf,* one of their divisions of time. In the past it was thought that the sun had been extinguished, and reproduced, several times. Thus history had been divided into four or five stages. The accounts surviving differ amongst themselves. According to one the first, called the Water Sun, ended with the flood, the second, or Earth Sun, ended with the destruction of most of the giants by earthquakes, the third or Wind Sun witnessed the destruction of surviving giants, the coming of Quetzalcoatl, who being rejected left the people who were transformed into monkeys and the world was convulsed with high winds; we live in the period of the Fire Sun, which will end in a general conflagration. Other accounts alter the order of these catastrophes.

Resemblances to this cosmology can be seen clearly in the traditional stories contained in the *Popol-Vuh.* The latter, which merely means Book of the Written Leaves, was inscribed by a native of Guatemala who had been converted to Christianity, in the Quiche or Kiche dialect of that country, which was one of the languages of the Maya group. It was copied in its original language and translated into Spanish by the Dominican Father Francesco Ximenez, both of which manuscripts, with other writings of the latter author are now in the Newberry Library of Chicago.[15] It has been translated into several European languages.

It was formerly thought by many archaeologists that this book was a mixture of Maya tradition with stories derived from the Old Testament. It is unlikely however that a native convert to Catholicism would know much about the Old Testament, and the study of comparative mythology shows that many early traditions of other parts of the world bear resemblances to the Old Testament, particularly to the early chapters of *Genesis.* There is now a very

[15] *Popol Vuh: The Sacred Book of the Ancient Quiche Maya.* English translation from the Spanish of A. Recinos, London, 1951. This differs very little from the original translation of Ximenez, who had the assistance of a number of natives, selected for their knowledge of the old mythology.

wide agreement that the book represents, almost wholly, native lore, and is a reproduction of part or whole of their sacred scripture.

Magico-religious Organisation. As in Egypt the whole country was organised in accordance with a magical or astrological diagram of the divine realm. The earth had to conform to the heavens. There were distinct traces of the dual organisation, as in all heliolithic cultures.

There are many resemblances to Egypt in the organisation of the hierarchy. The civic officers were closely associated with the priesthood, and the higher positions wielded the dual power over both.

Sacrifices. Vegetable, animal and human sacrifices were offered by the Azetcs, the Mayas and the Incas, but among the first named the number of human victims was vastly in excess of those immolated in a comparable period anywhere in the world.

American Pyramids. The earliest pyramids in the New World were constructed of earth, and some of them still survive in Mexico, dating from about 500 B.C.[16] The worship of the Jaguar-god has recently been discovered to go back to this time, long before the Aztecs. Pyramids of stone were put up in the next period, during which the cult of fire and rain gods were introduced and the feathered serpent, afterwards identified with Quetzalcoatl, flourished. The Toltecs followed with this identification about A.D. 900–1150 and finally the Aztecs from the later date to the conquest A.D. 1520. The pyramids of the two latter peoples are well built, of stone terraces.

The Pyramids of the Sun and Moon, at Teotihuacan, which are probably pre-Toltec lie among extensive ruins of an ancient city, the foundations of which have a circumference of some twenty miles. The larger of the two, the Pyramid or Temple of the Sun stands on a base 682 feet square, and is truncated-pyramidal in form, that is to say it has a flat top. The latter reaches 180 feet high. It is believed that it was surmounted by a colossal image of the sun-god, possibly furnished with a golden breastplate reflecting the sun's rays. The Pyramid of the Moon is somewhat smaller. It is connected with that of the Sun by a path called *the path of the dead,* on either side of which, covering an area of some nine square miles are numerous tumuli or small rough pyramids. The two large pyramids, like most large ones in America are broadly terraced, a

[16] H. de Terra: *Man and Mammoth in Mexico,* trans., London, 1957.

feature not found in the pyramids of Egypt, except in the stepped types, and even in the latter the steps are not so broad in proportion as are these terraces.

Probably the largest of all pyramids, as regard extent, is one standing not far from Puebla, called the Pyramid of Cholula. Its base is 1,423 feet square, but its height only some 164 feet. Its sides, as is usual, face the four cardinal points, and it was used as a mausoleum. It is of late (Aztec) date, and has even been alleged to have been put up during the reign of Montezuma, last Aztec emperor (1466–1520).

There are many remains of such pyramids in Mexico, and practically the same thing in Yucatan, whilst they reach a large size in the highlands of Peru.

CHAPTER VII

THE MAGIC OF INDIA

Indian Chronology. The earliest cultural period that has been much studied in India is called the Vedic, and dates from before 600 B.C. Some say it is very ancient. The gods of this period have been incorporated into the later pantheon, called the Brahminic, but bear much the same relation that the Titans do to the Olympians in Greek mythology. In the last century the doings of the Vedic gods were interpreted purely as nature myths by Max Müller, the famous Sanskrit scholar, but it is now apparent that this, to say the least, was a very one-sided interpretation. There are few monumental remains from the Vedic period, but the idea that images of the gods were not then made is now discredited.

The Magical Hierarchy. The mighty population of India, now estimated at over 350 million (nearly one seventh of that of the whole world) is largely under the control of the brahmins or brahmans, the members of the priestly caste. The latter, however, differ amongst themselves in many ways, and are not subject to any form of central organisation or supervision, as for instance was the case in Egypt.

Nevertheless, apart from those Indians that have been influenced by Western ideas and modernism, the whole country is still organised on the basis of caste, the latter being inherited, and the occupation of everyone is thus largely determined.

There are four main castes, each subdivided into numerous divisions.[1] The main castes may be described briefly, as follows, although it must be realised there are many variations, too numerous to mention.

The *brahmins* as we will call them, following Western custom, are supposed to be initiates into the secret knowledge of the *Atman*, the breath of God which infuses life into every human being; nowa-

[1] For an excellent account of these, before they and their customs began to crack up under the influence of modernism, see J. A. Dubois: *Hindu Manners, Customs and Ceremonies*, trans. 3rd ed., Oxford, 1906 (recently reprinted).

days however every man is a brahmin who has been born of brahmin parents and who has been duly invested with the sacred cord, a ceremony of initiation. The women of the caste are initiated by their marriage to a brahmin. There are many celibate brahmins, but all these have been married, and have given up the married state to live as ascetics.

There is some reason for calling the brahmins magicians, although nothing at all derogatory is implied by this. At any rate there is evidence for the belief that brahminical ceremonies have a determined effect when properly performed.

The second caste is that of the *kshatriyas*, or regal and warrior caste. From this is drawn the rajahs and maharajahs, and the officers of the army. They too are entitled to be initiated by the conferring of the sacred cord.

The third caste consists of the *vaisyas* (*vaishyas*) which includes the merchants and farmers. These, too, are entitled to initiation by means of the sacred cord, like the two preceding castes, and all three, because of this, are called *twice-born*. The cord is worn over the left shoulder and right hip.

The fourth caste consists of the *sudras* (*shudras*) and comprises the labourers. Most of these are not entitled to the cord.[2]

Apart from the castes there are certain Hindus, called outcasts, untouchables or *pariahs* who, for one reason or another, do not belong to any caste. They are avoided by other Hindus, and scarcely conform to their customs. For instance they are allowed to eat meat.

Sacred Prostitution. Almost any temple of any importance in India had attached to it a group of dancing girls, some eight to twelve in number. These women are said to be concubines of the priests, and to act as prostitutes among the congregation. The sexual act is here regarded as a sacrament, as an alternative to the more ordinary sacrament of marriage. They are sometimes regarded as married to the god, to whom the temple is dedicated. Dubois,[3] a Catholic priest, comments on their modesty in dress and public behaviour, which has nothing in common with that of prostitutes as known in Europe. They wear beautiful perfumed costumes, coiffures well

[2] The cord is also worn by the Jains, who do not belong to the Hindu religion, and are relatively few in number. According to J. Yarker (*The Arcane Schools*, Belfast, 1909) the cord was of different material in the three castes.

[3] *Loc cit.*

suited to set off the beauty of their hair, which they entwine with sweet-scented flowers, jewels adorn various parts of their bodies, they assume graceful and voluptuous attitudes but do not expose any part of their person in public. They were formerly, on the whole, much better educated than other women, especially in reading, singing and dancing. Twice a day they perform a sacred dance in the temple. They also take part in all processions, hymns, feasts and family ceremonies. They used to accompany distinguished people at social gatherings. R. P. Knight[4] says that they were selected at an early age for their beauty. Another account says that amongst them are to be found the most beautiful girls in the world. If offspring were born, the latter were also devoted to the temple, and if female followed the profession of their mothers.

Phallic Worship. It is in Hinduism according to current conceptions in the West, that there are the best examples of phallic worship that exist in the world today. This idea is, however, somewhat misleading. It is true that the Hindus, as many peoples did in ancient days, use sexual acts and objects in their religion, but this is purely symbolical. The sexual urge symbolises for them, being one of the more compelling of natural instincts, the power of their gods. It has been compared also, with the vivifying action of the sun on natural objects, and that is an alternative symbol for the same thing.

The *lingam* is the male organ, and the *yoni* the female. The former is usually represented as a pillar, the latter as a circle or oval, which resembled the figure known in the West as the *vesica piscis,* formed by the intersection of two equal circles. Singly or combined these symbols are worn on the person as amulets. They are also erected as monuments, usually combined, these often being of very large size.

The lingam is particularly the symbol of the god Siva. In one of the Puranas,[5] twelve places are mentioned at which this monument was to be seen. These have played a part in the history of India. Some are still in existence, accompanied by magnificent temples. Others have disappeared, having usually been destroyed by Mohammedan invaders. But apart from these twelve there have been and still are a vast number of other monuments of this kind. In fact they are common in most parts of India. They are generally care-

[4] *The Symbolical Language of Ancient Art and Mythology,* New York, 1892.
[5] Sacred books.

fully tended, and anointed from time to time with oil, or washed in milk or water.

There are also images of the gods with their wives, sometimes the former are shown embracing the latter. It must be recorded that some of these carvings appear very indecent to Western eyes.

The serpent is often shown coiled round the lingam, and in other cases is believed to be a substitute for it. Some Indians regard serpents as sacred. They do not all have a phallic significance however. For the serpent, owing to the fact that it casts its skin, is a symbol of regeneration.

The lotus is another important religious symbol in India. This represents the universe. Brahma is sometimes shown arising from or sitting on a lotus, springing from the navel of Vishnu. The lotus represents the three spheres of human experience, being rooted in the mud, extending its stalks through the water, and flowering at the surface, in the air. But the lotus flower does resemble the combined figure of the lingam and yoni, the fruit vessel or ovary standing up in the middle of the flower suggesting the upright column of the monument, and the rest of the flower the encircling base.

Cattle are sacred in India, and it is the greatest of crimes to injure or kill any one of them. It has been alleged that this was originally connected with phallic worship, but on rather slender evidence.[6] It dates back to the time when the Spring Equinox was in Taurus, the constellation of the Bull. This was the period when the Egyptians had their bull Apis as an object of worship, as a sign of fecundity. Stone figures of the bull are very common in India.

Hindu Temples. These are found in every city, town and village. Everywhere they are the centre of communal life. They are generally small, but some of the older ones are of large size. Many are of stone, heavily carved all over. It is a pious act to endow a temple, but patrons often pay for the construction of a number of small ones, rather than one big one. The oldest Hindu temples[7] that have survived are those of stone, constructed during the reigns of the Pallava kings, supposed to be between the 4th and 9th centuries A.D. More ancient temples, being largely constructed of wood (as they still are in Malabar) have probably for this reason

[6] The white bull Nandi is sacred to Siva, whose other symbol is the lingam, as we have seen. The image of this bull is seen everywhere in front of or near temples of Siva, just as those of the bird Garuda are seen before the temples dedicated to Vishnu.

[7] This does not include Buddhist *stupas*, or Buddhist and Jain *cave-temples*, which are mentioned later.

disappeared.[8] The oldest Pallava temples are artificial caves, carved out of solid rock (as were some Buddhist structures) but later monuments of the same dynasty were constructed of cut stone. However there are relatively few of this period.

Hindu Astrology. In our discussion of the star groups of Neolithic times and their evolution into the celestial constellations of today we said little about India. However it appears that astronomy and astrology were very highly developed in India at a very early date. The old idea that India derived astrology from Chaldean sources is now discredited. The star science of India differs fundamentally from that of the Chaldeans and the West which was derivéd from Chaldean sources. The Indians, in fact, have preserved two features which have been lost in the West, as follows :

(i) We have already mentioned there are two zodiacs : those of the constellations and of the signs. The Indians know this and they have pretty accurate measures of the precession of the Equinoxes. In spite of this, in their horoscopes (unlike the Western) they generally use the zodiac of the constellations.

(ii) The Hindus pay particular attention to the lunar divisions of the zodiac, of which they count twenty-seven.

[8] H. K. Sastri: *South Indian Images of Gods and Goddesses, Madras,* 1916.

CHAPTER VIII

YOGA

Sources of Yoga. The *Shastras* include the sacred books of Brahminism, but the term is also applied to commentaries and summaries of cognate subjects. Some of the latter deal with what are known as the shad-darsanas or six schools of Indian philosophy. One of the six is that dealing with Yoga, founded by the sage Patanjali. It is concerned with the union of man with the Universal Spirit, and shows how, in the attainment of such union, the individual acquires remarkable powers.

Patanjali was no doubt a historical personage, but is so much mixed up with legend that it is not possible to give him a date. Three dates are ascribed to him in Dowson's *Classical Dictionary of Hindu Mythology,* viz. about 200 B.C., 143 B.C. and A.D. 25. The fact that he fell from heaven in the form of a small snake, does not help us.

Patanjali's work on Yoga, generally termed his aphorisms, is a small one, and has on more than one occasion been translated from Sanskrit into European languages, including our own.[1]

It is generally conceded, however, that Yoga is a practical subject, in fact more than that, it is a way of life. It is also agreed that Yoga must be learned from personal tuition, rather than from books. One must, as in related subjects, always find and learn from a *guru, i.e.* a religious teacher.

There are many references to Yoga in the sacred scriptures of India. In the *Bhagavad Gita* Krishna himself refers to it. Yoga theory and Yoga practice are both very old. Yoga means union, and refers to union with the higher self, and ultimately with the Universal Spirit or God. In its aims it resembles mysticism in the West. But its methods are for the most part quite different.

Feats of the Yogis. The *yogis* or practitioners of yoga are mostly, almost exclusively, drawn from the *sannyasis* or brahmins in their

[1] See for example *Aphorisms of Yoga* by Bhagwan Shree Patanjali, trans. with commentary by Shree Purohit Swami and an introduction by W. B. Yeats, London, 1938, reprinted 1952.

fourth or last stage of religious life. They may wander about, sub-
sist upon charity, and wear little clothing. A few yogis are drawn
from Buddhist orders, but these are mostly found in China; Indo-
China and Tibet, and not in India. There are also Moslem prac-
tioners of similar arts; these are properly termed fakirs. Yogis are
of varying degrees of intellectual and spiritual development, and
some perform the most remarkable feats.

Yogis first practise control over certain desires, and this in many
instances leads on to great asceticism. There are eight steps, according to Patanjali, in renunciation: (i) *Yama* which includes non-
violence, truth-speaking, non-covetousness, non-stealing and non-
receiving (even of gifts) and continence; (ii) *Niyama* which includes
cleanliness, contentment, abstinence from desire, concentration and
study, recognition of God; (iii) *Asana*, the correct positions assumed
by the body and limbs for particular purposes; (iv) *Pranayama*,
control of the breath; (v) *Pratyahara*, introspection and control of
the senses; (vi) *Dharana*, concentration and control of the mind;
(vii) *Dhyana*, a higher stage of mind-control; (viii) *Samadhi*, a still
higher stage, ecstasy.

Some of these stages, however, become an end in themselves for
certain practitioners of yoga. The asanas necessary to pass on to the
next stage are probably few, but this subject has loomed large in
the popular presentation of Yoga. In the more simple of these
asanas the yogi sits with his thighs more or less horizontal, his legs
flexed, as in the position shown in most images of Buddha. There
are, however, variations relating to the position of the feet. There
are also different positions of the hands, sometimes termed *mudras*.[2]
There are about a dozen well known sitting asanas, some of which
have received popular names, such as the lotus, the lock, the cock,
etc. Altogether there are said to be eighty-four of these postures,
but some of them assume other attitudes than that already described
such as the cobra, with legs stretched out behind, and front of the
body raised, and the upside-down asana, in which the yogi stands
on his head. In a few, such as the lion, the yogi kneels, with his
knees forward. The noose asana calls for the placing of the
thighs under the arms, and the legs behind the head, a position
worthy of a contortionist.

Some ascetics sit in one of these positions for months or years.
Others have themselves suspended, either upside down or in some
apparently awkward position, such as suspended on a wire, balanc-

---

[2] The term *mudras* applies chiefly to hand-postures, but is also used in a
wider sense for any bodily attitudes.

ing thereon like a tight rope walker for hours, days, months or years. Others hold up their arms to the sky, until they lose all pain and they become immobile and useless. Others load themselves with heavy chains, confine themselves or parts of their body, usually the head, in iron frames or cages. Or they lie for days, months or years on beds of thorns, or iron spikes. Some walk about with dozens of arrows or spears embedded in their flesh. These self-torturers can hardly be described as yogis, but their behaviour may be compared with some forms of yoga, at least, inasmuch as that the ability to control the feeling of pain is here shown at an extreme degree.

Some of these feats have been equalled, or even excelled by ascetics following the Mohammedan religion. Such alone are properly termed *fakirs*. Many of these exist in Moslem countries, and only a few attain great powers. They often perform humble duties, such as cleaning of mosques and assisting with burials. They wear coarse brown or black clothing, and a black turban over which a red handkerchief is placed. But a small majority of these holy men have studied practical yoga, and whilst they and their Hindu counterparts have been accused of trickery there is no doubt that a few of them do things which have not yet been explained by Western science. They are also found among the Sikhs.

These practitioners (yogis and fakirs) have acquired a power over those parts of the body which function, according to Western ideas, in an involuntary fashion. For us only the striped muscle forming the muscles of the body is under the control of the will. But a yogi can control the heart and blood vessels (which we in the West can only do by auto- or hetero-suggestion and then not very effectively). They probably influence the circulation by feeling, rather than will, as Coué did in his auto-suggestion. But their ability transcends anything hitherto attempted in the West. Hereward Carrington[3] records that Hamid Bey, after numerous other feats, showed control over his blood circulation. Three physicians recorded, one the left pulse, one the right, one listened to the heart with a stethoscope. At first all were normal and, of course, showed the same pulsation. Soon however there was a change, the left wrist recorded 102, the right 84 and the heart 96 instead of all being near the normal 72.

Still more remarkable is the ability to throw oneself into a trance. One ascetic is reported to have planted a mustard seed on some soil on his lips, nor did he move until that seed had sprouted. Others have been buried alive for longer or shorter periods.

[3] Magic Men of India, *True Magazine*, May, 1926.

Hamid Bey is recorded by Carrington as having been buried alive for several hours. The fakir told Dr. Carrington that before burial the heart has to be slowed down until it beats only a few times a minute, otherwise he could not survive. The neck is manipulated, the tongue turns back into the throat, the body becomes cataleptic, breath is practically stopped. Apart from the stiffness due to the catalepsy the body appears dead. Hamid Bey said the state resembled that of a bear or turtle hibernating. The ability to do it was acquired by gradually extending an experimental trance period. The burial of Hamid Bey was recorded in the newspapers as having taken place in the garden of the New Jersey home of Mr. Walter A. Shannon. It lasted three hours.

One of the most remarkable feats of suspended animation in the human subject is that described as having been performed before the Maharajah Runjit Singh in Lahore in 1837. A yogi, much venerated by the Sikhs, named Haridas, was buried alive for forty days, after which he was dug up and revived. Before burial the yogi fell into a trance, then assistants stopped his nose, mouth, ears and eyes with wax and wrapped him in a shroud. He was lowered into a grave which was filled with earth, and a guard placed over it, to watch against trickery. When he was brought up he was somewhat emaciated, but otherwise was none the worse for his experience.

Attempts to imitate these feats have seldom been made in Europe and America. Houdini, the famous escapologist, shortly before his death, was buried in a coffin under six feet of water for an hour and a half. The amount of air in the coffin was only enough to last, under ordinary conditions, for about four minutes. Houdini said there was nothing relating to the supernatural in the feat; it was all a matter of keeping quite still, and taking short even breaths. Raman Bey, an Egyptian fakir was seen in London about the same time, similarly stayed under water at Carshalton for about an hour, and said it was only possible if he put himself into a hypnotic trance. In France about 1950 Michel Marechal, otherwise known as Yama Kevadi was recorded in press reports from Dijon to have stayed in a coffin under water for three hours, one minute and one second. In 1927 the first woman in the history of the world to be buried alive was interred under test conditions for motion picture news reels; this occurred in the United States, the lady, Mlle. Nijmi, was initiated and trained by Dr. Abd-el-Rahman El Adaros, Founder-President of the Society of Transcendent Science, Chicago.

There are two stages which the yogi can attain in developing the power to be buried alive. In the first he requires the help of assistants when he is to be revived, they bathe his body in warm water, and may even put his tongue (which during the trance has been in the pharynx) back into place. In the second and more advanced stage he can revive himself unaided.

One of the most remarkable instances of prolonged burial, followed by revival is recorded by Dr. Alexander Cannon,[4] the London psychiatrist. He was visiting a monastery in Tibet. One of the ceremonies witnessed was the revival of a man who had been dead, the doctor was told, for seven years. The monks assembled to the light of torches, arranging themselves in a circle and chanting. Their chief prayed, a huge stone coffin was brought in to the centre, carried by eight men. A stone slab, covering the coffin was removed, and Dr. Cannon was allowed to examine the body inside. He applied various tests, there was no pulse, no breath and the body was stone cold. To all appearance it was dead.

However the chief lama then began a recitation of certain strange words, and the eyes of the corpse opened, the body gradually sat up, and then assisted by monks walked towards the celebrant and bowed to him. Thereafter it returned to its coffin, lay down therein and became again as dead.

Levitation is one of the feats most often ascribed to the adepts in yoga; in this ability to raise themselves into the air they rival mediaeval saints and modern spiritualists. In the *Asiatic Monthly Journal*, March, 1829 there is an account[5] of a brahmin who could raise himself into the air and apparently sit there and could remain under water for several hours. The Indian rope trick is well known as a story, although few have seen it. A coiled rope is thrown into the air, uncoiling as it goes up. Its upper end remains suspended, miraculously. Then a boy climbs up to the top and disappears. The performance has been ascribed to mass hypnotism of the onlookers. Others say it has never been seen. On certain occasions large sums of money have been offered in India to anyone who would volunteer to perform it, but no one came forward.

Other feats ascribed to yoga, on the physical plane, include the ability to make oneself lighter or heavier, larger or smaller, to travel through space, to animate dead bodies, to become invisible oneself, and to make bodies invisible, to make objects appear, as if from nowhere, to read the past and the future, or events going on at the present time in any part of the world. Some of the practitioners

[4] *The Invisible Influence*, London, 1933.
[5] Quoted from E. Cobham Brewer: *A Dictionary of Miracles*, London, 1884.

may get wonderful effects by methods used by hypnotists in the West, others resemble spiritualistic phenomena. It is fair to add, however, that many yogis regard physical phenomena either as unnecessary, or as only means to higher ends. At any rate the object of yoga is to satisfy the higher aspirations of the yogi, and not to provide entertainment for the public.

Kinds of Yoga. Western authors make much of the classification of yoga into various subdivisions, according to the means adopted and the object to be gained. All however have importance according to the sacred books, and they are often combined by yogis. They are as follows :

(i) *Hatha Yoga* = yoga of health; this is somewhat akin to modern physical education in the West, and has been adapted for students of that subject; it includes exercises, postures, control of the organs and external and internal washing; it has some similarity with the nature cure movement.

(ii) *Mantra Yoga*=yoga of speech, this consists of the correct enunciation of certain sacred and mystical phrases in Sanskrit, such as the famous

"Om mane padme hum"[6]

These are repeated rhythmically, the number of times being carefully regulated. The process reminds one of the Rosary in the West; in fact various rosaries are used in Hinduism. It will also be recalled that Coué, the exponent of auto-suggestion, taught his followers to use a knotted cord, and to repeat suggestions over and over again. However Coué lacked the religious motive!

(iii) *Raja Yoga* = yoga of will, royal yoga. This can only be performed by those who are already advanced in hatha yoga and mantra yoga. The breath is brought entirely under voluntary control, and control of the emotions brings about the ability to alter the visceral functions, a matter already referred to. Meditations on the mystical syllable OM or AUM are used. The three letters of the latter are believed to represent the three members of the Godhead.

(iv) *Bhakti Yoga* =. yoga of devotion. Here the aspirant usually chooses one of the gods, to represent some aspect of the Supreme, and pays his devotion to the said god in a special manner.

(v) *Gnana Yoga* = yoga of knowledge. The latter refers to arcane knowledge of the Universe, as is taught in Brahmin theosophy. The

---

[6] "Hail thou Jewel in the Lotus, Amen." This is an almost exact equivalent of the first part of the *Ave Maria* of the West, Christ being the Jewel and Mary the Lotus. It is better known in Tibet than in India.

chela or pupil strives to acquire, not only theoretical, but actually
practical knowledge *e.g.* memory of past incarnations, reading of
the minds of others, etc.

(vi) *Karma yoga* = yoga of work. The yogi works in the outer
world, acquiring extraordinary skill in military and civil arts and
handicrafts; this form of yoga has something in common with Zen
in Buddhism.[7] It makes use of what we in the West would call the
forces of the Unconscious.

(vii) *Laya or Kundalini Yoga* = yoga of equilibrium. This yoga,
in addition to using all the preceding methods, succeeds in raising
the energy called *kundalini* or *serpent power*, which is said to be
lying coiled up, in a latent state, near the base of the spine. When
it is uncoiled it successively activates the *chakras* or *lotus-blossoms*
which are the centres of power (*shatki*) in the human organism.

Several other kinds of yoga have been described but they are of
lesser importance.

Sex Magic. There is one subject, allied to yoga, that needs our
attention. In yogic literature there are often allusions to the *Tantras*.
These we have seen are sacred books, appended to the Puranas, of
which four are well known, although some say there are as many
as 160. They take the form of dialogues between Siva and his wife.
The latter is called his *sakti*, and represents power or sex-libido,
symbolised as the wife of the god. The practical application of
these teachings is carried on mainly in Bengal and the Eastern
Provinces. The worshippers are called Saktas and are of two classes,
called right-handed and left-handed. The former use a statue or
painting of a naked woman in their daily devotions,[8] or an orna-
ment called *sri-kakra* in brass or stone depicting the external organ
of the female sex. They apparently inflame the sex instinct, sometimes in an abnormal direction.[9] Those of the left-hand path hold
their meetings in secluded places, and the object of devotion is a
living beautiful woman.[10] For this kind of tantric worship the five
makaras[11] are required: (i) *madya* = wine, (ii) *mansa* = flesh,
(iii) *matsya* = fish, (iv) *mudra* = gesticulations and (v) *maithuna*
= sexual intercourse. It need hardly be repeated that the eating of

[7] Not to be confused with the Zen sect.
[8] Sir George MacMunn: *The Religions and Hidden Cults of India*, London
(not dated).
[9] *Loc. cit.*
[10] *Loc. cit.*
[11] J. Dowson: *Classical Dictionary of Hindu Mythology and Religion,
Geography, History and Literature*, 7th edition, London, 1950.

flesh is prohibited to the vast majority of Hindus, and is generally looked upon as repulsive. Moreover the way in which the other matters are used is such as to suggest that these practices are not wholly approved by Hindu society, in spite of all we have said about their ideas on sexual symbolism. The left-handed saktis are also said to stimulate their passion with drugs and their meetings are said to degenerate into sexual orgies.

In one ceremony, formerly practised in certain places in India, men and women assembled in a secret place. Each woman then removed her upper garment, which was placed in a sort of basket. The latter was then circulated among the men, each of whom drew out a garment. The woman to whom this garment belonged became the sexual partner of the man who drew it, for the rest of the evening.

It is probable, however, that very few Hindus took part in such rites as these, which were by no means approved by the majority.

Tantric worship, however does tend to diverge from the public rites of the Brahminic religion. It includes a number of complex ceremonies which can only be properly performed by small groups or individuals. Such rites may be performed for private ends, thus becoming magical as opposed to religious. J. Marquès-Rivière[12] translates formulae for death and destruction, distinctly reminiscent of mediaeval witchcraft. The majority, however, are not of this nature. The magical methods are such as could be performed by monks living in the forests. For every purpose a *yantra* is drawn. This consists of a geometrical figure, in which Sanskrit letters are inscribed at certain points. To each letter was ascribed certain powers, and the arrangement of the letters in a particular pattern, within the geometrical framework, was supposed to radiate out a particular influence for good or ill, if the figure were used in the proper manner. Certain rhythmic prayers, depending on the power of sound, called *mantras* were also recited.

The sexual symbolism of the *Tantras* is by some considered as purely a philosophical representation of the way the higher self united with the lower man, this being represented as a sexual act. There is no doubt that such symbolism is often used in Brahminism. There is also no doubt that, at times, sexual practices in India have been strangely mingled with religion.

[12] *Rituel de Magie Tantrique Hindoue*, Paris, 1939.

CHAPTER IX

BABYLON THE GREAT

Babylonian Chronology. In the *Prophecy of Daniel* in the Old Testament the greatness of the city of Babylon is referred to. Situated on both banks of the River Euphrates it stood four-square and covered an area of 200 square miles, if we are to believe the records of Herodotus. The walls surrounding it, in modern measurements, were some 85 feet thick, according to the same historian. Twenty-five gates on each of the four sides of the city were constructed of bronze.[1] Two hundred and fifty towers were placed on the walls.

The word *Babylon* and the word *Babel* are the same in the Hebrew Old Testament. Babylon was built by Nimrod,[2] on the site of, or near where the tower of Babel was built.[3] It was in the land of the biblical Sennaar or Shiner, called Sumer by the archaeologists.

The land between the two rivers, Euphrates and Tigris, called from this position Mesopotamia, now in what is called Iraq, comes into recorded history under the name of the *Land of Accad and Sumer.* The latter was to the south, and its inhabitants the Sumerians were of Mongolian affinity and may have come from Central Asia in prehistoric times. The Akkadians, who had followed and in early times occupied only the north, were of Semitic affinity and may have come from the Caspian region. In those days the two rivers flowed separately into the Persian Gulf whereas today they unite before they reach the sea.

About 2750 B.C. the Akkadians, under Sargon I conquered the Sumerians, and the two lands were united under the Akkadian leader, but retained the Sumerian culture. Cuneiform writing, wedge-shaped marking on baked clay tablets, was already in existence in the south. The double empire lasted for about two centuries. It was in contact with people called Hittites on the north,

[1] The word is translated brass in the Old Testament, meaning bronze or copper.
[2] *Genesis,* x, 10.
[3] *Genesis,* xi, 1–9.

in present day Armenia. On the west were Amorites, in Syria. On the east in Persia were Kassites, and south of them the Elamites. The Elamites conquered Sumer and Accad, but failed to retain their sway. Then the Amorites gradually took over, and Babylon became the capital, this regime becoming stabilised under Hammurabi, the famous law-giver, about 2100 B.C. Thus the Babylonian Empire was established. This lasted, with a few temporary eclipses until 745 B.C. Meanwhile another people, the Assyrians, a purely Semitic people, had appeared in the north. For a long time they had an independent kingdom there. Finally under their king, Tiglath-pileser III, they conquered Babylonia and a conjoined kingdom was established. The capital was the great city of Nineveh in the north of Mesopotamia.

In 606 B.C. a combined force of Medes and Persians from the north and east, and a Semitic people called Chaldeans (perhaps a mixed remnant of the Akkadians) from the south and east overthrew the Assyrians at Nineveh. Assyria was ceded to the Medes under Cyaxares. A new Babylonian (Chaldean) Empire was established to the south under Nebuchadnezzar II. The story of the latter is given in the Old Testament. He carried away a large number of the Israelites into captivity. His imaginary transformation into an ox is one of the first instances of lycanthropy (the transformation of man into an animal) of which we have any record.

The new Babylonian Empire did not last long. Its ruler in some way upset the priesthood. He was feasting one night with a thousand of his nobles when a most extraordinary event happened.[4] A hand appeared and wrote mysterious characters on the surface of the wall, over against a candlestick. Not one of the court magicians being able to interpret them, the prophet Daniel was called in. He read the inscription as follows : "God hath numbered thy kingdom, and hath finished it. Thou art weighed in the balance and found wanting. Thy kingdom ... is given to the Medes and Persians." Before the night was out the ruler was slain, and the kingdom fell to the Medio-Persians. Shortly afterwards Cyrus, king of the Medes and Persians, released the Israelites, and ordered the restoration of their temple at Jerusalem.

Another Magical Hierarchy. When the Sumerian peoples first appear on the stage of history, as recorded in the numerous remaining cuneiform inscriptions, they appear as an aggregation of city-states, of which eleven "cities of royalty" each possess a separate

4 *Daniel,* Chapter V

throne. The latter was occupied by a *patesi* or governor who often assumed the high title of *lugal* or sacred king. This was the highest priestly as well as a royal office. Under him was a chief priest and next a temporal ruler. Babylon was not one of the cities of royalty, but Ur of the Chaldees, mentioned in the Bible as the native place of Abraham, was. Sometimes one, sometimes another of these royal cities dominated all the others. Sometimes there was rivalry, two or more of them being regarded as equally important. When Babylon became the capital the same organisation was retained, except that the highest rank was accorded to the ruler of the capital. Although he was called king or emperor it must be remembered that he held the highest priestly office and as shown from bas-reliefs and other carvings he spent most of his time performing religious ceremonies. He carried the shepherd's crook, and was called tenant-farmer of God, being responsible, through his magic, for all agriculture throughout his land, as in Egypt and China. Each year, at the spring festival, corresponding with our Easter, three important ceremonies were performed.[5] First there was a dramatic representation of the conflict between the chief god Marduk and the dragon of Chaos. During this the god is vanquished and slain, but is raised from death by magical ceremonies, and eventually overcomes the dragon. Secondly the king is brought before the image of Marduk, his insignia are removed, he is struck on the face by the high-priest. An omen was taken at this point, for if the blow produced tears all would be prosperous in the realm and vegetation would grow well during the next year. This is considered by some as a substitute for the sacrifice of the king. Finally there was a sacred marriage, where the king, acting the part of the god, was united sexually with one of the priestesses of high rank, representing the goddess.

A large part of the work of the priests was divination. The object of this was to ascertain, as far as possible, whether conditions were favourable or unfavourable for a particular action. For this purpose the calendar was consulted, which gave the appropriate astrological information. The phases of the moon were particularly important.

Women played the part of priestesses, these having particular functions, differing from those of the men. Some of them belonged to the order of sacred prostitutes, who played an important part at the great seasonal festivals.

The priests and priestesses wore elaborate vestments, if we are to judge from the carvings.

[5] S. H. Hooke: *Babylonian and Assyrian Religion*, London, 1953.

The Tower of Babel. We have already drawn attention to vast monuments having a connection with the dead, as well as a reference to the heavens, in discussing the pyramids of Egypt and America. These have been regarded as artificial mountains.

That the Babylonians built high towers is certain, and one of the last of them, *circa* A.D. 10, remains fairly complete to this day at Samarra. Pictures on cylinder seals show them in building. These towers were called *ziggurats,* and have survived under Moslem culture, in modified form, as minarets. Remains of another ziggurat were found at Babylon, associated with part of a temple; this is generally considered to have been the Tower of Babel itself.

Amulets and Talismans. The whole life of the Babylonians was plagued by evil spirits, and, judging from the numbers recovered, hardly anywhere in the world was the use of amulets and talismans more resorted to.

An *amulet* is an object which is believed to have a beneficial influence on its owner. It is usually small, and generally portable. Its shape, its material and any markings or inscriptions on its surface are generally believed to be significant. Amulets, to be efficacious, should be magically charged, or blessed by a priest in those cases where their action is believed to depend solely on the faith of the owner or wearer. They were formerly used, very frequently, with a view to the cure of disease.

A *talisman* differs from an amulet in that it is constructed for a specific purpose. When the object for which it is required becomes known to the magical practitioner, the latter chooses a suitable time, when the stars are favourable, and inscribes a suitable magical inscription on some appropriate material. Virgin parchment was used in later times, but this, of course, was unknown among the Babylonians.

Whilst the Babylonians, as we have said, had nothing quite like the mediaeval talisman, they seem to have had *talismanic sculptures.* We call them by this name because they seem to have had a specific purpose. Many are described by Budge[6] who gives samples of the complex rituals, including the incantations used, and the meaning of the symbolism.

Chaldean Astrology. In classical and even in mediaeval times the term Chaldean was almost synonymous with astrologer or astrological. When Alexander the Great captured Babylon in 344 B.C.,

[6] E. A. Wallis Budge: *Amulets and Superstitions*, London, 1930.

wresting the great city from the Medes and Persians who had held it since 539, he was presented with the astronomical records of that empire, dating back to 2230 B.C. Diodorus, a classical author, writing about 40 B.C. refers to observations of the Babylonians extending over 473,000 years. Cicero in his *De Divinatione* refers to these observations, giving the round number of 470,000. If this is not mere boasting it may mean that the Babylonians had calculated back and placed some event some 470,000 years before, for astrologers can calculate past positions, as well as future, from their knowledge of astronomical regularities, and can imagine what sort of events such positions may signify.

· That the Babylonians were, in fact, highly skilled in astronomy is evinced by the large collection of cuneiform inscriptions dealing with astronomical observations and their interpretations. In later or Chaldean times they had available as much information as is used by astrologers today.

CHAPTER X

SOLOMON AND THE JINN

Islamic Legends. Islam, the religion of the Moslems, is essentially based on tradition, and is very rich in legends. Although the founder Mohammed lived in the 6th century A.D. many of these stories may have originated much earlier, and they certainly refer to events of preceding epochs. Most in fact, apart from those relating to the prophet himself, deal with matters mentioned in the Old Testament, a few concern Christ and Mary his mother, although in a way rather different from the New Testament. Some legends are recorded in the sacred book of the Mohammedan religion, the *Koran*, but in addition to this all schools of the Moslems receive a considerable amount of traditional material not so recorded.

In the Western World the chief source of information on this subject, apart from the *Koran* (which has been translated from the Arabic into most European languages) are the fantastic tales collected together under the name of the *Thousand and One Nights* which were first brought to the notice of the Western World when, in 1704 to 1712 A. Galland published a French translation. Later they were translated into English by several authors, the best known versions being those of E. W. Lane and Sir Richard Burton. This cycle of stories is highly esteemed in the West, but apparently less so among the Arabs themselves. There has been much argument about the source of these tales. Burton dates the earliest from the 8th century A.D. and the latest as late as the 16th century. He is inclined to believe that they come from the Persian. Some think they may even be derived from India. But they are Arabian in every detail. As they are full of magical lore, and even give accounts of magical procedures, we must refer to them, if we are to be complete, although it is impossible to ascribe any real historical period to the stories. Many of the tales are enacted in the reign of the Caliph Harun al Rashid (763–809) who figures in a number of them, but others are set, as Burton says : "In times of yore and in ages long gone before" ...

The Islamic Cosmos. Various symbolic ideas were entertained as to the position of the earth in the universe. The Moslems in this matter excel in phantasy their Hindu and Buddhist brethren. There are seven heavens, variously described, and said to be composed of different precious stones and metals. There are seven hells, which seem to include purgatory, a place of probation for those awaiting admission to heaven, and according to some the earth itself is one of the seven.[1] The earth is surrounded by a great sea, beyond which is the circular Mount Qaf. It rests on the sacred stone Sakrat, the reflected light from which is said to cause the blue colour of the sky; a single grain of this stone is alleged to give magical powers to its possessor. The whole is said to be supported on the shoulders of a giant angel (cf. Atlas in classical mythology). This angel stands on a rock of ruby, which is supported by a huge bull, Kujata, with many eyes and feet, and the bull stands on the enormous fish Bahamut which apparently swims in chaos.

On this earth there are several classes of beings, besides humanity. The most frequently mentioned, in Islamic mythology, are the *jinn* or *djinn* whose bodies are made of smokeless fire as contrasted with angels whose bodies are composed of light. Burton equates the jinn with the salamanders or fire-spirits of Western fairy-lore. The jinn (*sing.* jinni) are of various ranks and orders. To the lowest rank belong the *jann* who are the least powerful. Most of these have been demoted from the next rank, just as apes and swine are often men transformed by magic. The second class is called *jinn*, the term here being used in its restricted sense. The third class comprises *shaitans*. The fourth and powerful class are called *ifrits*. The fifth and most powerful class are the *marids*. The jinn were created two thousand years before Adam; they reproduce their kind and die, but their lives are on the whole much longer than those of human beings. Many, however, are killed by shooting stars. Numerous jinn of all kinds live in the mountainous country of the Qaf,[2] but some have taken up their abode amongst men. They haunt wild places on the sea-shore and the banks of rivers, or live among ruins, old wells, latrines and ovens. The Arabs, when they visit such places, may ask permission of the jinn, so as not to offend them. There are good and evil jinn, and they are of various religions and sects, as are mankind. The good female jinn are usually called *peris*, a word derived from the Persian, and originally a term in the Zoroastrian religion. The whole of the jinn were originally ruled over by a series of monarchs called Sulaiman or Solomon. The last

[1] The numbers of heavens and hells differ somewhat in different accounts.
[2] A circular country surrounding the world in Islamic lore.

of these has been identified with the Solomon of the Old Testament. The creatures called *ghouls* have been included with the jinn. They haunt graveyards and prey upon corpses. They are usually female, and it is alleged they waylay travellers, and try to prostitute themselves to men. Other jinn also sometimes violate human beings (as what we will afterwards mention, as *incubi* and *succubi* in Western folk-lore). It is even pretended that mixed offspring may be produced, between a jinni and a human being.

The jinn have certain powers which mankind do not possess. They fly rapidly from place to place. They can easily make themselves invisible, and can also appear in different shapes of animals plants, clouds and vapour. On the other hand they can be controlled by human beings, who know how, and none had greater control over them than Solomon, to whom they were totally subjected. Individual jinn or groups are often bound to servitude by the possessor of a ring. Solomon had a most powerful ring of this kind, which he entrusted, whilst he washed, to his favourite concubine Amina. One day Sakhar, a devil or jinni, assumed the form of Solomon, and got possession of the ring. Solomon was dethroned, and Sakhar reigned in his stead. But after forty days Sakhar flew away and threw the ring into the sea. It was swallowed by a fish, but the fish was caught and served up to Solomon, who thus recovered the ring. Another well-known instance is that of Aladdin and his wonderful lamp. A ring with somewhat similar properties, albeit not so powerful, figures in the same story. Other instances of the control of the jinn by means of a ring occur in the *Thousand and One Nights*.

Besides the jinn, which play such an important part in Islamic mythology, there are beings much resembling human beings, inhabiting the realms under the sea. In the story entitled the *City of Brass* in the *Nights* not only are captive jinn brought to the Caliph, but also daughters of the deep are transported to his court, and placed in cisterns full of water. We are told that they died from the great heat. In the story about Julnar, the sea-born, we are given further particulars of the underwater realm, and of the mermen and mermaids that inhabit it.

Besides the creatures of fire and the inhabitants of water there were also spirits of air and earth. The former are often confused with birds. Solomon had dominion over men, jinn, winds, birds, beasts and reptiles. He was said to know the language of birds. This we are told by R. Guenon[3] was symbolic, and refers to a prerogative

[3] *Le Voile d'Isis, circa* 1930.

of high initiation. The language of birds was the angelic language, and is represented in the human kingdom by rhythmic language, in which the sacred books of the world were originally written. This is the origin of poetry which, at one time sacred, like the rest of the arts, only gradually became profane.

Islamic Magic. Three forms of magic are recognised in Islamic tradition: (i) *dawah* which includes incantations and exorcisms, which is lawful as long as its invocations only include the names of God, good angels and good jinn; (ii) *sihr* which depends upon the power held over evil jinn, and (iii) *kihanah* or fortune-telling. The second and third of these are regarded as unlawful.

Alchemy and Astrology in Arabia. Alchemy, the art of transmutation of metals and other substances is derived from Arabic words *Al Kimiya* meaning the magical craft of the Black Country,[4] the latter place being Northern Egypt, so called from the dark soil of the Nile delta, whereas Southern Egypt was the Red Country, because of the reddish colour of its desert sand. The practical objects of alchemy were three in number: (i) the making of gold and other precious substances generally effected by the *philosopher's stone*; (ii) the finding of the *elixir of life,* usually considered to be a liquid which, if taken, would cure all diseases and, according to many, would preserve life indefinitely; (iii) the creation of life by artificial means, and eventually the production of a living human being (such as the *homunculus* of Paracelsus, to be described later). without the aid of woman. Not all alchemists, it is true, pursued all these quests, but later, at any rate, they became the object of many.

Alchemy has been associated with the *Emerald Tablet,* elsewhere described, as an Egyptian production. The idea of analogy, mentioned in the tablet, is also an idea of alchemy. We know also that the Egyptians were workers in metals and precious stones. Among those whom early alchemical writers mention as having a knowledge of alchemy in times antecedent to exact history were Hermes the Elder (identified by some as Enoch, by others as Mizraim, the grandson of Noah) Hermes Trismegistus, identified by Diodorus Siculus, a classical writer, with the son of Mizraim[5]; Isis, Queen of Egypt; an Egyptian goddess already referred to; Agathadaemon, a Phonecian serpent deity; Pibechios, a god identified by F. Sherwood

[4] E. A. Wallis Budge: *Amulets and Superstitions,* London, 1930.
[5] F. Sherwood Taylor: *The Alchemists,* London, 1951.

Taylor[6] with Apollo; Cleopatra, Egyptian queen; Ostanes, legendary Persian sage; Moses, Hebrew prophet[7] and several obscure personages whom Taylor[8] supposes may have been historical persons. Of the latter Mary the Jewess may be mentioned, as she was the first to describe the *still*, the apparatus used for distillation, her description being quoted by Zosimus,[9] *circa* A.D. 300. The Arabs were acquainted with alchemy, which they probably derived from Egypt, as the Jews and Persians may have done. Certainly they afterwards became very famous for their alchemical writings, which influenced mediaeval Europe as we will see later.

The Arabs derived most of their knowledge of astrology from the Chaldeans. It was probably less altered than their mythological borrowings from the same source.

The Arabic zodiac was derived from the Chaldean and is therefore practically identical with ours. There are a few minor differences in the names, but the signification is the same, thus Virgo was an ear of corn, Libra was the purchase, referring to the use of scales in trading, Scorpio was the wounding, Sagittarius the arrow and so on.

The Arabic lunar mansions, on which the Arabs relied greatly, are different in name from those of the Hindus, although they begin at the same point, and occupy the same areas in the heavens.

The Arabs were also responsible for most of the names still in use for individual fixed stars. Although today all fixed stars are designated by the constellation to which they belong preceded by a Greek letter (or number after the Greek alphabet has been exhausted), or by their number in some catalogue, yet Western astronomers still often use a number of the Arabic names, somewhat modified in most cases. Such designations are full of magic, and often refer to qualities possessed, or.believed to be possessed, by the stars in question.

[6] *Loc. cit.*
[7] The grounds for supposing Moses to have been an alchemist are the biblical description of the way he disposed of the golden calf.
[8] *Loc. cit.*
[9] Taylor, *loc. cit.*

CHAPTER XI

THE CULT OF FIRE

Persian History and Legends. The cult of the sacred fire first began among the Persians, and ever since has been, at any rate in poetry and romance, closely associated with magic. It will be remembered that the Chaldeans ruled Mesopotamia in the 8th and 7th centuries B.C. To the east thereof, in the country now called Persia or Iran, were the Kassites, the Elamites and the Persians. To the north, and extending around the southern shores of the Caspian Sea were the Medes. Media had been established as an independent nation in 820 B.C. when it shook off the domination of Assyria. Later it was amalgamated with Persia. The Persian Empire, at its greatest extent, *circa* 525 B.C. extended into Europe, where it included Thrace (north of Greece), into Africa, where it included Egypt and Libya, and far into Asia, where it included modern Afghanistan and Baluchistan, reaching the borders of India. Somewhere in this vast area, but long before it became a single empire, the Magian religion began. It corresponds in time with the Vedic phase in India, and it is commonly believed to be due to a schism among people who spoke the Aryan languages.

The Magi. The Magian religion is commonly associated with the name of the great prophet Zoroaster, or more correctly Zarasthustra. He is believed to be an historical personage who lived about 600 B.C. and in whose time the sacred book of the religion, the *Zend-Avesta* was written down, either by the prophet himself or by some of his followers. But the religion of fire existed much earlier, and several teachers of the same name have been confused together by earlier Western writers on this subject. At any rate the last Zoroaster was only a reformer, who put the religion into a form that has survived to the present day, and is still practised by the Parsees, most of whom have had to forsake the land of their origin, and form only a relatively small community, centred in the region of Bombay.

It is called the *Mazdayasnian* religion, and the *Magian* religion, although the latter term is applied to pre-Zoroastrian cults by some.

From it we get our word *magic*. The priests are sometimes called *Magi*.

Mithraism. Mithra was one of the judges of the soul among the Magians. Mithra, Mitra or Mithras is also mentioned many times as a god in the Vedas, being in the *Rig-Veda* one of the twelve gods who preside over the months of the year. In the *Brahminic* pantheon he occupies an obscure place as his worship has practically died out. In Persia he was originally a sun-god, being termed "the genius of heavenly light." It is curious that the flag of Persia still bears the lion and sun, symbols of Mithra, although the religion is now Shiah Moslem. Even in Persia, it seems, Mithra has been demoted. There is evidence that he has, at times, been regarded as one of the seven amshaspands or even one of the supreme triad. Darius I who came to the throne in 521 B.C. placed the symbols of Mazda and of Mithra in equally conspicuous positions on the sculptured tablet above his tomb, and this practice was continued by his successors.[1] When the latter were conquered by Alexander the cult of Mithras was widespread in his great empire. It particularly flourished in Cappadocia and Phrygia.[2] It became very widespread however and in the first half of the 1st century Christian missionaries were competing with the emissaries of the Mithraic cult in the Roman Empire. Mithraism, in the beginning of the 2nd century A.D. had spread throughout the Roman Empire, for it was very popular with the Roman army, and soldiers sent to various outposts carried the cult. It even spread to Britain, as we know from the discovery of the remains of more than one Mithraic temple. Such temples are widespread over the whole of the wide area occupied by the Roman Empire. In them a conventional figure occurs repeatedly. It is the image of Mithra, in the form of a handsome young man, in Phrygian attire and wearing the famous Phrygian cap that afterwards became a symbol of liberty. He is plunging a knife into the breast of a bull on the back of which he kneels with his left knee. The beast is brought prostrate, to the

---

[1] Rawlinson, quoted by G. J. Bettany: *The World's Religions,* London, New York and Melbourne, 1890.
[2] During the period of the four centuries preceding the birth of Christ a number of kings in Asia Minor, took the name of Mithridates (the gift of Mithra). The most famous was Mithridates VII (131–63 B.C.) of Pontus and Cappadocia who opposed the Romans. He was said to have been incapable of being poisoned or infected, having taken an antidote containing seventy-two ingredients, prepared by his physician Damocrates. Hence the term *mithridate* for any comprehensive curative mixture.

ground, but rears his head upwards. A dog licks the blood flowing from the wound, a serpent and a scorpion crawl at his feet; there are sometimes other figures, and plants springing up from the soil fertilised by the blood. The scene is generally portrayed in a cave. There is little doubt that this represents a sacrificial act of a special kind, whereby the forces of evil are held in check, the fertility of the soil is ensured, and the welfare of mankind is made possible. Mithraic temples in Europe take an oblong form with the altar at the eastern end. In front of each was a pronaos or vestibule, at a lower level, so that the temple itself was approached by a few steps. On each side of the entrance was a human figure. On one side this figure holds a torch upwards, on the other downwards. Above the altar was a figure of Mithras, with the sun on his left and the moon on his right. Sometimes he has seven stars near his head, sometimes he holds a torch, sometimes a flaming sword issues from his mouth, as does the figure like the Son of Man in the Apocalypse,[3] who also holds seven stars and shines as the sun.

[3] *Apoc.*, i, 16.

CHAPTER XII

THE KABALAH

Temple Worship. Like every other great religion that of the Jews was originally hierurgic, *i.e.* they had a priesthood and a more or less complicated ritual. However unlike most peoples, they had a highly centralised cult, for the full enactment of the aforesaid ritual could only be carried out in a single place of worship. This, as we have seen, was at first the movable *tabernacle,* and later the fixed *temple* at Jerusalem, which was thrice erected and thrice destroyed, under the vicissitudes of history. This does not rule out smaller places of worship, such as were present in early times either on hills or under trees,[1] more especially in early times.

Like other great religions the Jewish involved a belief in spirits of various kinds, some of which were angels. The holy men of the Old Testament had to engage in encounters with evil magicians. Moses and Aaron had to engage in contests with the magicians of the pharaoh, during which the rod of Aaron turned into a serpent, which eventually swallowed up those produced by the rivals. Under the command of the Lord they placed ten plagues on the Egyptians in a miraculous fashion. Elias (Elijah) contends in a successful manner with the priests of Baal, being able to set fire to a sacrifice in a supernatural manner, whilst they cannot. Balaam is a sooth-sayer; miraculous speech is given to his ass, and he himself prophesies the Messiah, saying a star shall come out of Jacob, and a sceptre out of Israel. The raising of the spirit of Samuel by the witch of Endor, on being consulted by Saul, is another example of magic in the Old Testament. Finally the most remarkable feat of all was the act of Josue (Joshua) in making the sun stand still, the meaning of which has been variously interpreted by commentators.

The first of the ten commandments includes a prohibition of idolatry. This was so strongly condemned among the Jews and Moslems that there was a strong tendency, especially among the latter, to forbid even the making of images. However, we know that images were sometimes used by the Jews in the worship of God, as

[1] A. W. Oxford: Ancient Judaism in *Religious Systems of the World,* London, 1905.

for instance the two cherubim on either side of the mercy-seat, over the tabernacle and temple, where the presence of God was believed to dwell,[2] and the cherubim carved all round the walls of Solomon's temple.[3] However, such images were frequently looked upon with distrust. The brazen serpent, set up by Moses at the command of God,[4] which healed the Israelites bitten by serpents, was afterwards destroyed, as it had become an object of idolatry. The *teraphim* first mentioned as belonging to Terah, the father of Abraham, and frequently later, were consulted as oracles.[5] There is little doubt that images then, became associated with foretelling the future,[6] not to mention other abominable practices hinted at in various places in the Old Testament, that the sin of idolatry, in fact, had associations with black magic.

Secret Knowledge. The Jews distinguish between the external, or exoteric features of their belief, and the internal, occult, or esoteric aspects. In fact they marked out three grades of knowledge, (i) the law, expounded in the Old Testament, and particularly in the first five books, the *Pentateuch,* ascribed to Moses, which was supposed to be learnt by all Jews; (ii) the *Talmud,* which was studied by all priests and learned rabbis; and (iii) the *Kabalah* or *Kabbalah* (QBLH) which was secret knowledge, imparted to highly learned initiates only, and which has only partly been revealed in writing, and that only in relatively modern times. In addition to the Talmud, we may mention the *Midrashim,* which continued the theological discussions of the Jews from the 2nd to the 13th century A.D.

However, the Kabalah is the great repository of Jewish occult knowledge, and this in mediaeval times had a tremendous influence on both theologians and magicians, Jewish, Christian and Moslem. It is still taught and revered in arcane schools surviving to this day. The Kabalah or Qabalah (variously spelt) is a complete system of symbolism, angelology, demonology and magic. It discusses reincarnation and messianism, and in view of the latter, has become a bone of bitter contention between Jews and Christians, it having been alleged, by the latter, that it contains the whole of Christian theology, whilst it is a fact that a few Jews have been converted to the Catholic religion by its means. It must also be recorded that some Jewish philosophers of note reject the Kabalah altogether, and

[2] *Ex.,* xxv, 22 and many subsequent references.
[3] III *Kings* (= I *Kings,* King James version), vi, 29.
[4] *Numbers,* xxi, 8, 9.
[5] IV *Kings* (= II *Kings,* King James version), xviii, 4.
[6] *Zach.* (*Zech.*), x, 2.

call into question its fundamental assumptions. Amongst these are Moses Maimonides (A.D. 1139–1205) whose *Guide to the Perplexed* has often been reprinted in recent times, and H. Graetz (1817–91), the great Jewish historian.

The Kabalah is an unwritten tradition, and should be learnt from one who is not only a profound Hebrew scholar, but who possesses a flair for occult symbology. This particularly applies to the use of the kabalistic law of correspondences. The kabalists believe that every word, every letter and every point in the Old Testament script has a meaning and therefore the text cannot be altered. The writer once heard a learned kabalist quote Jesus, from the New Testament, regarding Him as a learned rabbi: "Till heaven and earth pass, one jot or tittle shall in no wise pass from the law, till all be fulfilled."[7] Now the kabalists believe there are many correspondences between words and sentences, between letters and numbers and between letters and other letters.

Kabalistic Writings. The kabalah was sacred tradition, going back to Abraham or, as some say, to Adam. It is not a written system at all. Nevertheless it was inevitable that, in course of time, it came to be written down, in whole or in part. The clearest exposition of the system as a whole, and the shortest is the *Sepher Yetzirah*. A very full exposition, rich in mythological symbolism, and the longest is the *Sepher ha Zohar*. A knowledge of these two books, or even the first of them alone, will give the reader a very good idea of the kabalah. Other works are either commentaries on these or connect up kabalism with other matters.

The *Sepher Yetzirah* was written in Hebrew. Its authorship is ascribed to Akiba or Akibha ben Joseph, a Rabbi of the 1st century. It first appeared in print in a Latir translation by William Postel, published in Paris in 1552, and only ten years later, in 1562, did the original Hebrew appear in print, at Mantua. Many other editions followed, and it was translated into a number of European languages, including English. Akibha was originally a shepherd in Palestine, but he became a learned man, founded the first kabalistic school, and when he died in A.D. 138 is said to have had some 24,000 followers. He was succeeded by his pupil Simon ben Yochai, himself a brilliant and famous teacher, surnamed the *spark of Moses*, one of the most famous of kabalists, who lived to about A.D. 160. In the latter part of his life Akiba suffered persecution,

[7] King James version: *Matt.* v, 18.

however, from the pagan Roman power and it is said that he took refuge in a cave, and was finally martyred by the Romans.

There is little doubt that the subject matter of the *Sepher Yetzirah* (*The Book of Formation*) was only systematised by Akiba and is very old indeed. The work is astonishingly compact and only occupies a very few pages. Yet it, more than any other work, embodies the very essence of the kabalistic conception of the Universe.

A work called *the Alphabet* is also ascribed to Akiba. In it the letters are represented as contending amongst one another for the honour of beginning creation.

In the 11th century the Spanish Jew, Ibn Gebirol, known as Avicebron, attained some fame as a philosopher. He was a profound student of the kabalah, wrote *The Fountain of Life* and *The Crown of the Kingdom* dealing with this subject. He died in 1070. By this time the visions of Daniel and Ezekiel had been explained in kabalistic terms.

In the 12th century the kabalistic School of Gerona was founded in the extreme north-east corner of Spain. It was established by a famous Rabbi known as Isaac the Blind and flourished from 1190 to 1210. He made reincarnation one of the chief corner-stones of kabalistic teaching, and expounded the Sephiroth in some detail. He taught the Rabbis Ezra and Azariel. The latter wrote a *Commentary on the Ten Sephiroth* about 1200. Rabbi Azariel was succeded by Nachmanides (b. 1195). The latter was famous for his work on three methods of interpretation: (i) using words for letters or the reverse (*Notariqon*), (ii) using numbers for letters and comparing words of the same numerical value (*Gematria*), and (iii) substituting letters for other corresponding letters (*Temurah*). Nachmanides was followed by the Rabbis Isaac Nasir and Jacob ben Sheshet who bring this school of thought to a close. However, there were several other Schools of the Kabalah in Spain. In the north-central part of the country was the School of Segovia presided over by the Rabbi Abulafia (1240-1292) for example. He is said to have announced[8] that the Epoch of the Messiah was to begin in 1290.

Not far away, at Guadalajara, north-east of Madrid, was the most famous school of all, from whence emanated, just about the year 1290, the greatest of kabalistic books, the previously mentioned

---

[8] I. Regardie: *A Garden of Pomegranates*, an outline of the *Qabalah*, London, 1932, tells us that Abulafia journeyed to Rome with the object of converting the Pope to Judaism!

Zohar, from the pen of the Rabbi Moses ben Leon, the leader of the School of Guadalajara. It was written in Aramaic.

Although it now seems certain that Moses ben Leon was the first to write it down (internal evidence shows that some parts at least must have been written in the 13th century) it is equally certain that much of it is much earlier. Regardie[9] quotes S. M. Schiller-Szinessy, a Cambridge University Reader in Rabbinic Studies, to the effect that much of the *Zohar* "goes back to Mishnic times." We have dated the latter as A.D. 70–200.

The *Zohar* is a massive work. It first appeared in printed form in the Hebrew language in Mantua in 1558, shortly after, in Cremona in 1560 and later at Lublin in 1623. In the following centuries other Hebrew reprints were made. It was partially translated into Latin in 1684 by Baron Knorr von Rosenroth, with commentary, under the title *Kabbala Denudata*. Translations into some modern European languages have subsequently appeared.[10]

The word *Zohar* means *splendour*. *Sepher-ha-Zohar* is the *Book of Splendour*. This is really the title of the main section of the work which, in its present form also contains appendices.

Later Kabalists. Moses ben Leon died in 1305. He was succeeded as head of the School by Menahem di Recanti (*d.* 1350), Isaac Loria or Luria (*d.* 1572) and Chajim (Hayyam) Vital (*d.* 1620). Loria has been described as a wonder-worker or magician. He is said to have been influenced by the prophet Elias (Elijah). He was born at Jerusalem in 1534 and died at Safed in the North of Palestine, 1572. He came of a German-Jewish family and was educated at Jerusalem and Cairo. At the age of twenty-two he took up the life of a hermit in Egypt, but returned to Palestine in 1569. He continued to favour an ascetic mode of life, and is known to have preached the importance of *intention* in carrying out wondrous works. This is a theme which passed to mediaeval magicians and many of them thought that ascetic practices, fastings, abstentions of various kinds, helped them to direct their intention on their work. To Luria is ascribed *Rashith ha Galgalim* (*The Origin of Rotations*) which is a kabalistic presentation of the reincarnaton doctrine, but he wrote relatively little, and most of our knowledge of him comes through his pupil Vital.

The latter was born at Safed in 1534 and died at Damascus,

[9] *Loc. cit.*
[10] The most complete English translation, by H. Sperling and M. Simon appeared in five volumes, 1931-1934.

1620. He was a rabbi in Jerusalem for a short while, but at an early age moved to Damascus, where for a time he was an exponent of the early advent of the Messiah, but pressure was put on him by rabbinical authorities to stop this part of his preaching. Thereafter he elaborated the more recondite parts of the Lurian System, and delved deeply into occultism. He wrote *Otz ha Chiim* (*Tree of Life*) a large manuscript in six parts. This was stolen by a relative, copied and distributed without the consent or even, at first, the knowledge of the author. It was, however, for a long time, retained by the Jews in Palestine. Eventually it was brought to Europe, 1772, and soon after printed at Zolkiew, Poland.

In the Middle Ages in Europe, as we have seen, there were many Christian students of the Kabalah. The most famous of these include Cornelius Agrippa (1486–1536), Guilliam Postel (1510–1581) and Athanasius Kircher (1602–1680), whom we will meet again in a later chapter. In this he was followed by a number of his disciples.

The messianic movement has persisted into recent times. For instance in 1889 Joseph Abdallah, a Jew of the Yemen, Arabia, announced his mission, and no doubt others might be recorded.

Essenes and Therapeutae. These were two religious orders, existing in the time of Christ, the Essenes in Palestine, the Therapeutae in Egypt. Accounts of the Essenes are given by Philo and Josephus, the latter of whom lived amongst them for three years. They appear to have had a philosophy akin to that of Pythagoras, but it is doubtful whether they believed in reincarnation. They were vegetarians and offered no animal sacrifices, engaged in crafts and agriculture, did not trade, held few or no personal possessions, had no slaves. There were both householders and monks amongst them and they had a system of rigorous initiations. They had strict rituals, and rigorously observed the Sabbath. They wore white garments, had frequent ablutions, but never anointed with oil.

Unlike the Essenes the Therapeutae were recluses, spending most of their days in meditation. They fasted long and frequently. Sometimes they came together for worship. Philo and Eusebius wrote about them, and the latter claims them as Christians.

CHAPTER XIII

THE GNOSIS

The Gnostic Heresy. In the very early days of the Christian dispensation there arose various sects of philosophers, all of whom exalted knowledge over faith. Most of them preached the doctrine that salvation is procured by knowledge, rather than by faith and good works. They were called *gnostics* and their doctrine *gnosticism.*

The gnostics distinguished knowledge or *gnosis* from faith or *pistis,* claiming the former to be superior to the latter. They generally regarded matter as evil, and the whole world, they believed, was produced, not by God, but by an inferior being, the *demiurge,* or even by an evil entity. Christ is generally conceived by them as a redeemer, in some way representing the true God, but not usually as wholly divine. The creation, they taught, was effected by emanation, in a series of stages, personified in various mythological figures called *aeons.* Christ was usually considered one of them. The whole collection of aeons, when complete, was termed *the pleroma.* Gnosticism is otherwise very varied in its teachings.

Numerous forms of gnosticism, some with little in common, one with another, appeared in the first two centuries of the Christian era. After that the various schools of thought were cultivated unchanged for a few centuries, then they died out, to be revived in modified form during the Middle Ages and even in modern times.

Simon Magus (Simon the magician) is usually reputed to be the father of gnosticism, but that only means he was the first well-known leader of a gnostic movement. He is mentioned in the New Testament[1] where he appears as a wonder-worker from Samaria, giving out that he was some great one, and bewitching the people with his magical practices. He was baptised, however, and then seeing the apostles administering the sacrament of chrism, he asked them to give him the power to do this, offering them money. Peter rebuked him for attempting to purchase sacramental powers, and ever after the offering of money with the aim of obtaining sacerdotal powers has been known as *simony.*

In the New Testament Simon Magus is represented as answering

[1] *Acts,* viii, 9–24.

Peter in a humble manner and requesting the latter to pray for him. However, in legend he is represented as boastful, calling himself the omnipotent, challenging the apostles at Rome, before Nero. The latter event is mentioned by several of the Fathers of the Church. He ascended into the air, in imitation of the ascension of Elias and of Christ, but whilst he was doing so the apostles counteracted his activity and he fell to earth seriously injuring his legs. Later he was reported as performing the yogic miracle of being buried alive. He told his followers he would rise on the third day, which again looks like an attempt to imitate Christ, in an all too literal fashion. His disciples buried him carefully, but St. Hippolytus, who tells the story, said they were still awaiting his resurrection. But the accounts of his death vary.

In two works ascribed to St. Clement of Rome known as *Pseudo-Clementines* we learn more of Simon Magus. He is there connected with John the Baptist. Jesus represents the sun and had twelve apostles corresponding with the twelve signs of the zodiac. John the Baptist represents the moon, and had thirty disciples, corresponding with the thirty days during which the moon completes its heavenly circuit. These disciples corresponded with various aeons. Owing to the fact that the moon does not occupy thirty full days, one of these disciples was a young woman. In one of these works she is called Helen, in another Luna, which is a name for the moon herself. John the Baptist, it will be remembered, met an untimely death. When he died he was succeeded by Dositheus, but Simon, by magical means, supplanted Dositheus, and then fell in love with Luna. Dositheus and Simon together with their thirty followers are mentioned by Origen.[2]

It was generally believed, among the early ecclesiastical writers that Helen played an important part in the magical system of Simon. Just as Simon himself represented the *power of God*, so Helen represented the *spirit of Truth*, and she was supposed to be a sort of reflection of Divinity. St. Justin Martyr tells us that Helen was originally a Greek prostitute. St. Epiphanius accuses Simon of making use of semen and menstrual blood in his magical arts.[3] He is also said to have had fire appearing above the water at baptism, which made his followers believe he had a form of baptism

[2] Thorndike: *History of Magic and Experimental Science*, vol. 1, 1929. To this author I am indebted for several of the records relating to Simon Magus.

[3] Referred to as a terrible sin in the *Book of the Saviour* adjoined to the Gnostic work *Pistis-Sophia* translated by G. R. S. Mead, 1896 and G. Horner, 1924.

superior to the orthodox. St. Hippolytus[4] tells more about Simon
Magus. He says he produced certain effects through the agency of
demons. He also explains his cosmogony. *Fire*, according to Simon
was the principle of all things, therefore God, as is described by
Moses, is likened to a burning and consuming fire. This perhaps
shows a Zoroastrian influence. Six aeons, roots or powers, proceed in
pairs from the Fire. Each pair consist, as it were, of a male and a
female, the former looking down on and taking care of its consort.
The first pair are *Mind* and *Intelligence* which in a certain sense
are heaven and earth. The second are *Voice* and *Name*, identified
with the sun and moon. The third are *Reason* and *Thought*, which
are air and water. These six roots contain the boundless power of
the Universe, but existing potentially, not in activity. Hippolytus
also says the followers of Simon Magus make use of spells and
philtres, induce demons to take dreams to people, and venerate
images, including those of Simon and Helen.

Serpent Worship. Another very early sect that mixed Christianity
with black magic appears to be the Ophites or serpent-worshippers.
It seems that the serpent was held sacred in Egypt, as were many
other animals. In many places in Egypt live serpents were kept and
venerated, as they were in temples of Asklepios (Aesculapius) in
Greece and Rome. But when the gospel was preached in Egypt
some of these serpent-worshippers, under the leadership of an
obscure personage called Eucrates by classical authors, combined
the Christian message with the serpent cult. They came to believe
that the world had been formed under the influence of Ialdabaoth,
who is none other than the planetary spirit of Saturn, and as such
the principle of darkness and restriction. The serpent that persuaded Adam and Eve to eat of the Tree of Knowledge was, contrary to the usual view, Christ or Wisdom, and the Fall was considered not as an evil, but as the liberation from unconscious limita-
tion to conscious freedom.

The serpent has certainly been considered as a symbol of wisdom
by many peoples, and occasionally figures as a prototype of Christ,
as in that raised up by Moses in the wilderness to cure the people
of snake-bite. But the Ophites had one singular custom, according
to Epiphanius. When they consecrated the host in the Holy
Eucharist they first caused a living serpent to encircle the bread
to be consecrated, at the same time quoting the words of St. John :

[4] *The Writings of Hippolytus,* etc., 2 vols., trans. Edinburgh, 1868-1869.

"And as Moses lifted up the serpent in the desert, so must the son of man be lifted up." (*John*, iii, 14.)

Celsus, a pagan philosopher[5] of the 2nd century A.D. wrote an attack on the Christian religion. Here he refers to a magical diagram which he said was used by Christians. In it the seven planetary spirits were represented by different animals : chimaera, bull, dragon, eagle, bear, dog and ass. The great Christian theologian Origen wrote a *Reply to Celsus*. In it he says that he has seen the diagram, admits it is connected with magic, but says it is nothing to do with true Christianity, but is an unhallowed product of some sect, probably the very insignificant people called Ophites.

Strange Teachings. Menander was another Samaritan of the 1st century and leader of a gnostic sect. Irenaeus and Eusebius say he was the successor of Simon Magus. His headquarters were at Antioch. His teachings seem to have been similar to those of Simon. He regarded the Primary Power of the Universe as unknown and perhaps unknowable, the World was made by Ennoia or Supreme Thought, acting through angels or aeons. Menander claimed to be himself one of the aeons, and to be able to control spirits. He is said to have promised his followers immortality and perpetual life in this world.

Towards the end of the 1st century a Jew called Cerinthus brought out a form of gnosticism adapted to explain the Old Testament. He was educated at and afterwards taught in Alexandria. His doctrines can again be gathered from references to them in the writings of the Church Fathers. He held that the creator of this world was not the supreme god, that he gradually fell from a high spiritual state, that the Jews were given their laws by a still lower angel. He originated the heretical view of Jesus, still held in certain theosophical circles, which distinguishes between Jesus and Christ. According to this Jesus was the natural son of Joseph and Mary. At his baptism the aeon Christ descended upon Jesus, as it were a spirit possession. Then Jesus opposed the angel-lawgiver of the Jews, but was seized and crucified by them. When Jesus was captured Christ deserted the body of Jesus and returned to the heavenly world, whilst Jesus was led away to be crucified. He combined these heretical ideas with others of a more orthodox character.

Early in the second century we find Saturninus, a Syrian, as leader of a gnostic sect. His followers were vegetarians, moreover

[5] Not to be confounded with the medical author of the same name who lived in the preceding century.

they abstained from marriage and the procreation of children, as they regarded sex as wholly diabolical. The world was created, not by God, but by seven angels, who worked on the basis of a vision which they had for a moment from above, but they only succeeded in producing a creature that went about on all fours. God then sent a spark of life to complete creation, and the creature walked erect. One of the seven angels was the god of the Jews. The Saviour was sent to redeem men from the power of this angel. The Saviour never had a human body, and was only a phantasm. Such we gather from the Church Fathers was the cosmic scheme of Saturninus. The chief centre of this movement seems to have been Antioch in Syria. It flourished there during the first twenty years of the 2nd century (A.D. 100–120 approximately).

Elxai, a Jew, is said to have formed another sect of the gnostics. In A.D. 101 Alcibiades brought a book of the revelations of this mystic from Apamea in Syria to Rome. This, unlike most gnostic works, upheld the books of Moses, but gave them an allegorical meaning. It purported to give communications from the Son of God, described as a figure 96 miles high and with a footprint 14 miles long, and a female companion, represented as the Holy Spirit, of corresponding size. These figures suggest kabalistic symbolism, although ridiculed by Hippolytus who describes them. The sect had various heretical practices, such as re-baptism, and also made a practice of dipping sick people in water forty times in seven days.

Basilides of Alexandria is considered one of the most influential of the gnostic leaders. His followers were numerous in Egypt, various parts of North Africa and Spain. Traces of them occur in Britain, judging from certain archaeological remains. He is said to have succeeded Menander, and to have been followed by his own son Isidorus. He is also alleged to have been instructed by St. Matthias and by Glaucus, one of St. Peter's followers. However that may be, his system diverges greatly from the orthodox. On the practical side it was, as usual, a matter of magical incantations, using images and the names of angels and spirits. Candidates for initiation could pass through three grades : material, intellectual and spiritual. Gems were inscribed with the figure of their supreme god, and they had two symbolic statues, reminding one of the Simon Magus cult of which that of Basilides may have been in some sense a continuation.

The Supreme Being in the system of Basilides was called Abraxas, a Greek word. Now the letters of the Greek alphabet, like the

Hebrew, correspond with numbers. And if we take the numerical value of the letters of the name Abraxas and add them all up we obtain the number 365. This is not only the number of the days of the year, but according to the Basilideans was the number of the aeons, the number of the heavens, the number of the various orders of spirits and the number of bones in the human body.[6] Abraxas was represented engraved on gems in the figure of a human body and arms, with a cock's head and snakes instead of legs. He carries a whip and a shield. Sometimes he rides in a chariot drawn by four horses. Sun and moon may be represented on either side. This being did not create the world, but approved of it, the work of creation being carried out by aeons, at least as far as the animal stage. The human spirit, it seems, did come from God, much as in the last system. However, mankind suffered, principally under the angel who presided over the Jewish nation, so the Supreme Being sent the first of the aeons, called Nous or Christ, who united with the man Jesus in the way previously described. The man Jesus lost the Christ before being crucified. Afterwards some of the Basilideans said it was not Jesus, but Simon of Cyrene who, it will be remembered in the gospel story, helped Jesus to carry the cross, that was crucified in His place.

Basilides was a strong supporter of astrology. He refers to the Star of Bethlehem as an astronomical phenomenon announcing to the Wise Men the coming of Christ. He also said, according to Hippolytus, that Christ's remark on one occasion, "My hour is not yet come," (*John*, ii, 4), is an obvious reference to Christ's use of astrology.

Carpocrates of Alexandria was another gnostic leader in Egypt who had a considerable following. One of his lady-initiates, Marcellina, carried the movement to Rome about A.D. 150. Images were widely used by this sect. There are references to images of Marcellina and of Epiphanes (son of Carpocrates) who died at an early age. Beside the image of Jesus Christ they placed figures of Pythagoras, Plato, Aristotle and other pagan sages. Like other gnostics Carpocrates thought God produced a succession of aeons, the latter acting on matter, represented as eternal. Jesus they said was in no way different in his origin from other human beings, considering Him as the natural son of Joseph and Mary. The natural instincts of mankind were not right or wrong, they were only rendered apparently so by opinions and dictates. Consequently

[6] It need hardly be said that this number is incorrect by any method of counting.

property and women were held in common. Carpocrates apparently employed incantations, philtres, drugs and spirit-messages.

Valentinus of Alexandria was perhaps the most successful of all the gnostics. He went from Egypt to Rome about A.D. 140 where he worked until A.D. 157. At the end of the century his followers were numerous in various places in Europe, Asia and Africa, but most of all in Cyprus. He died in A.D. 160. His system is somewhat complicated, and in it both Jesus and Christ are aeons, although different from one another. After the death of Valentinus his large following became divided up among a number of leaders, some of whom added further fancies to the already complicated system. The movement reached its maximum at the beginning of the 3rd century, but appears to have died out completely by the 5th.

One of the most remarkable of the successors of Valentinus was Marcus in the middle of the 2nd century. His acts and opinions have been recorded by Irenaeus, Hippolytus and Epiphanes. He was thoroughly versed in the magical arts and sciences. He considered numbers and letters of basic importance. The whole of truth was symbolised by the Greek alphabet. That is why Jesus was called the Alpha and the Omega. Numbers and letters correspond, as in modern numerology. Marcus also used herbs according to the numbers of their names. He said the seven vowels correspond with the seven planets. He invoked spirits (Irenaeus says demons) and prophesied by their aid. He encouraged his female initiates to prophesy, and chose them for this purpose by casting lots. He claimed to transmit magical powers to those whom he chose. He was accused of seducing women, using love philtres for this purpose, and claimed to be above the ordinary rules of sexual morality. Marcus played certain sacrilegious tricks with the Holy Eucharist. Sometimes he said Mass with two chalices, one large and one small. He would transfer the contents of the small to the large, when it would fill the latter and even overflow or almost so. Another trick was to transfer white wine into three cups, in one of which it became blood-red, in another purple, in another dark blue. The blood of the aeon Charis was supposed to drop into one of the cups. Epiphanes says it was done by evil magic and Hippolytus states that chemicals were used.

Other gnostics were teaching at about the same time, but they are less interesting from the magical point of view.

Devil Worship. The belief that the world was created by an evil power gradually led to attempts to propitiate that power. Finally a full-blown devil worship appears, as a gradual development of the gnostic movements. This took its rise in the Middle East, where its remains exist today, and must not be confused with the witchcraft movement in Europe with which it has no connection and from which it is very different. In fact the devil-worshippers of gnostic origin are held in bondage by fear; they are otherwise good-living, humble people (Mandaeans, Yezidees).

The teacher who started all this was not certainly gnostic,[7] although he has been called "the last of the gnostics."[8] He was Bardesanes of Edessa of Syria, A.D. 154–222. He is alleged to have been the teacher of St. Clement of Alexandria[9] and of Manes.[10] Bardesanes was a teacher of astrology, but on the other hand a strong supporter of the idea of human free will, so he made it quite plain that the stars do not rule everything, and cites the differences between the customs of different nations as proof of the fact. He wrote *The Book of the Laws of Countries* in Syrian. This still exists and according to Thorndike[11] has been translated into English. He also wrote many hymns, which were a means of fostering his teaching.[12] He denied the reality of the Body of Christ, and the resurrection of the body. He assumed the evil principle in the world was equal to the good, or almost so. It is this last view, which, as we have seen, gained a ground also in Zoroastrianism, that led to Bardesanes being regarded as the founder of the Yezidis.

Manes or Mani, the founder of Manichaeism, was born in Ecbatana in Media, and was of Persian extraction, and brought up in the Zoroastrian religion. He was converted to Christianity, but sooner or later came under the influence of Gnosticism, the idea of a powerful evil being, side by side with a good God, apparently appealing to him. He was no doubt influenced by Bardesanes, Basilides and Marcion, the latter bringing in a strict ascetic aspect. However, Manichaeism eventually had a well developed magical cult. For example Thorndike[13] refers to a Manichaean manuscript dating from about A.D. 900. This contains many references to the seven planets, the five elements, the five magical plants, the five types of beings with souls: men, quadrupeds, reptiles, aquatic and flying animals, the whole corresponding with five gods, with five

[7] Thorndike, *loc cit.*
[8] M. A. Canney, *An Encyclopaedia of Religions*, London, 1921.
[9] Canney, *loc. cit.*
[10] Thorndike, *loc. cit.*
[11] *Loc. cit.*
[12] Canney, *loc. cit.*
[13] *Loc. cit.* The manuscript was brought to light in 1913.

demons imprisoned by the gods. It states that the devil imprisons luminous forces in man, and these can be released by the five liberators brought by Mani : pity, contentment, patience, wisdom and good faith. There are many other numerical correspondences, based on other numbers, such as ten heavens, twelve great kings, etc. This of course is late, developed Manichaeism, but is probably a fair representation of the system. We know it was intensely astrological. St. Augustine of Hippo was, when a youth, a follower of Mani and an ardent astrologer. After his conversion to Christianity he wrote an attack on astrology, although admitting solar and lunar influence to some extent in natural objects. The Manichaeans had a hierarchy after the death of Mani with a high priest at the head as his successor, twelve apostles, seventy-two bishops, as well as priests, deacons and evangelists. Instead of baptism they anointed with oil. They had a Eucharist, but Sunday was to them a fasting day. Manichaeism spread rapidly in Asia, soon reached Egypt and Rome, and survived until the 6th century. It was not without political pretensions which in those days were intimately mixed with religion. So, like Christianity, it was severely persecuted. Manes himself came into conflict with the King of Persia. He was eventually arrested and flayed alive[14] by the Persians in A.D. 277. Mani is said to have written six works in Syriac and a Holy Gospel in Persian,[15] the latter in opposition to the New Testament, which he alleged was much corrupted. He stated that Christ was identical with Mithras, that He had visited the world in a phantom body, had promised to send the Comforter (Paraclete) and that he, Manes, was this comforter.

In A.D. 385 a Christian bishop named Priscillian was put to death at Treves with some of his associates on a charge of magic. He was the leader of a strong movement in Gaul and particularly in Spain which tried to combine gnostic or Manichaean ideas with the Catholic religion. He denied the reality of the birth and incarnation of Christ and believed the world to have been produced by an evil principle. Some works of Priscillian are still in existence. The prosecution was regarded by the bishops of Gaul and Italy with the utmost dismay, as at that time it had not been the custom to take severe action against heretics.

The Mandaeans or Christians of St. John are a sect that still exist in small numbers to the south of Bagdad. *Manda* is synonymous

---

[14] This is the usual story; Widengren (*Mani and Manichaeism*, 1961, trans. 1965) says he was fettered and died as a result.

[15] Canney: *loc. cit.*

with *gnosis*.[16] They are said to be of the sect of St. John the Baptist. It will be remembered that the succession from St. John the Baptist was claimed by certain gnostics, and this may have been continued until this day. Baptism is their chief sacrament but it is used repeatedly rather as an ablution for purification. They have four main kinds of ritual meals, with several sub-divisions.[17] Some of these use bread, but water mostly takes the place of the wine used in other rites, a number of other foods are included and sometimes a dove and a sheep are sacrificed. There is no rite of circumcision. They have five sacred books, of which one is devoted to astrology.[18] These Mandaeans retain many traces of the Chaldean star-lore and are sometimes called Sabeans (*Sabbas* locally). They ascribe particular importance to the Pleiades and to the Pole-Star. They have no permanent temples, but construct tabernacles of branches when required. They have several sacred books, some sections of which, according to Budge,[19] are as old as the first century of our era. Mandaean theology is undoubtedly derived from the Gnostic. Earth and man have been formed by a demiurge, who, according to Thorndike[20] was Ialdabaoth of the Ophites. History was divided into seven stages, corresponding with the planets. Jesus was supposed to have been produced by the planet Mercury. Numerology played an important part in the cosmology, especially the numbers 5, 7, 12 and 360.

The Yezidis or Yazidis have their headquarters in the province of Mosul in Mesopotamia, and are widely but more sparsely distributed over Kurdistan, Armenia and the Caucasus. Wherever they live we find curious shrines, topped with a long conical upright white spire, with deeply fluted sides. They are made of cement. Each is dedicated to a saint, but are not necessarily tombs of their holy personages. Certain caves and trees are also held sacred. They build small temples. They keep sacred snakes. The colour blue[21] has a strong repulsion for them. All who have visited them agree that they are friendly peaceful people, but they have this peculiarity: they are very much afraid of Satan, whose name must never be mentioned. They call him the Peacock Angel (Melek Taos or Malka Tausa). They have fine bird-like images of him.[22] He is one

16 Canney: *loc. sit.*
17 E. S. Drower: *Water into Wine*, London, 1956.
18 Canney: *loc. cit.*
19 *Amulets and Superstitions*, London, 1930.
20 *Loc. cit.*
21 Or possibly indigo, sacred to Saturn = Satan?
22 This bird has been identified with the fabulous *simorg* of the Moslems.

of the seven spirits, and the most importance is attached to him. There is no need, they think, to worship the Supreme God. He will never do one harm. The evil one must be propitiated. He may do good, and may do harm, but the Supreme God always does good. At any moment, they think, the evil one may be reconciled with the Supreme God. Even now he has been largely forgiven. They do not believe that Christ died on the cross, but include Him in their heavenly hierarchy. Their earthly hierarchy follows the usual lines with several grades of initiation in the hereditary priesthood and a supreme high priest. Both laity and priesthood are baptised, and the men are usually circumcised, but this is probably to bring them into line with their Moslem neighbours, and appears to be optional. The women are not veiled. They believe in reincarnation, and at least some of them think men can come back as animals, at least on rare occasions.

Besides Christ and various Old Testament prophets the Yezidis venerate a saint or shaikh called Adi ben Masafir, who died in 1155. The high priest, sometimes called *khalifah* from Moslem influence, is supposed to be a direct descendant of Adi. They have a sacred book called *Yalvah*, but it is hidden. Early in the present century a translation appeared, but this is regarded by scholars as spurious.[23]

Gnostic Remains. Most of our knowledge of the gnostic theories comes from the writings of the Fathers. At the same time there are archaeological remains which are commonly ascribed to the Gnostics, and which it is difficult to correlate with the patristic data. Most of them are stones found in Egypt and more rarely in Asia Minor and dated 250 B.C. to A.D. 400. They are of lapis lazuli, jasper, blood-stone, agate, cornelian, chrysoprase, beryl, onyx, rock crystal or merely granite, triangular, square or oval and they are engraved with various figures. Now it is quite obvious that those which have been dated B.C. cannot be correctly considered gnostic, and in fact they portray figures well known from earlier Egyptian mythology. These include Osiris, Isis, Harpokrates, Hathor, Thoth and Anubis. Later these grade over to Christian symbols. Figures of Osiris or Serapis are identified with those of Christ. Isis becomes Mary, Hathor becomes Sophia. It is different with Abraxas. These are later, and there is no mistaking the gnostic character of these amulets. Other figures such as the Ophite serpent, and the animals representing the seven planetary spirits appear, often mixed

23 Canney: *loc. cit.*

up with classical deities. Many of them are inscribed in Greek uncials, often with words derived from Hebrew. Such names as Iao, Sabaoth, Adonai (or Adonaus), Ialdabaoth, Elvens, Oreus and Astanphaeus were often employed in magic and survived in this connection until the Middle Ages. Among the Ophites they referred (according to St. Irenaeus) to the seven who were cast down, the chief of which was Ialdabaoth or Saturn. On the other hand Orthodoxy used some of these names, like the first three listed above, as designations of the Supreme God.

They were also used by the Sethites for the seven planetary spirits. The Sethites were a small Gnostic sect who honoured Seth, son of Adam, and even identified Seth with Christ. Now Josephus in his *Jewish Antiquities*[24] says that the offspring of Seth were the first of astronomers, or rather more correctly, astrologers, and that, in view of Adam's prediction that the world was to be destroyed, once by fire, and once by water, they wrote down their discoveries on two pillars, one of brick (to survive the fire) and one of stone (to survive the flood), and one of them remained in the land of Siriad (Egypt) in his day. Another legend says that the two pillars survived the Flood, and were discovered by Hermes Trimegistus and Pythagoras respectively. Two pillars play an important part in Gnostic, as in Kabalistic lore, and from these spread to Freemasonry.[25]

The *Pistis Sophia* is a Coptic codex of the 5th and 6th centuries, probably taken from a Greek original. There are Latin, French, German and English[26] translations. This book is remarkably free from the black magical elements, and it, in fact, condemns such practices, including the use of drugs. Unlike many Gnostic teachings the book is not opposed to the Old Testament teachings. It purports to be the teaching which Jesus gave after His resurrection to a company of the Apostles, together with the Virgin Mary, Mary Magdalene and Martha. Jesus answers many of the questions asked by them. According to the book Jesus was with them for eleven years after the Resurrection. It describes much powerful hierurgic work performed by Jesus, using the points of the compass, fire, wine and water. Not only details of natural phenomena are to be given to those who have penetrated the Mysteries, but a true Spiritual

[24] Chapter II, p. 27, *Works*, trans. London, not dated.
[25] J. S. M. Ward: *Freemasonry and the Ancient Gods,* London, 1921, has some references to these pillars.
[26] English by G. R. S. Mead, 1896, and G. Horner, 1924.

Science will be revealed. In fact the book contains the indications of the plot of a story whereby a female power, whc conferred on Jesus a vesture of light, is redeemed. The story reminds one of that of Hachamoth in the Valentinian gnosis, but is different in detail. The apostles are twelve powers and there is much detailed astrological symbolism.

CHAPTER XIV

DRUIDS AND FAIRIES

Keltic Culture. The Celts or Kelts, who represent a culture rather than, or as well as, a race, originated, like other Indo-European peoples in the region of the Caucasus. Plutarch gives authorities for the belief that the Kelts come from the Crimea. Some spread into the Balkan Peninsula, others reached the Alps and eventually descended on Rome, where, however, they were repulsed, the remnants migrating to the middle of Asia Minor where they formed the country known as Galatia. Others reached Denmark and Germany, from which they were displaced by the Teutons. More successful were those that entered what is now France and the Low Countries, and in the former they settled especially between the Seine and the Garonne rivers, the country being known to the Romans as Gaul. Others entered what is now northern Spain and Portugal. From Spain, Portugal, France and Low Countries they passed to Great Britain and Ireland.

The Keltic languages have survived in Britain and Brittany in France. They include Erse or Irish Gaelic spoken in Ireland, Scots Gaelic in Scotland, Manx in the Isle of Man, Welsh in Wales, Cornish (practically extinct) in Cornwall and Breton in Brittany. Keltic culture is best preserved in Ireland and Wales where it has been relatively little interfered with by invaders, but even here the modifications have been very great.

The Kelts had a complex social organisation, which reached its maximum development in Ireland in the 1st and 2nd centuries A.D. This has been described by C. S. Coon[1] on the basis of recent anthropological investigations. There was a feudal system, with the High King of All Ireland at its head, under him five Kings of each of the great provinces Ulster, Munster, Connaught, Leinster and Meath, under them Kings of the Counties, under them Kings of the Hills and Peaks, under them four classes of Nobles, under them Cattle-chiefs, under them Freemen and Craftsmen, and finally Bondsmen. The land was divided up accordingly, except that the last class held no land. Besides these landowners and bondsmen was

[1] *The History of Man*, London, 1955.

the learned class, called Druids. These had an independent hierarchy, regulating everything else, including the appointment of the
High King and all kings, nobles and chiefs, and acting as priests,
judges, physicians, educators, poets, astrologers and magicians.
They were said to write in Greek characters. They are also said
to have used the ancient *Ogham alphabet*, wherein the letters
consisted of vertical and oblique strokes, variously combined and
placed along a horizontal line. Classical authors, however, agreed
that druidic lore was not committed to writing but was learned by
rote. Consequently the training of a druid took a long time, some
say twenty years. Women were also enrolled among the druid
fraternity, since classical writers refer to Druidesses. There were
several grades of initiation, as in other priesthoods. Two of the
grades included Bards and Ovates (*Vates*). Whether these were pre-
liminaries to the grade of Druid we do not know, but it is certain
that poetry was highly cultivated as a religious exercise. Druidesses
may have been used as mediums for communicating with the other
world, as pythonesses were among the Greeks.[2]

Druidism also flourished in Great Britain and Gaul, before the
conversion of these countries to Christianity. Julius Caesar who was
in personal contact with the Druids (for he invaded England as is
well known in 55 B.C.), says that the Druids from Gaul went to
Britain for their training. There are also references to a training
college for Druids in Anglesey, which seems to have been the seat
of their chief. When the country was converted many of the
Druids became Priests and the Arch-druids Bishops.

Archaeological remains show that the inhabitants of Britain before
the Saxon conquest were by no means all naked savages, painted
with woad, as Caesar described them. They had passed through the
Bronze into the Iron Age, had beautiful pottery, textiles, implements
and armour. The clothing of the people showed their rank, the
number of colours worn being indicative of their status. The Druids
used implements of bronze and gold,[3] and their golden breastplates
and torques can be seen in our museums. They carried croziers, but
most of these are of schist.

The whole subject of Druidism has been under a cloud for more
than half a century among archaeologists. This is due to the
romantic writers of the 18th and 19th centuries, who persistently

[2] W. B. Crow: Druids and the Mistletoe Sacrament, *Mysteries of the
Ancients*, 14, London, 1944.
[3] See also the remarkable sun-disc, figure on p. 151 and on carriage p. 152,
Guide to the Antiquities of the Bronze Age, British Museum, 1904.

associated the Druids with the Cyclopean monuments, such as Stonehenge, and regarded the latter as being built under Druidic supervision. This view has now been abandoned. W. Stukeley (1687–1765), who was an early investigator of Stonehenge and Avebury, and W. Blake (1757–1827) artist and poet, were exponents of the view that Britain was the home of the Patriarchal Religion, and believed that religion was Druidism.

The modern view[4] is that Druidism was a tree cult, based on two facts: (i) that Europe, including Great Britain and Ireland were up to the time of the beginning of the Christian era covered with extensive forests in which the dominant tree was oak; (ii) that the acorn, the fruit of the oak, was the staple food of the inhabitants of this vast area. The classical peoples also had this cult originally, for Jupiter, the king of their gods, was an oak-god. But in Greece and Rome it was superseded by a corn and wine cult (personified in Ceres and Bacchus) and became sophisticated in more ways than one.

Druidic Ritual. The most peculiar feature of druidic worship is the veneration of the mistletoe, which is a semi-parasitic plant growing on trees, its seeds planted there by birds. It is not common on the oak, but in the druidic ceremony it had to be found thereon and cut off with a golden sickle. The cut branches of mistletoe were then distributed to the congregation. In 1944 the present writer put forward a theory of this ceremony, comparing it with the Christian Eucharist.[5] It was based on a remark of Elder[6] who pointed out that the Messiah was called a branch. The ancestral tree of the Messiah, known as the Tree of Jesse, and portrayed as a real tree in many mediaeval manuscripts, is represented by the oak. On this the mistletoe is planted by a bird. The latter is a symbol of the Holy Spirit, who plants the Messiah on the ancestral tree of Jesse. And only gold may touch the sacred plant, as the wine of the vine sacrament, after the consecration becoming Christ, is only allowed to come into contact with the gold inside surface of the chalice. It is also pointed out that several plants have a sacramental significance. We may add that the mistletoe was held sacred also by the Teutons, and was said to have been, in some legends, the plant that formed the cross, and originally of tree-like dimensions. Virgil indicates

[4] L. Spence: *The History and Origins of Druidism,* London (not dated but about 1950).
[5] Crow: *loc. cit.*
[6] *Celt, Druid and Culdee,* London, 1938.

that the mistletoe was *the golden bough,* around which in modern times Sir James Frazer wrote so extensively concerning the vegeta-. tion cult.

The Druids are also recorded as making giant wickerwork figures, placing animals or human beings therein, and burning them as a sacrifice. There is no doubt that such giant figures were constructed, carried in procession, and finally immolated. The practice was continued for many centuries in England, and the burning of effigies of Guy Fawkes on November 5th is a relic of this practice.[7] Whether human victims were ever included is disputed. Elder[8] repudiates the idea, Canney thinks it was exceptional, and refers to instances where a few drops of blood were drawn from the victim, and then only the dummy was burnt.

Great druidic festivals took place four times during the year. Bonfires were lit on these occasions. Beltane was celebrated at the beginning of May, it has been perpetuated in maypole ceremonies, the beginning of morris dancing, the election of May kings and queens, the great witches' festival, coinciding with St. Walburga's day (May 1st) in the Church, and the various junketings of the Labour and Communist parties on the same date. Lugnasad was celebrated early in August. In the Middle Ages it was Lammas or Gule of August, now largely transformed into August Bank Holiday. Samhain occurs at the beginning of November. In the Catholic Church it was replaced by All Saints (November 1st) and All Souls (November 2nd) and among Protestants by Guy Fawkes day (November 5th). Oimelc, known in Ireland as Earrach was celebrated at the beginning of February; it corresponds with St. Bridgit (February 1st) who had a fire shrine (her name is the same as one of the Keltic goddesses), and with the Purification or Candlemas (February 2nd) the day on which the blessing of candles occurs. There was also a festival three days after the summer solstice, and on that day, known in Christian times as the Nativity of St. John the Baptist there was celebrated a *fire-wheel ceremony,* when a blazing cart wheel was made to run down a hill, a custom that has survived until recent times. There was also a festival three days after the Winter Solstice, corresponding with our Christmas. S. C. Cox[9] says that the seasons were personified by the Druids, Spring by a youth, Summer by a middle-aged man, Autumn by an elderly and Winter by an

[7] Crow: *loc. cit.*
[8] *Loc. cit.*
[9] The Bards of Ancient Britain, *Gaa-Sophia* III, 1929.

old man, the last named having developed into St. Nicholas who is Santa Claus or Father Christmas.

One of the most peculiar practices of the Druids relates to *the serpent's egg*. This was one of their ritual objects, and is described, from personal observation in Pliny's *Natural History*. It is of the size of a small apple, with cartilaginous shell and pitted surface. It is, says Pliny, formed in summer when a number of snakes twine together, as a secretion from their bodies, mixed with saliva. When the snakes hiss, some of this substance is thrown in the air. It must be, he continues, caught on a cloth before reaching the ground, and carried away on horseback, as the serpents would pursue, until one has crossed a stream. This must be done on a certain day of the moon. The so-called egg has the property of floating against the current of a river. We have connected this egg, which certain bards say was competed for by two parties, the successful one carrying it across water, with various forms of funereal games, with the mediaeval ceremony of *pelota*, and the whipping of the spinning top representing Alleluia on the Saturday before Septuagesima.[10] But it is highly probable that many ball games had a religious significance originally, and this is one of them. The egg or ball may have represented the soul (or more exactly the causal body of theosophy) and the game represents the contest for this between the powers of good and evil.

Arthurian Legend. King Arthur and his court are surrounded with magic and mystery. We have already recounted how, according to the story, Merlin the magician brought over the stones of Stonehenge and set them up in Wiltshire (where they still are) in the reign of Aurelius Ambrosius. Shortly after this Aurelius died of poison, as a result of a Saxon plot, and Uther Pendragon, his brother, came to the throne. Uther fell in love with Igerne, wife of Gorlois, Duke of Cornwall. By the magic of Merlin, Uther is transformed into the semblance of Gorlois, and obtains access to Igerne, whilst Gorlois is away with Uther's troops. Gorlois is slain, and Uther weds Igerne. But Arthur's birth is the result of Merlin's magic. Uther died when Arthur was only fifteen. Owing to his age, and the mysterious circumstances of his birth, there was some doubt as to who should ascend the throne. Christmas and New Year festivals were celebrated in London, all nobles and knights being present, when a great stone with an anvil of steel set in it was seen outside the Church. In it was stuck a sword, and the stone was inscribed,

[10] Crow: *loc. cit.*

saying that whoso pulled out this sword was rightful king. Only Arthur could achieve this. Arthur was then crowned king, and had to engage in twelve great battles against the Saxons, in all of which he was successful. By means of Merlin's magic Arthur obtained a wonderful sword Excalibur or Caliburn from the Lady of the Lake, an enchantress who had a wonderful palace beneath the waters of a deep lake. The sword appeared above the water, grasped in an arm clothed in white samite, which disappeared below when Arthur took it. When Arthur died the sword was cast again into the lake, the hand again coming up to grasp it. The sword and its scabbard were stolen from Arthur by Morgan la Fée, a powerful sorceress, one of Arthur's sisters. He recovered them, but she stole the scabbard a second time and threw it into the Lake. The scabbard was a protection against loss of blood to anyone wearing it. Morgan la Fée sent Arthur a rich robe, with properties such that it killed the wearer (similar to that which was said to have led to the death of Hercules). Arthur was warned by the Lady of the Lake, and made the messenger, who brought it, try it on. She was burnt to ashes.

Arthur married Guenever or Guinevere, daughter of Leodegrance, King of Cameliard. As a wedding gift Leodegrance gave Arthur the famous Round Table which Merlin had constructed for Uther, who had given it to Leodegrance. This table was said to symbolise the zodiac, the world and the table of the Last Supper, and some said it had twelve seats or sieges. According to Mallory's account there were 150 places.[11] It came with a hundred knights, Merlin found twenty-eight more, and gradually the empty places were filled. Three of the seats were left empty for some time, two were of especial honour, the third was called the *siege perilous* and was destined for the knight that should succeed in the Quest of the Holy Grail; it would prove fatal for anyone else to sit in it.

Several enchantresses were associated with the mysterious lake. One of them, called Nimue or Vivien was doted on by Merlin, who taught her some of his spells. Either by accident or design she got Merlin into a cavity in a rock or a tree, closed the entrance, and was unable or unwilling to open it. Merlin was the most famous of

[11] On the eastern wall of the County Hall, Winchester hangs a gigantic disc of painted wood alleged to be the top of King Arthur's round table. It is divided into twenty-five compartments radiating from the centre, whereon is painted a large rose. The compartments are alternatively white and green, except for one at the top whereon is the figure of a king. An inscription surrounds the central rose, and names appear round the margin. There are references to such a table in late mediaeval history, but the table as it exists today probably dates from the Tudor period.

British magicians, and was frequently mentioned in mediaeval legends, not only of the Arthurian cycle but in others.

In Geoffrey of Monmouth and Malory we are told that Arthur was called upon to pay tribute to the Roman Emperor. He marched on Rome with a large force and having killed the Roman Emperor in battle was himself crowned Emperor by the Pope. The claim of a British king to the Roman Empire is not so preposterous as it seems today, inasmuch as one of Arthur's predecessors, *viz.* Constantine I was undoubtedly for a few years *de facto* both Emperor of Rome and King of Britain (A.D. 306–312).

Another great adventure which involved many knights of the Round Table was the Quest of the Holy Grail. But the legendary lore and symbolism of the Grail is so extensive that we will deal with it in a later chapter.

A very strange adventure in these stories is the pursuit of the Questing Beast by King Pellinore for twelve months and after his death by Sir Palomedes. The beast was called Glatisaunt. It made a noise like many hounds giving quest, and it had the head of a serpent, the body of a lizard in front and of a lion behind, and its feet were like those of a hart.

Among the very numerous knights of the Round Table mentioned in the romances were Sir Gawain, a most courteous knight, Sir Kay, in some stories a boastful foil for the other knights, in others a magician of great power, Sir Bedivere, King Arthur's butler who attends the king when wounded in the last battle and throws his sword into the lake, Sir Lancelot of the Lake, a great hero, but whose adultery with Queen Guenever is largely the cause of the break-up of the fellowship of the Round Table, Sir Tristram who fell in love with the promised bride of his uncle, King Mark, when bringing the lady from Ireland,[12] Sir Lamorake, a great fighter who also had a love affair with his own aunt, the wife of King Lot of Orkney, and Sir Galahad, the pure knight who attained the Quest of the Holy Grail.

The end of Arthur's reign was in this wise. Sir Lancelot and King Arthur were fighting in Brittany, and Arthur had left his nephew Sir Modred or Mordred as regent in Britain. The latter tried to oust Arthur from the kingship, and Arthur returned. There was a great battle in the West Country, Modred was slain and Arthur received incurable wounds. He was carried off in a ship across a lake in the district now called Glastonbury, then Ynysgwydrin. In

[12] The subject of Wagner's music-drama *Tristan and Isolda.* A love-potion or philtre is involved in the story.

the ship were three fairies or fates, and legend avers that he did not die, but will come again some day.[13] Constantine III ascended the throne of Britain.

The *Mabinogion*[14] is a collection of early Welsh legends, somewhat apart from the English. These contain very peculiar material, of a mythological nature. In one story Kilhwch seeks the aid of his cousin King Arthur and his knights in obtaining the hand of the beautiful Olwen, daughter of the tyrant Yspaddaden Penkawr. He can only do so by satisfying a number of extraordinary demands of the tyrant, which tax the resources of the whole retinue of Arthur to the utmost. One quest of several that they undertake is to obtain the razor, comb and scissors that are between the ears of the monstrous boar Twrch Trwyth (who was once human but has been transformed by magic) which rages over the country extensively and kills many of Arthur's knights. Several magical objects have to be obtained before it can be hunted, and help has to be obtained from the mysterious Mabon, son of Modron, who disappeared when three days old. He is found imprisoned. After the epic hunt, and many other adventures, all the requirements are satisfied.

There is some evidence that the peoples of continental Europe regarded Britain as the Land of the Dead. There are stories of a ferry which passed over what is now the English Channel with an invisible cargo, which weighed down the boat, and which returned, the boat riding higher, having discharged the spirits of the dead. Whether this was widespread or not (and it fits in with Britain being a Sacred Land), there are stories of encounters of British chiefs with the King of Annwn, the Keltic underworld. In one of the stories of the Mabinogion, a Welsh prince exchanged places with the King of the Underworld for one year.

Fairies. In British mythology fairies and druids are intimately connected, since druids were magicians and had commerce with spirits who afterwards figure in folk-lore as fairies. At King Arthur's court it is almost impossible to distinguish between fairies (fays, Fr. *fée*) and human beings. Arthur's sister is called Morgan la Fée, yet she is queen of an earthly kingdom, being the wife of Uriens or Vrience of Gore. Merlin is at one and the same time a fairy and a human being, because of his birth, and probably the some applies to Nimue.

Shakespeare's fairies puzzle commentators today, but there is no

[13] The same legend is told of other great culture heroes.
[14] Translated from 14th century MSS in 1834–49 by Lady Charlotte Guest; many subsequent editions.

need to assume that they do not reflect beliefs held in this country in the early Middle Ages. They form definite communities ruled by a king and queen. Oberon is their king, Titania their queen. There is a fairy court, Puck is one of their ministers or pages, Mab is the fairy midwife,[15] Leprechaun, the fairy shoemaker, Ariel is a fairy enslaved by a witch,[16] etc.

Fairies are usually very small. Most are described as little, if at all, above one foot in height, some being much smaller, comparable in size with insects according to some poetic descriptions. The very smallest are called pigwidgeons.

They have supernatural powers. Usually they are invisible. Those people having *second sight* could see them,[17] and others on special occasions. Even then they could vanish away if they wished. They also had the power, like oriental jinn, of transporting themselves very rapidly from one place to another.

They behave as human beings having a strong inferiority complex, which is in harmony with the view that they represent displaced persons belonging to a race that formerly owned the land, but had been ousted by newcomers. The Shakespearian fairies are essentially airy creatures. Their quarrels affect the atmosphere, and may cause fog or tempests,[18] on the other hand when they are pleased they cause more agreeable phenomena, such as the deposit of dew. The *Fata Morgana* is the name given to a sort of mirage which is seen under certain circumstances in the straits of Messina, between Sicily and the mainland of Italy, and on rare occasions elsewhere. Images of the landscape appear in the sky upside down. This is said to be due to a fairy of the same name, who is none other than the aforementioned Morgan la Fée.

Fairies feed on fruit and fight against insects, snails and frogs, parts of which they also eat. Fairy butter (also called witches' butter) is a gelatinous fungus of the genus *Exidia*. Fairies use toadstools as seats or tables. Fairy utensils are not often seen. Flints used by Stone Age Men were thought sometimes to have been used by fairies as arrow-heads in shooting at cattle. They were called

[15] She is called Queen Mab, but this is derived from *quean*, a midwife, E. Cobham Brewer: *Dictionary of Phrase and Fable*, 2nd ed., London, not dated. See Shakespeare's *Romeo and Juliet*.

[16] See Shakespeare's *Tempest*.

[17] According to Lewis Spence: *British Fairy Origins*, London, 1946, this was the sense in which *second sight* was originally used; afterwards it meant foretelling the future.

[18] A. Nutt: The Fairy Mythology of Shakespeare, 6, *Popular Studies in Mythology, Romance and Folklore*, London, 1900.

elf-bolts. Occasionally fairies leave articles which come into the possession of human beings. Such was the painted goblet, left by fairies on St. Cuthbert's wall in the garden of Edenhall, Cumberland. It was taken into the family of Sir Christopher Musgrave, Bart., who lived there, and was called *the Luck of Edenhall.* According to superstition all luck will pass from this family if ever it be lost or broken.

Fairies dance on the greensward. Occasionally rings are seen on the grass, where the latter is darker and more luxuriant. These *fairy rings* are supposed to mark the path of fairies, when they dance in circles. Really they are due to the outward spread of fungi from a central point and sometimes the fungi themselves are seen in circles and there may be bare or brown patches where the fungus has competed successfully with the roots of the grass. When the fungi die down they enrich the soil along a circular line of growth. They are chiefly caused by fungi of the genus *Marasmius* in this country.

The dances of fairies and their other celebrations were always believed to have taken place by night. When the cock crows they vanish. We can compare this with the nocturnal activities of witches, to be described later. Fairies were thought by some to worship the moon. The name Titania was given in classical times to Diana. She and her followers lived in the country as huntresses, but their life was somewhat akin to that of the fairies. Fairies were said to be fond of hunting.

Fairies visit women in childbirth, and there are many stories of good or evil spells cast on individuals at their birth by fairies, presents from fairies, also of fairy godmothers, who help in a magical fashion as in the story of Cinderella. They sometimes bless the bridal bed, but sometimes fall in love with mortals. If they do, the union is usually unfortunate, although children may be produced.

When annoyed fairies make milk turn sour, blight the corn and sometimes throw pots and furniture about. Thus they are identified with witches and poltergeists, to be described later. They would also nip people unawares, usually on the toes. Worst of all they sometimes steal away unbaptised children, leaving *changelings* in their place. The latter were fond of music and dancing, but were otherwise inferior, being fractious in behaviour or stupid, and sometimes had a voracious appetite. Whether the changeling was itself a fairy child, or comes from elsewhere is not clear.[19]

[19] A medical friend who is extremely well acquainted with the Highlands of Scotland tells me that the changeling theory was used to explain the birth of cretins and Mongolian imbeciles in otherwise normal families.

Fairy-money[20] has several significations : (i) certain places were supposed to belong to fairies; a farmer could not take over such land without leaving a piece of money, which was supposed to have been taken away by the fays; (ii) money was sometimes left with human beings by fairies, after they had gone away it sometimes turned to leaves or other worthless material (this was an old trick of the witches); (iii) the fairies evidently had a currency of their own; according to Brand[21] this consisted of "orbicular sparry bodies" as found on the banks of the Tyne, Newcastle, and now in the Leverian Museum.

Fairies could sometimes cause disease. An affection involving a hardening of the side of the body was known in the Middle Ages as the *elf-cake*. It could be cured by taking rootstock of the gladen (*Iris*) in white wine.

In Hampshire and Dorset the name *colepexy* (=*coltpixy*) is given to a mischievous fairy appearing in the form of a horse. The fossils known as belemnites are called *colepixies' fingers* and fossil sea-urchins *colepixies' heads*.[22]

Elementals. Whilst fairy-lore contains much relating to displaced aboriginal peoples it must be borne in mind that there are other theories of their origin. Some factors suggest that they are modified gods, others suggest a totemic origin.[23] But it must be remembered that all peoples of the world have beliefs in spirits which are neither men nor angels, good or bad. Such spirits are called *elementals*, or nature spirits in theosophical literature, and again these are distinguished from *elementaries* which are spooks or ghosts of human origin. The latter are said to be responsible for the belief in apparitions, spectres, shades, wraiths, banshees, bogies and boggarts. They are the lares, manes and larvae of classical times.

The elementals on the other hand, which appear to correspond somewhat with the classical penates, were independent entities. They live a long time, they are not immortal, but may become so by cohabiting with a human being. They are not all either good or bad, but may be either, like men and women. Bad ones were called goblins, hobgoblins, urchins, imps and poltergeists, the latter name being particularly applied to those who throw furniture about.

[20] J. Brand: *Popular Antiquities of Great Britain* II, New Ed., London, 1854.
[21] *Loc. cit.*
[22] *Loc. cit.*
[23] See Spence, *loc. cit.* for a discussion of these views.

There appear to be at least six classes of these beings :

(i) *Gnomes,* the spirits of earth; these were supposed to appear out of holes in the rocks; the miners of Cornwall and of Germany were afraid of or annoyed by them. In the latter country they were called *trolls, kobolds* or *dwergers.* The females were called *gnomides.* The gnomes were held responsible for roof-falls and explosions in mines. They are described as wearing brown or dark clothing and are ugly in appearance.

(ii) *Undines,* the spirits of water; they include the *oceanides* and *nereides* of the sea in classical mythology, the *elle-folk* of the Scandinavians, the females of which were called *elle-women* or *elle-maids,* the *merrows (mermaids* and *mermen)* of British fairy tale, the *naiades* of classical mythology who lived in fresh water, the *nixies* or *necks* of northern mythology and the *kelpies* who take the form of a horse. They are described as mostly of human shape above, but fish-like from the waist downward. Their hair is often green. The mermaid is often beautiful. Amongst them were *sea-monks* and *sea-bishops.* The former were distinguished by having a kind of cowl over the head, whilst the latter wore a mitre. It is thought that these have been suggested by particular kind of fish, whilst the mermaid herself is said to have been suggested by the dugong, a marine mammal, the females of which sometimes suckle their single young just above the water, holding it to the pectoral mammaries which occur in this species as in the human. The flippers are like arms, and the heads round like the human.

(iii) *Sylphs,* the spirits of air, these include the *fairies* proper or *fays,* probably also the less good-looking *brownies, elves* and *pixies.* In classical mythology we may place the *oreades* here, the nymphs of the mountains who attended on Diana. Female sylphs are called *sylphids.*

(iv) *Salamanders,* the spirits of fire; these include the *acthnici* which appear as globes of fire over the sea and on the masts and rigging of ships as St. Elmo's fires, also the *ignis fatuus,* the Will o' the Wisp or Jack o' Lantern, a flame appearing over marshland.

(v) *Dryads,* spirits of vegetation; these include the *dryades* and *hamadryades* of classical times; each tree was supposed to be inhabited by one of these spirits, who died with the tree itself.

(vi) *Fauns,* spirits of animal life; these include the *fauni, panes* and *sylvani* of the Romans and the *satyri* of the Greeks, the spirits of the totemic animals of totemic systems; from them are drawn the *familiars* of the witch. The fauns or satyrs played an important part in classical magic, as will be seen in the next chapter.

These must not be confused with what we can consider as the highest class of spirits, *viz* :

(vii) *Gods* and *Goddesses*, these although numerous were much fewer than the preceding; their images, sometimes with inscriptions, are sometimes found in Keltic parts, and they include those of Hu or Hesus, the great sky god, Keridwen, the Keltic Ceres, Grannos, patron of springs, Camulos, god of war, Lugh, god of light, Llyr and Manannan, sea-gods, Govannon or Goibniu, the craftsman, the Keltic Vulcan, Sul, patroness of hot springs, Brigit, goddess of the fire and hearth, the Keltic Vesta, Ogmios, the Keltic Hercules, and Cernunnos, the horned-god. The latter has been identified with the Christian devil, on the grounds that he was represented with cloven hoofs and horns.[24]

[24] Horns are, however, very common in mythological iconography. Moses, Bacchus and Alexander the Great are shown with horns.

CHAPTER XV

OLYMPUS AND THE SATYRS

The Labyrinth. Already in about 4000 B.C. there were people called the Aegeans in the Mediterranean region. They were sea-going folk and they had made their home in Italy as the Etruscans and along the coast of Asia Minor, at Troy for instance, and in the island of Crete, to the south of Greece. There were settlements at Tiryns and Mycenae, on the mainland of Greece, about 3000 B.C., but at that time Cnossos, capital of Crete was the main centre, trade communications having been established between Crete and Egypt by 4000 B.C., whilst by 2500 B.C. Cretan civilization had reached its zenith.[1]

This civilisation, the Cretan or Minoan as it is called, because at a later date the priest-king ruling the island often had the name or title of Minos, was a very distinctive one. It had a few general features in common with all early peoples, for instance a magico-religious cult centring around a mother-goddess and her divine son, with its priests and priestesses, and the bull-sacrifice was, at any rate in later times, an outstanding feature. But the symbolism was somewhat peculiar, as were the dress and customs of the natives. The religion was in some respects primitive, and attempted to establish a magical relation with elemental powers.[2] There were no large temples, but worship was on mountains, in caves, in rustic shrines and domestic chapels.[3] The palace was provided with running water and excellent drainage. There are remains of horned animals sacrificed, especially bulls, and bull-fighting was practised.[4] There were games, which may have been associated with magic, as we know[5] was the case with the original Olympic Games, founded on the mainland in 1222 B.C. The arts were highly developed, sculpture,

[1] H. G. Wells: *A Short History of the World*, 1922, revised Middlesex, 1946.
[2] G. R. Levy: *The Gate of Horn*, London, 1948.
[3] *Loc. cit.*
[4] According to H. G. Wells these bull-fights were similar to those of Spain later, even in the costumes of the fighters.
[5] J. E. Harrison: *Themis, a study of the social origins of Greek religion*, Cambridge, 1912.

carving, painting, jewellery attaining a remarkable elegance. The clothing, as H. G. Wells[6] points out somewhat resembled modern costume, for instance the women wore corsets and flounced dresses.

The *twin-symbolism* was highly developed in Crete. Everywhere we meet with the double-axe, the supreme symbol of the cult. This is a rod or staff, with two blades on either side at the top. Other symbols were a pillar, with two lions on either side, two birds, two griffins, two deer, two sea-horses, etc. The same idea is expressed by a head with two horns, or an altar horned on either side. Sea-shells were also used in religious symbolism and in magic.

Minos II, King of Crete, had the famous labyrinth constructed (1210 B.C.). This was not a new invention in Crete, there was one at Clusium in Etruria, one on the isle of Lemnos, one on the isle of Samos, both in the Aegean Sea, and one at Arsinoë in Egypt, so the idea was widespread. The one in Crete was built to house the monster called the *minotaur.*

Olympians. The stories of the Greek and Roman gods may, in part, be derived from this great and wonderful Cretan civilisation. In fact certain features of the mythos may refer to the peculiar social organisation of the Cretans. The gods were supposed to be immortal, but on the whole they act as mortals.[7] Yet the gods behave with a degree of freedom not granted to ordinary human beings. Is it possible that the exploits of the gods refer in part to a caste set apart from the populace—the class of the priesthood? In Greece and Rome, monogamy for instance was the rule, incest was taboo, and marital fidelity defended. Many of the gods, however, had many wives, they married their own sisters, as the Pharaoh and some very high dignitaries did in Egypt, and it was common practice for them to cohabit with mortal women, many of whom were married, yet whose husbands generally regarded these affairs as honourable. The husbands were often kings who were glad to become foster-parents to the offspring of a god. These facts suggest that in early times, probably in the Cretan forefathers of Greek religion there was a special caste of priestly personages, male and female, whose stories became incorporated afterwards in classical mythology. Crete was supposed to have been the birthplace of the king of the gods, Zeus (*Greek*) or Jupiter (*Roman*), and it may have been the seat of the high-priesthood of this peculiar cult.

The wonderful acts of the gods could then be interpreted as

6 *Loc. cit.*
7 The tomb of Zeus was shown in Crete.

originating from supposed magic, effected by this curious class of priests. Otherwise we hear relatively little of the priesthood, in spite of the fact that Greece and Rome were afterwards full of wonderful temples, and had a highly developed hierarchy. The gods and goddesses may have been the priests and priestesses of early times. Even in later myths there is some ambiguity as to whether an act was performed by one of the gods or goddesses, or only by his or her earthly representative.

Minos I who is said to have given laws to his subjects 1406 B.C., still in force in the days of Plato, is said to have been the son of Zeus and the mortal maiden Europa, daughter of a Phoenician king. Zeus is said to have assumed the form of a bull in order to gain Europa's love. After his death Minos I was made chief judge of the dead in Hades, the underworld. Can it be that in early days Crete itself was regarded in Greece as the land of the dead or sacred land, as Britain was so regarded in Gaul? The bull, from the time of this Minos, became the totem animal of the island.

The Oracles. The Aegeans invading Greece gave rise to Mycenean culture, which flourished 1600 B.C. to 1100 B.C. The two great historical events of this period, of which we have any record, are the *Argonautica*, or Quest of the Golden Fleece and the Trojan War. In the former all the heroes of Greece set out on a voyage on the ship *Argo* in search of the Golden Fleece. This story is rich in magic and afterwards served as a sort of bible to the alchemists. In the Trojan War, all the petty kings of the Greeks and their followers invaded Troy, because the wife of one of them, Menelaus, king of Sparta, who was the beautiful Helen, had been abducted by Paris, one of the sons of the king of Troy. After a long siege the Greeks captured Troy by the aid of the stratagem of the wooden horse.

The great epics, probably based on actual events in the Mycenean period, became idealised in the subsequent periods. During the Mycenean period the Aegean influence was predominant. The elemental deities held sway. Thereafter they were replaced by the Olympians. This is symbolised, according to Levy[8] by the conquest of the Titans by the Olympians. The Olympian religion gradually became the official or state religion; that which was publicly professed. But the old religion did not disappear. It was partly assimilated and incorporated into the official cultus. It was partly driven into secrecy, but it expressed itself as a secret cult, which was respected and looked upon with awe, in the form of *the Mysteries*.

[8] *Loc. cit.*, but the story probably has more than one symbolic meaning.

Lastly it was perverted, partly driven into underground, or into clandestine activities, classed as witchcraft.

From the earliest times many of the gods had their *oracles*. The latter were consulted by persons in difficulty, and, after a large sum of money had been paid to the priest or priestess in charge, the answer was delivered, either in words, as at the famous oracle of Apollo at Delphi, where the priestess, speaking the words as in a trance, was called the pythoness, or in signs and sounds, as at the ancient oracle of Jupiter at Dodona, where the signs consisted of the movements of an oak, and afterwards of objects, such as drums and cauldrons suspended thereon, imitative of the sound of thunder, appropriate to a sky-god. Some say the entrails of animals gave signs there. Another example is the oracle of Hercules at Bura, Achaea, where dice were used as signs. Less commonly the answers of oracles were determined by dreams of the querent. This was so in the oracles of Aesculapius at Epidaurus, Pergamum and Rome. Finally, some oracles resembled the modern spiritualistic seance, for the dead were consulted, by means of a medium. These were chiefly situated at places where there was a deep cleft in the earth, especially if volcanic vapour arose therefrom. These occur at Cinchyrus in Epirus, Taenarum in Laconia, both in Greece, at Heraclea in Pontus, Asia Minor, and near Cumae, Italy. In Epirus, by the way, there were rivers called Acheron and Cocytus, names also given to rivers in the underworld.

The chief oracles, apart from those mentioned were those of Jupiter in Crete, of Ammon (sometimes identified with Jupiter) in Libya, of Hera near Pagae, Megaris, Greece, of Minerva in Mycenae, of Apollo at Delos and the Tenedos islands in the Aegean, Claros on the coast of Greece, and at Patara, Lycia, Asia Minor, of Diana at Colchis in Asia Minor, of Hercules at Athens, and at Gades in Spain, of Mars in Thrace, of Pan in Arcady, of Venus at Paphos in Cyprus and at Aphaca in Syria. There was also a famous oracle of Trophonius at a cave named after this person, supposed to have been swallowed up in the earth, at Lebadea in Greece. He is said to have built the temple of Apollo at Delphi, and was later honoured as a son of the god. Another oracle named from personages not otherwise well known was that of the Palici, two alleged sons of Jupiter, in Sicily.

The great Egyptian god Serapis also had oracles, but not, it appears, in Greece.

Sometimes the oracles changed hands. The Delphic oracle first belonged to Tellus or Gaea, the earth goddess, who probably owned most of them at first. Apollo took over and ever after retained the earth-snake as a symbol. He is supposed to have killed it as soon as he was born. Oracles were supposed to be founded in a miraculous manner. Those of Jupiter at Dodona and Thebes were founded by doves, who flew to these places and spoke with a human voice. These doves are explained by Herodotus, as priestesses from Thebes in Egypt. Another account makes Deucalion founder of the oracle at Dodona, soon after the great Flood, in which he and his wife escaped in a vessel; it is not certain that this refers to the Biblical Deluge, as there are several floods in Greek history. It was also said that Deucalion consulted the oracle of Themis, one of the wives of Jupiter, which was in Attica, Greece.

Sorcery. Under this name we may class the selfish use of magical powers, and as the official magic was ostensibly for the benefit of society, it meant the unofficial exercise of such powers. It is not surprising that sorcery was most common, therefore, outside the main centres of Greek culture, and we learn that in Thessaly, to the north of Greece, it was extensively practised.

On his long journey home from Troy Ulysses (Odysseus) visits the island Aeaea, the home of Circe, the enchantress. She was the daughter of the titan sun-god, and married a prince of Colchis in the Caucasus. She murdered her husband, with a view to obtaining his kingdom, but was expelled by her subjects, whereupon her father provided for her a luxurious refuge in a lonely island. When the companions of Ulysses arrived she welcomed them, but turned them into swine by giving them certain herbs with their food. One messenger escaped, as he had not tasted the food, Ulysses also was not present, as he remained with his ship. On landing he meets Mercury the messenger of the gods, who has flown in to help him. Mercury gives Ulysses a herb called *moly*, believed to be of the onion family, a famous antidote to enchantments. This prevents him being transformed, he then persuades Circe to release his companions, and others she had previously enchanted. Another enchantress, called Medea, is associated with the story of the Golden Fleece.

Nymphs and Satyrs. There were a considerable number of minor deities, that had an important part to play in the cultural life and folk-lore of the Greeks and Romans. Of these the females were mostly called *nymphs*; the most prominent males were the *satyrs*.

Here we may also mention the *lamiae* who were certain witches or female monsters of Africa, who had the lower part of the body in the form of a serpent. They were bereft of speech, but their hissings are described as pleasant; they allured strangers and especially children, killed and ate them. The *empusae* and *strygae* are similar conceptions.

The Sirens (*Sirenes*) were nymphs who were said to have challenged the muses. They were great musicians, but were defeated in the contest. They were banished to a small island off Sicily. Anyone listening to them forgot all else, and died of hunger. The exceptions were Ulysses and the Argonauts. The former had himself bound to the mast of his ship and stopped the ears of his crew with wax, when they passed the Sirens on the long journey home. The Argonauts had Orpheus with them. He was a wonderful singer, and as they listened to him they passed the Sirens unharmed. The Sirens were represented as birds, with the faces of beautiful women. They were three in number.

Marine nymphs included the numerous *Oceanides* and the *Nereides*. The *Naiades* were nymphs of freshwater, and were supposed to inhabit rivers, lakes, springs, wells and fountains. Many of the river gods were represented as males. There were beings present in the winds, whilst the Cyclops, Cabiri, Curetes, Telechines and Dactyli were mysterious entities connected with fire and metals.

The Dryads, as we have seen, were nymphs of trees and were of various kinds according to the species. The *Hamadryads*, for instance, were said to have belonged to the oak. The *Meliades* presided over fruit-trees. The *Limoniades* ruled the vegetation of meadows and were said to dance in rings like the fairies among the Kelts.

Fauns were beings connected with the animal kingdom. Related to them were two classes of nymphs said to hunt with Diana, the goddess of hunting. The *Napaeae* were represented as beautiful but shy maidens, wearing short tunics, and the *Oreades* or mountain nymphs, attired at huntresses, being larger and bolder than the preceding. The term *Fauni*, in the narrow sense applies to capricious young males, with hairy bodies, following Faunus or Pan, and that of Satyrs or *Satyri* to males of mature or old age, with flat noses, very hairy bodies, hoofs, horns and tail, and pointed ears like those of an animal. They lay in wait for passing nymphs. They follow in the train of Bacchus, god of wine, and were heavy drinkers. In later art they were more humanised. Their chief was Silenus.

The Centaurs (*Centauri*) were represented as having the body and four legs of a horse, and the shoulders, arms and head of a man. They, like the Satyrs, were fond of women and wine but some of them, like Chiron, the tutor of Hercules, had great knowledge of archery, music and medicine.

The Spirits of the Dead were called *Manes* and were of several kinds. Part of the soul might haunt the living, part might be confined to Hades, and in some exceptional cases, *e.g.* Hercules, whose shade was supposed to be in Hades, the spirit might be received into Olympus (*apotheosis*). In Roman times a special ceremony, to celebrate the ascent of a human being to heaven was sometimes carried out, an eagle being used to symbolise the ascent.

Daemones or *genii* were spirits of men, especially what we now call their guardian angels. *Lemures* or *larvae* were what we now call ghosts, haunting abodes or other localities after death, or spontaneously appearing. *Lares* were spirits of their ancestors, who exerted a protective influence over the homes of the people. Statues of the lares, or of the chief lar, were found in all Roman houses and were honoured by offerings of food or flowers placed before it. There were also shrines of various lares in public places. *Penates* were deities selected for household or public worship, much as today saints are selected, to which churches and other institutions are dedicated.

The Pythagorean Order. The Ionic Period succeeded the Doric; it lasted 650–300 B.C. Following various catastrophes in Greece during the early part of this period, the Pelasgian religion, centred on Dionysos, in his aspect of a slain and resurrected supreme god (Zagreus) emerged. This in fact was called a re-emergence, as it is only a new expression of the elemental forces of man's being trying to assert themselves, under the stress of war and natural cataclysms. The mysteries of Crete, however, were combined with the rather different magic, more closely resembling witchcraft, derived from Thrace (corresponding roughly with the modern Bulgaria and Rumania). The use, not only of wine, but of various drugs, appears to have been incorporated from the latter source. However, at the same time, some of the Bacchic worshippers, seem to have aimed at purification of the body and mind from evil influences, with the ultimate aim of uniting man to God. This cult and philosophy is called Orphism, and was supposed to have been taught by Orpheus.

A certain amount of arcane science seems to have been taught in this school of philosophy. The fixed stars were symbolised by humming tops, the planets by whipping tops.[9] These with the dice, the

[9] G. R. S. Mead in his translation of *The Chaldean Oracles* quoted in a footnote to the English translation of E. Levi: *The History of Magic*, London, 1922.

ball and the mirror were said to be the playthings of Dionysus in the Mysteries. They were kept in the sacred basket, and touched by candidates during the initiation ceremony. The dice were probably the five Platonic solids (the five solids having equal faces: tetrahedron, cube, octahedron, dodecahedron and icosahedron) which are models for the structure of chemical substances. The tops were planets and were reflected in the lower world as atoms. The ball was the earth. The mirror symbolised reflection, showing how the higher is reflected in the lower.[10]

This sort of teaching was brought to its highest perfection by Pythagoras (582–497 B.C.). He was born at Samos an island in the Aegean Sea, and in early life distinguished himself at the Olympic Games. He travelled extensively, even in Egypt and Chaldaea, studying and collecting information from the priesthood. He eventually established a school of arcane science at Crotona in Sicily. He was skilled in medicine, music and mathematics. Numbers to Pythagoras had a qualitative as well as a quantitative significance.

Pythagoras evidently had some knowledge of hypnotism. He was said by Iamblicus to have had dominion even over birds and beasts, by the power of his voice and the influence of his touch. He subdued an eagle and a wild bear by these means. Pythagoras taught the dogmas of the immortality of the soul and reincarnation.

The School of Crotona grew in political influence and importance, but appears to have provoked a popular uprising. Fighting broke out, and Pythagoras is said to have been killed, but a more probable account tells that, with a few friends, he escaped to Metapontum, Italy and died soon after.

A few years later Xerxes I of Persia invaded Greece with an immense army (480 B.C.). With him came Ostanes, who, according to Pliny, introduced magic. However, it must have been a particular Persian variety of magic, as the latter, we have seen, was already widely believed in. It may, in fact, have been alchemy. A fragment of an alchemical work attributed to Ostanes still exists,[11] and early alchemical writers refer to him as a pioneer of alchemy. The invasion of Xerxes was repulsed, but alchemy thereafter seems to have been a pursuit of certain Greeks.

Plato, whose original name was Aristocles (429–348 B.C.) and Aristotle (384–322 B.C.), two of the world's greatest philosophers,

[10] C. Jinarajadasa: *First Principles of Theosophy*, 3rd ed., Adyar, Madras, India, 1923.

[11] According to a footnote by A. E. Waite in the English translation of Levi: *History of Magic*, 2nd ed., London, 1922.

upheld the dogma that man reflected the whole universe in himself, the microcosm as a miniature macrocosm. This was supposed to have originated with Hermes Trismegistus and was taught by Pythagoras.

Aristotle was tutor to Alexander the Great, of whom certain magical stories are told. Alexander's father was said to have been Nectanebus an Egyptian magician, who artfully seduced his mother Olympias (wife of Philip, king of Macedonia) under the form of the Egyptian god, Ammon. Alexander ascended the throne, after Philip's death, and became a world conqueror. He extended his conquests to India. He writes to Aristotle about the wonders of India, where he sees a dragon and visits talking trees and the fountain of the water of life. He sees Enoch sleeping on a golden bed. He descends into the ocean with two friends in a glass diving bell, and sees great monsters of the deep. He sees magical apparatus of ten kinds in Babylon.[12]

The talking trees were two in number and were called the tree of the sun and the tree of the moon. They grew in a temple in India, and were consulted as oracles by the priests. By them Alexander was warned of his early death in Babylon.

Later Classical Occultism. Cicero (b. 106—assassinated 43 B.C.), famous Roman orator and writer, was interested in occult matters. He was one of those who mentioned the sibyl's prophecy of a coming great teacher.[13] He is something of a sceptic. In his *De Divinatione* he opposes astrology and divination, in his *Dream of Scipio* he gives astrology limited approbation, and seems to think dreams may reflect the future.

Vitruvius, architect of the latter part of the first century B.C., author of the only work on building and architecture that has survived from ancient times, was a great believer in occult virtues and affinities, and in the power of numbers. He speaks highly of astrology, tells how it came from the Chaldeans, that Berosus the Chaldean priest opened an astrological school in the island of Cos, that Antipater pursued the science, then Archinapolus, and that the latter left rules for casting horoscopes, not from birth, but from the actual moment of conception.[14]

Virgil (70–19 B.C.) most famous of Latin poets, author of the

[12] E. A. Wallis Budge, trans. *The Alexander Book in Ethiopia*, London, 1933.
[13] Howitt, *loc. cit.*
[14] Thorndike: *loc. cit.*

Aeneid was, curiously enough, accounted a magician in mediaeval times. He was one of those that prophesied the coming of Christ. But his magical qualifications seem to be inventions of later times; he was one of the guides of Dante.[15]

Apollonius of Tyana, Cappadocia, Asia Minor, flourished in the middle of the 1st century A.D. He was one of the first Neopythagoreans. He was a wealthy man who visited Persia, India, Rome and Greece. At Ephesus he is said to have seen, by clairvoyance, the assassination of the emperor Domitian at Rome. Many other miraculous events were recorded of him. His life was written by Philostratus, a Greek sophist, living in Rome, about A.D. 217. Hierocles, a persecutor of the Christians under Diocleian, blasphemously attempted to show the miracles of Apollonius were superior to those of Christ, and was refuted by Lactantius and Eusebius. The latter says Apollonius worked with demons. According to a modern view,[16] there is no evidence that Philostratus attempted to parody the gospels, as formerly alleged. Apollonius was refused admission to the Mysteries on the grounds that he was a sorcerer. He had consorted with the magi of Babylonia, the brahmins of India and the gymnosophists of Egypt, but his biographer points out that the same was alleged of such eminent philosophers as Empedocles, Democritus and Pythagoras.

Apollonius also practised necromancy. He was alleged to have raised the shade of Achilles. He cured insanity. He was alleged to have raised the dead, for it is recorded that he revived an apparently dead maiden.

Apollonius when in Rome was tried by the order of the Emperor Domitian for sacrificing a boy. The crime was partly a political one, as Domitian's political rival Nerva had asked Apollonius to find out whether there was any chance of his becoming emperor. This, it was alleged, Apollonius proceeded to do by the inspection of the entrails of the aforesaid human sacrifice. When, at the trial, it was alleged that Apollonius was a magician, the latter replied that if he had been he would have thrown off his fetters by his magic power. However, before the trial was over Apollonius escaped, and he died in Asia Minor at an advanced age.

Apuleius, author of the famous *Golden Ass*, largely autobiographical, was born in Numidia, North Africa, A.D. 125. He studied at Carthage, Athens and Rome, and his scientific and medical

[15] He conducted Dante through Inferno, Beatrice conducted the poet through Purgatory, and St. Bernard through Paradise.
[16] Thorndike: *loc. cit.*

knowledge was mentioned by St. Augustine. After returning to
Africa he married a wealthy widow much older than himself, and
he was then charged with having won her hand by magic, and with
conspiring to kill her son. At the time Apuleius had been dissecting
a sea-hare (*Aplysia*), a marine mollusc used by the Romans in
poisoning. Fortunately he cleared himself of the charge. In the
Golden Ass the hero enters the laboratory of a sorceress named
Pamphile with a view to turning himself into a bird for a time.
Unfortunately he uses the wrong unguents and gets changed into
an ass, from which he can only be released by nibbling roses. It
is some time before he gets an opportunity to do this. The story
is probably only intended for amusement, but may have some
reference to initiation, and it is believed that Apuleius was an
initiate of several different rites, and finally became a priest of Isis.
He certainly was involved in the practice of magic, spirit control,
dream-interpretation and astrology.

Ammonius Saccas (*fl.* early 3rd century), a man of humble birth,
established a Neoplatonic school at Alexandria in A.D. 232 in which
Plato, Aristotle and the Christian revelation were held to be synthe-
sised. The perception of spirits, and the part played by the latter
in miracles is alleged to have been taught. Amongst several distinguished pupils of this school are Plotinus and Origen. The former
became, perhaps, the best known of the Neoplatonists.

Plotinus (204–270) travelled to Persia in 242 and to Rome in
243. He finally taught philosophy in Rome. He believed diseases are
due to natural causes, but thought that incantations benefited them
through sympathy. The stars are souls or gods, they are signs of
earthly events, but do not determine them.[17] The whole universe is
one whole; there is an interaction between all things, but not
determinism. He accuses the gnostics of a deterministic view, and
says they frighten people with it.

Plotinus was both a mystic and a practical occultist. On one
occasion he apprehended a thief among a number of suspected
persons, knowing nothing of the crime. The man eventually confessed. On another occasion a certain sorcerer, jealous of the success
of Plotinus, attempted to injure him by sympathetic magic. Plotinus
caused the spell to rebound on to its originator. After several

[17] Thorndike (*loc. cit.*) says that Plotinus arrives at what was to be the
usual Christian position in the Middle Ages, in reference to astrology,
namely the human will is free, yet allowing a large field to astrological
prediction.

attempts the sorcerer, one Olympius, a former student at the same school as Plotinus, ceased his efforts.

Plotinus is said to have had the ability to reach an ecstatic state, in which he received philosophical illumination.

Whilst Plotinus was favourable to the Christian religion his disciple Porphyry (233–301) was not so. He even expressed doubt on the existence of daemones (spirits) and in the reality of apparitions. On the other hand he opposed the sceptical view that gods were only personified stars and other natural phenomena. He wrote the lives of Pythagoras and Plotinus.

Iamblichus (died 333), a disciple of Porphyry, was an enemy of the Christian religion. In place of it he put forward what he termed *theurgy,* which is a kind of good magic, distinct from bad magic (sorcery) or neutral magic (enchantment) inasmuch as it serves mankind. Theurgy acts by *symbols* which are neutral things which correspond with hidden entities (gods, spirits), and by *signatures* which are relations, according to a law of correspondence between different things, *e.g.* the sun and gold, the moon and silver. Words according to Iamblichus have power, the names of spirits may be used to control them, and may lose their power if translated. Ancient prayers must be used unchanged.

Much of this is in harmony with the Catholic religion, but the resemblance does not stop here. Iamblichus evolved a mighty system[18] of what he believed to be orthodox theology, with ordered hierarchy and rigid ritual, with cloister and penance, with an even more detailed classification of spiritual entities than usually adopted by Christians, distinguishing gods, heroes, angels, archangels, archons, good and evil demons. The spirits are of different kinds according to the elements with which they correspond. There are also relations between gods and lower spirits. Unlike the gods the demons are not entirely separate from bodies, some are even associated with animals. Invocations draw men towards the gods, they do not bring the gods down to earth according to Iamblichus. Theurgy is not a physical science. Necessity rules many events in the world, and these are indicated by the stars. Gods, however, are not ruled by necessity, and human beings, inasmuch as they become god-like, can escape from necessity. Such were the ideas of Iamblichus.

After Iamblichus died his pupil Julian (331–363) ascended the imperial throne. Prior to this Christianity had been declared the

[18] O. Spengler: *Decline of the West,* trans. 2 vols., London, 1918, 1922, quotes Geffcken to this effect.

official religion (since the conversion of Constantine the Great, 321).
Julian himself was brought up as a Christian, but abandoned the
faith under the influence of Iamblichus. Hence he was called Julian
the Apostate. When he was made emperor, on the death of
Constans, Julian immediately proclaimed the restoration of sacrifices
to all the gods of ancient Rome. He tried to reduce divination to
an exact science, was a keen astrologer, and he devoted his energies,
with passionate zeal to the re-establishment of the Pagan Church-
State.[19] However, his life was cut short by war with the Persians.
Although he was successful he received a mortal wound; his successor was Jovian, who had been helping him in the war, but happened to be a Christian. The Catholic religion was quickly
restored.[20] In 388 a copy of Porphyry's work against Christianity
was publicly burnt by order of Theodosius, a later emperor.

Iamblichus, Porphyry and Julian all accepted Pythagorean
ideas of number-qualities. Iamblichus and Porphyry admitted the
value of astrological images.

Proclus (412–485) who called himself the last link in the chain
of hermetic philosophers taught mainly at Athens. He believed there
was one principle of all things, which expressed itself in the world
in triads. He again classified the gods, but opposed Christianity,
chiefly because he could not accept the doctrine of the creation.
There is, he averred, a magical sympathy between all things. One
works up to communion with the gods by first contacting lesser
spirits.

Proclus had a number of followers, some of whom were women.
The most famous was Hypatia, who, with her father Theon, a
mathematician, taught in Alexandria. She was the centre of society
in that city, where she was brutally assassinated by some Christian
monks in 415. Marinus and then Isidorus succeeded Proclus at
Athens. Isidorus removed to Alexandria and the succession was
continued for many years there, by a series of initiates known as the
Golden Chain.[21] But neoplatonism was also continued by such
Christian teachers as Synesius.

[19] The Roman State was a Church, says Spengler. He quotes Geffcken to
prove that Julian "devoted, and finally sacrificed, his life to the attempt to
establish this Church for all eternity."

[20] Spengler points out that Constantine the Great "acted simultaneously
as convener of the Council of Nicaea and Pontifex Maximus."

[21] Tennemann: *A Manual of the History of Philosophy*, trans. and
revised, London, 1878.

CHAPTER XVI

VALHALLA AND THE VALKYRIES

The Norsemen. The Norse, Germanic, Gothic and Vandal peoples, which we can roughly include under the name of the Teutonic, developed a distinctive cult and mythology which chiefly centred in Germany, Denmark, Norway and Sweden. We must turn aside from the main stream of culture to examine this, remembering that it influenced that stream to a great degree. Danes were invading Britain from time to time during the 9th to 11th centuries, Angles and Saxons during the 5th, the latter being the more successful, and setting up a line of Anglo-Saxon kings. Goths and Vandals conquered, for a time, large parts of Southern Europe, in Spain, Italy and the Balkans. Visigoths, for instance, sacked Rome in 410.

The Norsemen were warlike peoples. When not engaged in war they spent much of their time drinking, presided over by their chief, in halls set apart for their entertainment. After death they supposed that those that fell in battle would be transported to the great hall of Valhalla, where their chief god Odin sits enthroned. They were to be carried there on horseback by beautiful maidens called Valkyries.

Many, but probably not all of these Norsemen were of a specific anthropological type, with fair hair, florid faces, "flesh-coloured" skin, prominent noses and chins, features of the so-called Nordic race. But of course it is rather a language and cultural group, and the languages spoken were the Germanic varieties of the great Indo-Germanic or Aryan family. Their communities centred around the great halls of their chiefs, who were often also priests. These petty kings or priests were warriors, but also offered sacrifices, animal and sometimes human. The Norsemen had scalds, who were musician-poets, and sagamen, who recited poetry and prose without music. For the most part they did not have druids. These peoples probably originated with the Keltïc in the Caucasian region, and separated from them at an early date. There are vague references in the classics to a certain Odin or Odinus, a leader of the Teutons, who appeared in Germany and Denmark some 70 years B.C. The same name as we have seen is applied to their highest god.

Eddas and Sagas. The source of our knowledge of the early beliefs of these Teutons is to be found in the *Eddas* and the *Sagas.* The word *Edda*, originally applied to the rules of composition, is commonly used to designate two bodies of writings, emanating from Iceland. The *Elder* or *Poetic Edda* was first discovered about 1642, and was attributed to a historian named Saemund, but this ascription is now known to be incorrect. The 13th century manuscript of this, known as the *Codex Regius*, is preserved in the Royal Library at Copenhagen. There are certain smaller pieces of a similar nature, sometimes said to belong to this. The *Younger or Prose Edda* is a prose paraphrase of, and commentary on the preceding, and on other works now unknown, and was written by the historian Snorri Sturlson (1178–1241) about 1220 or 1230. Three manuscripts of this are known, the best is now preserved at Uppsala.

From sagas are probably derived many of our fairy tales, including, *Jack the Giant Killer, Jack and the Beanstalk* and many others. There is an Esthonian epic called *Hero* and a Finnish one known as *Kalevala*[1] which give modified versions of some of the sagas.

Gods as Magicians. It is obvious that the Norsemen had very little idea of abstract gods. Their gods are not immortal, even in the sense of the Olympians for instance. They all die, although there is some indication that they may some time be reborn. They are far from perfect beings. The greatest of them all, Odin, is constantly dependent upon talismans of various kinds. He frequently consults soothsayers. The powerful and supposedly popular god, Baldur, is killed. The god who kills him, Hodur, is represented as blind. The gods have a beginning. Some of their births are recorded. They all die at the end of an epoch, which was supposed to be in the future. This presupposes a sort of judgement-day, called Ragnarok, when the world and its inhabitants, including the gods, would come to an end.

Probably many of the Norsemen, in the early days, could neither read nor write. Small wonder then that they looked upon letters with awe. Even more than among other early peoples, script was regarded as having a magical power. Certain writings were merely used for communication among those that knew, but in addition it was widely held that some had a magical power, and these were called *runes.* The latter could be used for divination, by the casting of lots, when only the initiated would be able to interpret them.

[1] Collected in a book by E. Lönnrot only as late as 1835.

Others were supposed to have an evil effect on a person whom one wished to harm, acting as an adverse suggestion. Others would preserve from mishap, would procure victory over enemies, or would even cure disease, it was imagined. Odin, the supreme god, has to learn about runes from the magician Mimir.

Oracles of a sort were used. Their horse oracles, obtained by listening to the snorting and neighing of a horse seem to be in use in Germany, according to Tacitus.[2] But more important in the Teutonic world were certain prophetesses who wandered about, or lived in remote places and who were greatly venerated for their soothsaying.

The Magic Cauldron. Not all the soothsayers were in good repute, although the Northerners were more tolerant of their activities than were the Greeks and Romans. Both Gothic and Old High German distinguish witches, hags or "hedge-riders" from priestesses and prophetesses. It is particularly the witches among whom we read of the magical use of herbs, stones, animals, shells, teeth, claws and tails, still heard of in folk medicine at a much later date. Even at the time of writing it is possible to purchase a beautiful silver mounted rabbit's foot as a charm, and this superstition may have come down from our Saxon predecessors, although the practice is widespread. The cauldron of the witches, subsequently much in evidence, is foreshadowed by the large saucepan-like vessel used both by our Keltic and our Germanic ancestors. And when such authors as Shakespeare portray this cauldron with an evil significance, as in *Macbeth*, they are true to life, for it lends itself, not only to the brewing of so-called cures, but much more easily to the compounding of powerful poisons. That tremendous magical powers were ascribed to brewed potions, however, is evinced by the fact that Odin the supreme god, gains his wisdom by drinking from the cauldron of the magician Mimir. He is even willing to sacrifice one of his eyes (for a time) in order to obtain this great privilege. The sacred cauldron had a tremendous religious significance for the Norsemen.

In mythology the wisest of men, Kvasir, is murdered by the dwarfs Fjalar and Galar. They are going to be drowned by the giant Suttung, whose father, Gilling, has been slain by them, when they purchase their lives by giving up the cauldron, with its

[2] In his *Germania*. White horses, used for no other purpose than the oracle were kept at one place, according to him. He does not mention the locality.

magical contents, to Suttung. Henceforth the contents are known as Suttung's mead. Eventually Odin gains the cauldron and its contents, after taking the form of a snake and seducing Suttung's daughter Gunnlauth. To the draught from this cauldron also, some of Odin's remarkable wisdom is attributed, notably his knowledge of runes and poetry.

CHAPTER XVII

LOTUS, SWASTIKA AND PAGODA

Buddhism. No religion is richer in fantastic mythology and hierurgic ceremonial than Buddhism. Curiously enough, when Buddhist literature first became known in the West, in the last century, this faith was regarded as little more than a system of philosophic atheism, on the basis of certain passages from their sacred books, detached from their context. This view is now completely obsolete, and is a strange example of the armchair pronouncements of those who have no experience of field-work in anthropology. Everywhere in Buddhist countries are images of the Buddhas, not to mention the thousands of other sacred personages.

Buddhism is supposed to have been founded by a historical personage: Gautama Buddha, otherwise known as Siddartha or Sakyamuni (*circa* 563–483 B.C.). But although he is universally revered among Buddhists, he is by no means the chief of their pantheon. The latter is not altogether distinct from that of the Hindus, and at the head is a supreme triad. Of their three chief deities the Great Buddha of the West is the best known in iconography, but the three are shown together above the altars of their temples. The name Buddha is a title, and applies to all beings who have reached a certain grade in the heavenly hierarchy.

The historical Buddha called Gautama was the son of the ruler of Magadha, a kingdom of the Sakyas, a people akin to the Tibetans and quite different from the modern Indians, but lying in the north of India, in the part included in the modern Uttar Pradesh. Its capital was Kapilavastu, and near this Gautama was born. It was then a place of great riches and Gautama was brought up in luxurious surroundings, knowing nothing of hardship or suffering. He was married to a beautiful princess and had a son.

Although his father had taken precautions against Gautama seeing anything unpleasant, it soon happened that the latter discovered signs of the world's distress. These signs he encountered whilst on walks, and they were four in number (i) a senile man, (ii) a diseased person, (iii) a corpse and (iv) a monk. He was so upset by the contemplation of the first three, that he determined to become a monk, and for this purpose deserted his wife and young child. Furthermore he, for a time, practised certain austerities and mortifications, as was the rule among monastic establishments. One day, when faint from hunger through fasting, he decided to give up this method, so took a hearty meal. Thereafter he decided to try contemplation. This was much more successful. He reached a place called Bodh-Gaya, and he sat down there under a bo-tree or peepul (*Ficus religiosa*). Here he attained enlightenment. He had previously been a *bodhisattva*, that is one who was consciously seeking enlightenment. Now he became a *buddha, i.e.* one that is enlightened. Thereupon he was given the choice, either to enter *nirvana* and to leave this world, or to remain here and teach. He chose the latter course.

Gautama had been "on the path" towards buddahood for many lives—twenty-four to be exact—before the one in which he attained it. He remembered his experiences in these, and used them to illustrate his moral teachings and the action of karma. These tales are called *Jatakas*. A new buddha appears after a certain interval of time. The one following Gautama was still a bodhisattva when Gautama attained buddhahood. He is known as Maitreya, and was due to attain buddhahood after Gautama. Hence he is sometimes called "the coming Buddha."

In Christian legend of the Middle Ages in Europe the story of Gautama and the four signs of suffering, and his conversion to a religious life, has been ascribed to St. Jehosaphat.

Buddhist Kings. After the death of Gautama, Buddhism spread rapidly. The First Buddhist Council was held immediately after the demise of the founder, the Second soon followed. But what contributed most of all to the success of the movement was its recognition by King Asoka who succeeded to the throne in 273 B.C. and who eventually brought into his domain the greater part of India, Afghanistan and Baluchistan. Asoka, before he died in 232 B.C. made Buddhism the state religion. He left edicts on rocks and pillars at various places, and these have proved of great historic interest. The Third Buddhist Council was held under his auspices. His son, Mahinda, introduced the Buddhist scriptures into Ceylon. The Fourth Buddhist Council was held under Kanishka, another king who had a very wide rule from Afghanistan, Bokhara and Kashmir in the North to Madura in the South. His dates are uncertain, but he probably lived in the 2nd century B.C. In A.D. 634 Siladitya's Council was held at Kanauj on the Ganges. That Buddhism was widespread in India is evinced by numerous archaeological remains of indubitable Buddhist orgin. But it gradually disappeared from its land of origin. Already in A.D. 700 it is estimated that there were fewer Buddhists than Brahminists in India. By A.D. 800 it had practically disappeared there. It became, however, very popular with peoples of mongoloid extraction, and that was probably because it began among such a people, and not among caucasoids. The final blow came in 1197 when Magadha was overrun by Moslems, who destroyed a number of historical places of the Buddhists. The original monastery at Gautama's birthplace is now, curiously enough, in the hands of Brahmins, although it continues to be a great place of pilgrimage.

But Buddhism spread outside India. It is still the dominant religion in Ceylon. In Java it mingles with Hinduism and Mohammedanism. Otherwise it is only widespread among mongoloid peoples. Some of these are now under communist control, and religion is repressed to a varying degree, but by no means extinguished. In Ceylon, Burma, Siam and Indo-China Buddhism of the lesser vehicle (*Hinayana* or *Theravada*) predominates. This differs from Buddhism of the greater vehicle (*Mahayana*), which predominates in Tibet and Japan, in not accepting commentaries to the scriptures recognised at the Fourth Buddhist Council under Kanishka. However this has not prevented Buddhism in these countries from exhibiting its magico-religious nature, nor is it clear that here there was any very deliberate attempt to break with tradition; rather certain aspects of the religion were allowed to lapse. Consequently we must hesitate to compare this tendency in Southern Buddhism with the development of heresies in the Christian religion, since most of the latter were deliberate attempts to deny one or more dogmas of the Catholic faith. The Hinayana still has a complex mythology, and a correspondingly elaborate ritual. The monastic system dominates their social organisation.

Buddhism in Indo-China, in fact, is inextricably mixed up with Hinduism, and in Cambodia and probably in Java the greater vehicle was formerly predominant. There is everywhere a belief in spirits. Both in Ceylon and Indo-China horoscopes are cast, and there are elaborate rituals for counteracting adverse planetary influences. In Burma and Siam every male on leaving school becomes a monk, although some leave the monastery after a short while to resume life with the laity. There are kings of Siam and Cambodia, formerly there was a king of Burma and an emperor of Annam, now included in the republic of Vietnam. These kings were not only priests, they were formerly regarded as representatives of the Godhead, or even as if God himself.

The king of Siam was legally the owner of the whole country; he holds, as symbols of his supreme power, one or more white elephants,[1] the trident,[2] the discus[3] or the quoit and the umbrella. At his coronation which is a long ceremony and, like some high masonic initiations, performed in several different halls, he is called Master of the World, Sovereign of Life, August Great Emperor, Descendant of the Gods, Perfect Justice, August Commanding Summit and Excellent Divine Feet.

The king of Arakan (Burma) assumed the title of Emperor, possessor of the white elephant and of the two ear-rings. The latter were supposed to make him the legitimate heir to the kingdoms of Pegu (S. Burma) and Brama (which apparently refers to the territory around the mouth of the river Bramaputra in Bengal). He therefore claimed rulership over the twelve provinces of the latter, and their twelve kings were said to place their heads under his feet.[4] The Susuhnan of Solokarta, a ruler in Java was dignified by the title of *The Nail of the Universe*.

The king of Ava (Burma) was actually called "God." It is therefore not surprising that in writing to other monarchs he styles himself "King of Kings, whom all others should obey," he being "the cause of the preservation of all animals, the regulator of the seasons, the absolute master of the ebb and flow of the sea, brother to the sun, and king of the four and twenty umbrellas."[5] The latter were always carried before him, although most other Eastern monarchs were content to appear under a single one. Equally high sounding titles were however in use for other oriental potentates, including the former kings of Kandy (Ceylon).

The Temple of Heaven. Before the Revolution there was a complex religious organisation in China. European accounts of China describe that country as possessing three religions: Confucianism, Taoism and Buddhism,[6] but travellers reported that many Chinese

[1] The white elephant actually exists; it is an albino variety of the Indian species, having light grey skin, white hoofs, scanty white hair and pink eyes. Some individuals have red hair and some yellow eyes. Some are reported to owe their special features to disease, however.
[2] Corresponding with the trident of Siva in Hindu mythology.
[3] Corresponding with the discus of Vishnu in Hindu mythology.
[4] I. D'Israeli: *Curiosities of Literature*, new ed., London, 1867.
[5] I. D'Israeli: *loc. cit.*
[6] J. Hackin, *et al. Asiatic Mythology*, trans. London, 1932.

are attached to establishments of worship in all three. Further investigation showed, however, that these so-called religions are only branches of one cult of which the Emperor of China was the head or centre. As in mediaeval Europe there were three classes leading the whole community : (i) the monastic, represented in China by the Buddhist monks or bonzes, (ii) the secular clergy, represented there by the Taoist priests, who however also acted as physicians and magicians, and (iii) the Confucian officials, or mandarins, who held posts as prefects, sub-prefects, magistrates, etc., who corresponded with the nobility and chivalric orders, except that even these had, on certain occasions connected with their work, to conduct ceremonies involving the worship of certain deities. However the concept of worship in China was essentially a magical one, since every member of the hierarchy, in any of the three divisions, was believed to have power over certain divinities. The earthly hierarchy, as was usual in nearly all countries, was supposed to run more or less parallel with the heavenly hierarchy or pantheon of gods and spirits. But in China it was believed that every member of the earthly hierarchy not only had charge over those in lower ranks in the same hierarchy, but also had control over those spirits in the heavenly hierarchy, occupying a lower rank in the latter.[7]

It is true that in the history of China severe dissensions and rivalry between the leading classes of the community have been recorded. But these must be regarded as due to differences of opinion among members of a society having many principles in common. These wars are in fact comparable with those occurring in Europe between the forces of the Pope and those of the Emperor, both of whom were members of the same organisation, or in India between the followers of Vishnu and Shiva, both of whom were gods of the same pantheon.

There was in China an enormous collection of gods and spirits of various grades. Most of them are regarded as having once been human; in fact the dates of their deaths and their earthly careers are frequently recorded. Some have attained immortality, and will will reside in the heavens for ever. Those of the lower grades are only temporarily in the heavens and will have to re-incarnate on earth again some day.

Before the Revolution in China numerous religious ceremonies were observed by the Chinese, by the laity in their homes, by the mandarins in their offices, by the Taoist priests in their temples and by the Buddhist monks in their monasteries. But most impor-

7 J. Hackin, *et al., loc. cit.*

tant of all was the ritual performed by the Emperor, acting as high priest of the whole nation, in the Temple of Heaven at Pekin (Peiping). All these ceremonies were connected with agriculture and, as in ancient Egypt, fixed the times of agricultural operations. The Emperor himself took a yellow plough, yoked to a yellow ox, to begin the season's operations. Perhaps this is why the constellation of the plough played such an important part in mythology. But most significant of all was the sacrifice, offered by the Emperor at the Winter Solstice, near our Christmas Day. To the south of the city of Pekin is a large open space, surrounded by a low wall, in which are certain temples and the *altar of heaven*. The latter is circular and is three stages high. The top stage is 90 feet in diameter and the bottom 210 feet. The top stage is paved with stones laid in nine concentric circles, a single perfectly circular one in the middle. On the evening preceding the Solstice the Emperor was borne, in a chariot drawn by elephants, to the adjoining temple where he offered incense. Then he passed the night in fasting in a hall in the precincts. Early next morning he ascended the altar, attired in beautiful ceremonial robes, embroidered with the imperial dragon and other mystical symbols. Here he offered the sacrifice, consisting of silk, jade, flesh and wine, the latter of which were, in part, consecrated and consumed, whilst the rest were burnt as an offering. Music and sacred dancing accompanied the proceedings. It is curious that, after the Revolution, these ceremonies were continued for a time, by a priest appointed by the President, but they soon fell into disuse.

Until 1895 the Emperor of China and his family lived in a collection of palaces surrounded by beautiful gardens and lakes in a special part of Pekin called *the Forbidden City*. It was so called because only royalty and the royal entourage were allowed to enter. Therein were a number of throne rooms for official ceremonies that were of a more or less sacred character. One of the throne rooms contained *the Dragon Throne*, in front of a golden screen, and raised on a dais with steps. It was said to be of enormous value, being ornamented by golden dragons and images in precious metals.

Holy Men. Many extraordinary myths and legends surround the emperors and incarnate gods of China. It is difficult to distinguish between imaginary and historical personages. Among the latter however we must certainly reckon the three founders Sakyamuni (Gautama Buddha), Lao-tse and Kung-Fu-tse (Confucius). The lives of all three as recounted in Chinese books are full of miracles and magic. There is little doubt, however, of their historical existence, and they all lived at about the same epoch.

Jainism. Before following Chinese developments further we must not omit a curious development in India, which is responsible for the sect of the Jains. There are now only some two million followers of this religion, practically all merchants or bankers, mostly in West India and around Calcutta. Their religion inculcates an even greater respect for all living things than Buddhism. Jains are alleged to pray with muslin over their mouths, to prevent the swallowing of insects, and to carry a long brush, which they use to sweep the path along which they walk, in order to clear it of tiny creatures which might otherwise be crushed underfoot. They cannot till the soil for fear of killing worms. They must not boil water, or light fires for fear of destroying insects.

The Jain religion was founded by Vardharma, generally known as Mahavira (great man). He was born 599 B.C. at Vaisali (now called Basarh), some twenty-seven miles north of Patna in North-East India. He was the son of a minor king or chief, and became a monk, eventually attaining spiritual conquest over the passions. He died *circa* 527 B.C. at Pawa near Patna. His whole career is strikingly similar to that of Gautama Buddha, but there is little doubt that they were distinct historical personages. There are close parallels, also, between the Buddhist and Jain cults. The Jains, like the Buddhists, make great use of the *swastika* in their symbolism. The *lotus* is also common to the two religions, as it is also to Hinduism.

Myth and Magic in China. This country had been an empire from early times. In a general way it may have had the magical organisation similar to that of ancient Egypt, with a priest-ruler called the *wang*, responsible for the harvest and for the general welfare of the people. The earliest recorded dynasty in profane history is that of the Hsia 2205–1766 B.C. Then the Chow or Chou 1122–255 B.C. When the next dynasty the Chin or Tsin was set up in 255 or 256 B.C. the country was called China or Tsina, the great wall was built in the north to circumscribe the boundary and to keep out Mongolian invaders, and many canals and roads were made. The whole country was divided into thirty-six provinces, corresponding with the thirty-six decanates of the heavenly sphere (for earth was to correspond with heaven).

Of the nine sacred books of Confucianism the first is purely magical and has already been referred to. It was called the *Yi-King* and consisted of the eight possible diagrams formed by combining lines, each of which could be broken or unbroken. The unbroken lines signify *Yang*, the positive principle and the broken *Yin*, the negative principle. The diagrams themselves were invented by Fu Hsi[8] in the third millenium B.C. The commentaries in the *Yi-King* are due to Wen-Fang and his son Chou, the first rulers of the Chou dynasty, *circa* 1122 B.C.

The Taoist sacred books include the *Tao-Te-Ching*, already referred to as the work of Lao-tse himself, and definitely magical, and part of the works of Kwang-Tsze (Chwang-Tze) a contemporary of Mencius. According to some Taoists the concepts of the *Tao* is older than Lao-tse and originated with the Yellow Emperor, a semi-mythical ruler of China in the second half of the third millenium B.C. E. H. Parker,[9] a former professor of Chinese at Manchester, calls the Yellow Emperor the god and Lao-tse the prophet of Taoism. He says however that there is no evidence from the *Tao-Te-Ching* for the part played by the Yellow Emperor.

The magic of the Chinese is founded on a cosmic philosophy which involves the swastika and other mystical signs. In the beginning of the universe was the void, represented by a circle with nothing in it. From this manifestations are derived in the following way, by such philosophers as Chu-Hsi.[10] After untold aeons the great monad appeared in the void, represented by a dot. This reminds one of the first sephiroth of the Kabalah of the Jews. This monad divides into two, like the nucleus of a cell[11] and a cleft appears between the pair. As however the two halves are in motion the cleft does not remain in a single plane. Its section soon shows an S-shaped appearance. Now we have the well-known figure called the *pa-kwa* or *tomoye*. Similar figures can be obtained by making the dot divide into three, four or more units.

Mystical Signs. There is little doubt that the *pa-kwa* was a very ancient symbol in China, and refers to the division of the universe into polar opposites—the *yang* and *yin* of Chinese philosophy—represented by the white and black areas respectively. The *yang*,

[8] E. Sykes: *Everyman's Dictionary of Non-Classical Mythology*, London and New York, 1952.

[9] E. H. Parker: *The Taoist Religion*, London, not dated.

[10] Flourished *circa* 1130, discovered the true nature of fossils some 300 years before this became known in Europe (Leonardo da Vinci).

[11] Ray Lankester: *Secrets of Earth and Sea*, 2nd edition, London, 1923.

the white or positive principle was also represented by an undivided line and the *yin*, the black or negative principle by a divided line. By combining these two in different proportions Chinese philosophers tried to explain the nature of all things.

In Japan the divided circle was called the *tomoye* and the areas were coloured yellow and red. The symbol was regarded as indicative of triumph or honour. The two opposing principles were called *in* and *yo*. In Korea the divided circle appeared on the national flag, the two halves being coloured red and blue. Sometimes groups of three lines, broken and unbroken, were added at four corners.

Where the circle was divided into four by curved lines the figure known as the *ogee* results. When each of the four branches takes the form of the letter L we have the *swastika*. This word is of Sanskrit origin. In England it was known as the *fylfot* from the Anglo-Saxon. In Latin it was the *crux ansata*. In Greek it was the *gammadion*, because composed of four pieces, each of which resembled the Greek letter *gamma* (G, but written thus : Γ). In French it was called *croix gamée*, derived from the same idea. Among the Norsemen of Scandinavia it was given a name which means "the hammer of Thor." In Japan the swastika was called *manji*.[12] In China it was called *wan*. There is no doubt that the swastika had symbolic significance among the Maoris of New Zealand.

In spite of its extremely widespread distribution however it appears that the swastika is predominantly a Buddhist symbol. It was used in India before the Buddhists departed from that country. In gigantic carved footprints of Buddha discovered in an Indian temple the swastika figures prominently on the toes and soles. It is widely used in existing religious practices in Siam, Burma, China, Tibet, Korea and Japan.

Lotus. Another mystical symbol, prominent not only in Buddhism, but also in Brahminism and formerly in the ancient Egyptian religion, was the lotus (*Nelumbo speciosum*). It is also called a water-lily. It is a water-plant, distantly akin to our buttercups. The large flowers and leaves rise above the water, the rhizome is in the mud below the water, and the flower- and leaf-stalks pass through the water. A symbolical significance was seen in all this. The flower, too, is a *mandala*, *i.e.* it represents the physical universe. The pistil in the middle represented Mount Meru, which was supposed to be the centre of the universe. The stamens surrounding it represent mountains. The petals were continents, four large ones at the four

[12] W. Hayes: The Swastika, *Calamus Leaves* No. 1, Chatham, 1934.

quarters, each accompanied by two smaller ones on each side, as in the map of the Brahminic and Buddhistic universe. The flower represented the spiritual order, emerging from Chaos, represented by the waters. Its counterpart in mythology was the great mother goddess. Gautama and other buddhas are usually shown seated on the lotus. Brahma was represented as born on the lotus. Osiris floated on the lotus after his birth. Curiously enough the lotus no longer grows in Egypt, although venerated there for thousands of years, and still, in modern times, symbolic to some Egyptians.

Temples and Pagodas. Buddhist temples are very numerous, and some are of gigantic size. The general plan is much like that of a Christian church. The main hall is rectangular, with a rounded apse at one end containing an altar or rounded chaitya, supposed to contain a relic, after the manner of a Catholic altar.

A feature of the Buddhist region is the existence of numerous *caityas, chaityas, topes* or *stupas* as they are variously called. Modi-fied forms of these caityas form *dagobas* or *pagodas.* Caityas are often hemispherical structures, with a superimposed cone mounted on the middle. Sometimes they are supposed to represent the five elements of the Buddhist cosmology. In that case the base may be cubical, representing earth, on this comes a sphere, representing air, then a cone, for fire, at the tip of this a cup, indicating water, and finally, in this, an egg with the narrow end upwards, signifying the ether. Each caitya was originally supposed to contain a relic of Gautama, or of some Buddhist saint. But as they are so numerous this was not always possible. Many have been erected simply at places where holy personages have been supposed to have visited. They vary in size, from enormous monuments to small models, the latter movable. The large ones are mostly of stone. The small models are of clay, metal or wood. The interior of the caitya was supposed to be solid, except for a small cavity containing the relic. There are numerous magnificent pagodas in Indo-China, China and Japan.

Images. We have seen that sacred images play a large part in Buddhist religion. Before an image had any influence, however, it had to be consecrated, by a ritual designed to bring the spirit represented by the image into active relation with the latter. The images were sometimes clothed with various vestments, as among the Brahmins. Sometimes, particularly in China, internal organs were represented inside the images. Buddhist images were sometimes very large.

Relics. The cults of relics is less pronounced in Brahminism than in Buddhism. An example of a Hindu relic is the big toe of the left foot of Sati, the first wife of the Brahminic god Shiva, who abandoned her body in consequence of differences between her husband and her father Daksha. Afterwards she reincarnated as Uma or Parvati and thus returned to her spouse. The relic is preserved by the priests of Khali Ghat, near Calcutta.[13]

There are, or have been, many relics of Gautama Buddha. When he died his relics are said to have been divided into eight lots, for distribution to a corresponding number of priestly and royal communities. In the 7th century A.D. a Chinese Buddhist monk (A.D. 600–664) visited India and returned with 150 relics, many manuscripts and images.[14] A plate used by Gautama is said to be preserved at Anuradhapura, Ceylon. Not far away was kept his hat or mitre, some two feet high, at Konghanapura. His staff and one of his vestments are preserved at Nagarahara.[15]

But the best known relic is the left superior canine tooth, now preserved in the innermost of seven shrines in the Temple of the Holy Tooth at Kandy, Ceylon. Once a year it goes in procession, born under a panoply in a reliquary on the back of an elephant, accompanied by other elephants and attendant clergy.

Shinto, the Way of the Gods. The original inhabitants of Japan were very hairy people, the Ainu, akin to certain Caucasian peoples of Europe, and not at all to the mongoloids, of which the Japanese are typical representatives. The Ainu had an interesting bear-cult, with the sacrifice of that animal and the eating of its flesh. The idea that Shintoism was the original cult of Japan had been fostered only since the Imperial Restoration in 1868, when the Emperor asserted his powers over the Shogun, whose office had gradually (1192–1867) assumed supreme civil power. At that time the combination of Buddhism and Shinto (comparable with the combination of Buddhism and Taoism in China) was dissolved. This combination was called Ryobu Shinto. However the Shinto mythology[16] begins with the two positive and negative principles, here called *in* and

13 J. Rhys: *The Reliquary*, London, 1930.
14 The account of his travels was translated into French by S. Julien, 1853–1858.
15 P. Saintyves: *Les Reliques et les Images legendaires*, Paris, 1912.
16 The earliest source of Shinto mythology was the book *Kojiki*, compiled from legend by Ono Yasumaro in A.D. 712. This was followed by the *Nihongi*, published by imperial edict in 720. Both are in modified Chinese.

yo. These are obviously the Chinese *yang* and *yin*, and are at first combined in the cosmic egg, which is clearly the Chinese *pa-kwa.*

At certain Shinto shrines are young girls called *miko* who perform sacred dances. Some of them may be consulted like spiritualist mediums, for they hold communications with the dead, foretell the future, and may even claim to declare the will of the gods.

CHAPTER XVIII

THE LAMAS OF TIBET

Realm of the Lamas. We have already seen that in the wide stretches of Siberia the magico-religious system of Shamanism holds sway. To the south this system formerly extended. The earliest system of religion known in Tibet is that called Bon. This resembled in many ways the Shamanism of the North, including, as it did, the techniques for communicating with numerous spirits by means of devil-dancing and falling into trances. It was conducted by certain specially endowed individuals or priests, using the swastika. It has also been compared with Taoism. When Buddhism spread north the Bon was amalgamated with it, and its practitioners came to regard themselves as *lamas,* a name adopted by the priest-monks in the Mahayana Buddhism of Tibet, which is hence termed Lamaism. Nowadays even these Bon priests often regard themselves, and are so regarded by their clients, as part of the Lamaistic hierarchy, and they have been distinguished as the *black-hats* to distinguish them from the so-called *red-hats* or "unreformed" lamas who in large part succeed them and from the so-called *yellow-hats* who form the dominant church of Tibet today.

Lamaism as an early form[1] of Buddhism spread widely over central Asia. Most of this area has now come under the communist governments of Russia and China, and religious practices are discouraged, although not entirely suppressed. Before that time Lamaism not only flourished in Tibet, which was the unquestioned centre, but covered an enormous area.

In the Caucasus numerous Kalmuks adhered to this religion, but even in Tsarist days they had become officially cut off from Tibet, and their chief lama was selected by the Russian Government. A somewhat similar situation obtained among the Buriats of Siberia, around Lake Baikal.

Mongolia, which became wholly Lamaist in 1577, was under the rule of the Grand Lama of Urga, Outer Mongolia. The latter was

---

[1] The idea that it was only a late development, held by many Western writers at the end of the last century, has now been discarded by competent scholars, see D. Snellgrove: *Buddhist Himalaya*, Oxford, 1957.

selected by the Chinese Government at Pekin. Outer Mongolia is now an independent people's republic.

Manchuria or Manchukuo was conquered by China in 1644. The Chinese set up a new dynasty on the lines of the reigning house of China. This lasted until 1911. During the Second World War the Japanese again tried to set up an Emperor there, choosing the last, dethroned, Emperor of China (himself of the Manchu dynasty) for the purpose. Manchukuo is now part of the Chinese Republic. Before all this it was Lamaist, with Chinese affinities.

In China itself there were a few Lamaist regions in the West, in the province of Amdo which was formerly under Tibetan rule. There was also a large and powerful Lamaist monastery in Pekin itself, ruled over by a Grand Lama.

Khoten or East Turkestan, inhabited by Kirghiz tribes was also Lamaist, and is in the former kingdom of Sin-kiang, now under Chinese rule.

Ladak, in Kashmir, adjacent to Tibet, has also many lamas, but the rule of the country has been under a Hindu maharajah, whilst many of the inhabitants are Moslems. In Nepal there are also some lamas, although they are not encouraged by Gurkhas and other influential bodies. The country is ruled by a king.

Sikkim, a small country to the south of Tibet and the north of India was formerly ruled by lamas. It came under the rule of a maharajah, and in 1814 became a protectorate of Britain. Soon after India became independent, it became a protectorate of that country at the request of the maharajah, 1949.

Bhotan (Bhutan), a rather larger country, to the east of Sikkim was formerly ruled over by a Dharma-Rajah, who was an incarnate[2] Grand Lama, under whom was a maharajah. This dual rule virtually came to an end in 1885 and the maharajah was elected king in 1907.

In Tibet itself the government has been hierugic-magical since early times, although Western authors say the alleged Dalai Lamas prior to about A.D. 1400 are purely mythical. At any rate since about A.D. 1600 the Dalai Lama has been supreme priest-king of Tibet, and is generally acknowledged as a sort of Buddhist pope by Buddhists of all countries. He is called the *great gem of majesty* and is regarded as the incarnation of Avalokita or Avalokiteshvara one of the supreme gods of Buddhism. He resides[3] near Lhasa, the

[2] See later in this chapter for an explanation of this term.
[3] At the time of writing the Dalai Lama and many others of the hierarchy are in exile.

capital of Tibet, in the palace-temple called the Potala, designed to imitate the mythical residence of the god Avalokiteshvara. Next in office, in the supreme triad of government, is the Tashi-Lama,[4] the Grand Lama of Tashi-chunpo, called the *great gem of learning*. He is alleged to be an incarnation of Amitabha, the Buddha of Boundless Light, and Avalokiteshvara's spiritual father. Third in command is the King or Regent, who is also a Grand Lama. He is a reincarnation of one of the four beings attendant upon Avalokiteshvara and who formerly incarnated as ministers of the famous legendary ruler of Tibet, Sron Tsan Gampo, who himself figures as an incarnation of Avalokiteshvara. These four ministers are supposed to incarnate as the four heads of four monastic palaces at Lhasa, and from one of these four the King or Regent is selected. There are other members of the Government below these three, and these have included, at times, a few laymen. The two Ambans, or representatives of the Chinese government, also had some administrative rights and privileges, as well as acting as ambassadors.

The Black Hats. The priests of the Bon religion, popularly known as the *black hats*, continued to exist after the coming of Buddhism in Tibet, and were particularly abundant in the east of that country. There is little doubt but that they were profoundly influenced by Buddhist ideas. Formerly they were probably very little different from the *shamans* of Siberia. With the arrival of Buddhism they continued to be consulted by some of the Tibetans, who also patronised the lamas, and they themselves gradually came to assume the position of somewhat irregular lamas. Their chief rite seems to have been the sacrifice of dough images of animals and men, and it is believed that these were substituted, under Buddhist influence, for real animal and perhaps even human sacrifices which they formerly made. A figure of a Bon priest, given by Giorgi[5] shows him armed with a sword, bearing a shield, he is adorned with flags, wears a tunic, stole and breastplate. As already stated they used the swastika, worshipped dragons, possibly identical with the *nagas* (snake-gods) of Hinduism and performed dances for the propitiation of devils. The Bon represented the swastika with its arms pointing to the right (anti-clockwise), whereas all Buddhists make them point towards the left,[6] as if rotating in the clockwise direction.

[4] Sometimes termed Panchen-lama, but this title has been claimed by others.

[5] Reproduced by L. A. Waddell in his *Buddhism of Tibet or Lamaism*, 2nd edition, reprinted Cambridge, 1939.

[6] Waddell, *loc. cit.*

The Red Hats. According to Waddell[7] Lamaism was introduced into Tibet between A.D. 638 and 641, although native legends put it back to the 5th century and give the rulers a descent from Gautama's royal patrons. At any rate in the middle of the 7th century Tibet was ruled by a King, Sron Tsan Gampo, who had married two wives. One was the daughter of the King of Nepal, the other the daughter of the Emperor of China. Both these queens were ardent Buddhists. Under their influence the king obtained numerous Buddhist books from India, built temples and established monasteries.[8] After his death he was venerated as an incarnation of Avalokita, and his two wives as incarnations of the Tibetan Goddess of Mercy, Tara, the Nepalese Queen representing that manifestation of the goddess known as the green Tara, and the Chinese the white Tara. No further progress was made after the death of Sron Tsan Gampo's death in A.D. 650 until King Thi Sron Detsan (*b.* A.D. 728) ascended the throne. This mighty king, who ruled much of Western China, as well as Tibet, again sent to India for instruction, and he not only obtained books but also invited his brother-in-law, the guru Padma-sambhava, who was a professor at the great Buddhist University at Nalanda, India. Padma-sambhava[9] was an exponent of Tantrism and every form of magic and spirit-lore, for which his native land of Kashmir was famous. He arrived in Tibet in A.D. 747. He promptly visited all the most ill-omened sites in Tibet, exorcising the demons, allowing some of them to receive worship and sacrifice, on condition they became protectors of the new religion.[10] All the native deities were collected in the new assembly of gods, in which, however, the celestial buddhas held first place, followed by the boddhisatvas. Padma-sambhava himself is credited with almost unlimited magical powers. He had twenty-five disciples, each of whom had some particular supernatural gift.[11] Padma-sambhava means "the lotus-born one," he is the founder of Lamaism as known today. He is worshipped in eight forms and receives in Tibet as much honour as does Gautama, in fact more among several subdivisions of the red-hats.

The mission of Padma-sambhava was eminently successful, and he established Lamaism throughout Tibet in a form in which, with-

7 *Loc cit.*
8 According to Waddell monasteries only came later.
9 Described by Waddell (*loc. cit.*) as a wizard. According to W. Y. Evans-Wentz in *The Tibetan Book of the Great Liberation* it was not Padma-sambhava but a companion who was the professor at Nalanda.
10 Waddell, *loc cit.*
11 For list of their magical powers see Waddell, *loc. cit.*, pp. 51–52.

out very essential modification, it has existed ever since. Monasteries were established under his regime, although of course they continued to be set up for a long time afterwards. To this development, however, there was one set-back. In 899 King Ralpachan, grandson of Thi Sron Detsan, who had encouraged much translation from Indian sources, and had given the monasteries state-lands and the right to collect taxes, was murdered on behalf of his younger brother, who ascended the throne under the name of Lan-dharma. The latter was a great enemy of Buddhism, and has been called the Julian of Lamaism.[12] He desecrated temples and monasteries, executed monks or forced them to become butchers, and burnt their books. His persecution did not last long. In the third year of his reign he was shot with an arrow and killed by a lama disguised as a strolling black-hat devil dancer. The memory of this incident was afterwards celebrated in a modern Lamaist masquerade.[13] After this event the Lamaist Church soon regained lost ground, and in fact became stronger than ever. Numerous monks from India and Kashmir visited the country.[14]

Later, after the division between red-hats and yellow-hats the former became recognised, not so much by any fundamental differences, but by the special worship adopted for their own particular holy patrons (corresponding with patron-saints in Christendom). Each monastery had its particular cult-associations, with different tutelary deities. Some orders claimed to have special books of revelations, which had been hidden in caves by Padma-sambhava and were only discovered long after his passing. Most of the red-hats were allowed to marry. There were also, among the red-hats, a few ascetics, and to these belong those curious beings, reports of whom have excited great interest in the West, holy men who have had themselves walled-in, and fed only through a small opening, the object being to allow themselves to devote themselves to uninterrupted meditation.

Several great teachers appeared among the red-hats. The greatest was Atisha (980–1053) who, after studying the Tantra and the Mahayana in India and Pegu, arrived in Tibet in 1038, and with the help of a Tibetan disciple Brom-ton or Dom-ton (b. 1002) founded the Kadampa, which afterwards gave rise to the yellow-hats. Then, in the latter half of the 11th century the lama Marpa, who had visited India, and his pupil Milarapa (Milaraspa, Milarepa)

12 Waddell, loc. cit.
13 Waddell, loc. cit.
14 Loc. cit.

(1038–1122) who lived his life wandering about the mountains of Tibet and writing poetry, founded the Kargyupa, classed by Waddell as a semi-reformed school.

Meanwhile, to the north of Tibet the Mongols were growing more powerful. Their rise to military power culminated in the conquest of Gengis Khan (1167–1227). He was at first a ruler of a kingdom near Lake Baikal, now in Asiatic Russia. He conquered and slew the last holder of the title of Owanh Kohan, known in the West as Prester John, and seized his mighty realm. He conquered Korea, Northern China, much of Asiatic and European Russia, Bulgaria and Persia. He is not usually considered as a religious leader, but possibly he was some sort of Grand Lama. His grandson was the well-known Kublai Khan (1214–1294) who ruled over an extensive empire, extending from Southern Siberia in the North to the Indo-Chinese border in the South, including Tibet, but not Central Asiatic and European Russia. It was this Kublai Khan who first established Lamaistic rule firmly in Tibet, for he made the head lama of the Saskya monastery (fifty miles north of Mount Everest) supreme head, both of the spiritual and temporal powers of the country. He was required to officiate at the coronation of the Emperor of China.

The Yellow Hats. Tsong-kapa (1355–1417) the founder of the Gelugpa or yellow-hats (since his time the ruling officials of Tibet), was born in Amdo the Onion Country, now included in China, on the east of Tibet. Huc,[15] himself a Catholic missionary, says Tsong-kapa had contact with religious teachers from the West, and in this way he accounts for similarities between Catholic worship and yellow-hat Lamaism. Tsong-kapa belonged to the Kadampa and worked among this influential body. He began his work about 1407. He instituted many reforms and made the lamas celibates. He tightened up discipline, and clarified the organisation. He made the lamas wear the yellow cap and patched robes, an old custom from India. The hat had tails hanging down behind, and the length of these tails was an indication of the place occupied by the lama in their hierarchy. At first the Gelugpa, although a powerful organisation, had to contend with the rivalry of various groups of the red hats, but in 1640, with the help of a Mongol prince, the head lama of the De-pung monastery near Lhasa, named Nag-wan Lozan was installed as the spiritual and temporal ruler, with the title Dalai-

[15] *Travels in Tartary, Thibet and China*, 3rd ed., London, 1856.

Lama. *Dalai* means "ocean" and refers to his widespread powers.

The Lamaists believe in a bodily resurrection, in heaven, purgatory and hell, but they give many details unknown to the Christian scheme. They have a baptism of water and masses for the living and the dead (sanctifying bread and wine), marriage blessings, ordinations and extreme unction. There are confessions to special confessors, appointed by the head of the Church. They use holy water, candles, tapers, incense and various kinds of rosary. There is singing in church services with double choirs, chanting of psalms by the monks, monastic organisations not very different from some Christian monasteries, convents for nuns, vows of chastity, poverty and obedience. There are blessings given by lamas by extending the hand. They even make a movement of the hand over themselves closely resembling our sign of the cross. There are special services of exorcism. The clergy of the yellow-hat or Gelugpa Church are strictly celibate and tonsured. There are retreats, feasts, whippings for penance, processions, litanies, the use of images and veneration of relics of their saints. The cross is used and the vestments of the lamas include the dalmatic, the cope and the mitre. Speaking of these extraordinary resemblances, M. Huc,[16] an early Catholic missionary, says they even apply to details; for instance the thuribles or censers, used for burning incense, resembled in all respects those used in his own Church.

Huc and his companion Gabet opposed Lamaism, but before his time there were Catholic missionaries who had a more favourable attitude. The Jesuits in fact planned a vast scheme for the union of Christianity with Brahmanism, Buddhism and Lamaism. This might have succeeded, had it not been for the interference on the part of some Dominicans, Franciscans and Jansenists.[17] An example of the unity of cult between the Orthodox (Eastern) Catholic and Lamaist Churches was the presentation of magnificent episcopal robes by the Russians to the Dalai Lama in 1901 on the occasion of a treaty being signed between the two countries.[18]

It must be remembered however that modern Lamaism, even among the yellow-hats, does seek to propitiate evil spirits, as well as to seek the assistance of the good. There are numerous sacrifices. These are not generally directed immediately to the Supreme God, but to one, or generally more, of his lower reflexes. The offerings

[16] *Loc. cit.*

[17] Godfrey Higgins: *Anacalypsis*, 2 vols., London, 1836; reprinted 4 vols., London, 1878, *recently reprinted*.

[18] Spencer Chapman: *Lhasa, the Holy City*, London, 1940.

include bread, wine, flames, incense, perfumes, water and the sound of cymbals. The liquids are usually offered in the inverted top of a skull. The arrangement of the offerings is strictly regulated, and is very complex. In the aforementioned mass, besides wine and wafers, "pills of life" composed of flour, sugar and butter are used, also holy water, water tinged with saffron and sacred kusa grass (previously noted in India). The mirror, bell and the *vajra* or thunderbolt are also employed in this and other ceremonies. The *vajra* is one of the most characteristic of lamaist symbols. It is used for exorcism or blessing, in much the same way that the Greek orthodox bishop uses the small cross that he often carries in his right hand. The hand, as we have seen, is also often used without any ceremonial implement.

Mantras. These are oft-repeated prayers or ejaculations said in a rhythmic manner and the greater frequency of the repetition, it is supposed, the greater the effect produced.[19] The best known mantra is *Om mane padme hum* which has been translated as "Hail jewel in lotus, Amen." The jewel is the Supreme God, the lotus the "mother" entity or goddess, in the womb of whom He appears. Mantras are said with the aid of the rosary. The latter is, therefore, one of the things with which every lama must be equipped. It is also used by the laity. Each rosary consists of 108 beads for counting mantras, with three special beads to remind one of the Supreme Triad and other ideas reflected therefrom. Besides this the rosary has attached to it two rows of ten small perforated discs. One of these is terminated in a dorje, the other in a bell. When the 108 mantras have been recited one of the discs on the row ending in the dorje is moved. When all ten have been moved one of the discs of the row ending in the bell is moved, thus 10 × 10 × 108 repetitions of the mantra may be indicated on the rosary.

The beads of the rosary are made of various kinds of turned wood, notably pipul and sandalwood, but also of various hard seeds, semi-precious stones, crystal, glass, etc. The nature of the material varies with the organisation to which its owner belongs, and also to some extent with the deity worshipped. The yellow hats for instance use yellow wood of the bo-tree or pipul, or other similar wood. The red-hats use coral, at least for Padma-sambhava. The

[19] This is pure magic, but it is also very good psychology. It will be remembered that Coué, that great advocate of auto-suggestion, called for frequent repetition of favourable phrases, and even used a knotted cord, suggesting a kind of rosary. The vajra is also called *dorje*.

coral rosary usually has turquoise counters.[20] One of the most curious rosaries is one composed of discs cut out of a human skull. This is used for worshipping the slayer of the King of the Dead. A very rare kind is made from certain concretions found in the elephant. It is used in the worship of the King of the Dead himself. Waddell[21] also refers to a rosary of about fifty snake vertebrae, but says that this is only used in necromancy and divination.

Although some lamas repeat many thousands of mantras each day, they have devised means of producing what they believe to be the effect of still more numerous repetitions. They do this by revolving prayer-wheels, turning large prayer-cylinders and allowing flags adorned with mantras or symbols to float in the breeze. The prayer-wheels are covered with innumerable prayers, and every time one turns it, one is expected to gain as much merit as if one had repeated the same number of prayers. Prayer-wheels vary from small objects held in the hand to the immense cylinders set up in convenient places and which are turned by wind or water. Much scorn has been poured on these by bigoted Western writers, but W. Simpson, at the turn of the century, wrote a learned work[22] to show that the symbolism of the wheel is prominent in early Buddhism, and that it is closely connected with the lore of circular movements in all religions.

Reincarnate Lamas. The theory behind these is as follows. Every man is reincarnated, and every man reaps the reward of his efforts as he progresses from life to life. But in the case of some special Grand Lamas, but not all, a deity or saint incarnates in each of them, and when he dies, he reincarnates again in a child, who is sought out, and when discovered is raised to the same rank and office which he had before he died.

The way in which this is done may be illustrated by the procedure adopted when the Dalai Lama dies, although the details vary somewhat. The Dalai Lama, we have seen, is believed to be an incarnation of Avalokita (Avalokiteshvara). The selection depends upon several factors (i) any indication which the Grand Lama may have given before his death as to the district, community or family in which he expects to re-incarnate; (ii) the time of birth of infants who have been born after the death of the aforesaid; (iii) miraculous portents accompanying any of such births; (iv) selection of the

---

20 Waddell, *loc. cit.*; see this work for a full account of Tibetan rosaries.
21 *Loc. cit.*
22 *The Buddhist Praying Wheel*, London, 1896.

names of certain infants, made after much prayer and worship, by a selected company of very holy lamas; (v) lots cast by the same, the names being taken out of a golden vase, at random; (vi) hints given by the state oracle and (vii) the ability of the chosen infant to recognise property belonging to the deceased Grand Lama. It is generally believed that the last method alone is absolutely decisive, and the other six are only ways and means of reducing the number of infants to be tested. When the infant has been selected his family are well looked after. In the case of the Dalai Lama his father receives a dukedom together with considerable estates.

The three most important reincarnate lamas are the Dalai Lama, the Tashi Lama and the King or Regent. But the third of these is not always the same individual. As already explained he is chosen as one of four. The Dalai Lama and the Tashi Lama, incarnating respectively the high gods Avalokita and Amitabha, are by far the most important of the incarnate lamas. Next in importance in Tibet is probably the Saskya-Lama, head of an ancient monastery only fifty miles north of Mount Everest. He is an incarnation of the Bodhisat of Wisdom, Manjusri. His predecessors were at one time rulers of Tibet, before the Dalai-Lama was established as such.

An interesting female incarnate abbess rules over the Samding monastery at Yam-dok Lake in Tibet, which contains both monks and nuns. Her title is Dorje Pagma, which means "diamond sow" and she is an incarnation of the Indian goddess Vajra-varahi.

At the head of the large lamasery in Pekin is the Grand Lama known as Can-skya. He is believed to be the incarnation of Rolpahi Dorje who appeared as a Buddhist saint in the 16th century and ruled over Inner Mongolia.

Urgya-Kuren in Outer Mongolia is also the seat of a Grand Lama of much importance. He is the Khisson Tamba and is an incarnation of a famous being called Taranatha who appeared in the 16th century.

Bhotan, as we have seen, was formerly ruled over by the Dharma-Raja. He also had some recognised authority over the lamas of Nepal. His highest title, of which he had many, was "an avatar of God." Curiously enough another was "defender of the faith." Sikkim had, formerly, a reincarnate lama, at Labrang, who was head of the country, and another at Pemiongchi, but the system became extinct there before the end of the last century. In all centres there must have been very roughly some two hundred appointments or thereabouts, occupied by reincarnate lamas, the most numerous of course in Tibet.

Tibetan Astrology. Horoscopes are cast by the lamas, and in the larger monasteries there were specialists solely employed in this work. However, lamaistic astrology was never fatalistic. No matter how bad the influences, they could always be thwarted by getting lamas to read the scriptures, by performing or arranging for the lamas to perform certain rites, even sometimes calling in special devil-dancers to carry out a sort of pantomime, which was believed to crush evil spirits.

Divination in Tibet was adopted by everyone on all important occasions. Besides the horoscopes specially set up for really important events, divination by dice, by special divination boards, by rosaries, and even by the shoulder blade bones of sheep was adopted.

Oracles and Spirit Control. In all the larger monasteries there were lamas who were capable of falling into a trance, and making oracular pronouncements. Some of these were believed to work under the influence of the drug hashish or Indian hemp, but this does not appear to have been regular. One of these oracles became so famous that he was made a sort of state-oracle. He was given a monastery, with a number of monks as assistants, and received a high title. It is believed he was regularly consulted on important occasions of state. He was enrolled in the Gelugpa Church. There are, however, more numerous oracles and sorcerers among the red hats, and these unreformed lamas have a higher reputation for dealing with demonic influences among the general population, than the yellow hats.

These sorcerers use a most fantastic array of implements. They include mirrors and weapons, and the bones of men and animals. They chant long mantras. They erect devil traps which are placed on houses, looking like wireless aerials, but much more complicated. These sorcerers are also very good at exorcising ghosts, and some claim to control the weather.

Lamas of all denominations are skilled in effecting the release of the soul from the body, when anyone dies. There is a *Tibetan Book of the Dead* which has been translated into English and commented on by Evans-Wentz.[23] This work purports to show the art of dying, and the experiences to be encountered after death. It has some affinity with the so-called *Book of the Dead* of Ancient Egypt, which, as shown elsewhere, is not without its Christian counter-

---

[23] *The Tibetan Book of the Dead or the After-Death Experiences on the Bardo Plane, according to Lama Kazi Dawa-Samdup's English rendering,* by W. Y. Evans-Wentz, 2nd edition, Oxford, 1949, recently reprinted.

parts. The funeral rites in Tibet are very complex, and are designed to help, from this side, the deceased being in his journey from death to birth, for after staying on what is termed the *bardo-plane* or unseen world, and having certain experiences there, he will return to this world or one of the other five, for reincarnation. So the cycle continues.

Tree of Ten Thousand Images. In the great monastery at Kumbum, in Sifan, near the frontier of Tibet with China, is or was one of the most remarkable of all magical phenomena. It was visited and described by Huc.[24] It was called the Tree of Ten Thousand Images. It was enclosed in a square, formed of brick walls, near the main temple of the aforesaid monastery, and over it had been erected, at the expense of one of the Chinese emperors, a dome of silver. So astonished were Huc and his companion Gabet, that they were filled with consternation and perspiration trickled down their faces when they examined it. For on each of the leaves were imprinted well-formed Tibetan characters, all green, some darker, some lighter, than the leaf itself. The missionaries were unable to discover the least sign of deception. The bark was also covered with characters, and when it was removed further characters were seen below. The trunk was apparently old, three men with outstretched arms could scarcely encompass it, and it was about eight feet high.

The Tibetans say that this tree is the only example of its species in the world, and according to legend it sprouted from placental blood shed at the birth of Tson-Kapa. Waddell[25] calls it the white sandal (*Syringa villosa*) which would make it a member of the same genus as our ordinary garden lilac, but no evidence for this is given.

[24] *Loc. cit.*

[25] *Loc cit.*, but Waddell was a competent botanist, and a Fellow of the Linnean Society, at the rooms of which the present author had the privilege of a conversation with him many years ago; unfortunately I did not ask him about this tree.

CHAPTER XIX

ROME AND BYZANTIUM

Rome and Jerusalem. At the time of Christ Palestine formed part
of the Roman Empire, although its exact status was in a state of
flux. Herod the Great ruled in the first part of the 1st century A.D.
He had restored the Temple. This, *the Third Temple* of the Jews
was destroyed A.D. 70 when the Emperor Titus was at war with that
people. The Roman Religion, which was akin to the Greek, was
controlled at Rome by a college of *pontifices* (sing. *pontifex*) at the
head of which was the *pontifex maximus*. The latter office was so
important that, from the time of Augustus (*asc.* 27 B.C.) it was held
by the Emperor himself. This continued in the Christian era, until
early in the fourth century, when Constantine the Great made the
Christian religion, with the Pope at its head, the official one. But
St. Peter is supposed to have begun to reign as Pope in A.D. 42 and
was no doubt busy setting up a rival hierarchy. He was martyred ·
in A.D. 67 and succeeded by a line of popes, who were, of course,
subject for a long time to persecution. There was, however, at
Rome, a certain amount of support for the new religion. Tiberius
who reigned from A.D. 14 to A.D. 37 actually proposed to the Roman
Senate that Jesus Christ should be enrolled among the pagan gods
of Rome,[1] a process occasionally adopted with very eminent personages and known as *apotheosis*. When the conversion finally came,
under Constantine, many of the *pontifices* and *flamines* (higher
priests) became Christian bishops, and many of the pagan temples
were converted to Christian churches.

Magic[2] versus Miracle. The early Church Fathers had to contend
against accusations that the new religion was a magical one. They
also had to curb their own followers, who were producing uncon-
ventional and even heterodox accounts of Christ and his apostles.

---

[1] T. W. Doane: *Bible Myths*, 4th ed., New York, 1882, quoted from Bell
on basis of statements of the Church Fathers: Eusebius, Tertullian and
Chrysostom. The story was accepted by Mosheim: *Ecclesiastical History*,
Vol. I, London, 1842.

[2] Throughout this chapter the term *magic* is used to signify evil or black
magic.

We know that even during His life on earth Jesus was accused of casting out devils with the aid of the prince of the devils (*Matt.* ix, 34; xii, 24; *Mark* iii, 22). The apostles had to contend with the gnostic magician Simon, who tried to purchase magical powers from them (*Acts* vii, 9–24) whose attempted flight, before Nero, brought to an end by the prayers of Peter and Paul, has already been described. Another magician was Elymas (*Acts* xiii, 8–11) whom St. Paul deprived of his sight for a time, in order to prevent prominent people from being led astray by his activities. According to *The Golden Legend*[3] all the apostles had to contend with magicians. The burning of magical books by those converted is referred to in *Acts* xix, 19. In another passage (*Acts* xvi, 16–30) Paul and Silas are imprisoned because they have cast out a spirit of divination from a damsel, that gained her employers much money. But they are released by an earthquake.

Relics. No part of Catholic worship has been so bitterly attacked by Protestants as the cult of relics. It is pointed out that a large percentage cannot be authentic, that many of the alleged relics are duplicated or multiplied. But the use of relics is enjoined both in the Old Testament and the New. A resurrection was effected when the dead body of a man touched the bones of Elisha or Eliseus (IV *Kings* xiii, 21[4]). The sick were healed by cloths that had touched the living body of St. Paul (*Acts* xix, 12). As regards the so-called multiplication of relics, this is partly due to division of a large relic, partly by making of new relics by touching relics with other objects, which themselves become objects of devotion. Thus the cross has now been divided into innumerable small splinters, to be found in all parts of the world. The sacred bodies of the saints have been fragmented into numerous small parts. Besides it is not whether a relic is genuine or not that matters, but the faith and humility of the worshippers. One of the first to attack the cult of relics was the arch-heretic Calvin.

Images. In the West images in churches included both pictures and statues. In the East pictures were preferred, and these came to be heavily adorned with precious metals, thus forming the *icons* which are such a characteristic feature of the Russian Church today.

[3] A collection of the lives of the saints made by J. de Voraigne, a Dominican, in the 13th century.
[4] In the King James version II *Kings* xiii, 21. See also for the effect of a sacred staff IV *Kings* iv, 18–37 (II *Kings* iv, 18–37).

Long before the Great Schism the West and the East had acquired separate Emperors. On the death of Theodosius the Great in 395 the empire was divided between two of his sons, Honorius taking Rome and Arcadius New Rome, Byzantium or Constantinople, as it was variously called. By this time different art-forms were developing in the two areas. Constantinople vied with Rome in magnificence, but developed an art of its own called Byzantine, which afterwards spread to the Balkans and to Russia.

Prelates involved with Magic. Some of the popes have been accused of practising magic. There are in existence copies of an *Enchiridion* which claims that it was sent by Leo III to Charlemagne, and contains prayers possessing mysterious power. Levi[5] says it assumes a primitive revelation of the secrets of nature, comparable with religious revelation, which has, unlike the latter, been kept secret. It contains a series of symbols, which Levi interprets in terms of the Kabalah. Leo III reigned from 795 to 816.

The legendary female Pope Joan is supposed to have ascended the papal throne on the death in 854 of Pope Leo IV. The story goes that a young woman of studious habits conceived a violent passion for a monk, and in order to be near him she adopted male dress, and was admitted to the monastery. She and her lover were sent on various journeys, and at Athens he died. She, still in male disguise went to Rome, and became principal of an academy, receiving numerous honours for learning[6] and sanctity, finally being elected Pope. Unfortunately, she retained her amorous disposition, and secretly loved one of her cardinals or other associates. She became pregnant, but no one knew it, and she was prevailed upon to accompany the long Rogation processions. Whilst passing between the Coliseum and the Church of St. Clement she was seized with labour pains, and whilst receiving attention, gave birth to a child. Some say both mother and child died on the spot. At any rate the place where this event happened was marked as accursed, and subsequent popes always avoid it in their processions. Some say Pope John VIII was Pope Joan, but three other names of popes intervene between Leo VI and John VIII. Several who record this story say that the pontifical name of the female pope, which was John, was expunged from the list. It is noteworthy that in the Latin lists of popes there is no John XX. Is it possible that a correction was made at that time?

[5] Eliphas Levi: *The History of Magic*, trans. 2nd ed., London, 1922.
[6] According to Levi several books on black magic are ascribed to her.

Gerbert, a learned man, who reigned as Pope under the name of Sylvester II from 999 to 1003 was credited with being a magician, and even accused of attaining the papal throne with the help of the devil.[7] Moreover, the evil one promised Gerbert that he should not die, except at Jerusalem. One day, when saying Mass at a church in Rome the Pope was taken ill, and then recalled that this church was dedicated to the Holy Cross of Jerusalem. So he called his assistants together, arranged for his funeral and then died. In reality Gerbert was a student of science. The balance-clock, which was used until the pendulum-clock replaced it in 1650 is ascribed to him.[8] He wrote on the astrolabe, and was highly skilled in its use.[9] He studied the distances of the stars. He believed in astrology to some degree, but repudiated the idea that life is *determined* by the horoscope. One of his letters asking for a book on astrology to be sent to him has been discovered.[10]

A *grimoire i.e.* a work on black magic, showing how to utilise the services of devils to obtain hidden treasure, etc., was ascribed to a pope named Honorius. Usually said to have been by the third of that name it seems utterly impossible that Honorius III (reigned 1216–1227) was the author, for it was this pope that combated Albigenses, and established the Dominican and Franciscan Orders. Levi asserts,[11] however, that some old copies bear the name of Honorius II. Now this pope, on the official Latin list (*reigned* 1124–1130) is also quite unlikely to have been the author, as he surrounded himself with poets and learned theologians. Levi suggests therefore that the Honorius II in question is the anti-pope of that name, a man involved in the Lombard revolt against Pope Alexander II (*reigned* 1061–1073). But it is much more likely that the name Honorius was not originally that of a pope at all.[12]

That great Pope Gregory VII (Hildebrand) who succeeded Alexander II, and who is famous for bringing the rebellious Emperor Henry IV to submission, was accused of necromancy and prophetic arts. But the evidence for this is extremely slender.

Magical works in abundance have been ascribed to St. Albertus Magnus (1193–1280). They are fraudulent, and at least one has

---

[7] Levi, *loc. cit.*, from early writers whom, however, he completely discredits.

[8] W. L. R. Cates: *A Dictionary of General Biography*, 4th ed., London, 1885.

[9] Thorndike: *loc. cit.*, quoting William of Malmesbury.

[10] Thorndike: *loc. cit.*

[11] *Loc. cit.*

[12] *Cf.* Waite's footnotes to Levi, *loc. cit.*, pp. 298–299.

been placed on the Index. He was a Dominican theologian and also a natural scientist of no mean order. His observations on plant movements and on the human brain are still worthy of study. He is usually sceptical about natural lore, but occasionally somewhat credulous, as for instance when he tells of a human headed serpent slain on an isle off Germany. He does refer to occult matters. The divining rod was one. Fascination, he thinks, does occur, but it cannot influence one who has faith and devotion. Dreams have a meaning, but do not predict destiny. He believed in astrology, but of course opposed deterministic astrology. In this he was followed by his great pupil St. Thomas Aquinas (1225–1274). The latter was a greater theologian than Albert, but was not so well versed in natural science.

Albertus Magnus pointed out that magic was distinct from natural science. It therefore needs different methods. Aquinas distinguished magic from miracle. Demons are the agents of magic. They are always bent on evil, even when seemingly constrained by the magician to do good. It is legitimate to study magic to confute it, not to use it. Witchcraft sometimes has very unfortunate effects. It can, for example, produce impotence. Today we would say it could do this by suggestion. Fascination and the evil eye are accepted by St. Thomas. He also distinguishes divination from divine prophecy. Lot casting is not needed by those inspired by the Holy Spirit. Matthias was selected by lot *before* Pentecost, the seven deacons without lot *after*.

The making of a brazen head that could answer questions has been ascribed to St. Albertus.[13] It was perhaps some sort of auto-maton. The story goes that St. Thomas destroyed it, as he could not bear its incessant chattering.

On another occasion St. Albertus Magnus wanted to obtain a plot of land from the King of the Romans. He invited the latter, with his suite to a great feast. The weather was cold, and the ground covered with snow when the visitors arrived, but, much to their amazement, the feast was spread in Albert's garden. The guests were persuaded to take their places at the table, and no sooner was this done than the temperature rose, comfort was restored and the meal went on. Albertus obtained the land, on which he built a convent. It is believed that this incident really

[13] It has also been claimed for Roger Bacon, Guillaume de Paris and others.

refers to the first hothouse being constructed by Albertus in the grounds of the Dominicans at Cologne.[14]

Thorndike, in his monumental *History of Magic and Experimental Science*,[15] has shown that the early Christians were by no means opposed to natural science, as popularly supposed. Still more important, on the basis of his extensive researches from original sources, he alleges[16] that in the mediaeval and scholastic centuries, there was a constant seeking for something new and up-to-date, and precisely this period has been stigmatised as benighted and behind the times, whilst the Renaissance, which turned back to Greece and Rome, has been wrongly hailed as the beginning of modern science! Thorndike even shows that the Church did not frown on anatomical dissection, as some have alleged.

[14] J. H. Pepper: *The Playbook of Metals*, London, *circa* 1860.
[15] *Loc cit.*
[16] *Loc. cit.*, Vol. III.

CHAPTER XX

THE MAGIC OF THE CRESCENT

The Prophet: In the 6th century A.D. the inhabitants of Arabia were idolaters, following a debased form of the Babylonian or Chaldean religion. There were a number of loosely associated tribes, together with some Jews and some heretical Christians. Mohammed or Muhammad (570–632) was a member of the Quraish, the sacred tribe that had charge of the Kabah, a cubical building at Mecca, which contained and still contains a black meteoric stone, which was the centre of their cult. Mohammed's father died about the time of his birth, his mother died when he was six, so he was brought up, first by his grandfather, who was chief of the Quraish, and then by his uncle. He had many visions and dreams, and was believed to be guided by the archangel Gabriel. He married a widow Khadijah, considerably older than himself, and after she died a number of other wives. Khadijah encouraged him in his visions, but he began his mission rather late in life. The religion he founded, called Mohammedanism by some Christians, is known as Islam to its followers, who are often called Moslems. Mohammed had to flee from Mecca to Medina in 622, owing to the unpopularity of his teachings. This flight, called the *hegira*, marks the beginning of the Mohammedan era.[1] In 629, however, he returned to Mecca as governor, and ordered the destruction of the idols in and surrounding the Kabah, leaving the black stone as the centre of pilgrimage for his followers. The *Koran* was not written down until after his death.

Some say Mohammed performed no miracles, others say he did, and a few assert that miracles alone prove his mission. The best known is the cleaving of the moon, referred to in the *Koran* (liv. 1, 2). The popular version says Mohammed made the moon descend, pass through his sleeves, break into two, and pass back into the sky, where the two parts reunited. Thereafter the crescent, which was originally a Christian symbol, was particularly associated with Islam. The second most important miracle was the night-journey of

---

[1] The Mohammedan year, we may remind Western readers, is a purely lunar one and does not correspond with our year.

the prophet, mentioned in the *Koran* xvii, 1, which says that he was carried from Mecca to Jerusalem. But tradition reports that he took this journey on *Al Borak* a winged white animal like a horse (between the size of a mule and an ass) and visited all seven heavens. In the first he met Adam, in the second John the Baptist and Jesus, in the third Joseph, in the fourth Enoch, in the fifth Aaron, in the sixth Moses and in the seventh Abraham.[2] On one occasion Mohammed is alleged to have taken a scroll of the *Koran* from the horn of a bull. A dove was said to have whispered in his ear, a story popular among sceptics, who said he hid corn in his ear, on which the bird fed. He once dug out of the earth two jars, one containing honey and one milk, to prove, it is said, the earth's abundance. Other miracles were the assistance of angels given to Moslems in the battle of Badr, which is alluded to in the *Koran* iii, 120, 121 and others less spectacular in the tradition : miraculous food and water, movements of trees, cures, etc. The tomb of the prophet is at Medina. The coffin is said to be suspended in mid-air. But J. L. Burckhardt, who visited the enclosure at the beginning of the 19th century, denies this. Relics of the prophet are shown at various places.

The *Koran* is the only sacred scripture in which its own celestial origin is asserted.[3] The Islamic Doctors believe that it has existed from all eternity in the heavens, in the form known as the *Mother of the Book*. A copy of this was brought down to earth by Gabriel. It was on paper, but bound in silk and ornamented with gold and precious stones. Mohammed was allowed to see the whole work once a year. He dictated it to his followers, and they remembered it. After Mohammed's death all the remembered portions were copied down from verbal communications of the faithful. Many different versions existed, but under the caliph Othman one of the versions was accepted, and all others destroyed. The *Koran* is written in Arabic, of a style regarded as the purest. Small but beautifully prepared copies of the *Koran* are used as amulets. Verses from it are also written on vellum or parchment or engraved on metal or precious stones to serve the same purpose.

Magic in Islam. To raise the dead, to remove enchantment, to cure

[2] *Miskatu'l-Masabih,* quoted by T. P. Hughes: *A Dictionary of Islam,* London, 1885, reprinted 1935.
[3] P. Saintyves: *Les Reliques et les Images légendaires,* Paris, 1912. He is referring to sura iii, 2, 5. In iii, 2 the divine origin of both the Old and New Testaments is referred to.

disease, were admitted to be permissible forms of magic, *i.e.* spiritual magic. According to legend St. George, who is honoured as much by Moslems as by Christians, died and recovered several times before he was finally martyred. Examples of those freed from enchantment have already been given from *The Thousand and One Nights*. The fate of Lot's wife, who was changed into a pillar of salt, is referred to in the *Koran* vii, 72–82; xxix, 27–34; xxvi, 160–175; xxvii, 55–59.

A system of incantation called *dawah*, for the invocation of God by means of his sacred names, or rather those of his attributes, and the evocation of angels and good spirits has also been widely used and held lawful by Moslems. The object is to establish friendship between associates, love between those about to marry, to cure disease, and to cause success in good enterprises. But it is admitted that similar methods can give just the opposite results, in which case it would be unlawful. A person wishing to practise this system has to remove all animals from his house, refuse admission to strangers, perfume the place with incense, fast for forty days, refraining from certain foods and perfumes according to the work in hand. He must perform innumerable ablutions. He must always speak the truth, and maintain a humble disposition. He must possess and understand a set of magical tables, on which are inscribed the twenty-eight letters of the Arabic alphabet, their corresponding numbers, the names or attributes of God equivalent to them, the classes and meanings of the attributes, the qualities of the letters, and the corresponding angels, jinn, signs of the zodiac, planets, elements and perfumes. The art of dawah not only allows one to ascertain, from the letters of a person's name, as to how he will get on with another person, or how certain things will affect him, but it will call to the aid angels and jinn, and these will influence a person in the pursuit of good, and protect him from the forces of evil.

Astrology is also practised. It is legitimate only for certain purposes, and, as among Christians, is unlawful if it is used to predict the fate of individuals. Geomancy which is a mode of divination by random marks on the earth or on paper is also permitted with the same restrictions. Similarly auguration from the motions of animals is generally recognised. Omens from trifling events are often noted, and sometimes divination from opening a book at random. Finally palmistry and kindred occult sciences have received considerable attention from Moslem authors, although such books are little known in Christendom.

Amulets are worn by many Moslems, as a preservative against all enchantments. It is pointed out that even the Prophet seems to have believed in the evil eye. This is alluded to in the *Mishkat*, one of the traditional books of the Sunnis. We have seen that the *Koran* is carried as an amulet, and extracts thereon are copied and used. There are some passages which are favoured, as they are directed against witchcraft (suras cxiii, cxiv). The first of these has a reference to "blowers on knots." It is said to refer to the practice of witches and warlocks in Mohammed's day, and it is even said the Prophet himself suffered from it, until Gabriel told him how to overcome the evil effect. The evil practitioner tied knots in a cord, and breathed upon each the name of the person he wished to injure. In the case of the Prophet, Gabriel gave him the words which caused the knots to untie themselves, and release him from the spell.

Whilst the words of the *Koran* are generally agreed to have great power, some Arabs also make use, in their amulets, of some of the following : (i) the names of God, *viz.* the seven most sacred, or the ninety-nine attributes; (ii) the names of the suras (chapters) of the *Koran*, each of which has a symbolic name referred to in its contents; (iii) the names of their seven chief prophets,' *viz.* Adam, Moses, Jacob, David, Solomon, Jesus and Mohammed; (iv) the names of the seven planets; (v) the names of the four principal angels or cherubim, *viz.* Gabriel, the power of God, who revealed God's word to Mohammed and other prophets, Michael, whose name means "like unto God" who fights against devils and holds the balance on Judgement Day, Israfil, the angel of music, who is to blow the trumpet of resurrection on Judgement Day[4] and Azrael, the angel of death; (vi) the names of the seven planetary angels or spirits; these also include Gabriel and Michael, the other names are generally Raphael, Samael, Zachariel (or Zadkiel), Anael and Cassiel;[5] (vii) the names of the seven kings of the Jinn; (viii) the twelve signs of the zodiac; (ix) the four or five elements, earth, water, air, fire and sometimes the quintessence; (x) the twenty-eight mansions of the moon; (xi) the twenty-eight letters of the Arabic alphabet; (xii) numbers having an occult significance; (xiii) magic squares, *i.e.* squares containing numbers so arranged that each line, in any direction, adds up to the same number, which itself has a

[4] These first three angels warned Abraham of the coming destruction of Sodom.
[5] But see W. B. Crow: Astronomical Religion, 6, *Mysteries of the Ancients,* London, 1942.

particular significance; (xiv) symbols derived from Hebrew, Egyptian or Gnostic sources believed to have a magical effect; (xv) other images of men and animals and parts of the human body, such as the human hand, mostly used by the Shiahs, as the Sunnis are more strict about the prohibition against the honouring of images.

The amulets are made of all sorts of material. They may be written with perfumed ink on paper, parchment, etc., then folded flat in metal cases or rolled and placed in tubes of the same. The inscriptions may be stamped on metal, engraved on stone, or written on stones covered with wax, which are then exposed to acid, after which the wax is removed.[6] The best kinds, however, are beautifully engraved on precious stones.

Black magic is strongly condemned by the *Koran* and all Moslem tradition, but is believed to be practised, and very effectively. As among Christians it is thought to be due to the activities of the devil and his minions, which here include the evil jinn. The magician evokes these spirits. Disease and death are often, it is believed, due to black magic. Paralysis is frequently caused, parts of the body being said to be changed into stone. An example of this occurs in the story of the ensorcelled prince in *The Thousand and One Nights*. Persons are sometimes transformed into beasts, birds and fishes, or made to dote on some person or object. Examples of this may also be found in the same work. The discovery of hidden treasure by magical means is also referred to. That a person may become possessed by an evil spirit, and that the same spirit may be exorcised, was believed in equally by Christians and Moslems.

Sufism. The *sufis* or *sophees* bear somewhat the same relation to Islam that the yogis do to Brahminism. Within less than two centuries of the Prophet's death, his religion had apparently been tending to become more and more a matter of outward observance, and Abu Said Abul Khayr sought to bring Moslems back to the realisation of the mystical nature of their religion. It is difficult to define Sufism, however, for the movement soon broke up into many different schools of thought. Most of the Islamic philosophers are called sufis, and most of the dervish orders are supposed to practise Sufism. It also includes many poets. There are Sunni and Shiah Sufis, and the tendency is best known among the Shiites of Persia, where the Shah has been regarded as the Grand Sophee, or head of all the Sufis.

[6] See details, p. 69. E. A. Wallis Budge: *Amulets and Superstitions,* London, 1930.

The origin of the word *sufi* has been disputed. It has been suggested that it has been derived from the Arabic *safu* meaning "purity" or the Greek *Sophia* signifying "wisdom." But it most probably originated from the Arabic *suf*, meaning wool, in allusion to the woollen vestment called the pallium, worn by all Eastern bishops and possibly at one time used by philosophers.[7] At any rate the sufis have always been trained and initiated by qualified teachers called *Murshids*, and it is necessary for all who follow this path to place themselves under the direction of these preceptors.

The sufis have been accused of pantheism, and they certainly teach that God is in all things, and all things are in God. Some say there is truth in all religions, but Islam is the most complete. Behind the outward forms of religion, they hold, are spiritual truths and powers. Many of the precepts of religion are allegorical. They themselves use poetic symbolism. Thus wine, believed to be forbidden to Moslems, is often praised by them, but they say they really mean spiritual ecstasy. Love for them is not of the maternal nor of the romantic variety, but means devotion to the *Murshid* and yearning for God. Flowers mean various virtues, and so on. Some of the sufis, but not all, believe in the dogma of reincarnation. All aim at union with God, and final absorption into the Divinity, which they share in common with mystics of all ages and races. They frequently tend to spend much time in meditation. They often neglect worldly business, or regard it as unimportant. Some of them have been credited with control over the body, some of the feats reported of them rivalling those of the yogis of India.

Dervishes. This is a Persian term for members of Islamic religious orders, derived from their mendicant habits. The Arabic equivalent is *faqir*, Anglicised *fakir*, but as the latter term has been rather vaguely used we prefer the former. The Islamic religious orders are somewhat varied, and each has several degrees of membership. As with certain Christian orders some brethren, under certain circumstances, may live among the people, doing ordinary work, being only called upon to attend to the work of the Order at certain times. But more frequently, and particularly in the higher degrees the work of the Order is the sole activity. As usual the more menial offices are performed by probationers. All dervishes are more or less followers of the Sufi philosophy, all believe in a chain of succession from their various founders, and all have some sort of exercises called *zikr*, which are usually recited, either aloud, or in a whisper,

[7] *Anacalypsis*, 2 vols. London, 1836, 4 vols. London, 1878.

or even only mentally, and which may or may not be accompanied
by gestures or movements. Each Order has its own initiatory ceremonies, its signs of recognition, its tests and passwords. Some dervishes have abandoned the outward practices of Islam, but these are
classed as irregular. The late Dr. H. M. Léon, himself a Moslem,
says[8] there are thirty-three distinct orders of Dervishes, by which
we suppose he refers to those generally classed as such by Moslems.
They often wear long hair and most have beards.

Although Mohammed is said to have spoken against the monastic
life, it is probably only against the abuses thereof to which he refers,
as during his lifetime some of his followers formed a religious order,
and the great Dervish groups claim to have been founded by Abu
Bakr or Ali (the first Caliphs of the Sunnis and of the Shiahs
respectively).

Several of the Dervish orders take note of dreams and visions.
They are observed among candidates for initiation, and progress in
the Order is dependent upon these being regarded as satisfactory.

[8] *Masonic Secretaries Journal*, Sept. 1918.

CHAPTER XXI

KNIGHTS AND TEMPLARS

Chivalry. Whilst Islam was expanding, the world of the Christian religion, *Christendom*, was developing its organisation. It had its two sides, *spiritual* and *temporal*, which constantly interacted; the former was supposed to control the latter, but in practice this was not always the case. The Pope was the supreme head, as ruling the spiritual hierarchy, but since the time of Charlemagne (742–814), who became Emperor in 800, the latter office has been the chief of the temporal realms with some few exceptions.[1] Under the Emperor were the Kings, ruling countries, under them the Lords ruling parts of countries, *e.g.* Earls or Counts ruling counties and so on. This was the *feudal system*. In fact the whole of Christendom was divided and sub-divided several times into areas, each of which had its ecclesiastical head (such as a bishop for a diocese, a priest for a parish, etc.) and each had its temporal ruler.

But just as the spiritual hierarchy had its religious orders of monks and nuns, so also the temporal hierarchy had its *orders of chivalry.* Some of these became so famous that even the nobility esteemed it an honour to belong to them.

According to the findings of anthropology kingship is essentially magical. If so the orders of chivalry ought to be involved in magic, but by that we do not imply anything detrimental. Perhaps it would be better to say that they used symbolism of an esoteric nature. The organisation of the Order of the Garter has been compared with that of a witch-coven. All this means is that a highly religious cult has been imitated, to some degree, by a debased and diabolical one.

The extent to which the religious element entered into the work of an order of chivalry varied, and some orders, such as that of the Templars, were intermediate between chivalric and monastic orders.

Most of these Orders were founded by kings or ruling princes, and in Catholic countries it was the custom to get the confirmation

---

[1] Britain was one. The history of the Empire is somewhat complex, but is not important for our present purpose. A general view of the matter will suffice. Most of the greater kings, *e.g.* of Britain and Spain took orders only from the Pope.

of the Pope for each establishment. It is commonly thought that the chivalric orders are a relic of mediaevalism, but most of those recently existing were only founded between 1750–1850. However, those that are most clearly connected with magic are much earlier.

The Round Table. The stories of King Arthur[2] and the Knights of the Round Table are, as we have seen, known from mediaeval legends. In the last century it was thought that these legends had imported chivalry into a barbaric age, that Arthur was at most a petty chieftain, and the idea of his having a cultivated and highly civilised court fictitious. In the present century these views have been reversed; we need only refer to' the fact that most wonderful treasures of Keltic art have been made known, particularly among armour and jewellery, which show the Keltic culture of the Arthurian period was most sophisticated. This explains why such a complex civilisation is assigned to Arthur's court, both by the Welsh *Mabinogion* and by the English legends which developed independently.

The *Round Table* was constructed, according to Mallory, by the magician Merlin, at Carduel (the present Carlisle). It was given, as we have seen to King Uther, Arthur's father, who gave it to King Leodegraunce of Camelyard. When Arthur married Guinever, the daughter of the last named king, he (Arthur) received it together with 100 knights. Altogether, according to Mallory, it seated 150. The Knights of the Round Table included all the nobility of Arthur's court. Some of them were kings, such as Ban, King of Benwick (Brittany), Bors, King of Gaul, Meliadus, King of Lyonesse, and Pharamond, King of the Franks. Many were the sons of kings, such as Lancelot, son of Ban, Gawain, son of Lot, King of Orkney, Tristram, son of Meliadus, and Mordred, son of Arthur.

Charlemagne and His Paladins. When the Barbarians dismembered the classical Roman Empire of the West the Kingdom of the Franks included parts of France and Germany. It became extensive and was then sometimes called an Empire. The Merovingian Dynasty 481–751 were succeeded by the Carolingian 751–987. The second ruler of the latter dynasty Charles the Great or Charlemagne (742–814) was crowned Holy Roman Emperor by the Pope in 800. Not only was this a very important point in history, being a restoration of the classical Western Empire under Christian auspices, but it struck the imagination of the poets, and produced, during the

[2] Born 502, reigned 517–543.

Middle Ages, a mass of epic and romantic literature just as bulky and just as highly imaginative as that of the Arthurian period.

The knights of Charlemagne's court are called *paladins*. More than twelve are named, yet there are references to twelve who were constantly associated with the king, and are also called *peers*. They generally fought for the king, and often against the Saracens, who occupied large parts of Spain at that time.

The Templars. In 1099 the Crusaders established a Christian kingdom of Jerusalem. Under Baldwin II, the second king, the Order of the Temple was set up in 1118. It was confirmed by the Pope and formally recognised by the Council of Troyes, France, in 1128. They were called Templars because one of their aims was the rebuilding of the Temple of Jerusalem, having been granted a site on Mount Moriah, where it was believed this temple previously stood. They also undertook to protect pilgrims and fight for the Kingdom of Jerusalem. The first leaders of the movement were Hugues de Payens (1070–1136) and nine other knights. De Payens was elected the first Grand Master. The statutes and rituals of the Order were written or influenced by St. Bernard, the last of the Fathers and known as the Thaumaturgus of the West (1091–1153). They were officially put into final form at the aforesaid Council of Troyes. In 1146, under the third Grand Master, a General Chapter, held in Paris, was honoured by the presence of the King of France (Louis VII) and the Pope himself (Eugenius III). In 1172 the Pope gave the Templars the extraordinary privilege of being independent of the authority of any bishop outside, which meant that they had their own bishops and priests within the Order. In 1185 the Emperor Frederick Barbarossa became "Protector" of the Order. Within a hundred years of their formation the Templars had increased to some 15,000, and they had acquired lands and properties all over Europe. In some places they were exempted from various taxes.

The Templar Order was divided into provinces, the latter into preceptories and these into commanderies. Templars wore white mantles bearing a red eight-pointed cross. Their churches were eight-sided. Their symbol at first showed two knights on a single horse, indicating their poverty. Later it showed the head of Christ and still later an eagle. Each member took the usual monastic vow of poverty, chastity and obedience. The members were divided into priests, knights and serving brethren, who acted as esquires to the knights. The Grand Master ranked as a sovereign prince, and there were a number of officers.

In 1291 the Templars were driven out of the Holy Land, with the fall of Acre, which was captured by the Saracens. The archives of the Order were transferred to Cyprus, but by this time the Templars had rich establishments all over Europe. In Spain and Portugal some were still fighting the Moors.

Time passed and the Templars became richer still, and unpopular on account of their independence, for as we have said they were under no obligation to the ordinary priesthood, and paid no taxes to the civil authority. When a Templar gave offence to anyone it was almost impossible to bring him before a Court of Justice. People began to blame the Templars for the loss of the Holy Land. Then they began to ascribe to them secret rites of a magical nature. It is true that the reception of a Templar was held in secret.

When Philip IV ascended the throne of France in 1285 he found himself very short of money, and was angered by Pope Boniface VIII who refused to allow him to tax the clergy or the Templars. Boniface died, however, in 1303 and after the short reign of Benedict XI (1303–1304) Philip succeeded in getting one of his French bishops selected Pope under the title of Clement V in 1305. Clement was not allowed to reside at Rome, but had to set up his headquarters at Avignon.

One day the king received a letter from the governor of a place in Languedoc. It said that a citizen of Béziers, who had been accused of heresy and had been condemned to death, claimed to have a secret of unprecedented importance which he promised to reveal if his life were spared. The governor informed the king that, under the circumstances, he had deferred the execution of the prisoner. King Philip had the latter sent to Paris. His life was spared on condition he revealed something of importance to the State. The prisoner then disclosed that he had been imprisoned with an apostate Templar, also condemned to death, who had revealed to him before his execution that the crime for which he was to suffer was as nothing to the crimes he had been forced to commit on joining the Templars. These included sodomy, idolatry and a denial of Christ.

King Philip, already alarmed by the great powers of the Templar Order, eager to find some plausible excuse for seizing their funds, gave the criminal his life and laid plans for the suppression of the Order. He acted with great secrecy. He invited Jacques de Molay the Grand Master to Paris. The latter accepted the invitation, arrived with a great retinue and was treated with much respect. But on the night of the 13th October 1306 De Molay was arrested together with every other Templar in Paris, whilst orders, sent out in advance to all parts of the country, ensured that everywhere the same action was taken. Philip had even written to foreign rulers, so that, soon after, action was taken against the Templars in most parts of Europe. In Italy they were mostly suppressed, in England King Edward II was slow to act, but eventually the order was dissolved in a bloodless fashion, in Germany they were suppressed but treated very leniently on the whole, in Spain and Portugal they were tried, found innocent and restored under the name of the Order of Montesa in Spain and the Order of Christ in Portugal.[3] But in France the persecution was very severe. After a much delayed trial, and attempts to elicit confessions by means of torture, the Grand Master was burnt at the stake (March 1313) and many others suffered death in a similar manner. In 1311 the Order was declared disbanded by the Council of Vienne in France. It had previously been suppressed by a papal bull of Clement V.

The following accusations seem to have been made against the Templars :

1. *Secrecy.* That their initiations were held in secret was not denied, and attempts to justify some degree of secrecy might have been made. The early Christians kept part of the Mass secret.

2. *Denial of Christ.* The candidate was expected to trample on the cross, to spit upon it, or to deny Christ in words. The explanation is difficult, unless the Templars were an anti-Christian sect which is unlikely. There are two possible explanations, supposing the Templars intended to remain Christian : (a) Michelet[4] put forward the ingenious theory that the initiation of a Templar took the form of a drama, in which the candidate first appears as an unbeliever, and therefore denies Christ in the early part of the play, but as the action proceeds he is converted, and other symbolic acts *e.g.* clothing in Templar garb, show him to be admitted to the Faith; (b) there appear to have been some Christians who believed the cross to have been evil, because it was the instrument upon which the good Jesus suffered. This would explain the trampling or spitting on the cross, but not the verbal denial of Christ, if the

[3] In Portugal permission was granted for the continuation as the Order of Christ, on condition that the Pope retained the right to confer the same Order himself; it is therefore *also* a Papal Order.

[4] *Histoire de France*, 1838–1851.

latter really occurred. In the *High History of the Holy Grail*[5] the original of which dates from about 1200, a strange priest scourges the cross, much to the amazement of an orthodox knight looking on, and the explanation is that as Christ was crucified on the Cross, the latter was regarded as evil, contrary to the usual view. There may in fact have been those who held that idea, although we must admit it would have been strange if the Templars were among them.

3. *Alterations in the Canon of the Mass.* It was reported that the most essential part of the Liturgy had been mutilated. It is known that forms of the canon of the Mass exist which are so incomplete as to render the Holy Sacrament invalid. But it is unlikely they used such forms (which have a Protestant tendency). It is much more likely they used one of the lesser known but valid Eastern Liturgies, which may have been available in Jerusalem in their days, and that such were not understood in France. If they had cut down the Mass, because unbelievers, why did they not abolish it altogether?

4. *Various heretical beliefs.* It was claimed that, whilst in the East, the Templars had adopted various heresies from Eastern sectarians with whom they had come in contact: (a) Some said they derived dogmas from Islamic sects, and that they had even been influenced by the Assassins has been alleged; (b) Éliphas Levi[6] says the Templars were secret adherents of Johannism, which was a sect in the East who claimed St. John as the chief apostle and made him responsible for a number of statements that can only be regarded as blasphemous by Christians. The Johannites denied the virgin birth and the resurrection. Joshua (which is the name they gave to Jesus) was the son, they said, of Miriam, who was betrothed to Jochanan, but who was deceived by a certain Pandira or Panther. This story the Johannites have taken from a well-known Jewish account, given in the *Sepher Toldos Jeshu.* The son of Miriam was brought up by the Rabbi Joseph, who took him to Egypt where he was initiated into the priesthood, and where he eventually rose to the rank of sovereign pontiff with the title of Christ. This rank was passed on through St. John, they taught, through a line of pontiffs, and in the days when the Order of the Temple was founded the holder of the office was a personage named Theoclet, who was acquainted with Hugues de Payens and who passed on the succession to the latter, making the Grand Masters of the Templar Order secretly sovereign pontiffs; (c) Von Hammer, writing in 1818,

---

[5] Translated from the Old French by Sebastian Evans, reprinted London, 1910, 1913.
[6] *The History of Magic*, 1859, trans. 2nd ed., London, 1922.

brought forward evidence that the Templars perpetuated certain Gnostic dogmas. This seemed unlikely when it was written, but more recent evidence has been put forward to show Gnosticism persisted in many Eastern sects.[7] The Templar churches, notably at Erfurt, Schoengraben and Prague show Gnostic symbols, including the flaming star, the tau, the seal of Solomon, the square, the level and the triangle. Certain Gnostic or Kabalistic ideas may have been connected with that of rebuilding the Temple of Solomon.

5. *Idolatry*. The Templars were accused of worshipping an idol in the form of a head, called Baphomet, and a cat. There seems to be no doubt that some of the assemblies had such a head, that it was supposed to hold power, that they applied cords to it, and afterwards bound candidates for initiation with such cords. The head is described as bearded, with glowing eyes "like carbuncles." In some lodges the head had two or three faces. Others had to be content with a skull.

Why it was called Baphomet is a question which has never been solved. There are several theories : (a) Baphomet is a corruption of Mahomet. But this is most unlikely as the followers of the prophet never used images, least of all of the prophet himself; (b) Baphomet is derived from *baphe* (*Gk.* baptism) and *metis* (*Gk.* wisdom) according to Von Hammer; this seems equally unlikely, for why should an image be called by the name of an act? (c) Éliphas Levi says[8] the word was formed by writing in reverse order the initials of the words *Templi omnium hominum pacis abbas* (Father of the temple of peace of all men). But he takes the *three* first letters of the first word and *two* first letters of the last getting *tem o h p ab* joining them, then reversing them! This appears to be one of the oddest of Levi's odd conceits.

The cat is equally enigmatic. But we do know that somewhat later in history, when the witch-cult was in full swing, the officers of a coven sometimes dressed themselves up as various animals. This was also done, and still is, in ceremonies associated with folk-lore. It is hard to imagine an important chivalric order indulging in such antics. The cat was evidently a masked man, for in some cases it addressed the assembly.[9]

[7] See *e.g.* B. H. Springett: *Secret Sects of Syria and the Lebanon*, London, 1922.

[8] *Dogma and Ritual of High Magic*, 1856, trans. as *Transcendental Magic*, new ed., London, 1923.

[9] For further information about the cat in worship and occultism see M. Oldfield Howey: *The Cat in the Mysteries of Religion and Magic*, London, not dated but *circa* 1925.

6. *Abnormal Sexual Acts.* The serious allegation that the Templars indulged in such acts was never proved. It is possible that the candidate was kissed by the initiator, possibly even by the assembled brethren. But kissing was, and still is, a form of greeting in France. It is possible that the candidate was stripped of his clothing, which is by no means unknown in initiatory orders, and symbolises "the casting off of the old man" whilst the investment with the robes of the order signifies "the putting on of the new." Isolated accounts of indecent behaviour may have referred to irregularities of individuals, and have nothing to do with the beliefs or ideals of the Order. Certain hermaphrodite figures, alleged to have been used by the Templars have no reference whatever to sexual morality, but are well-known Gnostic symbols combining the positive and negative aspects of the universe.

7. *Political Status.* This is seldom mentioned, but was undoubtedly the real cause of the downfall of the Order. They formed a state within the various states. The intense loyalty of the Templars to their Grand Master, who ranked as a sovereign prince, was not, it was thought, compatible with their loyalty to the king of the country in which they lived.

CHAPTER XXII

THE HOLY GRAIL

The Troubadours. Today anyone may write poetry, and if it be made known and liked, the author is proclaimed a poet. It was not so in ancient days. We have already referred to the bards of the Druidic cult, and the scalds of the Norse. These had to pass an examination, and undergo an initiation into an order. The appointment was officially approved by the masters of the cult. The only thing barely approaching it today is the appointment to the office of the *Poet Laureate*. This harks back to late mediaeval times when some of the universities invested graduates in rhetoric and poetry with a laurel crown.[1] It is a distinction that goes back to Roman times when Apollo and some of the muses were shown crowned with laurel. This is therefore something characteristic of the Renaissance.

Before that time the poets had their guilds, to which admission was not easy. Wagner's opera *The Master-Singers of Nüremburg* deals with one of them, in an age when numerous rules had been imposed and there was a danger that these might stifle originality. Wagner deals with this problem, Hans Sachs becoming famous as the upholder of a free style of composition. This character was historical. The scene is set in the middle of the 16th century.

Before the Meistersingers of Germany were the Minnesingers (minstrels) of the 12th to 14th century. In the north of France in the 12th, 13th and 14th centuries were the Trouvères, inventive poets who wrote in the *langue d'oil* chiefly on amatory subjects. In the south of France (Provence) in the 11th, 12th and 13th centuries were the Troubadours who wrote on love and chivalry in the language called *langue d'oc*. There is some evidence that the Troubadours worked according to certain rules of the sacred tradition. They were mostly in deacon's orders, a few were priests, and a minority even bishops.[2] These clerics, however, did not belong to the regular clergy. Inasmuch as they had no fixed parishes or sees,

---

[1] The custom was long continued by the French Academy.
[2] Isabel Cooper-Oakley: *Traces of a hidden Tradition in Masonry and Mediaeval Mysticism*, London, 1900.

they wandered about, as did many knights in those days, and in fact it is at times difficult to distinguish between a knight-errant, a wandering knight in search of adventure, and a troubadour. Those in deacon's orders were supposed to act as a foil for the priests, but they soon came to be largely independent, and went about the country earning their living as jesters.

It is among the troubadours, the better class of whom were highly esteemed, that the stories of the Holy Grail originated. There are a very large number of known manuscripts on this subject. Some of them claim to be based on earlier manuscripts that have been lost. Caxton, the first English printer (1422–1491) and other early printers produced some of them, and translations were made later. The dates of the manuscripts are not known with certainty. The subject has become well known in England, as it was taken up by Tennyson. In Germany Wagner made use of the most esoteric of these legends.

The legend of the Holy Grail is associated with the stories of King Arthur and his Knights of the Round Table. The Grail story, in itself, is extremely mystical and esoteric, and has no very obvious connections with anything else. It is generally agreed by careful readers to have a high spiritual quality, perhaps surpassing anything else known in Christian literature. On the face of these manuscripts there is nothing unorthodox. Waite, who has examined them in some detail[3] says that if there are occasional traces of heretical ideas these are unquestionably accidental, due to ignorance. Yet Waite and a number of other authors seek to show that throughout the Grail literature there is an obscure tendency, which somehow does not agree with orthodoxy.

The Nature of the Grail. In most of the romances it is made quite clear that the Grail was the chalice used by Christ for the wine at the Last Supper, this wine being miraculously converted into the blood of Christ, as He declared (*Matt.* xvi, 27; *Mark* xiv, 23, 24; *Luke* xxii, 20). It was this cup which was used by Joseph of Arimathea to collect the blood of Christ as He was on the cross, or after His body was taken down. It will be remembered that Joseph of Arimathea and Nicodemus were responsible for taking down the body of Jesus, and placing it in the Holy Sepulchre (*Matt.* xxvii, 57–60; *Mark* xv, 45, 46; *Luke* xxiii, 50–53; *John* xix, 38–42). It has long been related in a legend that Joseph of Arimathea had come to Glastonbury in Britain and the romances accept this story, or say

[3] *The Holy Grail, its legends and symbolism*, London, 1933.

that some of the followers of Joseph came to this country, and brought the Grail with them.

Lucifer. There are some references, in the stories, which make it appear that the Grail was a stone. The explanation of this seems to be made plain in *Parzival* wherein we learn that the cup was made of the stone named *lapis exilis*.[4] The latter was in the crown of Lucifer, and he lost it when he was expelled from Heaven. Perhaps we may translate this as stone of exile, referring to the fact that Lucifer was exiled to the lower regions. Otherwise the stone was said to be the emerald, sacred to Venus, and it may be noted that Lucifer in the Classics was the name of the planet Venus when appearing as a morning star, *i.e.* just before the sun rises. Finally Venus is the planetary goddess of Friday, the day on which Christ was crucified, she is also Eostre, from whose name we derive the. word Easter, the festival of the Resurrection.

Grail and Dove. The Grail in all the literature is represented as being endowed with the utmost sanctity. When it appears a vision of Christ Himself is occasionally seen, sometimes as a child, sometimes with wounds as He was on the cross. Or there may be angels, or the appearance of three persons, representing the Most Holy Trinity. More often the apparition of the Grail is accompanied by beams of light and sweet odours and delightful sounds. In more than one description the coming of the Grail, which is miraculous, is preceded by the flying in of a dove, carrying a censer in its beak, and sweet perfume fills the air. There is often a procession, sometimes with other sacred objects : a platter or dish, sometimes carrying a severed head swimming in blood, a lance from which drops of blood continue to fall, and a sacred sword. The Grail itself is sometimes confused with the platter on which Christ consecrated the bread of the Last Supper. Sometimes the platter appears as well. Sometimes the Grail has a lid, like a ciborium. Sometimes the Grail was regarded as the dish on which the Paschal Lamb was served. If the platter bears a severed head, it is conjectured that it is that of St. John the Baptist, decapitated by order of Herod (*Matt.* xiv, 10, 11; *Mark* vi, 16; *Luke* ix, 9). The spear which regularly appears with the Grail is that with which Longinus pierced the side of Christ as He was on the cross, and of which we have already mentioned relics. The sword in the romances is said to be that which

[4] This name is also given to the philosopher's stone in an alchemical work ascribed to Arnoldus (Waite, *loc. cit.*).

was used to behead St. John the Baptist, although one would have thought a closer connection with the Passion would have been the sword with which Peter struck off the ear of Malchus, when soldiers came to arrest Jesus (*Matt.* xxvi, 51; *Mark* xiv, 47; *Luke* xxii, 50; *John* xviii, 10). It also appears in the Grail literature, that the sword was that of King David, and was placed by his son, King Solomon in a ship which also appears in one of the romances. In Wolfram von Eschenbach's *Parzival* the Grail is renewed in its power once each year by the descent from Heaven of a dove.

The most peculiar feature of the Grail, as it appears in the writings, is its property of sustaining the hungry. Joseph of Arimathea, during long years in prison, was kept alive solely by its means. In the *Morte d'Arthur* the Grail comes into the hall of King Arthur amidst sounds of thunder and "every knight had such meats and drinks as he best loved in the world." It is upon such passages that the Grail has been compared with folk-lore stories of feeding vessels, but it seems clear that it refers to spiritual rather than physical sustenance.

The Grail also had miraculous powers of prolonging life, and healing sickness. One of the Grail custodians, Titurel, is said to live for 400 years, appearing most of the time as a man of forty. The Grail was the stone that enabled the Phoenix to renew its life.

Lastly the Grail had an ability and a habit of appearing and disappearing, as if in a vision, and sometimes quite unexpectedly.

Waite repeatedly refers to the Grail as a reliquary. In that case the relic, kept inside, would be the Precious Blood. For the term reliquary is used for a receptacle containing a relic, and the relic is usually much older than the reliquary, its container.

CHAPTER XXIII

MEDIAEVAL AND RENAISSANCE ASTROLOGY

Origin and Antecedents. It is often said that Astrology originated in Chaldea. With our present knowledge of the antiquity of Indian astrology we can no longer hold this view. But perhaps the science did assume its Western form in Chaldea. It passed to the Greeks. In the island of Cos there was[1] a school of astrology founded by Berosus, who lived in the 3rd century B.C. It passed to the Christians, was accepted to a varying degree by the Fathers of the Church, all of whom of course rejected deterministic astrology, *i.e.* the prediction of the fate of individuals, which was regarded as a heresy. But even its early opponents generally admitted it to hold sway over natural objects, if not over the fate of man. Even Augustine who opposed personal horoscopes, admits the influence of the sun, moon and planets on nature, and cites the changes of sea urchins and oysters with the waxing and waning of the moon. Wedel[2] who has made a special study of the subject says that the knowledge of astrology preserved from antiquity in the Middle Ages was drawn, in the first instance, "from the Church Fathers themselves."

The Clementine *Recognitions* is full of astrology, and claims that the science is a great support for the Catholic religion. It of course opposes determinism, and upholds free-will. As often said later, the stars incline, they do not compel. The human being is a microcosm, or little world, that reflects the macrocosm, the great world—the cosmos, including the planets and stars, as we would say. This work also deals with miracle and magic. The difference is that miracle is the work of God, and does good, whereas magic is of evil intent and does harm.

Wedel[3] says that little astrology was known in mediaeval times, as compared with the ancient, but whether that was so or not the subject soon became popular. Thorndike[4] from the study of French

[1] T. O. Wedel: *The Medieval Attitude to Astrology,* New Haven, London and Oxford, 1920.
[2] *Loc. cit.*
[3] *Loc cit.*
[4] *History of Magic and Experimental Science,* Vol. I, New York, 1929.

literary history, confirmed by many works that in the reign of Louis I (r. 814–840), the successor to Charlemagne, there was no great lord "but had his own astrologer."

Western Astrology. Astronomy is the science of the heavenly bodies, Astrology the science of their influence on the earth and man. In the Middle Ages it seemed inconceivable that astronomy could be studied for its own sake; its data were only needed for its effects on this earth, in other words to help astrology. In Europe astrology in mediaeval times degenerated as it became more widespread, but its detailed study was preserved by the few. The most popular portents were comets. They were held to foreshadow the death of kings and other prominent people, as they did in ancient times.

But the true astrologers had a more scientific system. They had three great factors :

1. *The Houses of the Heavens.* These were obtained by first taking four points : (a) *the ascendant* (or *horoscope*[5] as it was formerly called) or that point due East on the horizon, at which point heavenly bodies are seen to rise, (b) the *imum coeli*, the intersection of the ecliptic[6] with the lower meridian,[7] (c) *the descendant* or opposite point to (a), *viz.* the point of the ecliptic on which the heavenly bodies are seen to set, and (d) the *medium coeli* or intersection of the ecliptic with the upper meridian, exactly opposite (b); a heavenly body reaching this point is said *to culminate.* Imaginary planes drawn through these four points from the centre of the earth divide the whole heavens (above and below the horizon) into four segments. Each of the segments was further divided into three, making the twelve houses. This factor in astrology which is unchanged with the movements of the heavenly bodies was thought by mediaeval occultists to symbolise God as the Heavenly Father.

2. *The Zodiac.* This is the track or belt in the heavens, in which all the seven planets move. The ecliptic or sun's path runs along the mid-line of this path, and the seven planets of the ancients never diverge more than 9° on each side of it, so this is as far as it is said to extend. The zodiac, of course, with the rest of the heavenly host of stars (the celestial sphere) appears to revolve around the Houses of the Heavens once in every twenty-four hours.

Being a circle the zodiac has no beginning, but a point is selected

---

[5] This term is now used, of course, to denote the whole chart.
[6] The ecliptic is the plane in which the earth revolves around the sun (or more accurately that in which the earth-moon centre revolves).
[7] The lower meridian is the plane passing through the lowest point.

which symbolises the upward urge of the annual cycle. This begins at the point at the Spring Equinox when the ecliptic crosses the equator and the days begin to get longer. Unfortunately, owing to the movement known as the *Precession of the Equinoxes* this point has moved many degrees over the centuries, so that the zodiac used in Western astrology (the zodiac of the signs) no longer corresponds with the constellations after which the signs are named.[8] The signs are twelve equal divisions of the zodiac. Beginning with the Spring Equinox they are named : *Aries*, the ram; *Taurus*, the bull; *Gemini*, the twins; *Cancer*, the crab; *Leo*, the lion; *Virgo*, the virgin bearing ears of corn; *Libra*, the balance; *Scorpio*, the scorpion; *Sagittarius*, the centaur-archer; *Capricorn*, the goat; *Aquarius*, the water-pourer; *Pisces*, the fishes. Each sign rules one part of the body : Aries, the head, Taurus, the neck, Gemini, the shoulders and lungs, Cancer, the stomach, Leo, the heart and back, Virgo, the intestines, Libra, the loins and kidneys, Scorpio, the genitals, Saggitarius, the hips and thighs, Capricorn, the knees, Aquarius, the legs and ankles, Pisces, the feet. This was often shown in the *melothesia* which was the figure of a man, marked with the twelve zodiacal signs. And as the only perfect man was Christ, so it came about that the zodiac was regarded as the symbol of God the Son. The twelve apostles corresponded with the twelve signs of the zodiac.

3. *The Seven Planets.* These include the sun which apparently moves through the Zodiac in one year and the moon which traverses the same cycle in one month. The sun and moon were called *luminaries*, but were treated in the same way as the true planets. Of these only five of course were known in the Middle Ages. They are as follows :

Mercury which moves most rapidly (next the moon) completing its cycle through the zodiac in eighty-eight days. Mercury never moves more than 30° away from the sun.

Venus is next, completing its revolution in 225 days; it never recedes more than 47° from that luminary.

The other planets move freely away from the sun.

Mars completes its cycle in about two years (687 days),

Jupiter in about twelve years (4,333 days[9]),

Saturn in between twenty-nine and thirty years (10,759 days).

The seven planets were symbols of the seven gifts of the Holy

[8] Recently certain students of astrology have said we should go back to the constellations. But if so what becomes of the symbolism of the signs. The Ram, for instance, symbol of upward urge, would no longer begin with the upward urge of spring !

[9] 47 days short of twelve years.

Ghost. Thus the three great factors in astrology symbolised the three Persons of the Most Holy Trinity. The planets or gifts were often shown as the seven-branched candlestick, an allusion to the symbols in the *Apocalypse*.[10]

The planets have different influences in the different signs, but always maintain their basic characters. The sun is male, regal, hot, dry and positive. The moon is female, cold, moist and negative. Mercury is often regarded as hermaphrodite, and as easily taking on the influence of signs and even of aspecting planets. Venus is female, benefic, warm, moist, fruitful and negative. She was the goddess of love and in astrology was termed the Lesser Fortune. Mars is male, malefic, hot, dry, barren and positive. He was the god of war and called the Lesser Infortune. Jupiter is male, benefic, warm, fruitful and positive. He was called the Greater Fortune. Saturn was a eunuch, he was malefic, cold, dry, barren and negative. He was called the Greater Infortune. These ideas had been passed on from the ancients.

Each planet rules one or two signs of the zodiac. The moon rules Cancer, the sun Leo, Mercury Gemini and Virgo, Venus Taurus and Libra, Mars Aries and Scorpio, Jupiter Sagittarius and Pisces, Saturn Capricorn and Aquarius. They also have other relationships to other signs.

The influence of the planets was very greatly dependent upon their *aspects*. These were the positions in the heavens in relation to one another. If planets were almost or quite in the same degree of longitude they were said to be in *conjunction*. The effect of this was said to vary with the planets concerned. The *opposition* occurs when planets are 180° apart and is a bad aspect, the *square* 90° is also very bad, the *trine* 120° is very good, and the *sextile* 60° is also quite good. The *semi-sextile* 30° is moderately good, and the *semi-square* 45° rather bad. All these aspects were taken over by mediaeval astrology from the ancients. It will be noted there were only seven of these aspects. Later others were added.

The basic texts in the Middle Ages were the works of Hipparchus (2nd century), Ptolemy (2nd century), Firmicius (4th century), Macrobius (4th–5th centuries), and Chalcidius (6th century). Ptolemy[11] was the most important and his geocentric theory of the heavens held the field until displaced by the heliocentric in the 16th century.

[10] *Loc cit.*
[11] He was an Egyptian (of Alexandria) who lived much later than the line of Egyptian kings that bore this name.

Some Mediaeval Astrologers. Martianus Capella (5th century) was an encyclopaedic writer in Carthage, North Africa who included astrology in his wide range of writing. St. Isidore of Seville, archbishop (560–636), one of the Fathers of the Church and the most learned man of his day, wrote about and accepted the action of the moon on plants and animals. The Venerable Bede, saint and doctor of the Church (673–735) studied and wrote about astrology. He tried "to Christianise" the zodiac, by replacing the names of the signs by those of the twelve apostles. The Blessed Alcuin (735–804) a native of York, finally an abbot at Tours, France, was also a student of astrology. Paul, the philosopher (9th century) upheld astrology about 850. Notker Labeo (950–1022) monk of St. Gall (Benedictine) dealt with the astrological mysticism involved in the fixing of the date of Easter. It will be noted that the cycles of the sun and the moon, as well as the days of the week are involved. Pope Sylvester II (Gerbert, 922–1003) has already been alluded to as suspected of magic; he was probably a scientist and wrote on the astrolabe, an instrument with sights for taking the altitudes of heavenly bodies. John XIX (r. 1024–1032) is another pope who is supposed to have dabbled in astrology.

· Hugh of St. Victor (1096–1141), a mystical and scholastic philosopher and theologian who wrote on the union of body and spirit and the symbolism of the ark, admitted that natural astrology was quite in harmony with faith, the stars influencing bodily complexions, health, the weather, the fertility of the soil and drought.

John of Salisbury (d. 1180) another ecclesiastical writer accepted astrology in principle, but he attacked certain aspects of it, such as making the signs masculine and feminine in quality, and strongly condemned any attempt to foretell the future.

Ibn Ezra, a Jewish writer (1092–1167), a native of Toledo, Spain, one of the foremost scholars of his day,[12] wrote astrological works that were very popular, and instrumental in spreading a knowledge of the subject throughout Europe. Just at this time the Arabic philosophers were becoming known, from their establishments in Spain, and the Arabic form of astrology, which makes use of the mansions of the moon, was becoming well known. Besides astrology was now universally respected, and in 1125 the first Chair of Astrology was established[13] at the University of Bologna, Italy.

Michael Scot (1175–1234), a priest and doctor of theology, who is

[12] Commemorated in Browning's *Rabbi Ben Ezra.*
[13] Burckhardt: *Die Kultur der Renaissance in Italien,* 10th ed., Leipzig, 1908, quoted by Wedel, *loc. cit.*

said to have been offered the Archbishopric of Cashel in Ireland, but refused because he did not know the Erse language, had the reputation of a magician. He was alleged to raise the dead, ride through the air on a demon-horse, and through the sea in a magical ship. In fact he was an eminent scholar, with a good knowledge of Arabic, and a philosopher who was expert on Aristotle. He was court-astrologer to the Emperor Frederick II. He also wrote on physiognomy.

Guido Bonatti (*fl.* 1223–1277) was also, for a time, court-astrologer to Frederick II. Both he and Scot were placed in Inferno by Dante. Bonatti wrote[14] a treatise on astrology, prefaced by a pious address to God and the Virgin Mary, in which he attempts to show that the Church Fathers and even Christ himself employed astrology. But he appears to have been a determinist.

Alphonso X (1226–1284), King of Castile and Leon from 1257, was noteworthy for his interest in astronomy and astrology. He had the famous astronomical data compiled, known as the *Alphonsine Tables*, about 1253. In his laws divination by the stars was allowed for those trained in astronomy, but conjuration of evil spirits and the making of waxen or metallic images, with the aim of harming people, was punishable with death. Incantations for good purposes were allowed and even encouraged. In 1256 Alphonso had a mediaeval manuscript translated from Arabic into Spanish, and from the latter a Latin version was prepared, as was usual in those days. It has been described by Thorndike[15] although known only in MSS. In these one Picatrix is mentioned, and he seems to have been the original author. He is described as "most skilled in mathematics" and "very learned in the arts of necromancy." It deals with astrological images, and the evocation of demons. Astrology is claimed as the root of all magic.

Pope Alexander IV (*r.* 1254–1261) was one of those who supported astrology in the 13th century. Pope John XXI (*r.* 1276–1277) was known as a writer under his name of Peter Hispanus. He was the author of several books on medicine, and shows therein a belief in the influence of the stars. The friars of the 13th century were often exponents of astrology. Wedel affirms[16] that at the Universities of Bologna, Padua and Milan the lists of professors of astrology are continuous from the early 13th to the 16th century.

[14] Quoted by Wedel: *loc. cit.*

[15] *Loc. cit.* Holmyard in his *Alchemy* (Penguin Books) 1957, says the original author was Al Majriti (Maslama ibn Ahmad) an alchemist, 10th century.

[16] *Loc cit.*

Scholastic Philosophy and Astrology. On the whole the scholastic philosophy was favourable towards non-deterministic astrology.

The two shining lights of the scholastic philosophy St. Albertus Magnus and St. Thomas Aquinas[17] both supported non-deterministic astrology. St. Albertus Magnus (1193–1280) according to Thorndike,[18] even tried to show St. Augustine supported this kind of astrology. Albertus used astrology for selecting suitable times for undertakings. He thought if anyone prognosticates from the planets those things subject to natural causes he serves a useful purpose. The order of nature is wholly under the influence of the planets and their configurations in the celestial spheres. With Augustine, therefore, he approves astrology in meteorology and medicine. But he who predicts the future of individual human lives is a deceiver, and ought to be shunned. Christ was exempt from the stars' influence, Albertus thinks, as His Incarnation was voluntary (other authors had claimed that the Lord had taken on fate as a man). Albertus did even allow, in his book on minerals, the engraving of stones with astrological images, provided due care be taken to avoid idolatry. With the aid of such engraved stones, it is true, the demons do act, but only to speed up natural processes. There is a good magic, in fact, as well as a bad. The Magi who visited the infant Jesus were good magicians not sorcerers. He seems to mean they were wonder-workers, like many of the saints. The *Speculum Astronomiae* was originally always ascribed to Albertus Magnus. It is wholly in support of astrology. Opponents of the latter tried to discredit it, but as Thorndike[19] points out, astrology and magic are sufficiently vouched for in the works on minerals. St. Albertus Magnus believed that the stars and planets are media acting between higher intelligences and this world. Angels do move the planets, but in the *Speculum* he does not class these spirits as rational souls.

St. Thomas Aquinas (1225–1274) says that the human intellect and will are not corporeal, and consequently are not directly affected by the stars. The body, on the other hand, certainly is. When man's body processes are disturbed the intellect is affected, but the will need not follow the inclinations of the bodily appetite. The

17 St. Thomas Aquinas was made the patron saint of a German astrological society, which was active some few years ago. For much more detail about these two great masters in reference to astrology, see Wedel, *loc. cit.*, and also Thorndike, *loc. cit.*

18 *Loc. cit.*

19 *Loc cit.*

majority of men, he concludes, are governed by their passions, and are dependent upon bodily appetites. It is in the latter that the influence of the planets is clearly felt. Few indeed are the wise, who are capable of controlling their animal instincts. Therefore astrologers, in making general predictions (which apply to many men) foretell the truth in the majority of instances. In making particular predictions (which apply to the individual) they often fail, for nothing prevents the individual from resisting the dictates of his lower faculties. Wherefore the astrologers themselves are in the habit of saying that "the wise man rules the stars" because he can control his own passions. This phrase about the wise man was common in astrological literature of the 13th and 14th centuries.[20] St. Thomas Aquinas thought that the planetary spirits might be honoured with a lower kind of veneration (*dulia*) such as is given to the saints, but not of course given the worship (*latria*) which is due to God alone.

The Franciscan monk, Roger Bacon (1214–1294), pioneer of experimental science, who attacked the frivolous distinctions of the lesser scholastics, stressed the importance of astrology in meterology, chemistry, medicine and agriculture. He asserts[21] that only fatalistic astrology had been condemned by the Church Fathers, and cites passages to prove they accepted the true science.

Peter of Abano (1250–1316?) was a Professor of Astrology at Padua. He wrote on philosophy and medicine, and introduced the idea of periodicity in history. At one time he was friendly with the Pope, but somehow got into trouble with the Inquisition. He was accused of heresy and black magic, but died whilst awaiting trial. His bones were burned after his death.[22]

Duns Scotus (1265–1308) was another scholastic who was drawn into the theological conflict (hence the appellation *dunce*, first applied to his followers by opponents). He was nevertheless an upholder of astrology, and of orthodoxy.

Thomas Bradwardine (1290–1349), Archbishop of Canterbury and mathematician, after attacking deterministic astrology, defends the true science. He upholds its value. He even claims, on the strength of the Pharisees and Sadducees asking Jesus for a sign from heaven (*Matt.* xvi, 1) that Christ approved of general astrological predictions, although this seems to apply to meteorological signs, and soon

20 Wedel: *loc cit.*

21 *Opus Majus*, quoted by Wedel, *loc cit.*

22 This is the usual account; Thorndike, *loc. cit.*, however, says after a trial he was not menaced by the Inquisition.

after Jesus says a sign shall not be given, but that of Jonas (*Matt.* xvi, 4).

For proof that nearly all Church writers in the Middle Ages accepted non-deterministic astrology, and that many practised it, reference should be made to the vast researches of Thorndike.[23]

House Divisions. We have seen that the houses of the horoscope are obtained by dividing the four quarters or quadrants of the heavens formed by ascendant, *imum coeli*, descendant and *medium coeli*. There are three principal methods that have been used in dividing, named after the astrologer who introduced the method as follows :

1. Placidus de Titis (17th century), an Olivetine monk[24] has been the most popular and his method is the one most used in recent times.[25] It is also called the semi-arc system. A *semi-arc* (*S.A.*) is defined as half the time (converted into degrees and ·minutes of space) that a planet remains above or below the horizon. The · diurnal S.A. is the time above, the nocturnal S.A. the time below. One-third of the S.A. is the extent of each house for that planet.[26]

2. Johannes Campanus (13th century) Italian mathematician. This method depends on the following. Imagine a great circle passing through the zenith (the point immediately overhead) and at right angles to the meridian. This circle and the meridian cut the sphere into four quadrants. These quadrants are each divided into three by circles intersecting at North and South points of the horizon. The cusps (=beginning points) of the houses are the degrees of the ecliptic cut by these circles.

3. Regiomontanus (Johann Müller, 1436–1476), Professor óf Astrology, noted for his *Ephemerides* and for helping Pope Sixtus IV to reform the calendar. Here the quadrant to be divided is that between the horizon and the meridian. The three-fold division is made by circles intersecting at the North and South points of the horizon. The cusps of the houses are the degrees of the ecliptic cut

[23] *Loc cit.*

[24] His great work *Physiomathematica* bears the *imprimatur* of several Church authorities.

[25] Raphael's *Table of Houses for Great Britain*, London, 1914, and *Table of Houses for Northern Latitudes*, London, 1933.

[26] Maurice Wemyss in his *The Wheel of Life*, Vol. I (not dated but *circa* 1930) points out that the Placidus method introduces a different principle for determining the cusps of houses, in relation to the *medium coeli*, from that used in determining the ascendant. He prefers the Campanus system and gives the table of houses (i) for London and (ii) for New York according to that system.

by these circles.[27] This system was also used by many including the English astrologer Lilly (see later).

The houses played an important part in the horoscope according to the signs on their cusps and the planets and signs within them :

I. The First House, the cusp of which was the ascendant, had a profound effect on the native (the individual subject of the horoscope). It ruled his personal appearance, his bodily characteristics, his outlook, in short it had to do with everything intimately connected with the native himself.

II. The Second House rules possessions, wealth, money and the treasures of the earth.

III. The Third House rules brothers and sisters, more distant contemporary relatives, neighbours, also short journeys, letters, writings, papers, newspapers and journals.

IV. The Fourth House rules the mother, the home, childhood, the grave, old age, houses and land, mines and underground places and the womb and prenatal life.

V. The Fifth House rules pleasure, courtship, holidays, amusements, theatres, games, children, schools and education.

VI. The Sixth House rules nutrition, health and disease, food and clothing, small animals, maternal aunts and uncles, servants and employees.

VII. The Seventh House rules marriage, the marriage partner (wife or husband), all partnerships, contracts, competition and open enemies.

VIII. The Eighth House rules death, loss, destruction or decay, also wills, legacies and bequests and the financial affairs of the marriage partner.

IX. The Ninth House rules religion, the Church, the priesthood, the Law and the legal profession, long journeys, books and long writings.

X. The Tenth House rules the native's position in the world, fame, honour and credit, also the father, occupation or profession, employers and employment.

XI. The Eleventh House rules friends, acquaintances, companions, associates and fraternal organisations.

XII. The Twelfth House rules prisons, hospitals, and asylums. It has to do with sin, suffering, penitence, confinement and exile, and also rules paternal uncles and aunts.

[27] The Regiomontanus System is given in *Zenit: Sonderheft 3, Häusertafeln nach rationaler Manier* (Regiomontanus), by Dr. Walter Koch, Düsseldorf, 1932.

Each house corresponds with one sign of the zodiac, beginning with the first which corresponds with Aries.

Renaissance Astrologers. The Renaissance witnessed a great revival of classical learning, with the development of some degree of scepticism. There were attacks upon astrology and other things almost universally accepted hitherto. Rolle de Hampole (1290–1349) an English hermit, disagreed with many of the claims of the Pope, with the subtleties of the scholastic philosophy and with astrology. Wycliffe (1320–1384), who rejected almost all Catholic beliefs, in his later works opposes the study of all law, grammar, logic and science and maintained the literal interpretation of Scripture. It need hardly be said he was among the most bitter opponents of astrology. Long after his death (from a stroke) his views were condemned by the Council of Constance 1415 and his body was disinterred, burned, and the ashes thrown into the River Swift.

Nicole Oresme (1330–1382) an orthodox prelate (Bishöp of Lisieux 1377) was noted as the translator of various classical works and was also an opponent of astrology. Henry of Hesse (d. 1397) another theologian also attacked the science.

There were, however, strong supporters of astrology. John of Saxony (14th century) turned upon the attackers and classified them into eleven sects, including one which maintains astrology is contrary to the Christian Faith.

A curious case was that of Cecco d'Ascoli (1257–1327) (Francesco degli Stabili) who was burnt at the stake at Florence in 1327. He had been Professor of Astrology in the University of Bologna. He did not deny the freedom of the human will, and Thorndike[28] is unable to state why he was condemned and thinks personal motives may have played a part. On the other hand necromancy has been mentioned as one of the charges by Wedel.[29] Cecco d'Ascoli wrote on astronomy and astrology and also composed an encyclopaedic poem *L'Acerba* attacking Dante's *Divina Commedia*. Dante (1265–1321) himself was a great believer in astrology.

Boccaccio (1313–1375) was also a supporter of astrology, but Petrarch (1304–1374) attacked both astrologers and physicians. Wedel[30] points out that Petrarch was living at the court of the Visconti at Milan and was well acquainted with their quackery. Curiously enough Petrarch himself was accused of magic (which he

[28] *Loc. cit.*
[29] *Loc. cit.*
[30] *Loc. cit.*

heartily condemned) because he was a great reader of Virgil. And to the popular mind, in those days, Virgil was chiefly known for his reputation as a magician!

Ruysbroeck (1293–1381), Flemish mystical theologian, called "the Ecstatic Doctor," was a believer in astrology.

Chaucer (1340–1400) wrote on the astrolabe, and John de Murs (14th century) built a giant astrolabe, some 15 feet in diameter.[31]

The Black Death, a terrible pandemic in 1345 was said to have been predicted by astrologers on the strength of a conjunction of Mars, Jupiter and Saturn in that year.[32]

By this time the Dragon's Head and the Dragon's Tail had come into general use in astrology. They probably come from India or China, where they are regarded as shadow planets, causing eclipses. They are set in the horoscope at the moon's nodes, and are permanently in opposition to one another. They are discussed by a 14th century astrologer calling himself Perscrutator.

The Emperor Charles IV (r. 1347–1378) was a great believer in astrology, and always had several astrologers at his court.

Cardinal Peter d'Ailly (1350–1420), nicknamed "Hammer of Heretics," who presided over the Council of Constance 1414–1418 (which condemned Huss) wrote many treatises on astrology. His geography *Imago Mundi*, 1410, was closely studied by Christopher Columbus before undertaking the journey which led to the discovery of America. D'Ailly helped the Pope to correct the calendar. He rejected what he termed superstitious astrology, *i.e.* that which denies free-will, or is associated in any way with black magic. The fact that such superstitious astrology does exist, he thought, does not invalidate the true science.

The learned Gerson (1362–1428), Chancellor of the University of Paris, was a pupil of D'Ailly. He wrote against superstitious astrology, in favour of the true science in his *Astrology Theologised* and attempted to show, in his *Examination of Spirits* how to distinguish true revelations from false. He included the use of astrological images in superstitious astrology, as with them, he thought, demons are active.

The 15th-century humanists, like Poggio Bracciolini (1380–1459) and Politian (1454–1494) believed in astrology. So did Cardinal Nicholas of Cusa (1401–1464) who anticipated the heliocentric theory of the solar system afterwards brought forward by Coper-

[31] Made known by Thorndike, *loc. cit.,* who says it was unnoticed by those who praised Tycho Brahe for his 6 foot 9 inches device.
[32] Trithemius: *Chronicon Hirsaugiense,* quoted by Thorndike, *loc. cit.*

nicus. It is true that he made disparaging remarks about certain astrologers, but he himself was engaged in applying the astrological idea of jubilees to Old Testament history, and with a view to predicting the coming of Antichrist, which he calculated for 1734.

Many astrological predictions were made between 1405 and 1435, to which Thorndike devotes a whole chapter in his large book.[33] Astrology was much practised by the friars in the later Middle Ages and they also had almost a monopoly of posts in the Inquisition. In the 15th century astrology had the approval of Popes Nicholas V (r. 1447–1455), Pius II (r. 1458–1464), Sixtus IV (r. 1471–1484) and Alexander VI (r. 1492–1503). It also interested King Henry VII[34] of England (r. 1485–1509).

Printing was introduced in the West in 1440 and greatly helped to spread information of all kinds. It particularly helped to spread astrological knowledge, as rudiments thereof were included in almanacs and calendars, which now began to appear. One of the earliest was the Shepheard's Kalendar, first printed in French in 1493, which, translated into English, appeared in 1506. In the 15th century both agriculture, and also medicine and surgery were completely bound up with astrology. No farmer would plant, no surgeon would operate, without consulting a calendar to ascertain a favourable position of sun, moon and planets.

From the 14th to the 16th century the wealthy banking and trading family called Medici ruled in Florence and Tuscany and became famous for encouraging the arts and learning. Cosimo de Medici, the elder (1389–1464) employed the Platonist Ficino to translate into Latin the works of Plato and the Neo-Platonists. Lorenzo de Medici, known as the Magnificent (1449–1492), lived a life of pleasure, devoted to music, astrology and necromancy. He was fond of festivals, and in one procession he arranged to have the seven planets personified. The University of Pisa was established by Lorenzo 1472–1473. At first there was no provision for teaching astrology, but students asked for it, and the Dominican theologian Pagagnotti was appointed to teach this subject.[35]

The power of the Medicis was challenged for a time by the miserable Savonarola (1452–1498). He drove Cosimo's son Pietro from power in Florence in 1494, but was soon himself brought low, excommunicated, imprisoned, tortured and hanged. Savonarola

[33] *Loc cit.*
[34] This was discovered by Thorndike from MSS. See his great work, *loc. cit.*
[35] Thorndike: *loc. cit.*

preached against all sorts of things which he regarded as corruptions, including astrology. Professor Pagagnotti replied. Later Pagagnotti was made a bishop in France.

The aforementioned Marsilio Ficino (1433–1499) is a good example of the Renaissance astrologer, highly cultivated and sophisticated. He was also a musician, performed on the lyre and was an accomplished singer. He was expert on the history of harmony, as exhibited in ancient days by David the psalmist, by Orpheus, Pythagoras (music of the spheres) and Plato. The priesthood of the ancient Persians, Egyptians and Chaldeans he pointed out was astrological, and the Magi who visited the infant Jesus were astrologers. Ficino accepted non-deterministic astrology on the grounds of the analogy of man to the world (doctrine of the microcosm corresponding with the macrocosm). One can, however, he believed, alter cosmic influences by magical means.

Count Giovanni Pico de Mirandola (1463–1494) was a protégé of Lorenzo de Medici and Ficino. Whilst very young he mastered Arabic and Hebrew, and acquired a considerable knowledge of the Holy Kabalah. He appeared in Rome in 1486 and publicly posted a list of some 900 theses dealing with logic, ethics, mathematics, physics, kabalism and theology which he proposed to defend, in public debate, against all comers. He was accused of heresy, but afterwards recanted. He fiercely opposed astrology. The astrologers predicted for him an early death, and he is said[36] to have died at the exact hour which the astrologers said would be fatal to him.

The Dominican Giovanni Nanni (Nannius 1432–1502) was an astrological writer of some interest, as he attempted to reconcile cosmic events with Scriptural history.

Many astrological predictions are extant in the 15th, 16th and 17th centuries. Astrology as such was taught in the universities, and many medical men concerned themselves with it.

The Reformation and the Heliocentric System. These two important movements in human thought had an adverse effect on astrology. They did not, it is true, cause the immediate disappearance of the science from the universities, but they have undoubtedly been a factor, even in Catholic countries. Thorndike,[37] speaking of the time before the Reformation says that "well certified instances of condemnations of astrologers as such by Christian authorities are exceedingly rare."

[36] C. Aq. Libra: *Astrology, its Technics and Ethics.* Trans. from the Dutch, Amersfoort, The Netherlands, 1917.   [37] *Loc. cit.*

The Reformation is usually dated from 1517, when Martin Luther (1483–1546) nailed his ninety-five theses to the church door in Wittenberg, Germany. The reformers were mostly averse to astrology. A notable exception was P. Melanchthon (1497–1560), who believed in astrology. He was one of the more moderate party, and even tried to reconcile Catholics and Protestants. Among the opponents of the reformers was Conrad Wimpira of Buchen (1465–1531), a poet, who believed in astrology.

The 16th century was a curious one. It produced great writers on the occult, like Trithemius (1462–1516), Paracelsus (1493–1541), Agrippa (1486–1535), Cardan (1501–1576), Nostradamus (1503–1566), Dee (1527–1608) and Della Porta (1538–1615). On the other hand it produced sceptics like Pomponazzi (1462–1525), Calvin (1509–1564), John Knox (1505–1572) and Erasmus (1524–1583). The last-named wrote an attack on astrology, and occult science, especially that of Paracelsus.

Paul of Middleburg (d. 1533) who was prominent at the Lateran Council 1512–1517 in connection with calendar reform, was an astrologer who issued predictions. He was Bishop of Fossombrone and in the last year of his life was called to Rome to be made a cardinal.

It was Pope Gregory XIII who finally corrected the calendar, in 1582. The new system only slowly penetrated Protestant countries. It was adopted in England in 1751.

Some Later Astrologers. Two very important books were published in the 16th century. One was the *Matheseos,* in eight books, published in 1551, and alleged to be by the 4th century Julius Firmius Maternus. The other was *Speculum Astrologiae* by Junctin de Florence, published in 1581. The author was a doctor of theology and almoner to Francois de Valois, the younger brother of Henry III of France.[38] Eminent believers in astrology in this century included Catherine de Medici (1519–1589) a daughter of Lorenzo the Magnificent, described as an adept in the art, and the Emperor Charles V (1519–1556). Thomas Linacre (1460–1524) famous in the history of medicine and, in later life O. Brunfels, the botanist, were believers in astrology.

About this time some attention was given to comets, new stars and chasms. Attempts were made to ascertain their supposed effects by noting their position, especially in relation to the signs of the zodiac. A new star appeared in Cassiopeia in 1572 which was

[38] A. E. Waite: *The Occult Sciences,* London, 1891.

brighter than any other heavenly body, except the sun, moon and Venus. This and other phenomena led to the expectation of the End of the World. Chasms are celestial lights which were interpreted by the ancients as openings or breaks in the firmament.[39]

In the first part of the 16th century many of the Popes expressed approbation of astrology. Julius II (r. 1503–1513), Leo X (r. 1513–1521), Adrian VI (r. 1522–1523) and Paul III (r. 1534–1549) were all very favourable. Pius V (r. 1566–1572), who has been canonised as a saint, warmly approved the worship of the seven planetary spirits.[40] But orthodoxy could never tolerate predictions of events, especially of the dates of death. The Council of Trent (1545–1563) strictly rules out astrological prediction, but say astrology may be used in agriculture, navigation and medicine. Pope Sixtus V (r. 1572–1585) issued a bull directed in the main against political predictions. Henry III, King of France, promulgated a decree, in 1579, forbidding makers of almanacs to prophesy, directly or indirectly, about the affairs of the state or of individuals. Under James I, King of England and Scotland, a law of 1607 forbade almanac writers to exceed the limits of allowable astrology, and imposes on the archbishop and bishops, or their agents, the duty of censoring such publications.[41]

Whilst laws were being passed to control the aberrations of astrology, science was moving in a direction which tended to undermine it, or more correctly, to make it more difficult to understand its basis. Nicolaus Copernicus (1473–1543), a lay canon and physician at Frauenberg, Prussian Poland, lectured at Rome in 1500, on astronomy. Soon thereafter he began to talk about the planets revolving around the sun (*the heliocentric theory*) instead of the earth being the centre around which the planets circled (*the geocentric theory*) as always taught since Ptolemy. It became obvious that the new theory would immensely simplify the planetary movements. It is the most adequate for treating purely astronomical problems in our solar system. For astrology, however, the geocentric positions are needed, which define the relations of the planets to earth and man. Both systems are valid for their particular purpose. It is incorrect to assert that the heliocentric theory is true and the

[39] D. H. Menzel (Prof. Physics, Harvard) in his sceptical book *Flying Saucers*, Cambridge, U.S.A., 1953. He says they were mentioned by Pliny, Seneca and Aristotle.

[40] References in Blavatsky, *loc. sit.* See also W. B. Crow: Astronomical Religion, *Mysteries of the Ancients* 6, London, 1942.

[41] John Timbs: *Predictions realised in Modern Times*, London, 1880.

geocentric false. They are only frames of reference for different purposes.[42]

Copernicus was urged, both by Catholics and Protestants,[43] to publish his novel views. Eventually in 1543 his *Revolution of the Heavenly Bodies* appeared. Copernicus lived to see its publication, but died very shortly afterwards. There is no evidence that he was persecuted in any way.

Galileo (1564–1642) was Professor of Mathematics at Padua and later at Florence. He was among the first to use a telescope. He discovered the four largest satellites of Jupiter, thus opening up a new class of celestial objects. He upheld the heliocentric theory. But he went much further than this. He denied the importance of the earth and man, and may be regarded as the founder of *materialism*, for he said that tastes, odours, colours and feelings are nothing but pure names, and are not real qualities, the whole world consisting of nothing but masses, shapes and sizes, moving in space and time. He was brought before the Inquisition, and forced to retract his views. He is generally pictured as a martyr to science, but it was his materialistic conclusions rather than the heliocentric system which was objected to. He was allowed to retire, and he became blind five years before he died.

Tycho Brahe (1546–1601) was another famous astronomer. But he was equally noted for his astrology, and cast horoscopes for Frederick II, King of Denmark and Norway. The latter was his patron and allowed him to build an Institute and Observatory, which he called Uraniborg, on an island in the Sound, not far from Elsinore. He rejected the Copernican system, believed the planets revolved around the sun, and the latter around the earth. He was the discoverer of the new star of 1572. He was also interested in science and medicine. He occupies an unrivalled position in the history of prosthetics. For in early life he lost a great part of his nose in a duel, and he reconstructed the missing part in an alloy of gold and silver, and constantly wore it. Like Paracelsus he held that the planets are represented in man, the sun in man's heart, the moon in his brain, Mercury in the lungs, Venus in the kidneys, Mars in the gall-bladder, Jupiter in the liver and Saturn in the spleen.

When his patron died in 1588 Tycho Brahe lost his subsidy and

---

[42] W. B. Crow: *Proteus*, Third Series, No. 9, Vol. 1, Nov. 1957. It is also incorrect to call the sun a centre, except for calculations. The sun is moving like everything else.

[43] Thorndike, *loc. cit.*

soon after his pension, and he left Uraniborg, which had become an important centre for astronomical studies, and retired to Prague, where he died. He was not a determinist.

Johannes Kepler (1571–1630) was at first assistant and afterwards successor to Tycho Brahe at Prague. He accepted the Copernican theory and discovered and published the three laws of planetary movement (two in 1609, the other in 1619). He also worked on optics and mathematics. At one time he made a living by casting horoscopes, but was genuinely interested in astrology and occult science. He was forever seeking revelations between the planetary orbits, and apart from the physical laws which he discovered he evolved a peculiar analogical relation between the planets and the five Platonic bodies in solid geometry. There are only five regular solid bodies, *i.e.* having equal sides and equal angles (cube, tetrahedron, dodecahedron, icosahedron and octahedron). There are five spaces between the six planets (Mercury, Venus, Earth, Mars, Jupiter and Saturn) in the heliocentric system. Kepler thought if these be fitted between spheres, each sphere carrying a planet, the correct distances of the orbits would be defined. In fact the errors of this system are very great. However Kepler was particularly satisfied with this system, as it places the earth, the home of man in God's image, between the two classes of these solids, primary (cube, tetrahedron and dodecahedron) and secondary (icosahedron and octahedron). It thus had a religious significance.[44] He also, following Greek philosophy, assigned the five bodies to the elements, and tried to find a reason for it.

The tetrahedron has four triangular faces, four points or vertices, six edges. Of all the five solids it has the smallest volume in proportion to its surface, and hence Kepler thought it corresponded with fire. It was supposed to occupy the space between the spheres of Jupiter and Mars.

The cube has six square faces, eight vertices, twelve edges. Its shape suggested stability, and hence it was assigned to earth. It was believed by Kepler to occupy the space between the spheres of Saturn and Jupiter.

The octahedron has eight triangular faces, six vertices and twelve edges. It rotates freely when held by two opposite edges, and this mobile character led to it being assigned to the element air. It was supposed by Kepler to occupy the space between the spheres of Venus and Mercury.

[44] C. Singer: Historical Relations of Religion and Science, in *Science, Religion and Reality,* ed. J. Needham, London, 1925.

The icosahedron has twenty triangular faces, twelve vertices and thirty edges. As it has the largest volume in proportion to its surface it was assigned by Kepler to the element water. It was supposed to occupy the space between the spheres of Earth and Venus.

The dodecahedron has twelve pentagonal faces, twenty vertices and thirty edges. It lies between the spheres of Earth and Mars. Whilst the other four signify the four elements, this represents the heavens or the universe. It is unique in possessing pentagonal faces, and if we take a pentagon and continue its sides we get the *pentacle*, a figure much used in magic. Moreover the sides of the pentacle are divided by the angles of the pentagon in the proportion of the *Golden Section*. The latter is a line so divided that the proportion of the lesser part is to the greater part the same as the proportion of the greater part to the whole. This ratio is supposed to occur in nature[45] and plays a very important part in occult speculations about the universe.

Kepler published these speculations on the spheres and Platonic solids in an early work entitled *Mysterium Cosmographicum* 1596. But apparently he valued them to the end of his life. His better known works were *Astronomia Nova* 1609 and *Harmonica Mundi* 1619 in which his astronomical laws were enunciated. But he took astrology seriously. He published calendars, and discovered new aspects. He is credited[46] with introducing the Vigintile 18°, Quindecile 24°, Decile 36°, Quintile 72° Tredecile 108° and Biquintile 144°, as new aspects.

The Final Phase. Although scepticism was growing the 17th century was still rich in astrologers, and those that believed in the science. Astrology still formed part of culture. There are many allusions to astrology in Shakespeare (1564–1616). Francis Bacon (1561–1626) accepted astrology, but thought it should be expurgated.

D. Fabricius (1564–1617) an astronomer who first described a variable star (the famous *Mira Ceti*) refused to accept the Copernican system. His son J. Fabricus (1587–1615) discovered sun spots, which caused a good deal of discussion at the time, as they were regarded as a blemish on the sun's disc.

A. F. de Bonattis published his *Universa Astrosophia Naturalis*

45 See W. B. Crow: *A Synopsis of Biology,* Bristol, 1960, 2nd. ed., 1964.
46 V. E. Robson: *A Student's Text-Book of Astrology,* 3rd. ed., London, 1925.

at Patavia, 1617, and gave a new method of astrological direction.[47]

Among eminent men interested in astrology in the earlier part of the 17th century were the famous general Albrecht von Wallenstein (1583–1634) and Cardinal Richelieu (1585–1642), the latter of whom employed the astrologer Morinus.

Nicholas Culpeper (1616–1654) a puritan who published an English translation of the *Pharmacopoeia* 1649, 1654 and a *Herbal* 1653 practised physic and astrology in London. The Herbal gives the astrological rulership as well as the supposed uses of many plants and has often been reprinted.

Valentin Weigel (Weigelius) published his *Astrology Theologised* in 1649. William Lilly (1602–1681) published annual almanacs, and *Christian Astrology* 1649. He was ridiculed by Samuel Butler in the latter's *Hudibras* (1663–1678). Lilly was a practitioner of astrology, the divining rod and of planetary magic. He predicted the Great Plague and the Great Fire of London, and was summoned before Parliament to see if he could throw light on the cause of the fire. Henry Coley became the adopted son of Lilly, and after the latter's death continued the almanac.

J. Gadbury (1627–1704) was another contemporary astrologer, much mixed up with the political plots of his day. J. Heydon (1629–*circa* 1685) was an astrologer and writer on Rosicrucian and Kabalistic subjects. He married Culpeper's widow. John Bishop's *The Marrow of Astrology* was published in 1688, with comments by Coley. The works of Sir George Wharton on astrological matters were published posthumously in 1683, edited by Gadbury.

Finally it may be mentioned that, although their works are important for modern mathematics and science, both Leibniz (1646–1716) and Newton (1642–1727) believed in astrology. Halley (1656–1742) the astronomer best known for the comet named after him, was another adherent of the science.

Astrology was still being taught in the University of Ceylon as late as 1959 according to press reports, which stated that attempts were being made to put an end to the teaching of this subject.

[47] Described by Sepharial in his *Science of Foreknowledge*, London, 1918.

CHAPTER XXIV

MEDIAEVAL AND RENAISSANCE ALCHEMY

Origin and Antecedents. The occult science of Alchemy bears much the same relation to Chemistry that Astrology does to Astronomy. It is not, as was thought in the Victorian epoch, the early strivings towards chemical science, although alchemists did make chemical discoveries. In the Middle Ages and earlier it seemed inconceivable that anyone should want to study the pure science of matter, Chemistry. The latter was only the means to an end. Alchemy was not a pure science. It was applied to human ends.

Alchemy had three main objects :

1. The transmutation of the base metals into gold, or more generally the conversion of abundant relatively useless material into rare useful substances. The transmutation into gold was generally believed to be possible provided one could discover the *Philosopher's Stone,* which was to be agent of the transformation. Sometimes instead of a stone, a red or brown powder (*powder of Projection*) was used.

2. The prolongation of life indefinitely, or more generally the cure of all disease and senility. This was to be effected by an agent, generally thought of as a liquid, called the *Elixir of Life.*

3. The creation of a human being from non-living chemical materials, such an artificial man being called the *android* or *homunculus*; or in more general terms to create living things from non-living.

It is interesting to note that modern science has to some extent achieved what the alchemists were trying to do. The transmutation of the elements is now effected, and it is even possible to produce gold, although it is not worth while to do so from a commercial point of view. Life has been prolonged to some degree by the discovery of the functions of vitamins and hormones, and the rôle of mineral salts. The artificial synthesis of living things (although only of ultramicroscopic viruses) has been effected from complex chemicals.

However the alchemists did not work along the lines of modern science. They constantly reiterated the need for prayer and religious devotion as affecting the work. The psychologist C. G. Jung after finding alchemical symbols in dreams, propounded the theory[1] that unconscious psychic factors entered into the work. The alchemist, according to this theory, was not only doing chemical experiments, but was undergoing his own psychological development at the same time. This theory would explain why it is difficult at times to understand whether an alchemical writer is describing actual chemical changes, or whether his account is purely symbolic. Some religious writers, too, like Boehme, express themselves in alchemical terms, but are obviously trying to describe spiritual development. Even among alchemists psychological states, like sin, suffering, sadness and joy are curiously mixed with conditions of matter. And just as in astrology planetary positions are reflected in psychological states, so in alchemy chemical changes are bound up with and correspond with such states.

We have seen that alchemy was practised in ancient Egypt and among the Taoists of China. It is from the former that alchemy takes it rise in the West, and Hermes Trismegistus was regarded as the chief founder of the science. Imaginative writers made Moses into an alchemist because the way he dealt with the golden calf (*Exodus* xxxii, 20) implies a knowledge of the subject. Cleopatra was obviously an alchemist, for she dissolved a pearl in wine. As she was an Egyptian she was reputed to have met Ostanes. Democritus[2] was an alchemist, for he wrote a book dealing with the preparation of gold, silver, gems and the purple dye. He invokes Ostanes from Hades in this work, so Ostanes must have been, they guessed, his master. The Emperor Caligula must have been an alchemist, for did not Pliny say that he made gold from orpiment?

In the Middle Ages works were in circulation which were obviously mediaeval productions but bore the names of some of these ancient authors (Moses, Cleopatra, etc.). Moreover the alchemists used classical symbols very freely. The Quest of the Golden Fleece for example was obviously a symbol of alchemical work.

Early Alchemists. The first genuine alchemical work that is at all well known is that of Zosimus of Panopolis, Egypt in the 3rd

[1] *Psychology and Alchemy.* Collected Works Vol. 12, trans., London 1952 (original German 1944).

[2] Democritus of Abdera, "the greatest of Greek physical philosophers" (Lempriere, ed. Wright: *Classical Dict.*, London, 1948) was said by Seneca to have prepared artificial emeralds and other gems, dissolved stones and softened ivory.

century A.D. He claims that alchemy was the divine art of the priest-kings and priests of Egypt, and they kept it secret. In his days Egypt was a Roman province.

Synesius, Bishop of Ptolemais 401 onwards, was apparently a real writer on alchemy and on dreams, and expressed his belief in re-incarnation. But a later treatise is probably apocryphal. Olympio-dorus who also flourished in the East in the 5th century has been credited with a work on alchemy mentioning Mary the Jewess and Synesius as authorities. Aeneas of Gaza, who wrote about 480, had a work on *Theophrastus*, dealing with immortality and resurrec-tion. He followed the Platonic philosophy, became a Christian in 485, and has several references to what appear to be alchemical processes.

Stephanus of Alexandria wrote on alchemy,[3] in the sense that he is talking about wonderful plants and minerals, and their transfor-mations, but does not seem to have carried out experiments. He was prominent at the court of the Byzantine Emperor Heraclius (*d.* 641) who was a great patron of learning. Archelaus another writer (*c.* 715) also uses alchemical imagery, but it is obvious that his theme is theological.

In the works ascribed to Geber or Jabir "Arabian Prince and Philosopher", however, practical experiments predominate. Geber lived about 721–776, but his supposed works did not become known until the 14th century, and although of Arabic origin may have been written by his followers. Some parts claim to be based on Apollonius of Tyana. They contain a certain amount of sound chemical infor-mation, they propound the theory that metals are formed by the union of sulphur and mercury, although by this he did not mean the substances now called sulphur and mercury. The sulphur in fact was the spiritual bearer of the hot and dry nature, the mercury of the cold and moist. The natures also combine with matter to form the four elements (fire, hot and dry; air, hot and moist; water, cold and moist; and earth, cold and dry). This theory was much favoured in the Middle Ages. Geber certainly claimed to effect the making of gold, without the aid of any supernatural agency. The planets, however, were supposed to influence the formation of metals in the earth.

Among earlier believers in alchemy Pope Leo III (*r.* 795–816) is counted. He was the pope who crowned Charlemagne as emperor, and he is said to have delivered to the latter an *Enchiridion*,[4] or

---

3 Trans. Sherwood Taylor, with commentaries.
4 Printed at Rome 1523 and 1606.

magical treatise. There are records of a letter from Charlemagne testifying to the power of this *Enchiridion* in warding off dangers from man and beast. Another believer in alchemy is said to have been Nicephorus, Patriarch of Constantinople (r. 806–815) who was a great opponent of the iconoclasts of his day.

Rhazes (850–923) was an Islamic physician, born in Persia. He wrote on many subjects, but much on alchemy and medicine. Unlike most alchemists, his descriptions are quite clear. His apparatus included many things, such as athanors (furnaces), alembics (stills), pestles and mortars, which were in constant use among mediaeval alchemists. He had a large collection of materials, and classed them in six classes : spirits, metals, stones, vitriols, boraxes and salts. The processes he describes, such as solution, evaporation, crystallisation, distillation and calcination are more easily understood by the modern chemist than those mentioned by later mediaeval alchemists. He believed in transmutation and interested the Emir Almansour, ruler of Khorasan, his native province, in the process. The Emir spent a lot of money. on equipment for Rhazes to perform gold-making. Unfortunately the alchemist failed to produce the precious metal. He was belaboured on the head with one of his own books, and afterwards suffered from blindness said to have been caused by this treatment. He died in great poverty.[5]

Several of the learned Arabic writers, who influenced the culture of the Middle Ages so much, wrote on Alchemy.[6] Avicenna (980–1037) studied alchemy, wrote on alchemical theory much as did Rhazes, but disclaims that he or anyone else could make gold. What they do make, he says, appears to be gold, but is spurious. Alfarabius (870–950) who is supposed to have influenced the scientific views of Avicenna, made a number of physical discoveries, including the fact that sound is connected with air vibrations. But he wrote on everything and had a remarkable knowledge of languages. Al Majrati (Maslama ibn Ahmad) wrote on the planisphere and the astrolabe as well as an alchemical work. Mohammed ibn Umail wrote alchemical works with curious titles translated as *The Silvery Water and the Starry Earth* and *Epistle of the Sun to the Crescent Moon*. Latin translations of these works were current in the Middle Ages but not much is known of the author. Both the last named authors flourished under the Spanish Caliphate of Al-Hakam II (961–976). At the end of the 10th century, also, Abu Mansur

[5] L. Spence: *An Encyclopaedia of Occultism*, London, 1920.
[6] The word Alchemy itself is of Arabic origin.

Muwaffah, a Persian, made many chemical discoveries. He distinguished between sodium carbonate (natron) and potassium carbonate, and he knew arsenic and antimony, although only in their compounds. He alludes to the use, in surgery, of a plaster composed of white of egg to which heated gypsum had been added.[7]

St. Dunstan (910–988) who was successively Abbot of Glastonbury, Bishop of Worcester, Bishop of London and Archbishop of Canterbury, one of the most powerful men of his day was popularly supposed to practise black magic. He no doubt carried out many chemical experiments. According to a legend the devil appeared to him one day whilst he was doing goldsmith's work. The saint happened to have a pair of iron tongs with their working ends in the fire, with these he seized the devil by the nose and held him for some time whilst he roared and cried. Gerbert, Pope Sylvester II (940–1003), as we have seen, was alleged to practise magic, and is also reckoned among the alchemists.

Curious Alchemical Works. Robert of Chester (11th century) was instrumental in translating the *Koran* into Latin, and the *Algebra* of Al-Khwarizmi, thus introducing a new branch of mathematics to the mediaeval world. He also translated an alchemical work, describing the successful making of gold in the presence of the son of the Caliph Yazid I (*d.* 682). Gerard of Cremona, Lombardy (1114–1187) translated many Arabic works, including those of Avicenna and Rhazes. Geber's works became known in the 12th century. In this way many Arabic terms entered into European treatises for the first time. The Mercury-Sulphur theory of the metals was widely discussed.

Artephius or Artephus is the name of a hermetic philosopher who died in the 12th century. He wrote on the language of birds, on the character of the planets, on the future and on the philosopher's stone. But the most extraordinary was *De Vita Propaganda* which he claims to have written at the age of 1,025 years. Apparently some believed him and identified him with Apollonius of Tyana, a magician born in the 1st century, already mentioned. Cardan said these books were written by a practical joker who wished to impose on credulous partisans of alchemy.[8]

St. Malachy (1094–1148) Irish prelate and friend of St. Bernard, and the aforementioned Michael Scot (1175–1235) are also alleged

[7] C. J. S. Thompson: *The Lure and Romance of Alchemy,* London, Bombay and Sydney, 1932.
[8] Spence: *loc. cit.*

to have studied alchemy. The latter wrote at least two works on alchemy, based on practical experience. He used living plants and animals in his experiments, which appear to have been somewhat grotesque. No doubt these gave him his reputation for black magic. He is mentioned in Boccaccio's *Decameron*. There is no doubt that he believed in transmutation.

Magic and Alchemy. Michael Scot was not the only one combining magic and alchemy. In the 13th century this was common. Pope Honorius III (*r.* 1216–1227) has been credited with interest in alchemy, probably because he was alleged to have been the author of a grimoire, but this is no doubt an error, as we have seen. Grosseteste, Bishop of Lincoln (*d.* 1253), however, seems to have believed in alchemy. St. Thomas Aquinas (1224–1274) thought alchemy a possible, but difficult art. St. Albertus Magnus (1193–1280) thought alchemical transmutation possible, but seems to imply that no one has yet carried out the process correctly. He calls for more knowledge and more systematic research. The order in which the processes concerned in transmutation occur, he thought important. He also describes many other useful chemical processes.

It is in the works of Albertus generally considered spurious that a mixture of alchemy and low magic occurs. These include *De Mirabilibus Mundi* (Marvels of the Universe), *De Secretis Mulierum* (Secrets of Women) and *Experimenta Alberti* (Experiments or Secrets of Albert). At a later date still more debased versions were produced containing nothing but an ill-assorted collection of odd recipes for medical, veterinary and agricultural purposes of the most superstitious variety. Instructions for using evil spirits and creating illusions are among the worst features of these spurious works.

Roger Bacon (1214–1294) was a pioneer of science, and was formerly represented as being persecuted. This is now known, as shown by Thorndike,[9] to be incorrect. Bacon's own account, only discovered as recently as 1897, shows that he was not imprisoned or ill-treated, as formerly thought. He was encouraged in his experiments, and shared his belief in magic with other ecclesiastics of his day. He was mainly a scientist. He knew about magnetism, as did others earlier. He investigated, but did not discover, gunpowder. He predicted suspension bridges, oarless vessels, vehicles self-propelled, flying machines, small machines for raising great weights, machines for drawing men together against their will, pre-

9 *Loc. cit.*

sumably to be used in war, machines for attracting objects, machines for walking on water, or even below it. These machines, he thinks, were made in antiquity and made in his day, except the flying machine, and knowledge of how to make that was possessed by an acquaintance. But on biological matters Bacon seems today more credulous. Animals predict the weather. Animals like snakes he supposed had quite fantastic powers of regeneration if cut up. He apparently takes the great age of Artephus quite seriously. Bacon was popularly supposed to be a black magician, but only by the ignorant or the jester. He figures as such in R. Greene's play *The Honourable History of Friar Bacon and Friar Bungay* 1594 and in *The Famous History of Fryer Bacon* of about the same date.

A number of alchemical works were ascribed to Bl. Raymond Lully (1229–1315). Lully was an occultist, but as it happened he disclaimed any belief in transmutation.

Arnold of Villanova (1235–1313) was acquainted with Lully, but was a firm believer in transmutation. He may have converted Lully to this belief. He discovered the poisonous nature of carbon monoxide and the toxins of decaying meat. He wrote some alchemical works in one of which he compares the process of transmutation with the life, death and resurrection of Christ. He was nevertheless a great experimenter. He was acquainted with bismuth. He was the first to use alcohol for making tinctures. He had some trouble with the Inquisition, for a theological work. After his death his writings were publicly burned. Many tracts ascribed to him are not genuine.

Vincent of Beauvais (*circa* 1190–1264), French Dominican scholar, wrote the *Speculum Majus*, the most complete scientific encyclopaedia of the 13th century. He wrote profusely on plants, animals and gems. He was not an experimenter, but only a compiler. He accepted the possibility of transmutation, the sulphur-mercury theory and believed that metals grow in the earth. His elixir of life he supposed to be a tree.

Some Makers of Gold. Successful and unsuccessful attempts at the making of gold are reported from the 14th century. One of the best known, largely from his own account, is that of Nicholas Flamel (1330–1417). He was born near Paris and spent most of his life in France. In early life he was a scribe, preparing and eventually publishing illuminated and other manuscripts, and writing and deciphering letters for the unlettered wealthy. He married one of his clients. One night he had a dream of a remarkable alchemical manuscript. Some time later he picked up, on a second-hand book-stall, the very manuscript about which, he believed, he had dreamed. It consisted of leaves of thin bark in a copper cover, illustrated with symbolic alchemical coloured plates. The latter depicted (i) a rod with two serpents swallowing one another, (ii) a cross on which a serpent was crucified and (iii) deserts, wherein there were fountains, and a number of serpents. There were numerous illustrations on other pages. The author of the work describes himself as Abraham the Jew, Prince, Priest, Levite, Astrologer and Philosopher. The curse-word *Maranatha* was pronounced against anyone who should cast eyes upon it, unless he were sacrificer or scribe. The text was in Latin, of twenty-one pages, the illustrations on each seventh.

Flamel became obsessed with this work, and pored over it night and day. After a time he sought help of others interested, but no one of his French acquaintances could make anything of it. Finally after some twenty years of unsuccessful brooding and experimentation his wife suggested that he should go to Spain and consult renowned Kabalistic Jews known to be residing there. He set out therefore, as a pilgrim to St. James of Compostella, and then spent nearly a year frequenting synagogues of Spain. There and on his way back he picked up numerous hints. He resumed his experiments with greater vigour than ever. On the 13th February, 1382, he succeeded in making silver. On the 25th April he made gold. Finally he claimed to have made the elixir of life. Some say he lived to the age of 116. He and his wife were reported in India in the 17th century. In 1761 they were at the Opera in Paris.[10] The reader will be interested to hear that Flamel is now dead. His body and tombstone, with other archaeological remains, have been described.[11] He left large bequests. Unfortunately, this pretty story has been interpreted in a different manner. According to Spence[12] Flamel was a money-lender. He acquired great wealth by negotiating loans for the French nobility, some of which involved dealings with Spanish Jews. The alchemical writings were a cover for his usury. If so we can only say he did the job thoroughly, for connoisseurs have studied his works assiduously.

But about this time gold-makers were certainly at work, as evinced by a decretal against them issued by Pope John XXII (r. 1316–1334). In this it is implied that their gold is counterfeit,

---

[10] Holmyard: *loc. cit.* reports this belief.
[11] Holmyard: *loc. cit.*
[12] *Loc. cit.*

and they actually have the temerity to stamp upon base metal the characters of public money. They are to be fined the amount which they have been proved to have counterfeited. Curiously enough an alchemist named John Dastin wrote to the Pope and one of his cardinals, explaining the value of alchemy.

Pope Innocent VI (*r.* 1352–1362) continued the campaign against alchemists and in 1357 imprisoned the alchemist Johannes de Rupecissa, who wrote four books on the subject. But the next Pope, Urban V (*r.* 1362–1370) is reported to have been a supporter of alchemy. Charles V, King of France (*r.* 1364–1380), was a student of alchemy.

Chaucer (1340–1400) deals with alchemy in *Canon Yeoman's Tale* and Gower (1235–1408) alludes to the art in his *Confessio Amantis.*

Very few alchemical works, we are told by Thorndike[13] were printed in the 15th century, the period of the incunabula (early printed works). Two of Geber seem to have been published, and manuscripts were written, which were printed later. These include the works of two English authors : *Compound of Alchemie* by George Ripley (*d. circa* 1490) first printed in 1591 and *The Ordinall of Alchimy* by Thomas Norton (*d. circa* 1480), a poem printed first in Latin translation at Frankfurt-am-Main 1618, then the original in 1652 in a collection of works (*Theatrum Chemicum Britannicum*) edited by Ashmole, founder of the Ashmolean Museum, Oxford.

Ripley's *Compound* is chiefly of interest as describing what he calls twelve gates leading to the discovery of the philosopher's stone. These are of some interest, as they show what processes were used by alchemists of the day. They are described as (i) calcination (heating at high temperatures and thus oxidising), (ii) solution (dissolving), (iii) separation, (iv) conjunction, (v) putrefaction (changing into an inert substance), (vi) congelation (crystallisation), (vii) cibation (absorption), (viii) sublimation (purification by vaporising and allowing the vapour to condense as solid), (ix) fermentation (changing by introducing a "seed," as adding leaven to transform dough), (x) exaltation (purifying), (xi) multiplication, (xii) projection.

Norton tells of another alchemist Thomas Daulton who was brought before King Edward IV, who was interested in alchemy. He told the king that he once had the agent of transmutation, and had made gold with it, but it caused him so much anxiety that he had thrown "the medicine" away. He had not made it himself. The

[13] *Loc. cit.*

king dismissed him, but one of the king's retainers kept Daulton in prison for four years, and even threatened to kill him if he did not reveal the secret, but he either could not, or would not, and he was eventually released and died soon after (*circa* 1470).

Many lost money on alchemical projects in the 15th century. There were many arguments about the legality of alchemical transmutation. There were no doubt many serious students of alchemy, but there were numerous quacks. It was against the charlatans that Henry VII of England (r. 1485–1509) issued a most severe edict. In Scotland the contemporary James IV (r. 1473–1513) interested himself in medicine, surgery, dentistry, alchemy and flying, all from the practical point of view. On the continent alchemists included Cardinal Nicholas of Cusa (1401–1464), Conrad Heingarter (*fl.* 1430) astrologer and physician, and Eck (who isolated oxygen 300 years before its "official" discovery).

Iatro-Chemistry. The abbot Trithemius (1462–1516) wrote on spirits and angels, divination, sorcery and alchemy, and shows himself well acquainted with the practical handling of these matters.

Paracelsus (1493–1541) whose real name was Theophrastus Bombastus von Hohenheim studied under Trithemius and then spent the whole of his life in the acquisition of knowledge and writing about it. He tried to find out about things for himself and had no respect for authorities. He mostly wrote in the vernacular, neglecting the usual Latin. He studied in mountains, mines, in fields and villages and among the poor as well as the rich. He questioned workmen of all kinds and even gypsies and hangmen. He travelled about, practising medicine. The only important post he held was city physician and Professor of Medicine at Basle 1527–1528. During his course of lectures there he had the works Avicenna burnt. He soon quarrelled with the city authorities and left the district. He died under mysterious circumstances at an early age. All the more remarkable, then, are his numerous publications. The complete works of which the medical, scientific and philosophical sections alone comprised fifteen volumes,[14] began to be issued in 1930 under the editorship of Karl Sudhoff (Professor of the History of Medicine in the University of Leipzig 1895–1924). And this does not include the numerous theosophical and theological works.

Paracelsus started a new era in alchemy. His basic idea is that all things in the universe consist of salt, sulphur and philosophical

[14] Reviewed by the present author in *Proteus*, London, 1931–1932.

mercury or azoth which in man appear as the bodily, the emotional and the intellectual factors. All matter, Paracelsus thought, had evolved from one primordial substance, which he calls *iliaster*. This is differentiated by an individualising or organising principle *the archaeus*. Human beings may be born from animals (perhaps an early prevision of the evolution theory). The making of gold and silver, he thought, was possible, although it was not his aim, which was to cure disease. He did state, however, that human beings can be produced, without natural father and mother, and can be grown by the spagyric art. Such a being is the *homunculus*. The details of its production are kept secret by the alchemists. It appears, however, that human sperm is necessary. This is placed in a sealed vessel with the other ingredients and is incubated by heating in horse manure for forty days, by which time a human being is formed, although as yet invisible and without body. Then the arcanum of human blood is added, and the organism is nourished on this for forty weeks. By that time a child is produced with all the characteristics of one born of woman, but much smaller, and requiring much more careful rearing.

The insistence of Paracelsus on establishing theory on actual observation was soon after to be emphasised by Francis, Lord Bacon (1561-1626) in his *Novum Organum* 1620. This was regarded as the substituting of the inductive method of interpreting nature, for the deductive method of Aristotle, which tended to argue from first principles rather than from observations. Hence both Paracelsus and Bacon, though very different, are both regarded as important in establishing the basis on which modern science works.

G. Agricola (1494-1555) was a German mineralogist who laid the foundations of industrial chemistry, in his great work *De re metallica*, 1530. He is said to have discovered bismuth. He described the different colours imparted to flame by different metals, and thus indicated the possibility of flame-tests.[15]

Another chemist of the period, who was not an alchemist, in fact opposed it, was B. Palissy (1510-1589) famous for his ceramic work, who died in the prison of the Bastille to which he had been confined for some religious heresies.

William Gilbert (1540-1603) known for his investigations on the magnet was another scientist of this period.

The famous Dr. John Dee (1527-1608) and his assistant Edward Kelley (1555-1595), best known for their crystal scrying, were

15 Thompson: *loc. cit.*

adepts in all occult arts including alchemy. They travelled about in Europe for some time, and for a while were engaged on a supposed attempt to make gold from iron on the estate of a Polish nobleman, from whom they received immense sums of money, without producing any gold in return. They were later at the court of the Emperor Rudolf II (r. 1576–1612) at Prague, the home at that time of many alchemists and mystics, where the Emperor had a laboratory under the direction of the court physician Dr. Thaddeus von Hayck. The latter was an expert at detecting alchemical fraud, which had now become rife.[16]

Charlatans. Numerous charlatans would endeavour to attract the attention of a wealthy person; when they had done so, obtaining expenses for the work of transmutation (which the alchemist himself could not afford), and finally decamping before the experiment had reached its conclusion. Sometimes a test was required before the alchemist was engaged. These might involve trickery. The most simple was to possess a dagger or even a nail the lower part actually consisting of gold fused on to the upper. The lower part had been painted over by a spirit-soluble paint, to resemble the upper. When the lower end was dipped in spirit the paint was dissolved, and the gold appeared. Another trick was to employ a crucible with a false bottom of wax, beneath which gold was concealed. When heated the wax melted and the gold was revealed. Another was to use a gold amalgam with mercury, which looks silvery, but when the mercury is evaporated the gold appears. This, however, requires considerable heat.

Monarchs and nobles gradually learned to detect these tricks. Death was the penalty in a number of cases, either for running away, or for trickery. There are records of alchemical charlatans being hanged or beheaded, and at least one woman was roasted to death in an iron chair. One "alchemist" was hanged on gilded gallows.

Nevertheless some alchemists appear to have been successful. The Emperor Ferdinand III (r. 1637–1657) is alleged to have obtained some of the philosopher's stone from an alchemist. From the gold thus made, medals, suitably stamped, were coined. This appears to have been a regular practice.[17] Some were even ascribed to Bl. Raymond Lully, although almost certainly fraudulently.

Sometimes alchemical books were written by poets, as works of

[16] See later, p. 260–262.
[17] For an account of such medals see Holmyard: *loc. cit.*

fantasy, it would seem, rather than as scientific productions. Some were full of pictures, some of which have been reproduced in modern times. An example is *Splendor Solis* (Splendour of the Sun) ascribed to one called Solomon Trimosin. The manuscript is in the British Museum, and pictures from it are reproduced by C. J. S. Thompson[18] and E. J. Holmyard.[19] The pictures were supposed to be prepared for the manuscript by Lucas von Leiden (1494–1533) the famous Dutch painter. The whole work was published some few years ago, but not dated, including the twenty-two pictures.

Cornelius Agrippa (1486–1535) himself addicted to magic and occult arts, and believed to have practised alchemy, did not approve of this poetic symbolism. He refers to the green lion, the fugitive stag, the flying eagle, the inflated toad, the crow's head of the black blacker than the black, the seal of Mercury, the mud of Wisdom and other countless absurdities[20] as he calls them. George Fabricius, in a publication dealing with metals issued in Zürich, 1565, and later at Alsted[21] gives an account of a plant with leaves of pure gold.

The Triumphal Chariot of Antimony by Basil Valentine was first published in Latin in 1624, but belongs to an earlier period, and was originally written in High Dutch. Other works by the same author exist. He was said to be a Benedictine monk, but his life is unknown. He appears to have discovered antimony, the name of which is alleged to be derived from its adverse effect on monks.[22] One of his works is described as *Of Natural and Supernatural Things, of the first Tincture, Root and Spirit of Metals and Minerals, how the same are conceived, generated, brought forth, changed and augmented*. Another was called *The Twelve Keys of Philosophy*.

Doctrine of Signatures. This idea was first put forward by Paracelsus. According to it natural objects are stamped with characters which indicate their medical uses. Thus lungwort (*Pulmonaria*) has leaves resembling lung tissue, and is useful for curing lung-diseases. Croll said pepper, because of its crown, represents head

[18] *Loc. cit.*
[19] *Loc. cit.*
[20] C. J. S. Thompson: *The Mystery and Romance of Alchemy and Pharmacy*, London, 1897.
[21] Described by Thorndike, *loc. cit.*
[22] J. H. Pepper: *The Playbook of Metals*, new ed., London, not dated but *circa* 1870.

and brain. Others represent the pathological condition, as lily-of-the valley, with its pendent flowers, suggested the weakness caused by apoplexy. The doctrine of signatures was worked out in great detail by Giambattista della Porta (1538–1615) in his *Phytognomonica* first published at Naples in 1588. Porta in this points out many subtle resemblances between parts of plants, especially their flowers and fruits and the limbs and organs of various animals.

The Final Phase. We include the 17th-century alchemists here, as many were still dominated by the alchemical ideas of the Renaissance. In fact, among some, such ideas persisted more or less through the 18th century.

Alexander Seton (*d.* 1603?) is one of the best known alchemists at the end of the 16th and the beginning of the 17th century. He was a Scot, but wandered over Europe, apparently performing successful transmutation. At the court of the Elector of Saxony (who was inappropriately named Christian II) he was tortured and imprisoned for refusing to give up the secret. He was rescued by Michael Sendivogius (1566–1646) who hoped Seton would teach him the art. Seton gave Sendivogius some of the powder of projection, but not the means of making it. Sendivogius, after the death of Seton, married his widow, published his writings and himself acquired some reputation for transmutation, until the powder was all used up.

A. Libavius (1540–1616) whose chief work was entitled *Alchemia*, 1597, was really a chemist, for he defines alchemy as the art of making magisteries and pure essences from mixed substances.

R. Fludd (1574–1637), a London physician and Rosicrucian carried out alchemical experiments. So did J. B. van Helmont (1577–1644) who invented the word *gas*. His son F. van Helmont (1614–1699) was an early writer on mineralogy, metallurgy and physiology. Both were reputed to have effected transmutation.

A. Kircher (1601–1680), German Jesuit Father, inventor of the magic lantern, did not believe in alchemical transmutation or human predictions in astrology. He accepted, however, the relation of man the microcosm to the universe or macrocosm, and other features of the occult philosophy. He wrote on antiquities, numismatics, inventions, spontaneous generation, plants and animals and earth-structure. He believed there were vast underground reservoirs of water and conduits and even subterranean air-reservoirs. He discredited the Emerald Tablet of Hermes. He wrote a romantic account of journeys to the planets and described their inhabitants.

J. R. Glauber (1604-1668) German physician and chemist, believed in the philosopher's stone and the elixir of life. He wrote on practical alchemy and discovered useful substances. Glauber's salt (hydrated sodium sulphate) is named after him.

J. Gaffarel (1601-1681) French occultist, is best known for a work translated as *Unheard of curiosities concerning the talismanic sculpture of the Persians, the horoscope of the Patriarchs and the reading of the stars*, published at Paris in 1629. He wrote other kabalistic works. According to E. Bosc[23] he left a manuscript entitled, in translation, *Universal History of the Subterranean World, containing the description of the most beautiful caves and of grottos, vaults, caverns and excavations of the earth.*

F. Cesi (1585-1630), a Prince, founder of the Academy of the Lincei (Lynxes), a famous Italian scientific association, wrote *Tabulae Phytosophycae*, which was posthumously published.[24] Starting with the Creator it deals with every aspect of plant life, ending with medicinal uses, all set out in tabulated form.

B. Hopffer (1643-1684) maintained that the chameleon feeds on air, the pyrausta and salamander on fire. A. Cademann wrote on the basilisk and other remarkable creatures in 1659. C. Haenel in 1665 on the phoenix. The latter creature was sometimes used, appropriately enough, as an alchemical symbol, since a substance may disappear during alchemical experimentation, and subsequently reappear.

The Baron de Beausoleil and his wife were great students of minerals in the first half of the 17th century. They travelled from Germany all over Europe with a body of miners prospecting for minerals with the aid of the divining rod. They eventually arrived in France, where they tried to draw the attention of the Government to the mineral wealth of the country. In 1626 the Baron's house was ransacked in a search for magical apparatus. He had written a work in 1617 concerning the first matter of minerals, in which he deals with the metamorphosis of metals. The Baroness wrote a pamphlet in 1640 called (in translation) *The Restitution of Pluto* in which she disclaims the use of magic and the aid of the devil in discovering places for mining. She admitted seeing dwarfs, only three to four palms high in mines in Hungary. Both the Baron and the Baroness died in prison.

[23] *Dictionnaire d'Orientalisme, d'Occultisme et de Psychologie*, Paris, 1894.
[24] Republished, Rome, 1904.

G. F. Borri (1627–1695) attempted to found a new religion, based on alchemy. He had some following in Milan, his native place, and attempted to capture the city but failed. He escaped to Switzerland, then Germany, Holland, Sweden and Denmark, practising as a physician and borrowing money with the object of preparing, as he said, the Elixir of Life. He was brought before the Emperor Leopold I (r. 1658–1705) who was ill, and whom he saved by detecting that he was being poisoned by fumes from poison impregnated candles. He was nevertheless arrested, and made to retract his heresies, which he did before a large crowd. He was then lodged in a castle for the rest of his life, under supervision, but this imprisonment was not very strict, for he was allowed to continue his alchemical researches and to receive distinguished visitors, among whom was the exiled Queen Christina of Sweden who was interested in alchemy.

The Emperor Leopold I and the Emperor Ferdinand III (r. 1637–1657) had alchemists at their courts, and interested themselves in alchemy. One alchemist in Ferdinand's entourage was apparently successful, medals were struck with the gold, and the alchemist, Richthausen, was ennobled under the alchemical title of Baron Chaos. Several other rulers had court alchemists at the time. A medal was also made from gold produced by W. Seyler for Leopold I.

The alchemist H. Brand discovered phosphorus in 1669, and thereafter there were a flood of investigations on luminous substances.

The chemist Helvetius (J. F. Schweitzer: 1625–1709), who was somewhat sceptical of alchemical claims, relates that he was once visited by a stranger, who gave him some powder of projection, which enabled him to produce some gold, which proved to be pure.

Many other alchemists lived about this time; and a number of writers using alchemical symbolism. Amongst the latter figures was one calling himself Eugenius Philalethes who is identified with Thomas Vaughan (1626–1666), a poet, brother of Henry Vaughan (1622–1695) the British mystical poet, called the Silurist, from being born in South Wales, the home of the ancient Silures.

Two other developments must be mentioned at the end of the 17th century. The *phlogiston theory* was put forward by J. J. Becher (1635–1682) and G. E. Stahl (1660–1734). This postulates that when metals and other substances burn they lose a substance called phlogiston.[25] The other development was the controversy over *spontaneous generation*. In other words doubt began to be cast on the idea that living things arise spontaneously from non-living matter.[26]

Robert Boyle (1627–1691) who wrote *The Sceptical Chemist*, 1661, is accounted one of the founders of modern scientific chemistry. He is not altogether free from alchemical ideas.

Sometimes called "the last of the alchemists" J. Price, M.D., F.R.S., carried out experiments with red and white powders, and presented some of the gold produced, as he thought, by their action, to the king in 1782. The Royal Society, as Price was a Fellow thereof, insisted on sending witnesses to see the experiments, which were repeated the next year after some delay. The experiments not being successful Price committed suicide.

There have been many experiments in gold-making since that time, notably in France and America. We have not yet seen the last of the alchemists.

[25] For the benefit of non-scientific readers it may be pointed out that this is in opposition to the modern idea that substances in burning gain a substance, usually oxygen, as they increase, not lose in weight. Curiously enough the latter fact was known in the days of the phlogiston theory.

[26] See W. B. Crow: Spontaneous Generation in *The Search Quarterly* III, 1, Jan. 1933, and more recent short account in W. B. Crow: *A Synopsis of Biology*, Bristol, 1960, 2nd ed., 1964.

CHAPTER XXV

THE ROSY CROSS

Symbolism of the Rose. The Rose is a very ancient symbol. But when, in the early part of the 17th century, those curious practitioners of the occult arts and sciences, known as the Brethren of the Rosy Cross, or Rosicrucians became known, they took for their badge or chief symbol the rose combined with the cross. Sometimes it was a cross with a rose in the centre. Less often it was a rose with a cross in the midst. Frequently the cross was the ordinary (Latin) cross *i.e.* one with lower vertical longer than the other arms. Now the combination of the rose and the cross is peculiar to the Rosicrucians, and is not known before the date of their public appearance.

The terms "rose" in symbolism has several distinct meanings and one may well ask what the Brethren of the Rosy Cross intended to signify. Here are some of the ideas on the subject :

1. The rose was the symbol of Venus, the goddess of erotic love. The late Roman legend tells of the origin of the rose from the blood of Venus, when wounded by Cupid's dart. It is safe to say that this has no references to the Brethren, as they were in no way devoted to Venus and Cupid. On the contrary they had to forgo the delights of erotic love, and according to most accounts were, originally at least, celibates.

2. The view has been expressed[1] that rose refers to the Latin *ros*, which means dew and cross means light, for the St. Andrew's cross X comprises the three letters of the word, *lux*, meaning light. It is true that dew and light play some part in alchemy, in which the Brethren were experts, but after all they did use the flower of the rose, and it is very prominent in much of their literature including their pictures.

3. The rose was the symbol of secrecy, and the Rosicrucians were very secret in their doings and claimed to possess important secrets. Roman myth is the source. Cupid gave Harpocrates a rose, when

[1] In a footnote to the translation of J. H. Mosheim : *Ecclesiastical History,* Vol. II, London, 1870. This view is originally due to Gassendi, an opponent of Fludd (see later).

the latter promised not to reveal the amours of Venus, the mother of Cupid. Harpocrates seems to be an Egyptian god, adopted by the Romans. He was the god of silence, and represented with a finger over his lips for this reason.

4. The present writer has suggested that the Brotherhood of the Rosy Cross were the esoteric exponents of the Protestant Religion.[2] Mystery, symbolism and occultism were in danger of disappearing in the Protestant reformation, and the Brethren were trying to save these aspects of religion. That they were bound up with Lutheranism appears in many of their documents. Now in the coat of arms of Luther there is a cross emerging from a rose. Moreover in that of J. V. Andreae, a Lutheran pastor who wrote one of the chief Rosicrucian works, there was a St. Andrew's cross, having roses at the four angles.[3]

5. Although the use of the symbol of the rose with the cross may have arisen in connection with Lutheranism, we will see later that Rosicrucianism is not necessarily bound up with the so-called reformed religion, and yet the Rosy Cross continues to be used, and this suggests more fundamental reasons, of a religious nature, why the rose and the cross should be associated.

The Virgin Mary is called *Rosa Coeli* (the rose of heaven) and five red roses on a rose bush, in Christian iconography, stand for the five wounds of Christ. In Christian tradition the rose originated from the blood of one of the martyrs. According to a Moslem legend, when Mohammed rode to heaven on his celestial steed, Al Borak, the sweat which fell to the earth from the prophet's brow gave rise to white roses, that from Al Borak produced yellow ones. In all cases the rose represents something extremely holy. It was in this sense, it would appear reasonable to suppose, the rose was regarded by the Brethren of the Rosy Cross.

The Rosicrucian Manifestoes. In the 17th century alchemy flourished to an extraordinary degree, and there were no doubt associations of alchemists. Documents were circulated in manuscript. One of these societies was named *Militia Crucifera Evangelica*. It was concerned with numerology and Bible prophecy, as well as with alchemy. Its leader was one Simon Studion, and its chief manuscript, called *Naometria*, preserved in the library at Stuttgart, has been examined by Waite. It shows that the sect was looking for a

[2] W. B. Crow: The Mysteries, *Mysteries of the Ancients,* 9, London, 1943.
[3] A. E. Waite: *The Brotherhood of the Rosy Cross,* London, 1924.

general or world reformation and Waite found in it a diagram containing a cross on a rose. It is an ultra-protestant document, referring to the supposed forthcoming crucifixion of the Pope. Waite is convinced that this belongs to the original society from which the Brethren of the Rosy Cross took their origin.[4]

However this may be, some printed manifestoes soon appeared which caused immense excitement, to judge from the discursive literature which followed. Three of these documents are supposed to have been printed, on behalf of the Order, in the first instance. It may be mentioned, that a few supporters of the movement, as well as opponents, say they were not official, and some even that they were a hoax. But they are generally regarded as genuine documents authorised by the invisible Brethren. They were as follows :

1. The *Fama Fraternitatis* was first printed in German at Cassel in 1614. One of the things that throws doubt upon it was that the publisher seems to have bound with it two other treatises (i) preceding it was a work called the *Universal Reformation of the Whole Wide World* translated from the Italian of the satirist T. Boccalini, which is a skit on all ideas of reformation and (ii) following it is a reply to the *Fama* by A. Haselmeyer, who had read it in manuscript.

The *Fama* is addressed to the Governors of Europe and the learned in general. It says that the Church has been cleansed, apparently referring to the Reformation, and suggests that a similar reform should be applied to science, discrediting Aristotelian and other old ideas. The Brethren hold the secret of transmutation, the ability to keep themselves and others free from all disease and many other secrets. They are assisted in their work by "elementary dwellers" *i.e.* those spirits which abound in nature and which are usually called *elementals.*

The Order of the Rosy Cross, the *Fama* explains, was founded by a great occultist known as Christian Rosenkreutz (Rosy Cross), who was born in the 14th or 15th century, and according to the legend lived for 106 years. He was a German of noble descent, educated in a cloister. At an early age he went on a pilgrimage to the Holy Land, accompanied by a monk. The latter died, however, on the way out, at Cyprus. Rosenkreutz continued the journey alone, reaching Damascus. There he was diverted from his journey

[4] A. E. Waite: *loc. cit.* Students of Rosicrucian philosophy will know that the Brethren themselves look much further back for their origin. We refer here only to its open appearance in Europe.

on hearing of some wise men at the Arabian city of Damcar. He visited the latter place, met the wise men, who appeared to have expected him. He improved his knowledge of Arabic there, learned much of physics and mathematics, and translated the mysterious book M from Arabic into Latin. After three years he left, taking his translation with him. He passed through Egypt into Fez, Morocco. There he stayed two years, taking lessons from more wise men on how to communicate with elemental spirits. He returned to Europe, via Spain. He did not stay with the Spaniards, as they thought little of his attainments. Some of them told him they had learned all about evoking the spirits, for had not Satan himself lectured in the University of Salamanca? Rosenkreutz returned to Germany where he lived the life of a hermit for some time. Then he enrolled four associates and thus started the Order of the Rosy Cross. The small group invented a secret language, healed the sick, and built themselves a House of the Holy Spirit. They enrolled four new members, and then dispersed, but met yearly. We are not told, in detail, their work, but it seems to have been largely medical.

Eventually Rosenkreutz died and was buried in a wonderful tomb. The latter was apparently forgotten for some time and only discovered much later, after the Order had grown considerably, during some building operations. A secret door was discovered over which in Latin was inscribed a behest to open after 120 years. As just this time had elapsed since the founder died the brethren decided to open it. On doing so they discovered a vault of seven sides, with an ever-burning lamp above, and a circular altar on the floor. There were also various inscriptions. Behind the walls were stored books, including some by Paracelsus, magical mirrors, bells and ever-burning lamps. There were also "artificial songs." Finally the brethren came upon the body of their revered founder, under the altar, clothed in ceremonial vestments, and holding the sacred book T. Finally the tomb was reverently closed.[5]

2. The *Confessio Fraternitatis* was published in German, in the next year, 1615. It and the preceding were supposed to have been issued in five languages. From internal evidence there is little doubt that the *Confessio* was originally, like its title, wholly in Latin.

[5] Waite points out that all this is symbolic. But he jestingly remarks that one who takes it literally might consider these "artificial songs" were phonographic records. That the ever-burning lamps were real inventions has been seriously discussed. They could have been electrical. Even the ancients have been credited with knowing electricity. What appears to have been an electrical battery has been recovered from ancient Babylonian ruins. The ever-burning lamps of the ancients have been discussed by several authors.

It contains thirty-seven reasons for making the Fraternity known.[6]

It mentions new stars appearing in *Serpentarius* and *Cygnus* as indications that the Universal Reformation is at hand, and says there are secret characters in Scripture and in Nature, the latter probably a reference to the Doctrine of Signatures. It was blasphemously alleged that the Pope had been cast down, but added that complete destruction was in store for him, for he was to be torn to pieces, and a final groan would end his "asinine braying!" It gives the date of birth of Christian Rosenkreutz as 1378.

3. This was printed at Strasbourg in the next year, 1616. It was only written in German, and called *Chymische Hochzeit Christiani Rosencreutz* (*Chemical Nuptials of Christian Rosenkreutz*). In spite of its title it does not deal with the marriage of Rosenkreutz. It is the story of a wedding, although a symbolic alchemical one, which Rosenkreutz is represented as attending as a guest.

These then are the three manifestoes of the Rosicrucians. The first two were anonymous, but the third (*The Chemical Nuptials*) was written by J. V. Andreae (1586–1654). He was a Lutheran pastor, and in one of his later works admits that he wrote *The Chemical Nuptials* when he was a youth. He regarded it as a youthful indiscretion. In fact in *Turris Babel* (Tower of Babel), 1619, ascribed to Andreae, he appears to have broken away[7] from occult activities and severed connection with the Brethren of the Rosy Cross. There is evidence that he formed a Christian Brotherhood, which repudiated the occult sciences.

The Invisibles. In their manifestoes the Rosicrucians gave no address. In the *Fama* those that wished to join the brethren were told to make themselves known by public writings, in order that the mysterious Fraternity could get in touch with them. Many did so. In fact up to the year 1620, from the publication of the manifestoes, a large number of letters, or more serious works, some deserving the designation of scientific theses, appeared. Great then were the laments of the many who received no invitation to join the Order of the Rosy Cross.

Robert Fludd began to write about the Rosy Cross in 1615. He was a Doctor of Medicine of Oxford and a Fellow of the Royal College of Physicians, London. He was an adherent of the Church

6 The number is specifically mentioned in the *Fama*, but in the *Confessio* the reasons are not numbered but must be deduced from the text, see Waite: *loc. cit.*

7 The very confused evidence about Andreae is discussed by Waite: *loc. cit.*

of England, but did not like religious controversy to enter the discussion. He regarded the symbolism of the Rosy Cross as primarily spiritual, and in his view it could be adapted to any religion. He connected it with the Holy Kabalah, of which he was a deep student. He speaks with authority about the Order, but if he was a member he concealed it.

Not all the early writers were favourable. A few absurdly claimed to find influences of the Jesuits at work in the Rosy Cross. A more popular idea was that Satan himself was behind it. A few made ridiculous claims, probably with the object of making the Order look silly. Waite[8] mentions a tract purporting to be signed by three brethren, who give their ages respectively as 576, 495 and 463 years, and another which ascribes to the Order not only actual inventions but also the ever-burning fire, perpetual motion and the squaring of the circle!

The Order of the Rosy Cross was introduced into England, France and the Low Countries. It eventually spread to Russia.

A Baconian Controversy. Sir Francis Bacon, Viscount St. Albans (1561–1626) has been associated with the Rosicrucians. He was Lord Chancellor of England 1618, but was banished from court and Parliament in 1621 for bribery and corrupt practices, to which he confessed himself guilty. He wrote many works, some scientific. One was the *Novum Organum* 1620 which proposes a new method in science, the inductive method, *i.e.* building hypotheses only on the basis of observed facts. It was supposed to replace the *Organon* of Aristotle, which, it was claimed, supported the deductive method, arguing from first principles, and looking for observation to confirm such principles. Bacon also wrote *The New Atlantis,* the description of an ideal community in which human life was ordered on what he believed to be scientific principles. He refers to a community of savants that he would like to see established. Some say this was an exoteric community, after his death realised by the founding of the Royal Society, 1662. Others says it was an esoteric society, and was realised by the establishment of the Order of the Rosy Cross. One objection to this is that, on the whole, Bacon was opposed to kabalism, alchemy and nearly all the occult arts.

As is well known it is claimed that Bacon wrote the plays ascribed to Shakespeare. But some go much further than this. They claim he wrote the works of Cervantes, author of *Don Quixote,* and practically the whole of Elizabethan literature, admitting he may

8 *Loc cit.*

have had help from his Rosicrucian brethren.[9] Further Bacon was the legitimate son of Queen Elizabeth I, who according to profane history never married, and as such rightful heir to the crown of Britain! Finally Bacon did not die in 1626, as alleged in history; his alleged death was a hoax. He did disappear after this, becoming a monk, of what order we have not seen stated! It is said that Rosicrucians often faked their own deaths, when they found it convenient. This no doubt enabled them to conceal the great age to which they were in the habit of living!

Anyone acquainted with the writings of Bacon finds it hard to believe that he ever had anything to do either with drama or occultism. The style is so different. The evidence, such as it is, is based on cryptograms and symbolic pictures in the alleged works. The literature is extensive, however, and there is even a Baconian Society, devoted to the study of Bacon from the esoteric point of view. There is no evidence, as Waite has shown[10] that Bacon was connected with the Rosicrucians in any way. He agreed with them as to the need for reform in science, he differed from them in being sceptical in most occult matters.

Rosicrucians and Writers. J. A. Comenius (Komensky 1592–1670) educator and bishop of the Unitas Fratrum,[11] who travelled widely in Europe is alleged to have been a prominent Rosicrucian. He was in England in 1641 having been invited by Parliament in connection with the setting up of a College on Baconian principles, but left for Sweden the next year when the Civil War between royalists and roundheads began. He wrote *Pansophiae Prodromus* 1639 and several educational works.

The philosopher René Descartes (1596–1650) was interested in the Rosicrucians, and speaks of his search for the brethren in one of his works. In some points his philosophy tended towards their ideas, but he remained a Catholic throughout his life.

Another philosopher, Baruch Spinoza (1632–1677), a Jew, had pantheistic ideas which influenced the followers of the brotherhood, according to Meyer.[12]

Baron G. W. von Leibniz (1646–1716), one of the greatest of

[9] A. E. Waite: *loc. cit.* cites claims that Bacon wrote "all that matters in English literature" from Chaucer's *Canterbury Tales, circa* 1400, to Carlyle's *Sartor Resartus,* 1833–34, including the last named!

[10] *Loc. cit.*

[11] Moravian Protestants.

[12] Quoted by Wittemans: *A New and Authentic History of the Rosicrucians,* trans., London and Chicago, 1938.

philosophers, who spent much of his time trying to reunite Protes-tants and Catholics, was undoubtedly secretary of a small associa-tion claiming to be Rosicrucian, in the early part of his life.

Elias Ashmole (1617–1692) archaeologist, author of a great history of the Order of the Garter was probably a member of the Rosicrucian Order. He presented a collection of antiquities to the University of Oxford, and they formed the nucleus of the Ash-molean Museum.

Thomas Vaughan (1626–1666), an alchemist, already mentioned, who wrote under the pseudonym of Eugenius Philaletes, claimed with a show of authority to know about the Rosicrucians.

Rose-Croix. According to many masonic writers there exists a close connection between Freemasonry and the Rosy Cross. But at the time of the foundation of the English Grand Lodge in 1717 both Orders appear to have existed separately. Craft Masonry soon thereafter was working its three degrees with their own particular ritual. The idea of degrees, each with (at least in theory) its own special ritual and symbolism, soon began to prove interesting to the Masonic fraternity, and numerous additional degrees were added on the continent, and some of these appeared in Britain, although not officially recognised by the Craft,[13] which is always said to consist of three degrees only.

Now these higher degrees, added to the Craft and not officially recognised in England, collected their symbolism from many sources. One of the degrees, first appearing according to Waite in France in 1754 or thereabouts, was entitled *Rose-Croix*. It was the eigh-teenth degree in a rite consisting at first in all of twenty-five grades including the three craft degrees.

But a further connection of the Rosy Cross with Masonry is evident. There was established an Order, open only to Master Masons, which worked nine degrees. Each degree was conferred after the candidate had mastered certain studies on the philosophy of the Rosy Cross. The headquarters of the Rite were in Berlin. Very indirectly this is the source from which was derived the *Societas Rosicruciana in Anglia*[14] founded by learned English Masons in 1865 in Middlesex. The latter afterwards had branches in the Provinces, in Scotland and in America. It is believed to

[13] Nevertheless some are highly esteemed, by the Craft, notably the Holy Royal Arch (often regarded as a supplement to the third degree) and the Rose-Croix.

[14] Often abbreviated to *Soc. Ros.*

have derived its succession from (i) F. M. White, Grand Secretary of English Freemasonry 1810–1857, who had been initiated by brethren deriving their succession from a Venetian ambassador who had been a Rosicrucian and (ii) Kenneth R. H. Mackenzie, one of the founder members, who had been initiated by Count Apponyi in Austria. They based their ritual on some old manuscripts, said to have been discovered at Freemason's Hall, London. The degrees were I Zelator, II Theoricus, III Practicus, IV Philosophus (these constituting the First Order), then V Adeptus Junior, VI Adeptus Senior and VII Adeptus Exemptus (constituting the Second Order), finally VIII Magister Templi and IX Magnus (in the Third Order).

In 1887 or 1888 some more Rosicrucian manuscripts were found, and these enabled members of the Societas Rosicruciana to get in touch with a certain Anna Sprengel, claimed to be a Rosicrucian adept, in Nüremburg, Germany. She gave the members an elaborate magical system, and enabled them to establish the Hermetic Order of the Golden Dawn, the headquarters of which were at Keighley, Yorkshire. This differed from the *Soc. Ros.* in that (i) women as well as men were admitted on equal terms, (ii) it openly claimed to practise magic, (iii) the chiefs of the Order were supposed to be secret, and to possess remarkable powers, including the ability to direct a magical current of force against erring members, capable of paralysing or even killing them. The degrees were practically the same as in the *Soc. Ros.* V was called Adeptus Minor and VI Adeptus Major, and there was supposed to be an additional degree X Ipsissimus above all the others. The Golden Dawn included some prominent people, including W. B. Yeats (1865–1939), Irish poet and Nobel Laureate. It was active until the beginning of the Second World War.

Some Other Organisations. Dr. P. B. Randolph (1825–1875), a prominent American occult writer of his day, said[15] to have been a friend of Lincoln, travelled extensively and claimed to have been initiated in the secret Syrian Order of the Ansars. In London he became a member of the *Societas Rosicruciana,* and appears to have known a number of well-known occultists. He soon returned to America and set up some sort of Rosicrucian Fraternity. He wrote on sex-magic in a book called *Eulis,* which met with much opposition. He is said to have committed suicide, but according to another account was murdered. Randolph was succeeded by Dowd, E. H. Brown and finally R. Swinburne Clymer, a descen-

15 In the anonymous *The Trail of the Serpent,* London, 1936.

dant of George Clymer who signed the Declaration of Independence. Dr. R. S. Clymer was head of the Sons of Isis and Osiris, the College of the Holy Grail and the Church of Illumination. He claimed that there was, in Nature, a force capable of transforming the whole Earth. This force was known to the ancients, and is possessed by the secret schools of today. He claimed to be in touch with a secret Council of Nine, who want to bring in a New Dispensation.[16]

In 1888 a very different organisation was set up in France. The Marquis Stanislas de Guaita (d. 1897) writer on black magic, founded a *Kabalistic Order of the Rose-Croix* in Paris. It was an occult university, conferring the degrees of Bachelor, Licentiate and Doctor of the Kabalah. On the death of the founder C. Barlet became the head, and he was succeeded by G. Encausse, M.D., better known as Papus. The last named died whilst on medical service during the latter stages of the First World War, and no more was heard of the organisation. Sar Peladan (d. 1918) was one of the original members of the latter, but in 1890 broke away therefrom and founded a *Catholic Rose-Croix Order*. He published a Journal in which he urged Catholic authorities to acknowledge the importance of the Ancient Mysteries, including the Grail and the Rosy Cross.

Dr. Rudolph Steiner (1861–1925) founder of the Anthroposophical Society is claimed by his followers to have been a Rosicrucian, and was certainly interested in the movement before he left the Theosophical Society. Max Heindel (1865–1919), said to have been associated with Steiner, established what he called *The Rosicrucian Fellowship* in America. His book *The Rosicrucian Cosmo-Conception* deals with the evolution of the universe and man, and occult forces concerned therewith. Heindel claimed he had contact with mysterious initiates.

In 1912 an Order of the *Temple of the Rosy Cross* was founded by Mrs. Besant, Mrs. Russak and Dr. Wedgwood, in connection with the Theosophical Society.

In 1915 an organisation that came to be well known, *The Ancient and Mystical Order of the Rosy Cross* (A.M.O.R.C.) was publicly established in New York by Dr. H. Spencer Lewis. The Order claims connections chiefly in France and Egypt, and gives it a very ancient lineage, to which we have referred. A.M.O.R.C. has been widely advertised, and much work is done by duplicated lessons and correspondence.

[16] *The Trail, loc. cit.*, also numerous books and pamphlets by Clymer.

CHAPTER XXVI

WITCHCRAFT IN EUROPE

Origin of Witchcraft. Apparently witchcraft has always existed, and has generally been severely punished. Millions of people have perished for sorcery or witchcraft in Africa,[1] and vast numbers in India, even in the last century.[2] In Europe, under Christian authority, there was not much persecution until the 13th century. It is generally agreed that the severity of punishment was greater amongst Protestants than amongst Catholics.

The view has often been put forward, in connection with witchcraft in Christian times, that it is the emergence of religious tendencies that had been repressed by the Catholic Faith. In other words it is the emergence of paganism, which has been stifled by the new faith, but still lives, as it were an underground movement. Against this view it must be pointed out (i) the Catholic Church was not opposed to the good aspects of the antique world; witness for instance how it took over Plato and Aristotle, how the Druids and Flamens became Christian Priests, how the Pope himself became Pontifex Maximus; (ii) The Catholic Faith does not repress beneficial religious tendencies, but tries to guide them along paths advantageous both to the individual and the society in which he or she lives. The repressed tendencies in witchcraft are therefore not those of paganism, but are those of psychopathology.

It is futile to look for traces, in witchcraft, of an ancient fertility cult. It is the Church that still blesses the fruits of the earth. The witches, on the contrary, destroyed infants, rendered married couples sterile, caused disease in cattle and blighted the crops.

Today many do not believe in witchcraft. But they admit the effects of hypnotism and suggestion. These effects may be more powerful than many, who have not studied them, may suppose. And they can be very deadly. For they affect the Unconscious, that part of the mind of which we are unaware directly, but which has been shown by psychologists to be of immense importance.

The origin of witchcraft is not connected with any particular

[1] J. M. Robertson: *Pagan Christs,* London, 1911, reprinted, 1928.
[2] J. C. Oman: *Cults, Customs and Superstitions of India,* 1908.

religion, but there have been witches in all religions. It is a rebellion against all religion, against Nature, against God. It is useless to argue about this. The witches themselves, at all times and places, tell us just this.

Biblical References. There are many warnings in the Bible against witchcraft. *Exod.* xxii, 18, prescribes death for witchcraft. The original refers to female sorcerers, and probably, even then, witches were better known than warlocks (male sorcerers). The subject is broached again in *Levit.* xix, 26, 31, and xx, 6, 27. In the last two passages destruction is promised to those who consult them, as well as to the sorcerers themselves. In *Deut.* xviii, 10, sorcerers or wizards are excluded from the community. Similar passages are *Mich.* v, 11, 12 and *Malach.* iii, 5. How Saul consulted the witch of Endor is well known (*I Kings = I Sam.*[3] xxviii, 7–25). Manasses (Manasseh) also dealt with soothsayers (*IV Kings=II Kings* xxi, 6).

In the New Testament we have already referred to the temptation of Jesus by the Devil, the contest of the Apostles with Simon Magus, and their exorcism of the possessed maiden. In *Acts,* xix, 19, there is the burning of magical books. Witchcraft is condemned in *Galatians* v, 20, and in *Apoc.* xxi, 8, and xxii, 15.

The literal interpretation of the death penalty for sorcerers and witches has been upheld by many theologians including the reformers Luther, Calvin and Wesley.

The Dianic Cult. Regino in the 10th century already refers to wicked women who attended meetings by night with the pagan goddess Diana.[4] Why should the witches associate with this beautiful lunar goddess, said to be the twin sister of Apollo and the goddess of chastity and of hunting? It appears that there was another side to her nature. She was so chaste that an evil fate met many who fell in love with her. But she so far forgot her principles as to enjoy the company of Endymion, a beautiful shepherd, whilst some rumours alleged that her favours were granted both to Pan and Orion. In fact the moon gooddess had a darker side to her nature. She in fact had three natures, thus called *Triformis* and was represented sometimes with the heads of horse, dog and boar. She was Luna or the moon in heaven, Diana on earth and Hecate in the infernal regions. In the latter character she presided over enchantments, and was also called *Trivia* from presiding over

[3] King James version.
[4] G. Tartarotti: *Del Congress Notturno del Lammie,* Rovereto, 1749.

cross-roads. Many superstitions were attached to the latter. Witches met at the cross-roads. To perform certain magical acts one had sometimes, it was said, to go to the cross-roads. It seems that witches invoked Hecate, goddess of witchcraft, and she appears in Shakespeare's *Macbeth* in connection with the witches. There is a reference to the evocation of Diana, by which is meant Hecate, in a pronouncement of a General Council of the Church in the 9th century, which also refers to women professing and believing that they ride on certain beasts for long distances to attend the meetings which were afterwards called *Witches' Sabbaths* (more properly *Sabbats*). The witches thus continued a moon-cult, which was condemned long ago in the Greek classics, wherein are references to Thessalonian sorcerers who have debased moon-worship, and who are skilled in the use of herbs, magic and incantations.

But there is another curious reference. A Church Council of Treves 1310 condemns any woman who pretends to ride with Diana or Herodiana. Later there are references to riding with Herodias. Now the latter is mentioned in the Gospels (*Matt.* xiv, *Mark* vi and *Luke* iii). She married first her uncle Philip, but left him for his brother Herod Antipas. St. John the Baptist said this was not lawful. When the daughter of Herodias danced before Herod he was so pleased with her that he promised, on oath, anything she might ask. The daughter, instructed by her mother, asked for the head of John the Baptist in a dish. Herod was saddened by this, but because of his oath caused John to be beheaded. Now Herodiana was alleged to be the daughter of Herodias.

The meaning of all this (i) that the witches indulged in dancing, (ii) like Herodiana they danced for an evil purpose. Herodiana is, from the second part of the name, connected with Diana.

Pacts with the Devil. The authority for such pacts is *Isaias* (*Isaiah*) xxviii which in the Vulgate translation reads : "For you have said we have entered into a league with death, and we have made a covenant with hell." Both Origen and Augustine mention these pacts and the scholastic philosophers distinguish between express and implied pacts. The former ˙consists in actually evoking the demon, the latter in merely expecting help from him. The demon here refers to any evil spirit, and there were vast numbers of such.

When the witch-cult was at its height anyone interested in joining might receive a visit from one dressed in black. He would be the devil, or more correctly the devil's representative. He would sometimes get the victim to sign a written pact, and the signature was almost always in the blood of the person signing it. Sometimes the whole document was in blood.[5] If the victim could not write, the sign taking the place of the signature was a circle, as the usual cross was now taboo. The pact sometimes had to be made at cross-roads. The agreement was that the devil should give the victim everything he or she desired, in the way of knowledge, wealth, success, pleasure and vengeance against enemies, and in return the victim would renounce the Catholic religion, repudiate his own Baptism, would worship the devil, abandon all desire for Eternal Salvation and utterly deliver his own soul to Hell at death. The pact was to last for seven or nine years, or for life. Sometimes the victim died after the expiration of a number of years, sometimes the pact was then renewed.

A pact with the devil or with any demons is not legally binding, according to the opinion of theologians. Sometimes it was repudiated and the victims reconciled with the Church. Even two of the saints were at one time guilty of sorcery. St. Cyrian of Antioch (4th century) tried to seduce a maiden by means of an evil spirit. She converted him, however, and both suffered martyrdom for the faith. St. Theophilus of Cilicia (6th century) actually signed a compact with the devil in his own blood. He was a church treasurer, highly esteemed, and was offered a bishopric, which he refused. Another was elected bishop, and under the new regime Theophilus was subjected to certain accusations. Indignant at the falsity of the charges Theophilus repaired to a sorcerer, who put him in touch with the evil one, with whom he made the pact. It was now discovered that the charges were completely without foundation, and Theophilus was re-instated. After much prayer and supplication, with penance and fasting, Mary appeared to Theophilus, and promised to intercede with Christ on behalf of the sinner. Eventually he was forgiven, the pact was miraculously returned and handed to the bishop who absolved the penitent, and burnt the document. Theophilus afterwards led a holy life for many years. Another holy man who at one time signed a pact with the devil was the Dominican, the Blessed Gil of Santarem.

The Faust Legend. This story is based on old Jewish legends.[6] It was first published by Spiess, 1587. Soon thereafter it was made

[5] The drawing of blood for making pacts is not peculiar to the diabolical ones. Pacts between friends or between lovers were sometimes made in this way. There was sometimes even the drinking of blood in this connection.

[6] H. M. Léon: The Origin and Development of the Faust Legend, *Proteus* No. 6, April 1932.

into a play: *The Tragical History of Dr. Faustus* by Marlowe, about 1589. The best known version was by Goethe, *Faust,* two parts, 1790–1833, only the first part of which recounts the legend, the second wandering off into the depths of occult philosophy. Some other plays on the same theme have been composed, but the operas are better known, *viz.* Spohr: *Faust,* 1816; Berlioz: *Damnation de Faust,* 1846; Gounod: *Faust e Margoerito,* 1859; Boito: *Mefistophele,* 1868, and Zollner: *Faust* 1887. Wagner wrote a *Faust* overture and Liszt a *Faust* symphony.

It is now believed that an actual person called Dr. Johann Faust or Faustus existed, that he was an alchemist, astrologer and magician, born at Knittlingen, Württemberg about 1480 and died about 1538.

In the original legend Faust first appears as an old disillusioned man. He calls up the devil by his magic arts, agrees to sign a pact whereby he is given twenty-four years of further life, during which he is to have much knowledge and unbounded pleasures. He has a number of adventures, but at the expiration of the time he is claimed by the devil and is carried down to hell.

In Goethe's *Faust,* Part I, Faust is first seen meditating in a high-vaulted narrow Gothic chamber, contemplating suicide. He is saved by the sound of holiday-makers, singing an Easter hymn. He goes for a walk with his assistant Wagner and they see a poodle which follows Faust home. Faust performs magic and the poodle is transformed into a devil called Mephistopheles. On a second visit a pact is arranged and signed in Faust's blood. Mephistopheles explains that blood has unique properties. They then go to a tavern cellar in Leipzig, where Mephistopheles produces drinks by magic, but a brawl ensues. They next go to a witch's kitchen, where there is a great cauldron, watched by apes. The witch arrives and after fantastic rites gives Faust a drink of the magical brew. Soon Faust meets a beautiful maiden Margaret, whom he tempts with jewels, produced by Mephistopheles, and eventually seduces. She kills their newborn child and is cast into prison. Meanwhile Faust and the devil attend the Walpurgis Night celebrations of the witches on the Harz mountains, and Oberon and Titania's Golden Wedding is performed. Finally Faust and Mephistopheles try to rescue Margaret from prison, but she has gone mad and refuses to be rescued.

The second part includes Faust's journey to the Mothers, the Conjuration of Helen of Troy, the Creation of Homunculus, the Classical Walpurgis Night and the ultimate salvation of Faust and Margaret.

Laws against Witchcraft. It is difficult in early Christian times to distinguish laws made against witches and against other heretics. In 314 the Council of Ancyra refers to witchcraft as a branch of pharmacy and forbids it, but the penalty was a few years' penance. Under the joint Emperors Valentinian and Valens in 373 there was a severe persecution of the Gnostics, who were accused of adultery, treason and poisoning by conjuration. Anglo-Saxon law exacted penance on bread and water for seven years if the victim of witchcraft died. Canute laid down banishment for witches, or death for the relapsed. The Council of Agde (Lower Languedoc) in 506 ordered excommunication of vampires, poisoners and sorcerers. The first Council of Orleans 541 condemned divination. The Council of Narbonne 589 put the greater excommunication on sorcerers and ordered public whipping for those consorting with incubi or succubi. Several councils condemned folk customs associated with devil-worship. The Council of Toledo 681 condemns those venerating stones, and burning torches to celebrate Spring. In the 7th century in England the Church had to prohibit offerings to devils, and the dressing up of people to represent stags or bulls. It also prescribed penances for the use of charms, love-philtres, poisons, and forbade the making of vows at enchanted places (clumps of trees, certain rocks, places where boundaries meet, etc.).

Pope Boniface VIII (r. 1294–1303) laid down that the Inquisition should deal with sorcery, if heresy was involved, *i.e.* black magic. Pope John XXII (r. 1316–1334) was attacked by poison, then by sorcery; there were sorcerers at work even at the Papal Court and three of them (including a bishop) were burned at the stake for the magical murder of the Pope's nephew (they used wax images, ashes of spiders and toads, gall of pigs, etc.). This Pope gave the Inquisition authority to deal with all sorcery and magic, but withdrew it after ten years. However in 1374 Pope Gregory XI (r. 1370–1378) again gave authority to the Inquisition to deal with all sorcerers and workers of evil in the occult. In 1484 Pope Innocent VIII (r. 1484–1492) issued a bull specifically against witchcraft.

In England acts of 1541, 1562 and 1601 were directed against witches. These acts made witchcraft and sorcery a felony, without benefit of clergy. The last prosecution under these acts was in 1712. The laws then became dormant and on someone attempting to revive them they were repealed in 1736. Few witches were burned in England. They were usually hanged. But on the continent burning was common, especially for those condemned by the Inquisition.

Some Famous Witch Trials. Chilperic I, Merovingian King of the
Franks (561–584) had a concubine called Fredegund, who was
suspected of killing his first wife Galeswintha. Chilperic's son by the
latter, Clovis, fell in love with a girl called Klodswinthe, whose
mother was supposed to be a sorceress. Fredegund had Klodswinthe
imprisoned, where she died, and her mother executed. Later Clovis
was imprisoned and stabbed to death, it being reported he had
committed suicide. Later Fredegund killed Chilperic himself. She
practised black magic, and on one occasion rescued a woman
charged before the Bishop of Verdun with being possessed of an
evil spirit.

In the reigns of Pepin the Short (r. 751–768) and his successor
Charlemagne (r. 768–814) numbers of people were prosecuted who
were alleged to have fallen from the sky, or had seen visions
therein.[7]

The first witch-trials in England were in the reign of King John
(r. 1199–1216). A certain Gideon was subjected to an ordeal with
red-hot iron, but proved his innocence. In Ireland in the same
reign Hubert de Burgh was accused of using charms to gain favours
of the King.

In France, under Louis X (r. 1314–1316) a number of people
were accused of using enchantments to harm the king, his brother
and certain lords. A witch was burnt, and her husband, in prison
as a warlock, committed suicide. Finally one of the king's ministers,
Enguerrand de Marigny was hanged. This led to such an outcry
that further proceedings were dropped. The king himself repented
and left money to the family of the last-named victim.

In 1324 certain citizens of Coventry were accused of trying to
kill King Edward II (r. 1307–1327) and his favourites by plunging
daggers into their wax images. After several adjournments the trial
was abandoned.

In the same year the case of Lady Alice Kyteler of Kilkenny,
Ireland, caused great stir. She had married four husbands. The
first three died under mysterious circumstances, and her fourth
husband Sir John le Poer had been reduced to a miserable state of
illness by her powders and ointments. Being warned of black magic
by one of the servants he seized certain keys of her boxes, and on
unlocking them found, to his horror the intestines of cocks, worms,
herbs, and nail-parings, brains, fat and 'clothing from the dead
bodies of babes. There was also the skull of a certain robber who
had been beheaded, and in this the aforesaid articles had apparently

[7] J. Garinet: *Histoire de la magie en France,* Paris, 1818.

been boiled. Sir John reported all this to the Bishop of Ossory, who immediately investigated and obtained evidence that the lady was mixed up with a group that denied the faith, propitiated demons, cursed their own spouses, killed and injured people. Lady Alice was said to have an unholy connection with a demon called Robert Artisson (*filius Artis*) "one of the poorer class of hell."[8] Moreover she was found to have in her possession what was believed to be a consecrated Host, on which the devil's name had been inscribed.

Unfortunately for the Bishop he was a newcomer to the country, and a number of relatives and friends of the Lady Alice held high positions in the district. Indeed attempts were made to trump up certain charges against him, but these were dropped. The Bishop was a protégé of Pope John XXII and we have already seen how this Pope had been disturbed by sorcery. However during the long drawn out attempts to prosecute her, Lady Alice escaped to England, and eventually found refuge on the Continent. Her maid who confessed to atrocities was burned at the stake, and one or two others subsequently fared likewise, but the majority of the offenders merely had to perform various penances. The Bishop later had to leave the country, and returned to Italy, where he died at a great age in 1360.[9]

That notable visionary, St. Joan of Arc (1412–1431), who led the French to victory over the English for some time was finally captured by the latter, and charged with heresy and witchcraft, for which she was burnt at the stake. In 1455 the trial was revised and she was declared innocent. She was beatified in 1909 and canonised 1920.

During the same period lived Joan of Navarre who was wife of King Henry IV of England and step-mother of Henry V. She was unpopular during the war with France as she was French and had French retainers. She was accused of witchcraft in 1418 and imprisoned, but released in 1422, whereafter she lived in state until 1437.

The Inquisition. The Church has always claimed the right to restrain those who were spreading false teaching (see *e.g. Acts* xiii, 8–11). In the early centuries this power was exercised by the bishops, acting through the civil power, which in those days was

8 Wright's *Narratives of Sorcery and Magic*, Vol. I, quoted in Ennemoser's *History of Magic*, trans., Vol. II, London, 1854.
9 Wright: *loc. cit.*

always completely subservient to the spiritual authority. But as matters grew more complicated, and heresies more varied, the *Sacred Congregation of the Holy Office,* or the *Roman and Universal Inquisition* was established, to relieve the bishops of this burden. It generally acted in conjunction with the bishops, and through the civil power. The first head of the Inquisition was probably St. Dominic, who was appointed to the post in 1215. But the whole organisation was re-organised in 1542. In Spain punishment under the Inquisition was termed auto-da-fé (act of faith); those burnt were dressed in a sort of chasuble and wore a kind of mitre, as if regarded as sacrificial victims, and perished with due ceremonial.

In order to explain the various subtle questions which inquisitors had to deal with in connection with witchcraft, two of their number, Henry Kramer and James Sprenger produced a book called *Malleus Maleficarum,* approved by Papal Bull, 1484.

The Inquisition is still in existence and now forms one of the twelve congregations of the Roman Curia.

The Original Bluebeard. The well-known story of Bluebeard appeared in the works of C. Perrault in 1697. It is supposed to be based on the history of Gilles de Rais, Marquis of Laval and Marshal of France (*d.* 1440) most of the known details of whom are very well established. His father died when he was only about twenty, and left him an enormous estate and a fortune comparable with that of the king himself. He became a marshal for his distinguished war service, for he had been one of the most zealous supporters of St. Joan of Arc. He went about and entertained in the most magnificent style imaginable. Two hundred horsemen accompanied him on his journeys; his gaily caparisoned hunting and hawking expeditions were the talk of the countryside. His castles were open for the entertainments of all comers. He had a private theatre, and whole troupes of actors. His private chapel was more richly appointed than any cathedral, and most of the fittings were of gold. His chief chaplain was a bishop, attended by many priests, and it was said that the marshal attempted to get the mitre for each and all of them. He was himself bold and handsome, had a bluish-black beard, and learned, if not wise, in the sciences of his day.

After entertaining for some years on lavish scale, and seeking all sorts of pleasures, he began to find himself in need of more money, so he sold some of his estates. This went on for some time, but his heirs began to object, and persuaded the king and parliament to prevent the alienation of the rest of the estates. Meanwhile he had secretly sent out for alchemists, who stayed with him for some time. At one period he had no less than twenty alchemists working for him, with the object of producing gold, without result. One day one of these workers hinted there was a more rapid method of getting wealth. He gradually suggested diabolical means, and Gilles de Rais was persuaded to try the devil. Very, very secretly Gilles and the adept betook themselves to a lonely spot at midnight. Gilles saw the adept fall into a sort of fit, but otherwise nothing happened. The adept explained that the devil had appeared in the form of a leopard, but Gilles had not seen him because he lacked faith. He also said that certain herbs were needed but they only grew in Spain and Africa. The adept was immediately despatched to try to get them, but was never seen again.

Gilles de Rais now consulted another alchemist, Prelati, as to the possibility of diabolical aid. He was advised to write a contract in his own blood, and sacrifice a young child. This he did and Prelati was supposed to contact a young devil called Barron. After numerous delays and disappointments Gilles de Rais announced he was going on a pilgrimage. It so happened that he had just married a young wife, his seventh according to Mézeray.[10] When he went away he delivered the keys of the castle to Lady de Rais, telling her not on any account to try to get into a certain tower, the door of which opened by a push-button mechanism.[11] Lady de Rais was to have her sister Anne with her whilst the Lord of the Castle was away. A child was expected.

Of course as soon as Gilles de Rais had gone the two ladies began to look for means of getting into the mysterious tower. They eventually found and worked the mechanism and began to examine the tower's contents. Much to their horror they found the remains of dead bodies of numerous infants, which had evidently been sacrificed. To make matters worse Lady de Rais upset a basin of blood, and stained her garments therewith.

Meanwhile Gilles de Rais had really been visiting Prelati, who was refusing to leave his own house. Prelati told De Rais he did not want to proceed further, as the devil was now demanding the sacrifice of the De Rais unborn baby. But De Rais, apparently now

[10] *Histoire de France*, Paris, 1643–1651.
[11] A curious variation of a well-known theme in fairy-tale, of the one forbidden key.

completely insane, insisted on Prelati returning with him to the
mysterious tower. They did so and seeing that Lady de Rais could
not disguise the fact that she had discovered the secret, prepara-
tions were begun for this most horrible act to be carried out.
Prelati laid out the implements of the sacrifice and according to
some accounts had actually begun the Black Mass. However it
appears that Lady Anne had been signalling to soldiers from the
top of the tower, and the soldiers had told her two brothers. Won-
dering how their sisters were getting on in the absence of De Rais,
and perplexed by the signalling, the brothers decided to visit them.
They arrived with their armed escort, shortly before the terrible
sacrifice was carried out. De Rais and Prelati postponed the act
of horror, and came down to greet the guests. But by this time
the disappearance of infants had become well-known to Gilles'
retainers. The ladies soon conveyed the dreadful news to their
brothers, who immediately surrounded them with their escort. De
Rais called upon his followers to attack, but in view of the terrible
rumours that had been getting about, effective resistance was out
of the question. A message was sent to the Bishop of Nantes,
Chancellor of Brittany. De Rais and Prelati were cast into prison
and were eventually tried before the said bishop, together with
the Vicar of the Inquisition and the President of the provincial
Parliament. At the trial the most horrible evidence was given.
Nearly a hundred children had been slain, after being indecently
assaulted. Prelati was burnt at the stake, Gilles de Rais strangled
and then partially burned, his body being taken out of the fire for
interment in view of his former services to the country. Another
assistant was also burned.

Further Witchcraft Trials. From 1453 to 1460 many witch trials
took place in the Diocese of Arras, France. The crime was called
vauderie after Robinet de Vaulse, one of the first accused. It
consisted in making pacts with infernal powers, and the usual
accusation of attending the witches' sabbath. Several were burned
at the stake, and many imprisoned, but in 1491 as a reaction had
set in, the sentences were reversed and relatives of the victims
compensated.

The beautiful and accomplished Jane Shore (1445–1527) mistress
of Edward IV was once accused of witchcraft. After the king's
death she and Lord Hastings espoused the cause of the king's sons,
the young princes imprisoned in the Tower. Jane Shore and
Hastings were accused of witchcraft. Hastings was beheaded. Jane

Shore was made to do penance and paraded through the streets of London, dressed only in a white shift, in a procession with the Bishop of London.

In 1515 in the Republic of Geneva, when it was still united to Savoy, no less than 500 witches were burnt in three months. In 1524 many witches were burnt at Como. Many witches and warlocks were practising in France about this time.

The well-known writer H. Cornelius Agrippa von Nettesheim (1486–1535) military physician, alchemist, and lecturer on the occult, who had been knighted by the Emperor was popularly supposed to be a black magician, and seems to have done little to dispel this belief. In 1530 he published a treatise on the vanity of the sciences, but in 1531 his famous *Occult Philosophy,* expressing a belief in magic, came out. The two works apparently express contradictory theories, perhaps with a view to confounding critics. In 1518 or 1519, whilst at Metz, Agrippa defended a woman accused of witchcraft. On another occasion, according to a widely circulated story, Agrippa left his apartments and whilst he was away a young student gained access to his room and began reading certain spells from his books. One of them was sufficiently effective to cause a demon to appear. The latter demanded to know why he had been evoked. The student, paralysed with fear was unable to cope with the situation and was strangled by the demon. When Agrippa returned he was horrified to find the corpse. Fearing that he would be charged with murder he evoked the demon and compelled him to restore the student to life for a while. This was done, and Agrippa took the student for a walk in the market-place, and during the walk the young man apparently had a seizure and died. However shortly after this Agrippa wisely decided to leave the district.

Another student of Agrippa was Wierus, a prolific writer on witchcraft, who stayed with Agrippa for some time after the latter had separated from his wife. He says a large black dog, popularly supposed to be the familiar of Agrippa, always slept with the latter. When Agrippa died Wierus is said to have renounced black magic, and dismissed the dog, which straightway rushed out and drowned itself in the river.

In the 16th century great credulity existed in reference to witchcraft. Levi[12] gives instances of a woman burnt for abnormal bodily conformation, a man for travelling by night in the form of a hare,

[12] *The History of Magic,* trans. 2nd ed., London, 1922.

another for turning into a wolf. Nine hundred witches are said to have been burnt in Lorraine between 1580 and 1595.

At the end of 1610 two young ladies, Magdelaine de la Palud and Louise Capud, whilst on a pilgrimage in Provence fell into convulsions. Magdelaine screamed, writhed and begged to be beaten, and trampled under foot.[13] She claimed to be affianced to the devil, by a priest named Gaufridi. Another account says Gaufridi had taken her to the witches' sabbath. The priest was sent for and before the next year was out he was burnt at the stake.

About this time H. Bouget (*d*. 1619) published his *Discours des sorciers*. He had acted as a judge at witchcraft trials, and he records preposterous charges, *e.g.* of a child of eight possessed of eight demons, and of a woman tortured because a piece was missing from the cross of her rosary.

In Scotland at the end of the 16th century Margaret Aiken, known as the Great Witch of Balwery, was accused of witchcraft. To avoid execution she claimed to be able to detect witches by a secret appearance in their eyes. Under supervision she was taken about the country for that purpose.

In 1576 Bessie Dunlop was accused of witchcraft and sorcery in Ayrshire, Scotland. A certain T. Reid had visited her, also a woman, claimed to be a Queen of Elfhane, a fairy title. She was convicted and burnt. In 1597 there was a big witch trial at Aberdeen.

In 1590 in Huntingdonshire a witch named Mother Samuel confessed under torture to being responsible for the death of Lady Cromwell, and for five little girls having fits. She, her grown-up daughter and her husband were all hanged, and their naked bodies exposed to onlookers.

In 1616 no less than nine witches were hanged at Market Bosworth, Leicestershire, for causing epilepsy in a boy.

About the same time Pendlebury Forest, near Manchester, held a reputation for witchcraft, and between 1613 and 1619 a number of the villagers were charged, and sent to Lancaster Castle for trial. Whilst they were there news was received of a plot to blow up the castle and to kill one concerned with the arrest. The destruction of the castle was avoided, but the victim died, it was said by sorcery. One of the witches died during the imprisonment, eighteen others were executed. In 1634 many people from the same district were again charged on the evidence of a boy. They were found guilty and would have been hanged, had not the judge sent some

[13] Levi, *loc. cit.*

of them to London, for further examination. In the end the boy confessed his accusations were a pack of lies. The story of the Lancashire Witches has been told by the English novelist W. H. Ainsworth and by several others.

King James I of England (r. 1566–1625) was a great enemy of witches. He wrote *Daemonologia*, Edinburgh, 1597, and on one occasion prosecuted an assize who had acquitted a person accused under the acts.[14] A new law had been enacted under Elizabeth I, 1563, encouraged by preaching of leading prelates, but under James I the law was stiffened further, so that 40 per cent of those indicted went to the gallows. Bothwell's rebellion against James I was supposed to be aided by witchcraft, in spite of its failure. A whole gang of witches and warlocks were concerned in a magical plot to cause a storm at sea with the idea of wrecking King James who was bringing his bride from Denmark.

Witchcraft prosecutions were no less numerous on the Continent at that time. From 1627 to 1629 no less than 157 witches were burnt at Würzburg, Germany.

[14] R. Trevor Davies: *Four Centuries of Witch Beliefs* says James I largely recanted his witch beliefs and his successor even more so. When the Royal Society was founded 1662, a sceptical view was adopted. The Roundheads, on the contrary were strong believers and supported the witch-finder Matthew Hopkins.

CHAPTER XXVII

MORE WITCHCRAFT AND THE BLACK MASS

Demon Possession. Readers will be familiar with this from the New Testament. Some remarkably striking cases are however recorded in the 17th century, and strangely enough in nunneries.

One of these is connected with Urbain Grandier, burnt alive for causing the possessions in 1634. He was a priest at Loudon and had been at variance with his bishop. Levi[1] says he appealed to the king, won his case and returned to Loudon entering the town bearing a branch of laurel. Cardinal Richelieu, it is said, had also had some trouble over Grandier.

Now it so happened that Grandier was in the habit of visiting the convent of Ursuline nuns at Loudon, and when their confessor died he expected to obtain the appointment. He was disappointed, and soon after the new confessor took up his post the trouble started. First the Mother Superior and then some of the other nuns, twelve in all, began to behave in what we would now call a hysterical fashion, but worst of all, in a way that was utterly indecent. Exorcists were called and some devils of high degree, even including one of the fallen seraphim, were found to be possessing the afflicted nuns, and these devils one and all declared, in no uncertain terms, that they had been sent by Grandier. It is worth remarking that some of the nuns had lucid moments and three declared at the trial that Grandier was innocent. But the judges preferred to listen to the evidence of the devils speaking through the victims, with the result that Grandier was sent to the stake.

During the proceedings against Grandier it was thought advisable to ascertain whether any part of his body was insensitive to pain, that being a certain sign of one given over to the Evil One. The surgeon called in to perform the examination was called Manoury.[2] The latter was returning one night from a visit, with his brother and another person, when he suddenly cried out that he could see the ghost of Grandier, and began to tremble all over. He was put

[1] *Loc cit.*
[2] According to Vigny's historical novel *Cinq-Mars*, 1826, he performed the examination with great barbarity, startling details of which are given.

to bed but continued in a state of frenzy, believing Grandier to be at his bedside, until he died a few days later.

A few years after the death of Grandier a similar affair occurred in a nunnery at Louviers, Normandy. Some of the possessed women accused two priests of bewitching them. One of these priests had died. Nevertheless his body was tied to the stake and burned along with the living man in 1644.

Witchcraft Persecutions Extend. About the middle of the 17th century the number of witch prosecutions seems to have been considerably increased by the employment of professional witch-finders. The best known of these was Matthew Hopkins who was responsible for the execution of about 100 persons in Essex, Suffolk and Norfolk between 1645 and 1647. All those suspected were examined for marks and insensitive places on the body.

Dr. Lamb was a noted sorcerer in England, who escaped prosecution. He became, however, so unpopular that he was torn to pieces by an infuriated mob in 1640. He was alleged to have supplied poison with a view to effecting the death of James I.

Rebecca West was a witch and the daughter of a witch. She claimed to have married the devil. She was hanged in 1649.

In 1654 twenty poor women were put to death as witches in Brittany. In 1669 seventy persons were condemned to death, including fifteen children, for attending great meetings of witches at a place called Blockula in Sweden.

A number of persons were executed in Scotland for witchcraft during the 17th century. As not unusual, witches and devils were there referred to as fairies. Major Thomas Weir was strangled and burnt at Edinburgh in 1670, at the age of seventy, for incest and bestiality, and his sister Jean hanged in the same year for incest and witchcraft. In 1696 John Reid, in prison awaiting a trial for witchcraft was found strangled, and it was said that the devil had claimed his own.

In England about 1664 a number of witches were accused in Somerset, and in 1682 three poor women from Devon were sentenced to death for bewitching certain persons, injuring cattle and wrecking ships at sea by means of their art.

In France, it is recorded, Louis XIV (r. 1638–1715) commuted the death penalty to life imprisonment, on a number of Normandy women who had been accused of riding on broomsticks.

Witchcraft beliefs were entertained by the early colonists of America. In 1683 there were witchcraft trials in Pennsylvania. In

1692 some negro servants were charged at Salem, Massachusetts. Soon thereafter a white woman was hanged and the authorities called in the assistance of the prominent Congregational clergymen[3] Increase Mather (1639-1723) and his son Cotton Mather (1663-1728). The result was that large numbers of the population were accused and executed, one man perished because he did not believe in witchcraft and another who had been employed in arresting suspects, because he had refused to continue the work. Cotton Mather wrote remarkable works, in one of which he claimed that the devil could assume the guise of quite innocent persons. Finally people occupying high positions were accused, and even the wife of the governor. At Boston one of the suspects, however, counter-attacked by taking out an action for defamation of character. This was the beginning of the end of the prosecutions, and although Cotton Mather made an attempt to revive them, the agitation died down, and in fact a revulsion of feeling took place.[4]

Some Later Cases. Throughout much of the 18th century the death penalty for being a witch prevailed in Europe, and even where this was withdrawn persons suspected of witchcraft were liable to be thrown in water, a recognised practice for finding of witches. Possibly the last witch-burning in Scotland was in Sutherland in 1722.

In France a scandalous affair occurred in 1731. Catherine Cadière, a young woman of Toulon, was in the habit of falling into trances, and showed marks on her body, technically known as the *stigmata*, which were believed to represent the wounds of Christ, only occurring on very holy persons. Great was the sensation therefore when Catherine accused her confessor, a Jesuit J.-B. Girard, of seducing her by means of black magic. He was tried before the Parliament of Aix, but was acquitted.

In Würzburg in 1749 a nun, Maria Renata, was burnt for witchcraft. In Poland nine old women were hanged for witchcraft in 1775. The last witch to be burnt in Europe, under the law, is said to have been in the canton of Glarus in Switzerland in 1785, under a Protestant tribunal. These are among the last to suffer the death penalty, out of an enormous list.[5]

After the penalty was withdrawn a number of crimes were still

[3] Lewis Spence's *Encyclopaedia of Occultism* says of the two Mathers: "The fanatical and diabolical cruelty of these two men has probably never been equalled in the history of human persecution."

[4] See Spence, *loc. cit.*, for a concise account of further details.

[5] Many, but by no means all of the cases are referred to and some des-

committed in which witchcraft or black magic was associated. Moreover people sometimes took it on themselves to be revenged against alleged witches or warlocks. In 1863 an old paralysed Frenchman was ducked as a warlock at Castle Hedingham, Essex, and died. In 1875 an old woman was killed with a pitchfork by a half-insane man at Long Compton, Warwickshire. He asked for the body to be weighed against the Church Bible, as proof she was a witch (an ancient belief).

The Witch Burning at Clonmel. As this was probably the last case in Europe, occurred as late as 1895 and is connected with fairy-lore, it is of some interest. The victim was Bridget Cleary who at first resided peacefully near Cloneen, County Tipperary. Her body extensively burnt was discovered on March 22nd, buried in a cramped position, near her husband's house, in swampy ground, after he and other relatives had been charged with assault. They were then charged with murder, but found guilty of manslaughter, the husband receiving twenty years' penal servitude, the others lesser sentences. It appears that Bridget became ill, a doctor was called, and bronchial catarrh and nervous excitement were diagnosed. A priest was also called, he suspected hysteria and mental derangement, administered the last rites, and two days later said Mass in her room. Her husband had been told by his mother that the latter used to visit the fairies, and he suspected his wife had been doing the same. In fact he thought she had been replaced by a fairy changeling. He said she was two inches taller than his wife. He kept asking her whether she was really his wife, and in spite of some replies in the affirmative he, with others, passed her over the fire, and was accused of throwing lamp oil on her and igniting it. She had also been treated with herbs. Moreover her husband and two others of the accused had gone three nights to the fort at Kylenagranagh, a place haunted by fairies according to local tradition,[6] in order that they might see her and bring her back in place of the changeling.

The whole affair reminds one of the theme of the changeling in fairy-lore, except that in most fairy-tales the changeling is given in place of a child, not an adult.

Dr. Sprenger estimates the total number of witches slain in

cribed in H. C. Lea: *Materials towards a History of Witchcraft*, reprinted, three volumes, New York and London, 1957.

[6] The "Witch-Burning" at Clonmel, *Folk Lore* VI, 4, Dec. 1895. Further details are given therein.

Europe during the Christian epoch as about 9,000,000. This is a relatively small number for nearly two thousand years.[7]

The Witch at Home. Of course there were all sorts of witches, young and old, rich and poor. But the typical witch, *i.e.* the sort of person most likely to be accused of witchcraft was an old woman, with wrinkled face not devoid of hair, with defective teeth, squint-eyed, squeaking voice and scolding tongue.[8] She wore a dark rough garment and a skull cap or sometimes a pointed conical hat, the latter derived from the old traditional headwear of the magician, but here almost invariably black. She carried a spindle, or was often seen weaving, a feature derived from Greek mythology, wherein the three Fates or Parcae are generally old women one holding a distaff, one a spinning wheel and one a pair of scissors to cut the thread of life. The witch always had a cauldron, in which to prepare her drugs and philtres. In one corner of the room would be seen a broom of hazel twigs, or better still, of witch-hazel, a plant dedicated to witchcraft. There would be one or more small animals, believed to be possessed of evil spirits, the *familiars* of the witch. The familiar could be a dog, a cat, a hedgehog, a mole, a frog or an insect, said to be nourished on the blood of the witch. The witch usually lived in a thatched cottage. One of the ways of defending oneself against the attacks of a witch was to steal some thatching from her roof and burn it. The earliest account of chimneys as we know them is in 1347.[9] They were at first very wide. This would account for the idea that witches flew out of the chimney, rather than through the window or door. In most instances the latter was not available as above it was to be found, according to the custom of the day, the cross or pentacle.

As a sample of the ingredients of a witches' brew we cannot do better than mention some of the things used by the witches in Shakepeare's *Macbeth.* They included the venom of a toad, the fillet of a snake, the eye of a newt, the toe of a frog, the wool of a bat, the tongue of a dog, the fork of an adder, the sting of a blind-worm, the leg of a lizard, the wing of an owlet, the scale of a dragon, the tooth of a wolf, the mummy of a witch, maw and gulf of the ravin'd salt sea shark, the gall of a goat, part of a tiger, blood

[7] It is said that more than this number were executed, not for witchcraft, but for political reasons, during the Second World War, 1939–1945.

[8] Gaule, 1646, quoted in Brand's *Popular Antiquities,* new ed., Vol. III, London, 1849.

[9] J. Beckmann: *A History of Inventions, Discoveries and Origins,* trans. 4th edition, London, 1846.

of a baboon, nose of a Turk, lips of a Tartar, liver of a Jew and a finger of a babe strangled at birth. The plants used were root of hemlock dug in the dark, and slips of yew slivered during the moon's eclipse.

The mandrake (*Mandragora*) mentioned in Shakespeare's *Romeo and Juliet*, *Othello* and *Antony and Cleopatra*,[10] is a plant, the underground part of which is supposed to resemble the whole human body, except for the head, which would take the place of the overground shoot. When pulled from the earth, it was said, it utters a scream so terrible, that anyone hearing it dropped dead. Consequently to gather it a trick was adopted. A dog was tied to the overground part and some food placed out of reach of the dog, but visible to it. Then the operator rode away. The dog struggled to get the food, uprooted the mandrake and dropped dead on hearing the shriek. Then the operator returned and collected the uprooted specimen. Naturally it was very expensive. It has a narcotic action. Two other plants were used by the witches. They were the thorn-apple (*Datura*) and henbane (*Hyoscyamus*). All three plants belong to the potato family. Thorn-apple was used by the witches in ointments with which they anointed themselves before going to the witches' sabbath. It gives sexual hallucinations, apparitions and the sensation of flying, followed by confessions of guilt. Henbane contains the same active principle and was sometimes mixed with it, as Albertus Magnus mentions. Henbane is mentioned in Shakespeare's *Hamlet* as the poison used to destroy Hamlet's father. Aconite or monkshood (*Aconitum*), a most deadly plant of the buttercup family, also seems to have been employed by witches.

The Witches' Sabbath. More correctly the assembly of the witches was called the *Sabbat*. According to some accounts there were two kinds of meetings (i) the *esbat* which was an assembly of twelve witches and a leader called the devil, *i.e.* a *coven*, thirteen in all, which took place frequently, and (ii) the *sabbat* which was a united assembly of several or many covens. The meeetings, at any rate the sabbats, were always held out of doors, at remote and inaccessible places, often on hillsides or on clearings in a forest. There is some evidence that they used places with megalithic monuments, where available. They may have assembled at the cross-roads before proceeding to their destination. Some of the localities where they met have a tradition of connection with the fairies. The lesser festivals

[10] It is probably also *the insane root* of Shakespeare's *Macbeth*.

may have been determined by the phases of the moon. The meetings began at midnight and terminated before cock-crow. Both fairies and witches, as is well known in folk-lore, cannot be seen after cock-crow.

The witches prepared for the sabbat by removal of all clothes and anointing the whole body, from the crown of the head to the soles of the feet with their special ointment. This was of fat (preferably human) and contained the drugs, as already mentioned. It might also be made black, by adding soot, and disgusting by adding such things as the blood of goats or bats, or even given a definitely evil character (and this seems to have been common) by adding the fat of murdered unbaptised babes.

The witches then flew off on their broomsticks through the air. Theologians have debated, at great length, whether they really left their beds or did not. Probably some, after the anointing, fell into a sort of stupor, and dreamed about going to the sabbat. On the other hand there is no doubt that others did actually assemble, each witch, no doubt, being in a dreamy condition, owing to the drugs. Those who believe in levitation will have no difficulty in believing that they flew to the meeting-place. And if so why not on broomsticks?

As it was at night, a fire and torches illuminated the meeting place. At the sabbat a leader dressed in black, sometimes with horns and hoofs, answered for the devil. There was a roll-call. Each individual gave the *kiss of shame* on the hind-quarters of the devil, whereon there was sometimes represented a second face.

Instruments were played, notably the fiddle, pipes and tambourine. Hughes[11] says in Scotland the Jew's harp was used. Dancing took place, and the same author says *La Volta* was a favourite tune, brought from Italy into France. There is also evidence[12] that the round dance, that survives today in children's games, and even the waltz, may have originated from dances performed at the witches' sabbat.

Mr. Hughes is of the opinion that a blasphemous parody of the Mass was enacted at the sabbat.[13] He says that Hosts consecrated in Church were stolen, or that if an apostate priest were present consecration took place on the spot. There are many references to the most damnable misuse of the consecrated Host by witches for

[11] Pennethorne Hughes: *Witchcraft,* London, New York and Toronto, 1952.
[12] Margaret A. Murray: *The God of the Witches,* London, not dated, but *circa* 1930.
[13] *Loc cit.*

diabolical purposes. Sometimes only a parody of the Host was made, *e.g.* with a slice of black turnip mentioned by Hughes.[14] The Lord's Prayer was sometimes repeated backwards.[15]

Finally the devil was expected to have sexual congress with all the witches. At their trials the witches invariably describe this as painful, and the body of the devil as cold to the touch. It seems obvious that artificial methods were used. Finally the meeting concluded in a more general orgy of wantonness.[16]

The witches knew one another by special names or nicknames,[17] for had they not renounced their baptismal names?

Some very large assemblies of witches took place at certain localities. The Brocken or Blocksburg in the Harz mountains is one of the most famous. Early 18th century maps of Germany are decorated in this region with figures of witches on broomsticks.[18] Goethe describes the Walpurgis night festival of the witches there. The Blokula in Sweden was another famous place, already mentioned. A house was established there for witches, as reported in the witch-trial connected with this meeting-place. Another famous place was near the summit of Puy-de-Dome, Auvergne, France.

The witches apparently observed some of the Christian festivals. Their chief celebrations were undoubtedly what the Germans call Walpurgis Nacht, *i.e.* the Eve of St. Walburga's Day, or Roodmass in England. St. Walburga's Day is May 1st. The night before this was the witches' great festival, and the reason has nothing to do with the saint. April 30th was connected with Hades or Pluto, god and king of the infernal regions, and his festival was celebrated on this day. In the Church it is dedicated to St. Donat or Aidoneus who is a dragon-slaying saint, signifying the casting down of the evil one to the lower regions. That no doubt is why the witches chose it.

The Discovery of Witches. Two very crude methods were ducking, and weighing against the Church Bible, which must, in the old days, have been of enormous weight. Both methods were popular with the uneducated, and were denounced by theologians. The ducking of witches must not be confused with the ducking of scolds. In the latter the scold was bound down, seated in a chair, on the end of a plank which was lowered several times into the water. A witch to be tested, on the contrary, was cross-tied, *i.e.* the right hand was

[14] *Loc cit.*
[15] *Loc cit.*   [16] *Loc. cit.*
[17] For a list of these see Hughes, *loc cit.*   [18] Hughes, *loc. cit.*

attached to the left foot, and the left hand to the right foot. She was then thrown in water. If she floated she was deemed guilty. If she sank she was not guilty, and was fished out as soon as possible.

There were much better ways of identifying a witch. It was said that a witch could not shed tears. When one of their number has been received by the devil he gives them a prick, nip, scratch or bite, drawing blood. Thereafter the devil's mark was supposed to be on the body and the witch could not bleed. Red or blue marks were supposed to be due to the devil's claws. A small circular red mark was due to a prick. Sometimes the mark took the form of an animal: dog, mouse, bat or toad. Or it was like a hare's footprint.[19] There is no doubt that old scars, corns, warts, haemorrhoids, birthmarks, moles and supernumary teats were regarded in some cases, as proof of witchcraft. The additional teats (*polythelia*) are not at all uncommon and some women have additional breasts (*polymastia*). These were said to give suck to familiars. Hughes thinks the witches may have used tattooing.[20]

Incubi and Succubi. An *incubus* is an evil spirit that visits women, and has sexual relations with them. The belief is based on *Genesis* vi, 4 which is interpreted to mean certain angels came down from their high estate to cohabit with the daughters of men, from which unions sprang the giants. The belief in incubi is upheld by many theologians including St. Augustine and St. Thomas Aquinas. The former identifies them with the sylvans and fauns of pagan mythology.

There are very many stories of women being visited by evil spirits, who sought to tempt them to sin in this way. Such women often resisted the attacks, and called in the help of the Church to fortify themselves against them. In other cases absolution was obtained from the Pope, after transgression, as in the case of the abbess Magdalena Crucia of Cordova in 1545, who confessed to thirty years' intimacy with a devil. More often than not these sinners remained obdurate, and were sent to the stake.

A *succubus* is an evil spirit taking the form of a female and having sexual relations with men. Succubi appear more rarely than incubi. In folk-lore they sometimes appear as fairies. An example was Melusina who married a man on condition he never saw her on a Saturday, for on that day of the week she became a

[19] Hughes: *loc. cit.*
[20] *Loc cit.*

serpent. But one Saturday he did see her, and thereafter she vanished.

Offspring of incubi and human women were sometimes produced. There are various theories as to how this might occur, the best known being that these demons could transport human semen, and use it as if it were their own. Others believed that the offspring could develop without any physical contribution from the male subject.

Monstrous births and even the supposed births of animals, from human mothers, were explained in this way. But the offspring was sometimes human, and in some respects prodigious. Antichrist will be born after this manner, according to many accounts. In fact about 1600 several rumours spread in Europe that Antichrist had actually been born, with descriptions of his reception at the sabbat and personal features, such as his clawed feet, pointed ears, ability to speak all languages and work magic.[21]

According to L. M. Sinistrari[22] incubi and succubi are not demons and are motivated by lust alone, and not malice, unless discouraged. They are the spirits called *Follets* in France, *Folleti* in Italy and *Duendes* in Spain. The offspring of these beings and human females have been supposed to include: Romulus and Remus, the founders of Rome; Servius Tullius, sixth King of Rome; Plato, whose birth was rumoured to have been miraculous; Alexander the Great, the story of whose strange lineage we have related; King Seleucus of Syria, founder of the Seleucid Dynasty; Scipio Africanus, the great military leader; Augustus, the first emperor of that name; Aristomenes of Messina, the famous general; Merlin, the great magician and Martin Luther, the reformer. Others would add Ptolemy I, Zoroaster and all those heroes who had gods for father and mortal mother.

The Abbé Montfaucon de Villars (1635–1673), who was murdered near Lyons, France, for no known reason, wrote some very peculiar works dealing with those fairy-like beings technically termed *elementals*. These, as we have seen, are of several kinds. In his work entitled *Comte de Gabalis*, 1670, dealing in romantic fashion with the life of the aforementioned alchemist Borri, the author deals with the nature of salamanders, which is fiery, of sylphs, airy, of undines, watery and gnomes, earthy. These are described in some detail. But the most original part of the work

21 For further details see S. Baring-Gould: *Curious Myths of the Middle Ages*, New Edition, London, New York and Bombay, 1897.
22 Quoted by Lea, Vol. II, *loc cit*.

consists in the following assertions : (i) these elementals are beautiful, intelligent and friendly to wise men; (ii) before the Fall of Adam and Eve they were subject to Adam and in communication with him; (iii) this ancient communication may be restored by certain simple rituals; (iv) marriages may take place between elementals and human beings; (v) the offspring of such marriages are of heroic quality; (vi) elementals are not immortal unless they marry human beings; if they do a human being may make his elemental marriage partner immortal, or he may lose his own immortality and become mortal like an elemental, the matter being optional (those predestined to hell are advised to select the latter option). It will be seen that, by introducing the ideas of loss of immortality and predestination in this way, the Abbé was overstepping the limits of orthodoxy, but by this time he was devoting all his time to writing and the work was regarded as so amusing that no action was taken.

The Were-Wolf. The idea that a human being could be transformed into an animal was widespread among the ancients. We have already noticed Apuleius who was changed into an ass, and the companions of Ulysses whom Circe changed into swine. It was thought that powerful witches could do such things, and many witches were alleged to turn themselves into wild animals, particularly wolves. This is mentioned in Pliny. Sometimes it was voluntary, sometimes involuntary, the result of a curse. The phenomenon is technically termed *lycanthropy* which, according to derivation means the transformation of a man into a wolf or vice-versa. The worst kind of witches were thought to indulge in it, as their behaviour whilst in the form of wild animals gave them means to satisfy their malice.

One of the most celebrated cases of lycanthropy was that of Gilles Garnier, a native of Lyons, and tried at Dôle in 1573, found guilty and burnt at the stake. Under torture the accused confessed that he changed into a wolf, in this condition had killed and torn to pieces a girl of twelve years of age, had eaten part of the body and, after resuming human form had taken the rest home to his wife. He also admitted attacking another child that was rescued but died, he had torn off the leg and thigh of another boy and eaten him, and in human form had strangled a boy and would have eaten him if not prevented.

Another famous case occurred at a village in the Auvergne mountains in 1588. A gentleman suspected his wife of witchcraft.

One day a huntsman told the gentleman he had been attacked by a large and ferocious wolf, but that he had beaten it off and cut off one of its paws. He opened his bag to show the paw, when he was horrified to find a woman's finger with a ring on it. The gentleman then went to find his wife, and found she was hiding her hand behind her apron. She showed part of the hand had been severed. She was taken into custody, tried and burnt at the stake.

There are several theories in explanation of lycanthropy, as follows:

1. Witches, warlocks and other personages disposed towards evil at times dressed themselves as animals as a means of disguising their nefarious activities.

2. Bewitched persons imagined themselves and were imagined by others to have become animals, which they imitated in their behaviour. In some cases mass-hypnotism seems to have been involved. St. Macarius, who disenchanted a woman turned into a horse, in another instance met a young woman believed by her husband and bystanders to be turned into a stoat. The saint is here said to have lifted the veil from those who saw her in this condition, telling them she was still a woman and that they had been deluded.

3. Several cases are reported where it is certain that, whilst the wild animal appears elsewhere, doing mischief, the human being ensouling the creature lies sleeping. These cases can only be explained on the theory advanced by Eliphas Levi[23] that during sleep a part of the sleeper which Levi calls the sidereal body (now known as the astral body) leaves the physical body and can appear elsewhere (astral projection) and can assume the form of an animal.

The Vampire. This word, which is now applied to a blood-sucking bat, was also applied to a dead and buried person who was supposed to arise out of the grave every night except Friday, and to go about in a stealthy fashion, whilst others sleep, sucking their blood. The word *vampire* may be of Slavonic origin. Certain it is that, whilst belief in vampires was world-wide, in Europe it was best known among those peoples adherent to the Greek or Eastern Church, *viz.* the peoples of Russia, Montenegro, Serbia, Wallachia,

[23] Quoted by F. Hamel: *Human Animals*, London, 1915. This work contains a great deal of occult lore relating to lycanthropy and cognate subjects.

Bohemia, and certain parts of Hungary. Those under this denom-
ination popularly believed[24] that (i) the dead bodies of ordinary
people soon decayed after death, until only the bones remained,
(ii) those of very holy person were preserved in their natural colour
and consistency for an indefinite period and emitted an agreeable
odour[25] and (iii) the bodies of excommunicated persons turned
black, swelled out and were distended like a drum, and gave out a
very offensive smell. However, according to some, vampires come
from the third class. On opening the graves of these their com-
plexion was found to be ruddy, their veins distended, and their
blood not coagulated. In fact a slight incision yielded a copious
supply of blood, as from a young person.[26] The bodies of mur-
derers and suicides were particularly liable to become vampires.
But, horribly enough, there were many vampires who had become
vampires solely by having their blood sucked, during life, by
another vampire, or even if after their death, an animal jumped
over the corpse, or if a bird flew over it.

The way to prevent a vampire approaching and harming a
healthy human being is to have some garlic at hand.[27]

Various methods were adopted to stop the activities of vampires.
They were buried at the cross-roads, a large nail was driven across
the head, through the temples, a stake was driven through the
heart, the head was cut off, or the whole body burnt.

Vampirism reached its height in the period 1723–1735, when
an epidemic of the phenomenon occurred in south-east Europe,
being particularly prevalent in Hungary and Serbia.[28]

Occultists usually explain the vampire as the astral body or
etheric double of the dead person, which under certain circumstances can be seen as a phantom.

Flagellation and Dancing. In 1259 an irregular religious sect
appeared at Perugia in Italy. They first claimed to be merely peni-
tents, but soon spread the idea that salvation was to be obtained,
both for themselves and others, by whippings continued for thirty-
three and a half days in memory of the number of years in the
earthly life of Christ. The whippings were only effective in the
event that blood was drawn. They soon began regular marches in

[24] Dudley Wright: *Vampires and Vampirism,* London, 1924.
[25] This was also alleged of many saints in the Roman Church.
[26] Wright: *loc. cit.*
[27] As mentioned in Bram Stoker's *Dracula,* a romance giving an excellent
account of vampirism.
[28] Wright: *loc. cit.*

Italy, Hungary, Germany, Flanders and Holland. They paraded in a practically naked condition, and lashed one another as they proceeded. They carried figures of skeletons, and from this their exhibitions came to be known as *the dance of death.*

In 1374 a dancing sect appeared in the region of the Lower Rhine. They appear to have had the same dances as the witches, *i.e.* hand in hand in circles, or in pairs as in the waltz. They danced for hours, until completely exhausted, even in the streets or in churches. They said the dance was in honour of St. John. The movement spread through France and the Low Countries.

In 1349 Pope Clement VI issued a bull against the flagellants.

In 1414 one Conrad Schmidt preached that all spiritual authority had passed from the Church to the flagellants and denounced marriage and all the sacraments.

In the 16th century there were several outbreaks of dancing mania in Italy, but they were ascribed to the bites of the Italian tarantula (*Lycosa tarantula*) which is not usually very serious. The old idea was that anyone bitten falls into a state of intense depression and may die. However, he can be aroused by certain kinds of music, when he dances until exhausted. This is repeated on successive days, for a week or more, by which time the patient finds himself cured, and without memory of the bite or the dancing. The music used is still preserved in the dance called the *Tarantelle.*

The Black Mass. We have seen that various parodies of the Holy Sacrifice of the Mass were performed at the witches' sabbat. It is unlikely that these had an organised form, or that there was a common ritual. The "devils" might just carry out sacrilegious acts of various kinds. But, as the Mass is the most powerful of the sacraments, it was perverted to magical uses. It was argued that if the Mass in its normal form could effect miracles for the good of the community, it could be perverted to serve selfish, unworthy and evil ends when modified in a devilish fashion. Perhaps this was not consciously asserted, but it is implied by such rites as we have seen were performed for Gilles de Rais.

The Black Mass as an organised ceremonial seems to have developed in France in the 16th century. Catherine de Medici (1519–1589), who was the daughter of Lorenzo de Medici, and thus brought into contact with magic in her earliest days, married, at the age of fourteen, a prince who afterwards became Henry II, King of France (*r.* 1547–1559). She was beautiful and accomplished, but after his death in a tournament, at the age of forty, seems to have consigned herself to the devil. Her young sons were brought up to be effeminate and licentious. She has been accused of being more or less responsible for the Massacre of St. Bartholomew, of stirring up conflicts between Catholics and Protestants and even of encouraging first one side then the other.[29] There is little doubt that Catherine had black masses performed. Her son Charles IX (r. 1560–1574) is said to have done likewise. On one occasion a sorcerer called Trois Echelles was condemned to death during the reign of this king. Charles, according to Bodin,[30] pardoned him, on condition he gave an account of the sabbat, and mended his ways. He did so, but soon after relapsed and was hanged. Henry III (r. 1574–1589) the brother of Charles IX, who succeeded him, who was responsible for the murder of a cardinal and a duke, and who took sides with the Huguenots, was openly accused of sorcery and homosexuality. This was based on the discovery in a grove in the Forest of Vincennes of two silver figures of satyrs, each holding a bowl, in which incense had been burned, these statues had their backs turned to a golden cross, some $3\frac{1}{2}$ feet high, in which was set a piece of wood, believed to be a relic of the True Cross.[31] Meanwhile the king's enemies were employing magic against him. Mass was said with an image of the king on the altar. Prayers were said against the king, and at that moment a knife was plunged into the image. The king failed to die. Eventually a fanatic named Jacques Clément, after having had visions telling him to kill the king, succeeded in assassinating him, and was seized and put to death, laughing like a maniac.[32] This put an end to the dynasty of the Valois.

Under the House of Bourbon we hear of the scandals of Gaufridi and of the nuns of Loudon and Louviers, already mentioned. In all these cases there were allegations of attendance at the Black Mass. In the Gaufridi case, the Host was said to be offered to the devil and the Precious Blood sprinkled over the vile congregation with the cry "His Blood be on us, and on our children."[33] In the Louviers case there seems to have been a *Book of Blasphemy* to serve as a missal, the Host and Chalice were defiled, and the bread

[29] Websters *Biographical Dictionary,* Springfield, Mass., U.S.A., 1943.
[30] J. Bodin: *De Magorum Daemonomania,* Basle, 1581.
[31] Further details are given in Montague Summers: *A Popular History of Witchcraft,* London, 1937. This quotes contemporary pamphlets.
[32] P. de l'Etoile, quoted by Eliphas Levi: *The History of Magic,* trans. 2nd ed., London, 1922.
[33] Montague Summers, *loc. cit.*

for consecration was of a reddish hue.[34] One enormity was the stabbing of the consecrated Host with knives, and this was by no means the most offensive act of sacrilege.

In the long reign of Louis XIV (r. 1643–1715), famed for splendour, there was a very dark side under the surface. An epidemic of poisoning spread from Italy into France. It was particularly used to get rid of unwanted husbands. The poison was a solution in water of arsenical salt, and it was well known under the name of *Aqua Tophania*, after an Italian murderess who used it on a large scale, or *Manna of St. Nicholas of Barri*, which was the name used to elude the customs, it being alleged to be a miraculous medicine oozing from the tomb of that saint. Moreover there was an organisation for getting rid of new born babies. Two women were running this trade. They were known as La Voisin and La Vigoreux. They termed themselves midwives, and also went in for fortune-telling. They were burnt at the stake in 1680. La Voisin also organised Black Masses. She had a furnace at her house for the disposal of the bodies of unwanted babies, and on some occasions a child was sacrificed during the Black Mass, its blood being mingled in the Sacred Chalice.

Many priests were executed for celebrating these monstrous rites. The altar was covered with black, there were black candles. Beneath the altar cloth was a mattress, and when the rite was celebrated a naked woman was placed on the altar, her legs hanging down in front. Her arms were stretched out and grasped two of the candlesticks. Her head rested on a pillow. The priest consecrated the bread and wine in the usual way, but after the consecration they were polluted in a manner too indecent to describe. Another kind of Black Mass was one in which the Host was mixed with ashes from a cremated murdered child, and blood from another. Then there was a Mass of Virility in which blood, flour and very disgusting substances were mingled with the Sacred Species, for making love-philtres.[35] These Masses are known to have been celebrated by the notorious Abbé Guibourg, from reports of trials, and no doubt were common at the time. It also seems certain that, on at least one occasion, the Black Mass was celebrated, at the instance of the Marchioness of Montespan, the king's mistress, with a view to her retaining the king's affections, and that she herself was placed on the altar.

An extraordinary variant of the Black Mass was practised by the

34 Montague Summers, *loc. cit.*
35 J. K. Huÿsmans: *Là Bas*, Paris, 1891. Trans. London, 1943.

Abbé Beccarelli. At this lozenges were distributed which were supposed to make the recipient change sex. He was discovered and sentenced to serve in the galleys for seven years.[36]

Another form of the Black Mass called the Mass of St. Secaire is said to be derived from Basque or Gascon folklore. It is described by Huysmans, Montague Summers[37] and H. T. F. Rhodes.[38] Huysmans and Summers derive the name from St. Cesarius of Arles (470–543), a notable opponent of evil magic. The host is triangular in form, and instead of wine, water is used, drawn from a well into which has been thrown the body of an unbaptised babe. The sign of the cross is made with the left foot, on the ground. The intention of this evil mass is the death of some person; it is one of the worst forms of black magic, and anyone celebrating it can only obtain absolution from the Pope himself, and that with great difficulty.

Huysmans[39] mentions instances, in 1843, 1855 and 1874 where societies were discovered, wherein women regularly went to Mass, received the Most Holy Sacrament in the mouth, subsequently disgorging it, whereafter it was subjected to hideous pollutions. He mentions a society of black magicians, established in America, under the direction of a Scot named Longfellow.[40]

Huysmans[41] also claims to have attended a Black Mass himself. It was said in a deserted chapel. On the altar was a crucifix bearing a grotesque figure, with absurdly long neck, and face painted to show a grin. The incense was of rue, henbane, thorn-apple, nightshade and myrtle. Black candles emitted an equally unpleasant stench. The celebrant wore a red biretta, decorated with bison's horns of red material, and a blood-red chasuble, bearing the figure of a goat. Blasphemous words were shouted, the Host was consecrated and thrown on the floor and clawed by the congregation.

The celebrant at this horrible affair is believed to be a real priest called Roca. In the story he is named Docre. He is said to have possessed a Missal of the Black Mass, on parchment, bound in the tanned skin of an unbaptised babe, and with one cover impressed with a large Host, consecrated at a Black Mass. Further he feeds consecrated Hosts to animals. This devilish act was long known to witches and warlocks. But in the story (almost certainly based on

[36] Huysmans: *loc. cit.*
[37] *The History of Witchcraft*, London, 1926, reprinted 1956.
[38] *The Satanic Mass*, London, 1954.
[39] *Loc. cit.*
[40] Not to be confused with the poet of that name.
[41] *Loc. cit.*, written as fiction but believed to be autobiographical.

fact) the sacrilegious priest also feeds the animals on poison, in graduated doses, until the whole body of the creature is impregnated with venom. White mice, so dealt with, were then bled, and their blood used as poison. Fowls and guinea-pigs, similarly treated, were killed, and their fat taken as poison. Fishes treated with poisons acting on the central nervous system, or producing symptoms resembling those of tetanus, were taken out of the water, died, were allowed to putrefy, and distilled to give an essential oil, one drop of which applied to the skin induces dementia. He was also accused of making a paste composed of Sacramental Bread, mixed with flour, meat, mercury, acetate of morphia and oil of aspic.

But poisoning was effected, by this wretch, not only by contact. The black magician employed a rather rare kind of clairvoyant, so it was believed, who could travel in spirit, when hypnotised, for hundreds of miles, and yet carry the fatal poison to the victim.[42] It was alleged that this sort of devilry was being practised by not only one, but by a number of renegade priests. It was claimed that one man, at least, had a means of warding off the attacks of these black magicians, and of providing an antidote. He is called Johannès in the book, and has been identified with Abbé J.-A. Boullan whose story will be outlined later.

[42] Huysmans, *loc. cit.*

CHAPTER XXVIII

BLACK MAGICIANS AND DREAMERS

Abra-Melin the Mage. A serious and important magician was Abraham the Jew (1362–1460?) who lived in Germany, probably mostly at Würzburg. He is known from a manuscript preserved in the Library of the Arsenal, Paris. This was in French and purports to be translated from Hebrew. From the French it was translated into English by S. L. Macgregor Mathers.[1] Abraham had two sons to one of whom he bequeathed his knowledge of the Holy Qabalah, to the other his magic. The manuscript deals with the second. The first part recounts his wanderings, and explains how, after studying under many masters in Eastern Europe, Arabia and Egypt he at length attained the true art under Abra-Melin in the latter country. It also tells how Abraham was able to help, by magical means, several celebrated people. He facilitated the marriage of the Emperor Sigismund, and allowed a familiar spirit to serve him. He produced two thousand horsemen to help Frederick, Elector of Saxony, when his realm was being invaded. He delivered the Earl of Warwick, under threat of death, from an English prison. He helped the antipope John XXIII (r. 1410–1415) to escape from the Council of Constance, which condemned him.

The second and third parts of the manuscript give the magical techniques, which are in many ways peculiar. He makes use of a vast crowd of evil spirits including the four princes Lucifer, Leviatan (Leviathan), Satan and Belial and the eight sub-princes Astarot (Astaroth), Magot, Asmodee (Amodeus), Belzebud (Beelzebub), Orien, Paimon, Ariton and Amaimon and their numerous servitors. But he says magic should only be used for good ends, and to prepare for the visible coming of these devils he first calls down a crowd of good angels including his own Holy Guardian Angel, who gives him the necessary precautions for dealing with the devils. And to prepare for the invocation of the Holy Guardian Angel he retires to a secluded spot, adopts austere habits, and prepares an altar standing in an oratory. On one side is a window

[1] *The Book of the Sacred Magic of Abra-Melin the Mage,* London, 1898, Chicago, 1932.

which opens on to an uncovered terrace or balcony, on which the spirits appear. Lamps and incense are used, and holy oils for consecrating a silver lamen on which an angel writes instructions. The magician wears a white linen tunic, over which is a crimson or scarlet silk robe, both with sleeves. He is encircled with a girdle, wears a crown or mitre and carries a wand. A child of less than seven years old carries the lamen to the altar.

Notwithstanding his repeated assertions that only good magic must be performed, Abraham gives instructions on how to know things past and future, how to see visions, how to use familiar spirits, how to excite tempests, to fly through the air, to transform oneself and others into animals and to cause armed men to appear. He excuses the inclusion of matter that may be subject to abuse on the grounds that he wants his account to be a complete exposition of magic.

Grimoires. The Abra-Melin manuscript is relatively intelligible as compared with many magical documents which have had a wide circulation. Certain of these, of a very idiotic and puerile description, have been assigned to Aristotle and St. Albertus Magnus. The so-called *Admirable Secrets*, ascribed to the latter, has some interest but the *Egyptian Secrets* and the *Great* and *Little Albert* are extremely futile. The latter has often been printed and is a collection of receipts, most domestic, of an incredibly silly description. *The Greater Key of Solomon the King* probably dates from the 14th or 15th century. It purports to have been in Hebrew, but the originals are in Latin, from which translations into English, French, German and Italian have been made. Josephus said King Solomon wrote magical books, but this work has nothing in common with the legends of Solomon. It gives, very crudely, the influences of the planets, the conjuration of good and evil spirits, the construction of circles, pentacles, etc. for magical purposes, means of rendering oneself invisible, finding treasure, obtaining favours, the use of incense and magical weapons. *The Lesser Key of Solomon the King* or *Lemegeton* (17th century) gives the names, orders and offices of evil spirits and spirits of astrological divisions of time and the heavens, as well as certain conjurations. *The Grimoire Verum*, 1517, is partly based on these two keys, and includes confused instructions for evoking devils as well as less harmful matter. *The Grand Grimoire* is a futile and absurd collection of data on tricking the devils into man's service. *The Grimoire of Honorius*, already mentioned imitates catholic ceremonies in a confused attempt to raise the dead or control devils. *The Sixth and Seventh Books of Moses* bear no relation whatever to the Pentateuch, they are illiterate and imbecile collections of symbols, many sprawling about in all directions interspersed with conjurations, diabolical names, psalms and references to the *Talmud*.

The *Arbatel* is a magical work which appeared at Basle, Switzerland in 1575. Only one part of the original is extant. It deals with the control of spirits presiding over the natural world and its processes. These are called Olympic spirits, and of them there are seven chief: Aratron, Bethor, Hagith, Och, Ophiel, Phaleg and Phul, each with his servitors, of which the total is 196. Each chief corresponds with one of the planets.

Psychics. Mother Shipton (1487–1562?) of Yorkshire, reputed witch and prophetess, whose biographies are sometimes believed to be purely imaginary, was said to foretell the death of Cardinal Wolsey, the Civil War, the Fire of London, the invention of the steam engine and the telegraph, and the end of the world which she predicted would take place in 1881.

Nostradamus (1503–1566), French physician and astrologer, published, as was frequent in those days, annual prophecies. But he is more famous for his *Centuries* 1555 which gives in rhyme and in symbolic form a number of historic events up to the present day, including the death of Henry II of France in a tournament, the French Revolution, the rise and fall of Napoleon and of Hitler. Nostradamus was no mean figure, being consulted by Catherine de Medici and by Charles IX of France, her son.

The most famous of this class of individuals, whom we call *psychics*, as they apparently used faculties of the mind little understood, as well as the data of astrology and kabalism, were the famous Dr. John Dee (1527–1608) and his assistant Sir Edward Kelley (1555–1595). Dee was educated at the University of Cambridge, and afterwards proceeded to Louvain where he obtained his doctorate. After a short while on the Continent, where he came into contact with Mercator, he returned to England, and was prominent at the court of Edward VI, to whom he had dedicated two books. He took holy orders in the Church of England. Nevertheless on the ascent of Mary to the throne he was invited to calculate her nativity and that of her sister Elizabeth. However, soon after he was accused of magic and treason, and was imprisoned for a time, although soon acquitted. When Elizabeth came to the throne he was selected to choose a suitable day for her coronation. He was also consulted by the queen about a wax image of Her Majesty found in Lincoln's Inn Fields, with a dagger struck into the breast, evidently intended to harm the queen by sympathetic magic. Dee was expected to counteract the magical attack. He also reassured the queen on the appearance of a new star and a comet. He wrote on mathematics and travelled as far afield as St. Helena.

On his return he tried crystal-gazing, using a large piece of polished coal. Soon he began to see spirits. But he could never concentrate enough to see these and at the same time write down their messages. He therefore proposed to employ a scryer, *i.e.* a person having such psychic qualities as could "read the crystal." He soon found a satisfactory one in Edward Kelley. The latter was a Lancashire man who had been convicted of coining, and had had his ears cut off as a punishment. This he used to conceal by wearing a black skull cap bearing side lappets, which gave him a rather imposing appearance. Kelley moreover claimed to have some of the powder of projection, which he had found, with an old alchemical manuscript, in Wales. Scrying soon began on a large scale, together with alchemical experiments. The latter was soon noised abroad, and many eminent men were convinced that Dee and Kelley were making gold. Soon the rumour went round that they had found the elixir of life in the ruins of Glastonbury Abbey.

About this time a Polish count, called Laski, was visiting the court of Elizabeth, and was taken to see Dee and Kelley by Elizabeth's favourite, the Earl of Leicester. The count was a great believer in the occult, and soon was completely under the sway of Dee and Kelley. The spirits manifesting in the polished coal gave out that great political changes were imminent in Europe, and that Laski was to become a king. This was done in a gradual fashion, so as not to arouse suspicion, but soon Laski invited them to visit his estates in Poland, and in 1583 they set out with their wives and families for the Continent. The messages from the angels continued, and records of them were made. Incidentally it may be noted that these records contain a number of words of the angelic language, called Enochian by modern occultists, and believed to be the language spoken in Atlantis.

When the party arrived in Poland the angels began to concentrate on gold making and the political transformation of Europe, for which purpose funds were obviously necessary. Laski began to mortgage his estates. But unexpected difficulties developed. Eventually Laski, in order to get rid of Dee and Kelley, offered to introduce them to the Emperor Rudolph II. The latter, as we have seen, was intensely interested in alchemy. Laski also had to provide funds to get Dee and Kelley to the Emperor's court at Prague. The Emperor received them with delight, and soon conferred a knighthood on Kelley. They stayed a few months at Prague, pretending to be trying to make gold. But soon complaints were made that the Emperor was employing heretics, and one day the Papal Nuncio demanded their arrest. The Emperor, however, ordered them to quit the country within twenty-four hours. They did so, and now began a wandering life, earning their money mostly by casting horoscopes. They stayed for a time with the King of Poland, and then with a Bohemian count called Rosenberg.

During these wanderings the angelic messages continued. But one day Kelley suddenly broke off his scrying, and declared that the angels were really devils. He refused to say what they told him, and after an argument, packed up his belongings and went into other lodgings with his wife and family. Dee was heartbroken, and after some ineffective attempts to get his son to read the crystal was plunged in the depths of despair. However Kelley reappeared. He again consulted the crystal, and again expressed extreme horror. However, after much persuasion from Dee and his family, Kelley revealed the message. It was that Dee and Kelley should share their wives in common. The ladies were disgusted, but Dee pointed out that their livelihood was at stake, and after endless arguments they had to agree. The arrangement did not last long. Dee returned to England, Kelley wandered about both in Bohemia and Germany, being imprisoned in both countries. He injured himself in trying to escape from the German prison, and died of his injuries. Dee held some minor posts in England until his death. Dee was responsible for some works which are still studied by occultists. The best known is *Monas Hieroglyphica,* 1564.

Behmen and the Behmenists. Jacob Behmen, or more correctly Boehme (1575–1624) was a mystic, born near Görlitz, Prussia. In his early life he was a shepherd, then a shoemaker. In 1599 he became a master shoemaker and married, and had several children. Later in life he dealt mainly in gloves. He studied the mystics and alchemists, began writing in 1612 and produced many works. They explain the origin of the cosmos, and the nature of man, using alchemical symbols. He considered that Heaven and Hell are states of being and exist potentially in man whilst he lives, and only become manifest after death. He was not concerned with practical alchemy in any way; the alchemical symbols were only used to show the spiritual state of man. As the divine Grace operates in the spiritual world in the same way that the divine Providence does in the natural, so men are purged of sin as metals are purified of dross. This has been called his fire-theology.[2] His views got him into serious trouble with authorities of the Lutheran Church, to which he was attached. His system has been termed theosophical, dealing, as it does, with the Holy Wisdom, but it is considerably different from modern Theosophy, being based on Christian Scriptures.

Boehme had a number of followers, even during his own life-time. But he had many enemies. His beautiful tomb was violated soon after it was erected, and the monumental and symbolical cross[3] destroyed.

One of Boehme's followers named Kuhlman was burnt at the stake in Moscow in 1689. The latter professed to have communications both with God and the devil, wrote remarkable books and visited various countries of Europe, including Britain.

J. G. Gichtel (1638–1710) was another follower of Boehme. He was at first an anabaptist, and was banished from Regensburg (Ratisbon), Germany in 1668 and went to live in Amsterdam. He here published Boehme's works in 1682 and led an ascetic sect called the Angelic Brothers, who did not believe in marriage. His writings were published in 1722 in seven volumes, under the title of *Theosophia Practica*. He taught that mystic contemplation was a surer guide than Scripture, and enabled one to attain an angelic state.

John Pordage (1625–1698), a physician and preacher, attempted to systematise the views of Boehme, and also claimed to have direct revelations from God. He was interested in alchemy and astrology and wrote *Mystic Divinitie*, 1688. Pordage and his associate Thomas Bromley, who also wrote of Boehme, were associated with Jane Lead (Leade or Leadly, née Ward, 1623–1704) in the foundation of the Philadelphian Society in 1697. Jane Lead had previously issued a record of a number of her prophetic visions. She continued these, predicting the rise of a Philadelphian Church, depicted in the *Apocalypse*, wherein the members should possess

---

[2] J. L. Mosheim: *Ecclesiastical History*, Vol. II, trans. London, 1842.
[3] For a description of this cross and attached symbols see pp. 29–30, F. Hartmann: *Personal Christianity a Science: The Doctrines of Jacob Boehme*, New York, 1919.

miraculous powers. The sectarians would forget their differences and unite in brotherly love. They would be ruled by a triangle of love-elders, the first a priest, symbolised by a golden circle, the second a prophet, represented by a circle of silver, and the third or executive head, a king, symbolised by a mild and gentle fire.

William Law (1686–1761) a religious controversialist, author of the well-known book : *A Serious Call to a Devout and Holy Life* edited a third translation of Boehme's works in 1755, and was greatly influenced by them. Law is said to have been spiritual director of John Wesley (1703–1791), and his brother Charles Wesley (1707–1788), founders of Methodism. Law opposed all theatrical performances and wrote a book on this theme.

Sir Isaac Newton (1642–1727), the great physicist and mathematician, was much influenced by Boehme. Apart from his scientific work Newton was a deep student of prophecy and wrote a detailed manuscript entitled *Observations on the Prophecies of Daniel and the Apocalypse of St. John,* which has been described by Sir David Brewster.[4] Herein he claims analogy between the natural things mentioned in the *Bible* and the body politic. Thus the heavens represent thrones and dynasties, the sun kings, the stars subordinate princes and rulers, the moon the common people, animals and plants indicate nations. The four beasts are four empires, the lion with eagle's wings Babylon, the bear Persia, the leopard Greece, the beast with the great iron teeth Rome. Further the details are symbolic. Thus the four heads and wings of the Greek empire were four kingdoms, the ten horns of the last beast the ten divisions into which the empire was split in the reign of Theodosius the Great. There is much more on these lines, for the work goes into greater detail than most writings on prophecy, and that is saying a lot. It is probable that Newton's physical interests began with his search for occult phenomena. Newton was called "the last of the magicians" by Lord Keynes.[5] Newton believed in alchemical transmutations, at least in early life.[6]

Scientist and Seer. Unfortunately no account can be given here of the extraordinary visions of Emanuel Swedenborg (1688–1772). He

[4] *Life of Sir Isaac Newton,* London, 1828, new ed. 1855.
[5] Newton Tercentenary Celebrations, 1947, p. 27, quoted by Thorndike: *loc. cit.*
[6] Thorndike, *loc. cit.*

was a scientist and mining engineer in Sweden, contributing several mechanical inventions and works on geology, physics and anatomy. In 1743 he began to see angels and other spirits, and even the Lord Himself. In 1747 he resigned his position as assessor of mines on half pay to devote himself to theological writing and descriptions of his other-world experiences.

Occultism in France. Napoleon I (1769–1821) was somewhat attracted to the occult. He had his horoscope read by Marie Lenormand (1772–1843) who had predicted his marriage with Josephine. Marie was known as La Sibylle du Faubourg Saint-Germain and was consulted by Czar Alexander I of Russia and many other eminent personages. She even claimed to have helped in cementing the Triple Alliance, signed at Aix-la-Chapelle between Austria, France and Russia in 1818.[7]

Among French Catholics the 19th century was a period of great expectations. Several unbalanced persons[8] tried to give indications of a new dispensation of one kind or another. Rose Tamisier (*b.* 1818) made it known that she had received numerous visits from the Virgin Mary, who had instructed her to convert the infidels of France. Her body became marked with the stigmata, not indeed of the usual type, but with the form of a cross, a heart and a chalice, and at one time, according to report, a picture of the Virgin and Child appeared imprinted. All this caused intense excitement among neighbours, and no little bewilderment among Church authorities. But when Rose caused a picture of Christ descending from the cross to shed blood investigations were begun in earnest. The picture was in the small church of St. Saturnin-les-Aptes and a chemist E. Collignon was called in to prove the mystery. He found that blood from a leech, having lost its power of coagulation, could have been made to penetrate the picture and produce the apparent miracle. He even imitated the latter with success. Rose was arrested and tried for swindling and outraging public and religious morals, fined five hundred francs and costs and imprisoned for six months.

Rose Tamasier was suspected of belonging to what had been a small Catholic society of religious enthusiasts, which was becoming celebrated about the time of her trial (1851). The origin of this

[7] In her autobiographical *Dernières Prophéties,* 1843.
[8] Several are mentioned in Levi's *History of Magic* and Huysmans' *Là Bas.*

society is obscure. Up to 1839 their leader had been a certain Martin de Gullardon who had visions of angels. He died in that year and Eugène Vintras (1807-1875) was appointed to succeed him. Vintras was a manager of a cardboard box factory and a visionary. His appointment was the result of a visit from one whom he identified with the archangel Michael. It is alleged[9] however that the messenger was an agent of the royalist supporters of the imaginary Louis XVII, supposed successor of Louis XVI who was guillotined in the Revolution. It was the result of this royalist support that the society over which Vintras presided gained in popularity and increased in numbers. Vintras set up an oratory in his factory, and outwardly his society made a great show of piety. He called his institution *Carmel* and *l'Oeuvre de la Miséricorde*. Levi[10] however accuses him of having celebrated sacrilegious masses in which all present were in a state of complete nudity and during which at a certain point in the ceremony there were cries of "Love! Love!" followed by an orgy. The same author quotes a leaflet accusing Vintras of homosexual practices.

In 1842 Vintras was arraigned at Caen, accused of swindling, and sentenced to five years in prison. After serving his sentence he spent some years in London, but returned to France in 1863.

The sect was condemned by the Pope in 1843 and in later life Vintras was head of the sect. It ordained both priests and priestesses. Both celebrated Mass, but with slightly different ritual.

When Vintras died, a Catholic abbé J. A. Boullan (1824-1893) who had quarrelled with the theologians and had joined Vintras, was appointed as the latter's successor. Boullan held the view that the sacraments utilise forces which work like physical forces, but that they act for good or ill. He was constantly complaining of attacks by these forces, not only from Rome, but also from the Rosicrucians. When Boullan died he was under the impression that he was being attacked by the latter.

The Rosicrucians in question were the followers of the Marquis Stanislaus de Guaita, already mentioned. Huysmans in his famous *Là Bas* is supposed to have presented a description of Boullan under the name of Dr. Johannès. The latter is represented as a white magician and the only person capable of curing the ill effects produced by his abominable enemy Canon Docre, whose black

9 Eliphas Levi: *loc. cit.*
10 *Loc. cit.*

magic is described as very terrible.[11] Docre however, in the book, is identified with a real Canon Roca.

De Guaita, however, reverses the picture.[12] Roca for him is a good man, opposed to the evil Boullan. The latter is accused of teaching his followers that sex is the key to salvation. Nor is this confined to normal relations between married persons. In addition to this he taught, according to De Guaita, that under conditions of sanctity in Carmel relations that would otherwise appear sinful might be contracted (i) with members belonging to the opposite sex, (ii) with members of the same sex, (iii) with celestial beings and (iv) with elementals, much after the manner of the marriages between humans and elementals described in De Villars' *Comte de Gabalis* already referred to.[13]

The Sale of the Absolute. Hoene Wronski (J. M. Wronski 1778–1853) was a Polish mathematician of some standing. He was also a philosopher. Originally a disciple of Kant he studied the kabalistic system and came to develop some extraordinary views of his own. He formed the idea that the object of all occult fraternities is to direct the course of history, and even to participate in the act of creation, which, according to his philosophy, is a gradual process. These brotherhoods, he thought, could not influence governments directly, but must use indirect means. Consequently they are all secret. This leads on to the idea of Hidden Masters, who are supposed to be motivating power politics, an idea which has played a part in the thought of later occult groups.

More than this, Wronski brought forward the idea he called *Messianism.* Many other authors have talked about a second Messiah in the form of an individual. According to Wronski, whilst Christ was the Messiah to save individuals, a second Messiah must be a nation, to save nations. He thought Poland might become a candidate for this national messiahship, and in this connection notes the peculiar sufferings that have been inflicted and may still be inflicted (this was truly prophetic) on this unfortunate nation.[14]

Finally Wronski imagined, that by delving into kabalism, he had discovered the secret of the universe, and had unlocked the key

[11] We have already quoted details, see p. 256.
[12] Stanislas de Guaita: *Le Temple de Satan,* Paris, 1891.
[13] See p. 249.
[14] For some account of later Messianism see W. Lutoslawsky: *Pre-existence and Reincarnation,* trans. London, 1928.

to the Absolute. He sold this secret to a wealthy individual named Arson for 150,000 francs. After receiving some 40,000 or 50,000 francs the secret was handed over, but for some reason or other the rest of the money was not forthcoming. Wronski then wrote a pamphlet[15] entitled : *Yes or No—that is to say, have you or have you not, yes or no, purchased from me for 150,000 francs my discovery of the Absolute?*

Magic at the Russian Court. The Russian Church is an offshoot of the Byzantine (Greek Orthodox). At first it had bishops under the control of Byzantium (Constantinople, now Istanbul). Later some of these were raised to the rank of archbishops and even metropolitans, finally a patriarch was appointed (Patriarch of Moscow). Meanwhile the Czar, who was the recognised temporal head of Russia had been gaining in power. It was intended, by the clergy, to make Moscow the third Rome (Byzantium being the second). Finally the Czar however acquired the supreme power over Church and State, and this was the position until the Revolution.

There was always a great deal of mysticism and occultism in the Russian Church. Some of the clergy were not particular about associating with magicians, and mediums were freely consulted. The last five czars (Alexander I, Nicholas I, Alexander II, Alexander III and Nicholas II) and their consorts were remarkable for their interest in occultism, and made contacts with mystics, occultists and mediums both in and out of the Russian Orthodox Church.

Alexander I (1777–1825) who ascended the throne in 1801 was much influenced by Baroness von Krüdener. This mystic, who had some sort of an organisation in Switzerland, visited many European cities and was undoubtedly influential in cementing the Holy Alliance signed between Russia, Prussia and Austria in 1815. Baroness Krüdener combined the vision-seeing of Swedenborg with the beliefs of the Moravians, and made a number of successful predictions, notably the return of Napoleon from Elba, and his subsequent expulsion.

The next arrival was Sister Salome (Madame Bouche née Therese des ‘Isard) who was at the Russian Court from 1819 to 1821. She was a member of a French occult society (Society of St. John). She predicted the failure of Napoleon's Russian campaign and his subsequent fall. She persuaded Alexander I to have talis-

15 Quoted in translation from the English version of Levi.

mans of pure gold prepared.[16] These were impressed with the triangle, as the symbol of the Holy Trinity. They were distributed from time to time to princes.

Nicholas I (1796–1855) who succeeded his brother Alexander I was much influenced by the aforementioned Hoene Wronski. The latter addressed two publications to this Czar, dealing with the destiny of the Slav peoples.

Alexander II (1818–1881) who succeeded his father Nicholas I in 1855 was interested in all forms of divination, but particularly astrology.[17] D. D. Home, the great medium was one of those consulted. He said he could not continue to advise the Czar, but that a German would do the work. Later a German medium called Baron Langsdorff (d. 1908) told the Czar in 1880 of a bomb outrage that might take place at a dinner at which he was expected. The Czar delayed his arrival for half an hour, during which a terrible explosion took place. The next year the medium was sent on an important mission in Paris. During his absence the Czar was killed by another bomb.

He was succeeded by his son Alexander III (1845–1894). The new Czar recalled Langsdorff, and held seances with him almost daily until 1886, when the medium retired owing to poor health. Under this influence an alliance was concluded with France. The medium fell into trances, but also used an instrument, called a *psychograph*,[18] a rotating disc moved by the fingers of the medium, to facilitate the rapid selection of letters of the alphabet, spelling out the words of a message. This was invented by the spirits, and was subsequently adopted by other mediums.

Towards the end of the reign of Alexander III a Russian priest named John of Cronstadt (1821–1908) became very popular both at court, and among the people. He was supposed to perform miracles, and certainly carried out many works of charity. He was unable to save the life of Alexander in his last illness.

Alexander's eldest son was Nicholas II (1868–1918) who succeeded on his father's death. He and all his family were murdered by Bolsheviks in the Revolution. The Czar and his wife the Czaritza were deeply involved in mysticism and magic. After the failure of John of Cronstadt they called in a magus of Lyons, France, Nizier Anthelme Philippe, known as le Maitre Philippe (1849–1905). This

[16] J. Bricaud: *Le Mysticisme à la Cour de Russie*, Paris, 1921.
[17] Bricaud: *loc. cit.*
[18] Bricaud: *loc. cit.*

individual was undoubtedly a remarkable personality.[19] When at school a priest told him he had diabolical powers, and at the age of thirteen he performed marvellous cures. He married in 1877 and a daughter of this marriage married a doctor interested in Kabalism, but she died at an early age. Philippe became a medical student, but towards the end of his course of instruction news had reached the college that he was already practising occult medicine, which was regarded there as charlatanism, so he was not allowed to complete his fifth inscription.[20] He was subsequently allowed to open a clinic and courses of lectures at Lyons under the auspices of the Practical School of Magnetism and Massage at Paris, run by the celebrated hypnotist H. Durville, helped at times by the equally celebrated occultist and kabalist G. Encausse, otherwise known as Papus. He was, on several occasions fined for practising medicine without a licence.

Le Maitre Philippe classified diseases, rather after the manner of Paracelsus, into three classes : those of their origin which may be (i) physical, (ii) astral and (iii) spiritual. But in all cases he seems to have detected a kind of moral responsibility for each disease.

Philippe was called to Russia and journeyed there late in 1900. There his faculties of clairvoyance and clairaudience, enabling him to diagnose, even at a distance, astonished and enthralled the Czar. He predicted that a male heir to the throne would be born, and this prophecy was soon fulfilled. Philippe finally received the honorary Doctorate in Medicine of the University of Moscow, and permission to visit the royal family without special appointment.

However opposition was raised to the magus, on the grounds that he exerted political influence over the Czar, and in 1901 he returned to Lyons, continuing there to correspond with the Russian court. In 1903 he was in Russia again, conducting seances on a large scale and founding a Martinist lodge with the help of the Czar and the King of Denmark. He returned to Lyons for some reason, having been given a superb automobile[21] as a parting gift from the royal family. In 1904 his daughter died, and this so upset him that he retired into obscurity, dying himself the next year.

Attempts were now made to interest Nicholas in Russian Ortho-dox mystics, or at least in Russian occultism. For a time he held

[19] For a further account of his life see J. Bricaud: *Le Maitre Philippe,* Paris, 1926.
[20] *Loc. cit.*
[21] Bricaud: *Le Maitre Philippe, loc. cit.*

sessions with Mitia Koliaba, a dumb crippled monk who communicated only by gestures, which were interpreted by another monk, Elpifidor, or Egorov of the same monastery. Then attention was focussed on a priest calling himself Heliodorus, a learned man, supposed to work miracles, and the leader of a group considered heretical by many theologians. He had been a friend of Philippe, and his policy was so pro-French that there was political as well as religious opposition.

However help was coming from Siberia. Not only so, but it was rumoured at court that the new prophet had been predicted by Philippe, so the newcomer ought to be pleasing to both parties. Grigori Rasputin (1871–1916) was the newcomer. He had been born in the province of Tobolsk in Western Siberia as the son of poor peasants and when he grew up worked at first as a groom. He married and had a family, and was regarded by some as a drunkard and libertine, but nevertheless claimed to have had a vision of the Mother of God, whilst doing some farming work in a field. Soon after this a remarkable change came over Rasputin. He joined the sect of the Khlysty, left his wife and family and became an itinerant preacher.

In some manner, not now determinable, Rasputin had acquired tremendous hypnotic powers, and a persuasive way of reconciling the doctrines of the Khlysty with those of the Orthodox Russian Church. Moreover he was an able speaker, with a manner that was as direct as it was uncommon.[22] As he wandered around the country he became known as a miracle worker. Soon he was invited among the nobility and clergy. But two persons, particularly, who had great influence in Russia at the time, helped him greatly. One[23] was the monk-priest Iliodor, Russia's most famous preacher, and a most vigorous opponent of Western influence in Russia and of all foreign interference. The other was S. Badmaev, Doctor of Tibetan Medicine, one of the Czar's leading medical advisers. The latter worked at the magical and alchemical laboratory of his elder brother in St. Petersburg, where they dispensed Tibetan medicines, otherwise unknown in the West, obtaining remarkable cures. Badmaev studied, not only the physiology and pathology of his patients, but also their politics, which he charted carefully,[24] and thus gave

[22] R. Fülöp-Miller: *Rasputin*, New York, 1929.
[23] He afterwards opposed Rasputin, and wrote works against him, calling him "the holy devil."
[24] See Fülöp-Miller, *loc. cit.*, who also gives further details of the Tibetan medicines.

much useful information to the Czar for making state appointments.

Now it so happened that the heir to the throne, the Czarevitch, suffered from haemophilia, a disease in which slight wounds or bruises produce long and serious illness. Owing to the illness the Czarevitch was not allowed to ride or indulge in outdoor sports of any kind, and his play was restricted. Even Badmaev could not cure him. One day when the child was seriously ill with the complaint, and was lying inert, apparently near death, the Czar and Czarina were persuaded to allow Rasputin to come and see the invalid. Rasputin appeared in the royal apartments in due course, kissed the Czar and Czarina according to the Russian custom among friends, said a few prayers before an icon, and then approached the bed of the invalid. He told the Czarevitch that there was nothing really wrong with him, that he would soon be up and about, and would be able to play all sorts of games, in particular he began to talk about horses. The Czarevitch soon began to listen attentively and Rasputin recounted all sorts of adventures. The child began to improve from the first interview, and whenever he had a relapse Rasputin was called in to make him better.

Soon Rasputin acquired great power at the Russian court, and many of his friends received official appointments, both in Church and State. As most of the newcomers were hitherto unknown and uneducated, this caused dismay. Although Rasputin was never severe with his enemies, he and his friends were disliked by many. He had a large following of women, and very scandalous stories were circulated. Worst of all was the power which Rasputin seemed to possess of instantly hypnotising most of those with whom he came into contact.

Eventually a group of noblemen plotted to destroy Rasputin, whom they regarded as a menace to the security of the State. He was invited to a party by Prince Yusupov, who had gained his confidence. Rasputin was plied with wine, and finally given cakes containing cyanide. The poison, however, did not work,[25] and

---

[25] There are two theories as to why this was so: (i) Cyanides only act when they liberate hydrocyanic acid (prussic acid) when acted on by the hydrochloric acid in the stomach. A few people have at times no hydrochloric acid, and this may have been the case with Rasputin; (ii) the cyanide may not have been fresh; when not so it changes into the harmless carbonate.

Rasputin was finally shot. The Prince was banished to a remote part of Russia, and at the time of writing is living in America.[26]

The Revolution began in 1917 and the Czar abdicated. The murder of the Czar and his family took place in 1918. There is no evidence that Rasputin had any intention of fostering revolution, but it is held by many that his extraordinary activities weakened an already tottering throne.

[26] He died recently.

CHAPTER XXIX

SOME MAGICAL FRATERNITIES

Freemasonry. We do not intend to include the Masons in the magical fraternities. No one would consider Craft Masonry in England as working black magic! Nevertheless Masonry is throughout symbolic. It is well known that Masons wear symbolic jewels and aprons, that they use the instruments of architecture as symbols of moral teachings, that their tracing boards are highly symbolic, as are even the positions of officers in their lodges. The use of hand grips, passwords and signs made by placing the limbs or parts of the body in particular attitudes is well known to the uninitiated.

A. E. Waite,[1] noted masonic writer, clearly indicates that the secrets of Freemasonry are of a sacramental character. This is perhaps the main reason for the opposition of the Catholic Church to Freemasonry. Other reasons may be the allegedly severe penalties of Masons against those of their number who betray their secrets, and the fact that some degrees of Masonry (not in the Craft) are believed to refer to vengeance[2] against popes and kings, as a reprisal for the suppression of the Templars. Moreover Masons admit believers in any religion, and on the continent do not even require belief in God. This latter point, of course, would not apply to English Freemasonry.

At one time Freemasonry was practised with the consent of the Church. In fact the Masonic guilds, whilst under the guidance of the Catholic hierarchy, were instrumental and absolutely essential in building the great cathedrals.

At the Reformation the Masons came under the influence of the Rosicrucians, but to what extent is disputed. There were certainly many Rosicrucians in England who were Freemasons in the 16th and 17the centuries.

According to Sir David Brewster[3] popes "conferred on the

[1] *A New Encyclopaedia of Freemasonry,* New and Revised Edition, two volumes, London, 1920. There is also a still later edition.
[2] *Loc. cit.*
[3] Quoted by Dudley Wright: *Roman Catholicism and Freemasonry,* London, 1922.

Fraternity of Freemasons the most important privileges and allowed them to be governed by laws, customs and ceremonies peculiar to themselves." Since 1738 there have been a number of papal pronouncements against Fremasonry.

Templar Revivals. When Jacques de Molay, the Grand Master of the Templars was burnt at the stake in 1314, and the Order of the Templars was dissolved and disappeared, it is probable that many Templars survived, and continued Templar rites in secret. We have seen that it was continued in modified form quite openly in Portugal under the title of the Order of Christ. But in other countries it went underground.

Some attempts have been made to derive Freemasonry from the Templars. *The Rite of the Strict Observance* was founded by Baron von Hund (1722–1776) in Germany about 1754. It had peculiar claims: (i) that when the Templars were suppressed certain brethren escaped to Scotland, where they were admitted to Craft Lodges in existence there, (ii) they restored Templar Freemasonry in that country, (iii) Freemasonry originally contained the mysteries of the Templars, (iv) a succession of Grand Masters was passed on,[4] (v) correct rites of Masonry are maintained only under the Strict Observance, (vi) Masonry is not a democratic institution, as usually supposed in modern times, but is governed in the Strict Observance by superiors, (vii) the superiors or governors of the highest grade are unknown, they not only rule the order, but put forth special occult teachings from time to time.

The Strict Observance was very successful in the second half of the 18th century. It spread rapidly in Germany, France, Switzerland, Italy and Russia. The Strict Observance added several Templar degrees to those of the craft. Finally J. A. von Starck (1741–1816) tried to introduce Catholic dogmas into the order, and to include a Catholic priestly grade, presumably because the original Templars were Catholics. After considerable negotiation Von Starck resigned from masonic activities, and the Strict Observance refused further obedience to unknown superiors. Some of the followers joined the Martinists, but the others continued in lodges which adopted the ordinary rules of Masonry, and became undistinguished therefrom.

At the beginning of the 18th century an order working what appears to have been genuine Templar ritual was in existence in

[4] Waite, *loc. cit.*, says this list of Grand Masters is, he believes, still in the custody of the Grand Priory of Helvetia.

France. This order had the Duke of Orleans as its Grand Master, and possessed a charter which claimed its descent from the original Templars. This charter, beautifully written and illuminated, contained the signatures of a continuous succession of Grand Masters, from Larmenius to the Duke of Orleans who took office in 1705. Larmenius, the charter states, was selected by Molay, just before the martyrdom of the latter, to succeed him, and on his death was made Grand Master by the remnant of the fraternity which existed in secret.

The Duke of Orleans sent two of his Templars to Portugal to obtain recognition of his Templar Order by the Order of Christ. The King of Portugal, as head of the latter, made inquiries of the Portuguese ambassador to France, and as the latter gave an unfavourable report the two emissaries to Portugal were ordered to be arrested. One escaped, via Gibraltar, one was captured and banished to North Africa where he died.

This Templar Order was not masonic.[5] The Duke of Orleans was succeeded by the following: Duke of Maine 1724, Bourbon-Condé 1737, Louis Francis Bourbon 1741, Duke of Cossé Brissac 1776.

About 1790 the Order was in abeyance, and the charter was found in a desk, purchased from the estate of a relative of Brissac, by a Freemason named Ledru. He with others revived the Order. Claude Chevillon was offered the Grand Mastership, but he accepted only the title of Vicar (in 1792), and signed the Charter as such. He soon resigned and Bernard Fabré-Palaprat was selected as Grand Master in 1804. Soon after, the order purchased a certain amount of bric-a-brac, which they claimed were relics of the original Templars. They included a small copper reliquary, containing burnt bones, a bowl, a tall ivory cross, three mitres, richly wrought, the Templar standard, a sword, spur and helmet.

One of the Knights of Christ was friendly with Fabré-Palaprat, and another attempt was made to obtain recognition from the King of Portugal, but again without success. The first three degrees of the order, as worked under Palaprat roughly correspond with those of Craft Freemasonry. There were five higher degrees. Palaprat, after a while, accepted the *Levitikon*, an apocryphal Gospel, ascribed to St. John, already referred to (see under Templars). This caused a split in the Order, some following these teachings, believed to have been heretical, others remaining true to the Catholic Faith. Both these bodies died out after the middle

[5] Ward: *loc. cit.*

of the 19th century. About 1920 an English mason, F. J. W. Crowe, purchased an old document described by the dealer as a Knight-Templar Certificate. It proved to be the aforesaid Charter of Larmenius or a copy thereof, and is in cypher. It was presented by its discoverer to the Grand Priory of the Temple of England.

Templar Orders in Sweden, Denmark and Germany, which started in the last century, purport to derive their succession from a nephew of Jacques de Molay. They resemble the Strict Observance. Templar Orders were also active in Poland where they were associated with revolutionary activities.

One notable Templar order at a later date will be considered later.

Ancient and Accepted (Scottish) Rite. This is known in England as the Ancient and Accepted Rite. The term Scottish is added in the U.S.A. and elsewhere, as Scotland has long been famous for its study of these degrees. The rite uses a great deal of Christian symbolism.

Continental Masons in the 18th century were great students of symbolism, and in Clermont, France, in 1754 a chapter of twenty-five degrees including those of the Craft was established. Later it spread to Germany and the U.S.A. and seven new degrees were added, bringing the number to thirty-two. Finally in 1825 the Grand Council established a thirty-third degree, bringing the number up to that symbolised by the years in the life of Christ. The rite is now found in most countries.

The original headquarters of the Ancient and Accepted Rite were founded at Charleston, U.S.A. Two noted masonic authors occupied leading positions there. They were Albert Gallatin Mackey (1807–1881) author of the well-known *Encyclopaedia of Freemasonry* which has passed through several editions, and Albert Pike (1809–1891) who wrote *Morals and Dogma of the Ancient and Accepted Scottish Rite,* among other works. Mackey and Pike were interested in occult phenomena. They were said to have an image of Baphomet, and the skull of Jacques de Molay, brought from Europe in the early days of the rite by one Isaac Long.

Towards the end of the last century some extraordinary stories were circulated about Mackey and Pike. These are now regarded as fictitious. Mackey claimed, it was said, to be a reincarnation of De Molay, and for some years on each March 11th, the anniversary of the death of De Molay, he went into a trance, during which the skull was said to speak, and to emit flames. Another allegation was that Mackey had in his house a box called *Arcula Mystica*. The latter was one of seven, each in the possession of a director of the rite. Inside was a sort of telephone, and seven statuettes, each corresponding with one of the directories, and with one cardinal virtue. On pressing down two of these, one corresponding with his own directory, and one to the directory with which it was wished to communicate, the corresponding box at the other end is caused to whistle, and a small silver frog in the box emits flames. Messages were then transmitted. As this was before the days of the transatlantic telephone the story was designed to ascribe magical powers to Mackey and his associates. Pike was also accused of magic. He was supposed to have described a seance, held by an association he belonged to, in which a medium possessed of 330 spirits floated naked through the air, in the company of the devil Astaroth, and gave forth astounding revelations!

Order of the Palladium. All these extraordinary stories, and many others were due to a group of authors under the leadership of G. A. Jogand Pagès (1854–1907). He wrote under the name of Leo Taxil, and also supplied the material for the works of Bataille and Margiotta. Pagès started his literary career as an anti-clerical, and his first romances relate scandalous stories of priests and prelates. His chief work of this period deals with the love affairs of Pope Pius IX. He was received in the first degree of Freemasonry, but before progressing beyond it was expelled by the fraternity. In 1885 he pretended to turn Catholic, and after a retreat was received into the Church. He then commenced a series of writings of a strongly anti-masonic nature. He first turned his attention to the question of women in Freemasonry. There have been a few masonic rites which admit women to what were termed degrees of adoption. There was, for instance, the Order of the Palladium which was established at Paris in 1837. This gave Taxil his idea of Palladian Freemasonry. From all other accounts the Order of the Palladium was an insignificant affair, but Taxil put forward five hypotheses: (i) that the relation of men and women masons was of a scandalous nature; (ii) that the Order of the Palladium was a cosmopolitan association, attached to the headquarters of the Scottish Rite at Charleston; (iii) that the object of the order was the practice of Satanism; (iv) that it was the secret force controlling all masonic orders and (v) that it was politically subversive. Taxil even invented a Palladian Grand Mistress, called Diana

Vaughan. She was the descendant of Thomas Vaughan the alchemist and Rosicrucian, who visited America,[6] and there contracted a demonic marriage, and from this union Diana was said
to be descended. She herself contracted demonic liaisons, according
to the alleged customs of the Rosicrucians. Moreover she was said
to be closely associated with Albert Pike.

All this created a widespread interest. Taxil was received by the
Pope, and was questioned at an Anti-Masonic Congress at Trent
(the seat of the last General Council) in 1887. By this time, Taxil
alleged, Diana had been converted to the Catholic Faith, and he
was strongly urged to allow her to appear. He replied that her
life was in danger, on account of her betrayal of the Palladists.

In 1897, however, Taxil gave a lecture in Paris. He admitted
the whole of his stories of the Palladium were a hoax. Diana
Vaughan was merely the name of his typist, and she was neither
a Mason nor a Catholic. The meeting broke up in disorder, but
Taxil had escaped under police protection.

There are some other references to Black Magic in connection
with the Directory at Charleston. In Huysmans' *Là Bas* there is
a reference to the *Société des Ré-Thèurgistes Optimates,* a diabolical
order, with its seat in America, and stated by Huysmans to have
had ramifications in France, Italy, Germany, Russia, Austria and
even Turkey. It must be remembered that *Là Bas* is a work of
fiction, although containing many references to actual events in
the history of black magic. The head of this diabolical order was
said by Huysmans to be a Scot named Longfellow.[7] The latter was
said by Margiotta and others to have been associated with Pike.

The Illuminati. Illuminism and the Illuminati are terms which
have two different meanings. One applies to the faith and faithful
of some followers of Swedenborg. The other, like the world enlightenment, suggests the light of the mind, but actually refers to the
dreary and dull cult of materialism. Little space need be wasted on
such Illuminati, but they must be mentioned as they are invariably
referred to in comprehensive accounts of Occultism.

The Illuminati of Bavaria, as we had better term this sect, were
founded by Adam Weishaupt (1748–1830) Professor of Law in the
University of Ingoldstadt. Weishaupt was educated by the Jesuits,
but became a materialist in early life. He conceived the idea of

[6] There is no evidence that Thomas Vaughan ever visited America.
[7] Not to be confused with the poet of that name.

using subtle methods, in imitation of his conception of Jesuitry, but with the opposite object. He also borrowed from the Masons. There was a good deal of superficial symbolism. He superposed on the Craft the degrees of Illuminatus, Illuminatus Dirigens, Epopt (or Priest), Prince (or Regent), Magus (or Philosopher) and Rex (or King), and conferred them. The Order started in 1776, but did not make much progress until 1780 when an influential Freemason was enrolled. Thereafter it spread rapidly among members of the Masonic Fraternity. The dupes found, however, on reaching the higher degrees, that materialism and republicanism were being taught, and some reported the matter to the Elector of Bavaria. He banished Weishaupt. Some attempts were made to revive it in other German states, but it disappointed those in search of the supernatural and died out.

A Mysterious Character. Comte de St. Germain (*circa* 1710–1784) was a curious and mysterious character who travelled in various countries of Europe (including England) in the 18th century. He was engaged in various political missions, and was at one time employed by Louis XV, King of France. He alleged he was the son of Prince Ragoczy of Transylvania, whilst Levi[8] states that he was the natural or adopted son of a person who called himself Comes Cabalicus, from whom De Villars originated his character of the Comte de Gabalis.[9] The Comte de St. Germain was a painter, a chemist and an alchemist. He did not make gold, but produced wonderful gems. He also enlarged existing jewels, and removed flaws from the same. He carried out remarkable technical processes, for instance he could impart great brilliance and ductility to copper, and his paintings of gems displayed the fiery gleam of the real article. He pretended to have a knowledge of the philosopher's stone, and liked to talk with his associates about his experiences in the far distant past. He provided the sick with medicines and children with delightful sweetmeats and toys. He was always impeccably dressed, seldom ate in company and his conversation was exceptionally brilliant, being adorned with wit and candour.

St. Germain conformed outwardly to the practices of the Catholic religion with the utmost fidelity. He was nevertheless a high-grade Mason, and a member, perhaps the head, of the Order of St.

[8] *History of Magic, loc. cit.*
[9] We have elsewhere suggested the identity of the so-called Comte de Gabalis

Jakin or St. Joachim.[10] An existing account[11] of an initiation conducted by St. Germain suggests that the ritual included alchemical, kabalistic and spiritualistic elements, and ended with a very candid address.

Cagliostro's Egyptian Masonry. Count Alessandro di Cagliostro (1743–1795) was born at Palermo, Italy, of poor parents. His original name was Giuseppe Balsamo.[12] He was educated under religious auspices, and in a Benedictine monastery learnt the art of an apothecary. He appears to have been practising magical rites at an early age, and at the age of seventeen succeded in making a rich goldsmith part with a considerable sum, in consideration of performing a ritual designed to unearth buried treasure. He escaped with the loot to Messina, where he took the title of Count Cagliostro, which had been borne by one of his mother's ancestors. At Messina he met with a magician and alchemist named Althotas, who attracted him as the latter was dressed in oriental robes. The two having become friendly set out for Egypt, where Cagliostro, according to his own account, was initiated in a cave beneath the Pyramids. They subsequently journeyed to many places in Asia and North Africa, finally arriving at Malta, then the seat of the Order of St. John of Jerusalem. Here they assisted the Grand Master Pinto in alchemical experiments, but after a while Althotas died. Cagliostro returned to Italy, married Lorenza Feliciani, and then travelled about with her in several countries of Europe. They twice visited London. They often apparently had ample funds, which they largely distributed to the poor and needy. Cagliostro dispensed medical services, free when necessary.

Cagliostro claimed to have been made a Mason in London during his second visit. There is an account,[13] also, of both Cagliostro and his wife being initiated, in grand style, by the Count of St. Germain, as already referred to. At any rate Cagliostro was initiated by St. Germain. He began to claim that he could make gold and silver,

10 According to Waite (*Ency.*) this however was really a Catholic order. Others have said it was the name of what had previously been known as the *Initiated Brethren of Asia.*

11 See article on Cagliostro in Spence: *Encyclopaedia of Occultism,* London, 1920.

12 This is denied by Trowbridge in *Cagliostro: The Splendour and Misery of a Master of Magic,* 1910. But on the other hand Funck-Brentano in *Cagliostro and Company,* trans. 1902, gives an account of a visit of Goethe to the Balsamo family, and says they entrusted him with a letter to give to Cagliostro.

13 See article on Cagliostro in Spence, *Encyclopaedia, loc. cit.*

could prolong life, could renew youth and beauty, and conjure up the spirits of the dead. He began to tell stories of his own early life, alleging or hinting that he had been present in Palestine in the time of Christ.

Cagliostro became known as a magician, and as such became acquainted with distinguished people. He appeared at the court of Louis XVI where he revealed visions by getting his subjects to gaze in mirrors, or in pools of water. He set up an alchemical laboratory. He was already on intimate terms with the Cardinal Prince de Rohan (1734–1803) who was interested in Masonry and was in search of some form of Masonry that would not conflict with the Catholic Faith, and which could be recognised by the Pope.

Whilst he was in London Cagliostro had acquired some rituals of an *Egyptian Rite of Masonry* written by George Cofton.[14] There is no evidence that the Rite had ever been worked. Cagliostro adapted it, and after a few abortive attempts to gather adherents in London, he succeeded in getting it going at Lyons, Strasbourg, and Bordeaux. He attained considerable success, and then established a Temple in Paris, where distinguished people were initiated, and considerable interest set up among Masons. The degrees for men were only given to Master Masons in good standing, and were three in number, with names similar to those of the Craft. The first degree included instructions upon health and disease, the use of occult forces, the seven metals, the seven colours, the seven planets, the invocation of God and many other things relating to symbolism. The second degree included the *Sic transit gloria mundi* formula, which is used in the coronation of a pope, and the opening of the mouth, which is found in the making of a cardinal, as well as in ancient Egyptian ritual. The lecture of this degree gave the two methods of regeneration, physical and spiritual, which enable one, so it was said, to live on indefinitely. The third makes use of a young child as a medium, who is supposed to go into a trance and announce messages from the seven planetary spirits. In this degree the Presiding Officer moves around describing circles with his sword, and reciting magical formulae. The Phoenix and the Rose are the important symbols. Cagliostro was head of the Rite, and was termed Grand Copht. There were also adoptive degrees for women, and the Countess Cagliostro was head of this

[14] According to C. Photiades (in his *Count Cagliostro: an Authentic Story of a Mysterious Life,* London, 1932) Cofton was an Irish Catholic priest "who died in the odour of sanctity."

section. During the initiation of the women they were stripped of their clothing, then clad in loose white garments. Their bare arms and legs were tied to symbolise the bondage to which they were subjected by men. Then the cords were cut to signify their liberation. They were then taken into a room where they met with men who tried to tempt them, but when these were repulsed they came before the Grand Mistress who congratulated them. Finally a vast sphere of gold descended from the roof, it opened, and out stepped the Grand Copht, representing Truth, in a state of nature, holding a serpent in his hand, and bearing a shining star on his forehead. The females led by the Grand Mistress then also abandoned all clothing, and Truth gave a short address, after which he ascended upwards in the golden ball.[15]

Unfortunately these pretty proceedings did not last long. Cagliostro and his friend De Rohan were accused of being involved in the affair of the diamond necklace. This was an extremely valuable piece of jewellery, and De Rohan was led to believe, by a woman impersonating the Queen, that the latter was going to purchase it. De Rohan was persuaded to be security for the purchase, but when he signed the document the necklace disappeared. The culprits were the Count and Countess de Lamotte, who had found a woman to impersonate the Queen. Count Lamotte escaped with the diamonds to London, before payment became due. Countess Lamotte was flogged, branded and imprisoned, but also escaped later to London.

Cagliostro went to Rome, and at first made his living as a physician. But after a while he attempted to set up a Temple of Egyptian Masonry there. As soon as it became known he was arrested and tried by the Inquisition. He was imprisoned for life and died soon after. His wife was also imprisoned and died one year before her husband.

Ancient and Primitive Rite of Memphis and Mizraim. About 1758 some French Masons, students of esoteric symbolism, conceived the idea of collecting together all rituals under a single jurisdiction, but very little came of it in practice. These were the days when learned people were becoming aware that beyond Classical Mythology lay a wide field of symbolism, especially the Ancient Egyptian. This had scarcely been known hitherto. Great books like Dupuis : *L'Origine de Tous les Cultes,* 1795, were being prepared.

[15] See Waite and Spence (*loc. cit.*) for references to full descriptions.

The *Rite of Mizraim*[16] was founded in 1805 at Milan, as a sort of rival rite to the Ancient and Accepted. It spread to France in 1816. Attempt were made to have it recognised by the Grand Orient of France, but without success. It had at first eighty-seven degrees, to which three others were subsequently added. It amalgamated with the Rite of Memphis in England in 1875. It was then worked as the Ancient and Primitive Rite, under John Yarker (1833–1913) in England, and the official publication was called *Kneph*. It only gave degrees to Master Masons in good standing. Nevertheless it came into conflict with Grand Lodge.

The degrees of Mizraim are of considerable interest from the viewpoint of the occult. The first three are those of the Craft. The next five (4°–8°) are elaborations of the master grade. 9°–13° utilise various modifications of the title *elect*. 14°–21° utilise the title *écossais* or Scottish. 22°–28° involve architectural symbolism. 29° and 30° are Scottish. 31°–33° contain the symbolism of arch and ark. 34°–41° are chivalric degrees. 42°–45° include the officers or commanders of chivalry. 46°–51° are Rosicrucian, two of them being particularly curious, 49° called Chaos the First and 50° Chaos the Second. 52° introduces astrological symbolism, 53° is philosophical whilst 54°–58° dwell on alchemy, 54° being Miner, 55° Washer, 56° Blower, 57° Founder or Caster and 58° Adept. 59°–66° introduce ruling grades. 67°–77° are called mystical but introduce many Hebrew names and symbols. Thus 69° is connected, according to Ragon[17] with the old Jewish Feast of Lights. The degrees 78°–90° are administrative and kabalistic.

The Oriental Rite of Memphis[18] was represented as of Eastern origin, having been brought from Cairo to France in 1815 by Sam Honis. It was not really active in France until J. E. Marconis (1795–1868) established it in Paris. He tried to get the Grand Orient to recognise it, but they would only do so on condition its lodges confined their activities to the usual three Craft degrees. This was regarded as an affront to the system, and Marconis after a time worked it independently of Grand Orient. It was even introduced into England and the U.S.A. It is the largest quasi-masonic rite and eventually had as many as 97 degrees.

Under Yarker in England the orders of Memphis and Mizraim

[16] Mizraim is the Hebrew name for Egypt.
[17] Quoted by Waite: *loc. cit.*
[18] Memphis was for a long time the sacred and royal capital of Egypt, hence the name of the rite.

were amalgamated and had a Rite of Adoption, in which Mme. Blavatsky held a high degree.

The Golden Dawn. We have already referred to the *Societas Rosicruciana in Anglia*, a Rosicrucian Society only open to Master Masons. They worked a ritual, but apart from the effects it produced, they could not be considered as practising magic. The G .·. D .·. (*Golden Dawn*), however, was established by some members of this *Societas Rosicruciana* with the definite object of practising magic.

In 1884 one of the members of the *Societas Rosicruciana*, the Rev. R. F. A. Woodford, found some manuscripts, written in cypher, with rough diagrams which indicated that their contents might be of Rosicrucian interest. Some say he bought these papers on a bookstall in Farringdon Street, London, others that he found them in the archives of the *Societas Rosicruciana*, or the library of some masonic body or individual. Woodford showed these papers to Dr. W. R. Woodman and Dr. W. Wynn Westcott, who were officers of the *Soc. Ros.* and profound kabalistic scholars. Subsequently another prominent member of the *Soc. Ros.*, S. L. MacGregor Mathers (later known as Count MacGregor of Glenstrae, *d.* 1917) was called in to assist.

The papers contained the name and address of Fräulein Anna Sprengel of Nüremburg, said to be a Rosicrucian Adept. Correspondence was entered into with her, and after some delay a charter was transmitted enabling Woodman, Westcott and Mathers to establish a Temple of Isis-Urania of the Golden Dawn in London and to act as the three chief officers thereof. This happened in 1888. Later other temples were established in England and New Zealand. There was also one in Paris.

It must be understood that the G .·. D .·. was very different from Masonry. The penalty for breaking the oath consisted of being subjected to a magical "current of will" which would cause the unfortunate offender to fall dead or paralysed, as if blasted by lightning. The G .·. D .·. admitted men and women on equal terms. One of the most prominent members was the wife of MacGregor Mathers, who was the sister of Henri Bergson, the famous French philosopher. Some well-known people joined the G .·. D .·. They included W. B. Yeats, poet and Nobel prizewinner, A. E. Waite, the well-known writer on occult, mystical and masonic subjects, Florence Farr, the actress, Miss Horniman, the wealthy daughter of the founder of the Horniman Museum, of which

Mathers was in early life curator, Peck, Astronomer Royal for Scotland, Arthur Machen, the writer, Allen Bennett who afterwards became a Buddhist monk in Ceylon, and Aleister Crowley, poet, mountaineer and magician, of whom we will hear later.

Each member was known in the Order by a Latin motto, chosen by himself. Each degree of the Order had a remarkable ritual of its own,[19] but before being admitted to each degree the candidate had to prove, by tests, that he had acquired competence in practical magical processes. The latter were numerous and included invocations and evocations, clairvoyance, clairaudience, scrying in the spirit vision, making talismans, divination, symbolism of the Tarot and the Kabalah, using the Enochian Tablets (one hundred squares, covered with symbols, obtained by Dee and Kelley during their scrying), playing Enochian Chess (an Eastern form of chess, with images of the gods as chessmen), the various Rosicrucian scales or systems of colour symbolism and how to use them, the making and consecration of magical weapons, geomancy, astrology, the assumption of god-forms and many other studies. The degrees of the G.·. D.·. were as follows: the first to be taken was introductory and called Neophyte $0=0$,[20] next follow Zelator $1=10$, then in succession Theoricus $2=9$, Practicus $3=8$, Philosophus $4=7$. Few members passed beyond the latter. Strictly the degrees $0=0$ to $4=7$ alone comprised the Golden Dawn. But beyond this was the Inner Order, known as the *Rosae, Rubae et Aurae Crucis*. This included three degrees, very difficult to attain, especially the last two. They were Adeptus Minor $5=6$, Adeptus Major $6=5$ and Adeptus Exemptus $7=4$. The Order was supposed to be ruled over by unknown chiefs of an altogether superhuman nature. These belonged to the Mysterious Third Order of the Silver Star (Argentinum Astrum or A.·. A.·.) and these superior beings alone could attain the last three degrees of Magister Templi $8=3$, Magus $9=2$ and Ipsissimus $10=1$.

In 1891 Dr. Woodman died rather suddenly, and in 1897 Dr. Wynn Westcott resigned unexpectedly. Dr. Westcott was a London coroner and his resignation was due, it was said, to criticism against any coroner being a practitioner of magic, his activities in the latter sphere having somehow been made public. These events left Mathers undisputed head of the Golden Dawn. He alone held the

[19] The rituals were published in Crowley's *Equinox*, and in revised form in I. Regardie: *The Golden Dawn*, 4 vols., Chicago, 1937-1940.
[20] The first figure is surrounded by a circle, the second by a square, but for simplicity we omit this.

exalted grade of Adeptus Exemptus, the highest degree open to ordinary human beings, and he was the link with the unseen superiors. The latter he contacted mainly by using Mrs. Mathers as a medium, but he also once met three of these Masters in the Bois de Boulogne, and was confirmed by them as head of the Order.[21]

Mathers had moved to Paris about 1899 where already he had founded a temple of the G∴D∴.

In 1898 Aleister Crowley (1875–1947) became a member of the Golden Dawn, and by the middle of the next year he had reached the grade of Philosophus. When Mathers went to Paris Crowley began to come into conflict with other members and when Crowley also went to Paris in 1900 and was initiated by Mathers to the degree of Adeptus Minor, he found on his return, that the members of the London Temple refused to give him access to papers to which his degree entitled him. Crowley hastened to Paris and Mathers sent him to the London Temple as his envoy, ordering the recalcitrant members to submit unconditionally. Crowley arrived at the London Temple in the garb of a Highland chieftain, wearing kilt, dirks and tartan, his face concealed with a heavy mask.[25] He obtained the papers, but the rebels, by legal action, retained the possession of the Temple premises. They broke with Mathers, and formed a schismatic body called the *Stella Matutina*, which, however, broke up into several sections and finally disintegrated.

We have already seen that Mathers translated the *Book of Abramelin*, dealing with magic. Crowley set up a temple in Boleskine near Loch Ness in Scotland, for the express purpose of practising the magical rituals described in that work. His chief object was to invoke his Holy Guardian Angel. About this time Crowley had begun to identify himself with the Beast of the Apocalypse, whose number is 666. He often called himself Therion (*Gk.* beast).

Crowley was a great traveller. He had visited Mexico and had climbed in the Himalayas. In 1904 he was in Egypt with his wife (the sister of Sir Gerald Kelly, the artist), who was acting as his seeress. In their apartments they began to invoke the gods of Egypt. Messages from the latter impelled them to visit the Cairo Museum. There in the galleries they stopped before an image of

---

21 So he recorded. The effect of meeting them, he reports was difficult to sustain. His breathing was affected, and various and almost unbearable sensations were experienced.

25 Regardie: *My Rosicrucian Adventure, loc. cit.*

Horus, in the form of Ra-Hoor-Khuit, painted on a wooden stele of the 26th dynasty.[26] They were particularly interested in that, because, just before, the seeress had received a message from the gods, saying they were to invoke Horus, and curiously enough the museum number of this exhibit was 666. A few days later another message came through the seeress. Crowley was to go into his oratory and write down what he heard. He did so for three successive days. The writing, or so he believed, was dictated to him by a being called Aiwass, an angel of the highest order. This writing was much later published as the *Liber Legis*, or *Book of the Law*. It purports to be the holy book of a new dispensation for mankind, which was to be founded by Crowley with the aid of a facsimile of the stele in the museum—"the stele of revealing." The book is apparently brutal and blasphemous in its attacks on existing religions, but Crowley maintained to the last that he could never understand these passages. It also contained a puzzle, couched in terms of numerology. One of Crowley's followers, a former mathematics lecturer in South Africa, spent a great deal of time trying to unravel the mystery. This unfortunate individual committed suicide.

One result of the great revelation in Cairo was that Crowley now reckoned he had attained to a higher degree in the G∴D∴ and he wrote to Mathers telling him that the secret chiefs had now conferred the headship of the visible order on himself.

Crowley did not, at first, take his new mission in the world as seriously as he did later. But from that time on he would greet everyone, even total strangers with the words : "Do what thou wilt shall be the whole of the law." The proper reply to this was "Love is the law, love under will," but few ever gave it. These quotations are from the *Liber Legis*. However, Aiwass seems to have borrowed from Rabelais, and when in 1920 Crowley set up his establishment in Sicily, for the practice of sex-magic, he called it the Abbey of Thelema, a name taken from the same author.

In 1906 Crowley was in China. There he carried out further magical rituals, which resulted, so he supposed, in his being raised to the degree of Master of the Temple. In 1916 whilst in America he went one step further, attaining the grade of Magus. The ritual for this was crucifying a toad, with blasphemous references to New Testament texts. Finally in 1921 in Sicily he attained the last degree, Ipsissimus; this involved invoking Insanity itself.[27]

[26] J. Symonds: *The Great Beast: The Life of Aleister Crowley*, London, 1951, reprinted.

[27] J. Symonds, *loc. cit.*

Henceforth Crowley regarded the A.·. A.·. as under his control.

Order of the Temple of the Orient. Crowley was a member of the Ancient and Primitive Rite, and attained the highest degrees therein. There is no evidence that he tampered with this rite in any way.

It is different with the Order of the Temple of the Orient, known as the O.·. T.·. O.·. The latter was founded by a German Karl Kellner (*d.* 1905) in the year 1895. It was an order practising sex-magic, in the belief, which in our view is mistaken, that the original Templars had this practice. The O.·. T.·. O.·. was said to have been based on the *Hermetic Brotherhood of Light,* an American Order supposedly basing its work on Randolph's *Eulis,* already mentioned. The O.·. T.·. O.·. worked ten degrees, distinguished by being indicated by Roman numerals. Kellner was succeeded in 1905 by Theodor Reuss, a German newspaper correspondent, a high initiate of the Ancient and Primitive Rite.

In 1912 Crowley was contacted by Reuss, and accused of revealing the secrets of the O.·. T.·. O.·. in some of his writings. It was not difficult for Crowley to prove that he knew nothing of the O.·. T.·. O.·. or its secrets, but he was persuaded to join, and before long he was the representative of the Order for Ireland, Iona and all the Britains, with the tenth degree (Supreme and Most Holy King) and taking unto himself the sacred name Baphomet (a name by which he often signed his letters thereafter). He was also asked to rewrite the rituals.

The next year, 1913, Crowley set out for Moscow with a theatrical party called the Ragged Rag-Time Girls. In Moscow, under the influence of the Liturgy of St. Basil of the Russian Church[28] he was inspired to write the Gnostic Catholic Mass. This extraordinary production, enacted by both a priest and a priestess, part of which is in Greek, is based on the ideas of the new dispensation which was supposed to begin with the revelation of *The Book of the Law.* Among the "saints" mentioned are Simon Magus, Roderic Borgia (Pope Alexander VI), Adam Weishaupt, Dr. Reuss and Sir Aleister Crowley. The same treatment was meted out to the rituals of the O.·. T.·. O.·. and the publication of translations of this Mass and the said rituals caused consternation among the oriental templars. But in a short while the First World War broke out and the German branch of the Order died out. Crowley went to America, where he is said to have published anti-British propaganda. His own version was that he was writing such transparent

[28] Or so he told the present writer.

rubbish as to act altogether in the opposite way. When he returned to England no action was taken against him. He continued to work the O∴ T∴ O∴ with a small following and even had a few representatives in Germany and the U.S.A.

The official organ of the A∴ A∴ and the O∴ T∴ O∴ was the *Equinox*. Therein[29] it was announced that the O∴ T∴ O∴ is a body of initiates in whom are concentrated the wisdom and knowledge of a number of bodies including the Hermetic Brotherhood of Light, the Rites of Memphis and Mizraim, the Scottish Rite, the Martinists and the Sat B'hai.

A Theurgic Rite. Martinez de Pasqually (1700–1774) was a profound student of the Kabalah and of the writings of Swedenborg. He was of Portuguese or more probably of German extraction, but was born in the south of France. He is also said to have been of Jewish descent, but this is probably a mistake due to his use of kabalistic symbolism, for he was a most devout Christian. He travelled extensively in early life. In 1760 he appeared at a Masonic lodge at Toulouse bearing a charter written in hieroglyphics and purporting to possess magical powers. He aroused interest, but the brethren were suspicious. The next year he appeared at a lodge at Bordeaux, and succeeded in convincing the brethren. In 1766 he established the headquarters of the new rite at Paris, and soon after a few lodges were established in several French towns.

The new system was called in French *Rite des Élus Coëns*. This has been translated as Rite of Elect Priests. *Cohen* is the Hebrew for *priest*, *Cohenim* being the proper plural, but *Coëns* was apparently an attempt to render this into French. The peculiarity of the rite was that, after being received therein, the members gradually acquired occult powers. There were probably seven degrees, and in the highest the initiate attains the ability to converse with angels, and even with Christ himself. The highest degree was connected with the Rosy Cross, and the unknown superiors who gave the hierglyphic charter are suspected[30] to have been Rosicrucians. The highest initiate was expected to practise magic, with all the usual paraphernalia, of fasting, observing special times, reciting magical formulae, wearing elaborate vestments, describing circles on the floor of the temple, prostrating himself at certain points, burning candles and special incense.

[29] Vol. III, 1 Detroit, Michigan.
[30] Even Waite, usually a sceptical author, admits this possibility. See not only his *Ency.* but also his *Saint-Martin, the French Mystic*, London, 1922.

In 1772 Pasqually went to St. Domingo in the West Indies, where he had been left some property. He never returned, for he died there two years later. J. B. Willermoz succeeded him as head of the rite. But he never obtained the magical effects of his predecessor. He and his colleagues devoted most of their time to the Rite of the Strict Observance, in which Willermoz became a Provincial Grand Master. It will be remembered that this rite also depends on unknown masters. The Elect Priesthood finally came to an end with the French Revolution.

The papers relating to the Elect Priesthood passed from Willermoz to his nephew, from the latter to his widow, from her to an occult student named Cavernier, from whom Papus (Dr. Encausse) obtained them.[31] The latter attempted to revive the rite.

Martinism. Louis Claude de Saint Martin (1743–1803) was a French author on occultism and mysticism. He came from an aristocratic[32] and wealthy family. His mother dying at a very early age he was brought up by his step-mother who encouraged him in his studies. He entered the army, became a Mason, and finally a prominent member of the *Rite des Élus Coëns.* He was not only influenced by Pasqually, but also directly by Swedenborg and Boehme, especially later in life. He was closely associated with Willermoz. He appears to have been of independent means after leaving the army, although at times holding certain educational appointments. He never married.

It must be remembered that Saint Martin lived in the heyday of materialism, which he did all he could to combat. Like Swedenborg he emphasised the necessity of good works, in addition to faith. He believed that a divine quality resides in humanity, and that this only needs arousing for the effects of the Fall to be counteracted. In his early days he was interested in the occult, especially in the phenomena exhibited in the Rite of the Elect Priests, but later in life displayed less interest in this and withdrew into mysticism or the development and study of the Inner Light.

Saint Martin had a large following in the last century. His ideas were studied under the title of Martinism, and there were several Martinist societies. He is said to have founded a Martinist Rite, by modification of that of the Élus Coëns. He was certainly a high member of that rite, and in his first book *Des Erreurs et de la*

31 Waite: *Saint-Martin (loc. cit.)*
32 He was not however a Marquis, as sometimes stated.

Vérité he is already supposed to be recording the wisdom of the master who appeared in bodily form in the temple of the rite, and who was called the Repairer, and supposed by some to be Christ Himself. Some of his books, including the aforementioned, were written under the pseudonym of The Unknown Philosopher.

. Now the Martinist Rite is said by several well-known authors, including Clavel and Ragon to have been founded by Saint Martin the aforementioned mystic. It has got in masonic literature as the *Rectified Rite of St. Martin,* and is said to have had at first ten grades and to have been reduced to seven. But Waite[33] tells us that it was named after the real Saint Martin, a saint of the Catholic Church, who according to legend divided his mantle to assist a beggar on one occasion. So the name merely refers to the charitable activities of a certain lodge. We leave masonic historians to argue this matter amongst themselves, but it does seem that later in his life Louis Claude de Saint Martin withdrew from lodge and temple activities.

However, even in his lifetime, he had a profound effect on esoteric fraternities. In 1773, within a masonic lodge at Paris, a *Rite of the Philalethus* was set up, a system of nine degrees, beyond the Craft. It was founded by Savalette de Langes, Keeper of the Royal Treasury, and had a very distinguished membership, including the Prince of Hesse and others of the nobility, Cagliostro, Mesmer, Court de Gebelin[34] and Saint Martin himself. They had a splendid library and a cabinet of natural history, and studied all the sciences especially the occult. There were twelve degrees, including the Craft. The additional degrees were 4° Elect, 5° Scottish Master, 6° Knight of the East, 7° Rose Croix, 8° Knight of the Temple, 9° Unknown Philosopher, 10° Sublime Philosopher, 11° Initiate and 12° Philalethes. It is obvious that they had drawn a wide field of symbolism into their rituals, and Saint Martin must have been gratified at finding his own pseudonym as the name of one of the degrees, which no doubt involved the study of his teachings. On the death of Savalette de Langes in 1788 the rite went out of existence.

Gérard Encausse (1865–1916) the well-known writer on occultism, under the pen-name of Papus, was born in Spain but came to France at an early age. He graduated as a Doctor of Medicine, in the Medical Faculty at Paris, writing a most extraordinary thesis

[33] *Loc. cit.*
[34] (1725–1784) Author of *Le Monde Primitif* 1773–84 and other works.

on Philosophical Anatomy[35] in completion of the degree. We have already noted his connection with the Kabalistic Rosy Cross, but he was interested in almost every branch of occultism, and wrote extensively thereon. He was not a Mason, but claimed to have been initiated into Martinism by his friend Henri Delaage, author of a work on secret societies. The latter obtained his knowledge from his maternal grandfather De Chaptal, who claimed to have been initiated by Saint Martin himself. It is probably a case of passing on of certain papers, rather than a ceremonial initiation.

The Order which Papus established was called *Ordre des Silencieux Inconnus*. It had three degrees, and after taking the third a member was able to enrol new members. It appears that this was sometimes done by post. There were no fees, and the Order spread rapidly in several countries. In 1902 a large proportion of the American members broke away and formed an association admitting Masons only. Several other splits then occurred. During the First World War Dr. Encausse died of illness contracted whilst on war service.

[35] *L'Anatomie Philosophique et ses Divisions précédée d'un Essai de Classi-fication méthodique des Sciences anatomiques*, Paris, 1894.

CHAPTER XXX

THE DIVINING ROD AND THE PENDULUM

Dowsing. The term *rhabdomancy* means divination by means of a rod, and refers to one method among very many used in divination generally. The particular use of a rod for finding water, metals and other substances among the rocks of the earth is called *dowsing.* As this is most frequently used for finding water it is often referred to as *water-divining.* The operator, called a water-diviner, holds a cleft stick in his hands, usually one branch of the Y-shaped stick in one hand, the second in the other, whilst the third or free end dips downwards and forwards. When at work he wanders about and the stick moves of its own accord, presumably by involuntary muscular action. As this is not yet understood, the phenomenon must be classed as occult. Many modern students of the subject believe the movements are due to the action of unknown or incompletely known radiation. Others suggest it is due to occult faculties, comparable with those of clairvoyance, telepathy, etc. It must be emphasised that the operator must not make any voluntary movement, he must aim at being passive and must allow himself to be acted upon by influences from without or within, in fact he may be in a condition analogous to a trance.[1]

Not everyone can be a successful water-diviner. There are varying degrees of sensitivity.

Basil Valentine (late 15th century), best known as an alchemist[2] in one of his lesser known works[3] devotes a considerable portion of his text to divining rods, and describes seven different rods, corresponding with the seven planets.

Baron de Beausoleil (*d.* 1643) a foremost authority on mining, travelled widely with his wife, also sharing his knowledge, in Europe and America. They used divining rods and rings. They were suspected of sorcery and persecuted, as we have seen. In her

[1] A. Wiesinger: *Occult Phenomena in the Light of Theology,* London, 1957.
[2] See chapter on Alchemy.
[3] *Novum testamentum,* known from the posthumous French translation, Book 2, 1651.

book *La Restitution de Pluton*, 1640, the Baroness gives five methods which she and her husband used for detecting water and deposits of ores *viz.* (i) digging; (ii) looking for certain types of plant; (iii) tasting waters flowing from ore deposits; (iv) noting vapours which arise from ores when the sun rises and (v) the use of instruments, the latter including the seven planetary rods of Basil Valentine and sixteen other kinds.

Robert Boyle (1627–1691), noted physicist, a believer in metallic transmutation, is the first to describe the divining rod in England.[4] He mentions that it was a forked hazel twig, and the movement was involuntary. A dipping of the rod indicates the presence of ore below the operator.

Radiesthesia. Whilst the forked divining rod has long been used in field work, and is not likely to be superseded for that purpose, a number of new instruments have been introduced for more critical work. The material of which the rod is made makes little difference. The wood of peach, willow, hazel and witch-hazel has been favoured in the past. Among animal substances whalebone has been used frequently. Tromp[5] describes a loop-shaped wire as efficient. Maby used a rod, bent at right angles at $\frac{1}{3}$ to $\frac{1}{4}$ from the end; the shorter part swivels inside a hand-grip. The horizontal part tends to swing inwards on entering a dowsing zone. Many other shapes of rods are described by Tromp.[6] Artificial dowsing instruments are useless, unless they are motivated by human activity.

It is the *pendulum*[7] which is used for precision work. It was formerly used in India, and its present form usually consists of a strong but flexible thread $4\frac{1}{2}$ to 6 inches in length, with a ring or knob at the top[8] for holding it, and a weight, usually conical and pointed downwards, at the lower end. The latter may be made of wood, ivory, whalebone or metal. In fact it makes no difference of what it is composed, although if of metal Mermet[9] recommends an alloy of metals, which he has patented for this purpose, because it

4 Spence: *loc. cit.*
5 Whilst divination with the rod has been called *rhabdomancy*, Tromp (*Psychical Physics*, 1949) has coined the term *pallomancy* for divination with the pendulum.
6 *Loc. cit.*
7 *Loc. cit.*
8 Not essential and not always used.
9 *Principles and Practice of Radiesthesia*, 1935, trans., London, 1959.

is a combination of metals rarely met with in nature, which he thinks is advantageous. He also makes his pendulum weight hollow, to contain a *witness*. The latter is widely used with the pendulum, either in it or near it. It is a sample of material, usually liquid, as like as possible to the material being sought after. Thus if one were prospecting for natural oil, one would place a sample of this oil in the weight of the pendulum, or hold a vial of it in one's hand. The witness is thus used to fix *intention*.

Among the French workers with the pendulum, during the first half of the present century, it became clear that they were dealing with sensitivity to radiation, and Bouly coined the term *radiesthésie* for this phenomenon in 1927. Later in the same period the word was translated into English as *radiesthesia*. This implies sensitivity to radiation, and response to radiation. Both the sensory impressions and the movement which is the response are unconscious for the most part. But as dowsers do feel conscious sensations it is probable that the unconscious impressions are sometimes accompanied by feeling (i) that certain muscles are contracted (from small sense organs in the muscles called *kinaesthetic organs*), (ii) cold (from small sense organs in the skin) and (iii) pins and needles sensation (*paraesthesia*) which is a sensory response of abnormal and sometimes a pathological state of affairs, (iv) of nausea due to stimulation of endings in the hollow viscera (*coenaesthesia*) and of (v) headache due to changes of blood pressure in the head.

The main indications of the pendulum are usually three in number, (i) parallel backwards and forwards, (ii) clockwise circular revolution and (iii) anti-clockwise circular revolution. Elliptical movement is intermediate between (i) and either (ii) or (iii). Seldom does (iv) rotation occur, because this would twist the thread. The meaning of these movements varies with the operator. Each operator has to learn by experience what a particular movement means to him. Usually a movement of revolution means an influence, and a rotation backwards and forwards is neutral. Clockwise movements often indicate something beneficial to man, and anti-clockwise the reverse, but this does not always apply.

The pendulum has been studied in France, in the first half of the present century, mainly by Catholic priests, and not only for finding water and minerals (Mermet) but also in medical diagnosis. Since 1935 a number of societies have been established, as well as many journals, especially in France, and the first British Congress[10] was held in London, 1950. The scientific study of the radiations affecting living things has been termed *Radionics*. Many physicians, scientists and engineers have assisted in the development of this new science.

Some extraordinary claims have been made in this field of investigation. With the aid of *witnesses* a very wide field of investigation has been opened up, and finally there has been developed an entirely new method, whereby results are obtained, not by wandering about with a pendulum, over the countryside, but by using this instrument over a map or photograph, which is said to give results as good as those obtained in the field. Tromp[11] rightly claims that this involves clairvoyance, and he thinks the pendulum only serves to bring the operator into a trance-like condition. Very successful results were recorded by the Abbé Mermet with maps, even though he was a most renowned field operator. This indirect method is termed *teleradiesthesia*.

Theories of Action. Most of the later workers assume that radiation of some kind is emitted by minerals, plants, animals, including human beings and also by many artificial products. They also believe that the diviners or operators are sensitive to the radiations. But we will survey the chief theories that have been put forward in the history of the subject, noting that some of these theories are not necessarily incompatible with one another.

1. P. Melancthon (1497–1560), best known in connection with the Reformation, was one of the few "reformers" who interested himself in occultism. He believed that there was a sympathy between certain trees and certain metals and minerals, and therefore that twigs of such trees could be used to find these ores.

2. A. Kircher (1601–1680) a German Jesuit Father, whose extensive scientific writings have already been referred to, advanced the theory that "the movement of the rod is due to unconscious muscular action."[12] He actually carried out experiments in 1654 to show this.[13] He balanced the rod, so that it could move practically without friction. Water and metal were then placed in various positions in the vicinity. No movements took place at all, and Kircher concluded that the rod itself was not active, that it must be moved

---

[10] *Proceedings of the Scientific and Technical Congress on Radionics and Radiesthesia,* London, 1950.
[11] *Loc. cit.*
[12] Tromp, *loc. cit.*
[13] Spence, *loc. cit.*

by the human being, and as the latter was not consciously willing to move it, its action must be due to unconscious movements. This conclusion is universally accepted by scientific workers, whatever other views they may hold on the subject. This finding is supported by the observation, first noted by J. de Royer[14] in 1674, that the nature of the material forming the rod has practically no importance.

3. In 1781 P. Thouvene,[15] physician to King Louis XVI, suggested an electrical theory of the movement of the rod, and in 1791 Galvani made his famous discovery that electricity had something to do with the movements of isolated frogs' muscles when brought into contact with two different metals, an observation to which his attention had been drawn by his wife. This led to more recent theories[16] dependent upon the idea that the rod or pendulum can be used to detect differences in electrical potentials occurring naturally.

A. E. Baines, in a work[17] published in 1918, described experiments on natural electrical potentials. His conclusions were (i) that non-living things usually have zero potential, although many of them can be artificially charged with electricity and (ii) that living things contain charges of different kinds, positive and negative in different parts, these charges being preserved by insulating membranes, which remain intact during life. An apple, for instance, has a stalk and core negative, the flesh positive.[18] There is a membrane separating and insulating core and flesh, and another outside (the skin). When the apple is cut these charges begin to be lost, and after a time the apple, without its charges, becomes inedible.

4. A number of authors[19] ascribe dowsing phenomena to the reception, by the human body, of short Hertzian waves. For instance Lakhovsky[20] had geranium plants which he infected with a bacterium which caused on them certain growths. Two lots of plants were then observed, one the control, the other treated with electric wiring which generated Hertzian waves of two metre wave

[14] Tromp: *loc. cit.*
[15] Tromp: *loc. cit.*
[16] For details see Tromp: *loc. cit.*
[17] *Studies in Electro-Physiology*, London, 1918.
[18] See figure in original or in Wethered, *An Introduction to Medical Radiesthesia and Radionics*, Rochford, 1957.
[19] See especially experiments recorded by J. C. Maby and T. B. Franklin in their *The Physics of the Divining Rod*, 1939.
[20] G. Lakhovsky: *The Secret of Life*, 1932, trans. 2nd ed., 1951.

lengths, and only the plants so treated recovered. He then invented a *multiple wave oscillator* which utilises such waves for curing disease in man. But if man be sensitive to this kind of radiation, it may explain dowsing. J. C. Maby has long claimed to explain dowsing in this way. In 1934 and 1936 J. Wust and W. Wimmer in the University of Münich, Germany, published extensive works designed to show that dowsing is due to the hitherto unknown effect (called by them *Magnetoism*) of waves of between 0.9 cm. and 52.4 cm. wave length. They tested most of the chemical elements, and found a different wave length radiation was emitted from each.

5. A French worker with the pendulum, A. Bovis, apparently believed that matter of all kinds, such as metals, micro-organisms, plants, animals, blood, secretions and drugs, emit waves of small wave-lengths, as he claimed to measure such in Angström units.[21] The waves are different in diseased tissue. The measurement was made in a simple apparatus called a *biometer*. This consists of a rule, marked out to correspond with the aforesaid units. The specimen is placed at zero point on this. The pendulum is placed over the rule, and a point found at which it oscillates transversely. This gives the reading. This apparatus and method is still used, but more recent workers prefer to speak of degrees Bovis rather than commit themselves to the hypothesis that the readings actually give Angström units.[22]

6. In 1933 A. de Vita reported experiments which suggest a greater degree of atmospheric ionisation (independent of moisture) in regions where the sensitivity of the dowser occurs. R. Jemma in 1934 confirmed this.[23]

7. The most modern theory of radiesthesia maintains that radiation is produced from everything, and that what the dowser experiences, when the rod or pendulum moves, is a change in radiation.

Od, Odyle or Odic Force. Baron Karl von Reichenbach (1788–1869), a German industrial chemist, who first extracted paraffin and creosote from wood tar, carried out and recorded[24] some interesting experiments with specially sensitive human subjects.

[21] One Angström unit $= \dfrac{1}{10,000,000}$ of a millimetre.

[22] Wethered, *loc. cit.*

[23] Both sets of experiments are quoted from Tromp, *q.v.* for references.

[24] *Odisch-magnetische Briefe*, Stuttgart, 1852, translated under the title of *Letters on Od and Magnetism*, London, 1926.

Reichenbach found that such sensitives can feel a cool current near the north pole of a magnet, and in the dark distinguish a bluish vapour or flame. From the south pole a warm stream and orange colour were emitted. But this phenomenon is not confined to magnets. It is well demonstrated on rock crystal; one end of the crystal sends out the cool blue emanation, the other the warm orange one. Many other substances show similar phenomena. A few substances produce other colours, gold and silver emit white, cobalt blue, and copper and iron red. If the sensitives remained in darkness two or three hours they could detect light from plants and animals. The human body also appeared to glow, the right side (especially the extremities) shone blue, and the left orange. The sun, moon and planets were supposed to emit, besides their ordinary light, some sort of additional emanation, which could be detected by sensitives in suitable experiments. The radiation causing these phenomena was called Od, Odyle or Odic Force, and distinguished from electricity, magnetism and known physical radiations. They were named after the supreme god Odin, of Northern mythology, as ruler of all nature, because they appeared to be universally distributed. Reichenbach's experiments were confirmed by De Rochas (*b.* 1837), noted French hypnotist and psychic investigator, and by William Gregory (1803–1858), a professor of chemistry in Edinburgh University.

The Human Aura. In 1911 Walter J. Kilner (1847–1920) a physician of St. Thomas's Hospital, London, published a book entitled *The Human Atmosphere,* a second edition of which came out in 1920. In this he claimed that the human body is enveloped in a mist "the prototype of the nimbus or halo." It had long been visible to clairvoyants, but hitherto no one else had seen it. By Kilner's method, which depends, he claims, on natural science alone, it is open to inspection by all, and ninety-five per cent of those who tried it, under his supervision, could see it. The author had previously been interested in N-rays, and their effect on calcium sulphide.

To see the aura, as the human atmosphere is generally called, two methods were used : (i) to look at the body through a screen of two layers of glass between which is interposed a *dilute* solution of a dye,[25] (ii) to look through two layers of glass, between which

[25] Other ways of using the chief dye were found to be unsatisfactory as gelatine or collodion stained with the dye caused the latter to decompose almost at once.

is *strong* solution of the dye, at some bright object, then to look at the human body without the screen. The latter method, the author warns us, must not be used for more than one hour daily, otherwise the eyes become very painful.

The dye used for seeing the aura as a whole was originally dicyanin. It was used in alcoholic solution. Later workers have discovered other dyes that are equally, if not more, satisfactory. For some purposes Kilner also used carmine. H. Boddington discovered a glass of the same colour as Kilner's dicyanin. This glass is made in Czechoslovakia. It can be placed in goggles, thus dispensing with the liquid solution of the dye.

Psychometry. The word *psychometry,* which today is sometimes used in its literal sense, merely for the measurement of psychic faculties, was coined in 1842 by John Rodes Buchanan for a special faculty. Buchanan was at one time a lecturer to medical students in an American college, and he noticed that drugs and metals had a psychological effect on himself, so one day he tried experiments with his students. He found the majority, some eighty per cent, were affected. They could distinguish metals merely by touching them, without other tests. He found that drugs held in the hand gave some effects similar to those which would have been produced had they been administered as medicines by the mouth, although to only a slight degree, and temporarily. Further, diagnosis could be made very frequently, in various diseases, if the student merely held the patient's hand for a short while. If an object belonging to some person, even if enclosed in a cover, were held against the forehead of the operator, the latter could often tell quite a lot about the person concerned. Letters written by the subject were most productive of results, in spite of the fact that the operator could not see the writing. Personal details obtained in this way were often so detailed as to prove embarrassing. The operator could even imitate the subject's facial peculiarities and mannerisms. Buchanan became convinced that every object carries its history, that this history is preserved in an etheric or astral counterpart of the object, and is retained indefinitely. Professor W. Denton (*d.* 1883) a geologist, collaborated in these experiments. He found one man in every ten was quite sensitive, and four women in ten. Denton gave his subjects meteorites and fossils. In this way he confirmed cosmic, geological and evolutionary theories and developed new ones. For instance, from a few fossil bones, a sensitive could reconstruct a picture of the environment in which an extinct animal lived, its food, and even its external appearance.

Buchanan to some extent foreshadowed Kilner's discoveries of the human aura, and the alleged investigation of brain structure from radiation. We hear of him also in connection with phrenology.

CHAPTER XXXI

MESMERISM AND HYPNOTISM

Animal Magnetism. Everyone nowadays has at least a vague notion of hypnotic phenomena, especially how a person may be influenced by another, by means of movements, touches and fixed looks. Ancient bas-reliefs from Egypt show an operator making passes in front of a subject, and there is little doubt that the action is hypnotic. There are also figures showing the laying on of hands.[1] There are even pictures indicating that mass-hypnotism was used. Gindes refers to a Greek engraving showing the centaur Chiron placing a pupil under hypnosis.[2] Imposition of hands was for two purposes, *viz.* (i) initiation, or the passing on of power, and (ii) healing. Both were the prerogatives of priests and kings. Healing by what was known as the *royal touch* survived in England until the reign of Queen Anne or later.

The hypnotic trance was also known in ancient times, as for instance in the *temple sleep* prescribed for invalids in the Temple of Aesculapius in classical times.

In the Middle Ages a number of authors refer to a universal magnetic fluid by which living beings influence one another, much in the same way, it was thought, that the planets influence plants, animals and men. This view was held by Pomponatius and J. B. Van Helmont. Somewhat similar views were put forward by Paracelsus, Kircher, K. Digby and Fludd.

In 1679 Gulilemus Maxwell wrote on magnetic medicine, following a suggestion of J. G. Burggrar in 1611 that the mumia of Paracelsus was really magnetic in its action. In 1673 Sebastian Wirdig had said that many cures were effected by an all pervading *spiritus vitalis.*

There is no doubt that many successful healers have operated by mere touch, or the use of some simple means of appealing to the imagination. Valentine Graterakes or Greatrakes (1629–1683) an Irishman was one of these. At the age of thirty-four he dreamed repeatedly that he had a gift of healing goitre by touch. He tried it

[1] This practice is mentioned in the Ebers papyrus, second millenium B.C.
[2] B. C. Gindes: *New Concepts of Hypnosis,* London, 1953.

and was very successful, then extended it to numerous other diseases. He became famous, and went to London, and for a time was at Court. He left a record of his cures. Later J. J. Gassner (1727–1779), a Catholic priest, became famous in South Germany for his remarkable cures. He used a diamond-studded crucifix, and performed exorcisms as well as ordinary cures. He even caused other remarkable phenomena, such as making uneducated peasants suddenly speak long passages in Latin, and altering the pulse rate and stopping it for a while. He was visited by Mesmer.

F. A. Mesmer (1734–1815) was the discoverer of what he termed *animal magnetism*, and which his followers termed *mesmerism* in his honour. Mesmer was born near Lake Constance, on the border of Switzerland, and although originally intended for the priesthood, he studied medicine in the University of Vienna. He attained his doctor's degree with a thesis entitled *The Influence of the Planets on the Human Body* in 1766. Such a subject was remarkable at that time, and it was probably only acceptable because one of the leading professors, Van Swieten, although famous in medicine, was also interested in the occult. Mesmer was also acquainted with M. Hell or Hehl (1720–1792), a Jesuit, who was Professor of Astronomy at Vienna. Hehl was experimenting with large steel plates and magnets, and loaned some of them to Mesmer for his medical work. The latter found that the magnets were very effective in curing certain patients. Mesmer reported this to Hehl. Shortly afterwards Hehl published some account of the healing power of magnets, much to the disgust of Mesmer, who thought an astronomer had no right to interfere with medical matters. At first Mesmer cured by contact with magnets, then he found that contact was not necessary, and finally that objects other than magnets would produce the same effects, provided they had been charged, as he believed, with magnetic fluid. The latter, he concluded, is also present in the human body, and could be conveyed by touch.

Antagonism having been aroused in Vienna, Mesmer went to Paris. Here he acquired a large following, and he held his séances in a large room. A large bucket containing bottles of water was placed in the middle. Iron rods were dipped into the water at one end, and were held by patients at the other. Mesmer wore a lilac robe and carried a magnetic wand. Plaintive music was played. Many of his patients went into convulsions, but remarkable cures were effected.

The Medical Faculty of Paris soon became alarmed at these strange proceedings, and clamoured for the government to take action. Two commissions were appointed to investigate the matter. One consisted of members of the Faculty of Medicine and of the Academy of Sciences, together with a few independent persons. It included the eminent Benjamin Franklin,[3] the notorious Dr. Guillotin[4] and the ill-fated Lavoisier.[5] The other commission was drawn from the French Royal Society of Medicine. Both reported unfavourably. The first admitted that favourable results might accrue, however, from imagination. A little later Mesmer left Paris for Germany. He died at Morsburg and apparently was more appreciated there, as his German colleagues erected a monument over his grave.

But Mesmerism did not die. It continued to interest many, among whom were some outstanding physicians. It gave rise to two schools of thought : (i) the physiological, which considered that it was due to physical factors, magnetic or akin to magnetic, affecting the human body; (ii) the psychological, which maintained it was due to mental factors. As the former school is now practically extinct we will consider it first.

Metallotherapy and Magnetotherapy. Dr. Elisha Perkins (1741–1799) was a successful medical man in Connecticut, U.S.A. He was the delegate of his county to the Connecticut Medical Society in 1795 and to them he reported a discovery he had made. It was the effect of metals on living tissues particularly muscles and nerves. When a muscle is touched by metal it suddenly contracts. When a metallic instrument is used to separate the gum from a tooth, prior to extraction, pain suddenly stops. Perkins had tried various metals and combinations of metals for relieving various affections. Finally he had evolved (and later patented) his *tractors.* Each consisted of two rods of metal, closely bound together, one end was rounded, one pointed, one side was curved in a semi-circular form, the other side was flat. One of the two metallic components was composed of copper, zinc and a little gold, the other of iron, silver and a little platinum. These instruments were to be drawn away from the pained part towards the extremities. In obstinate cases friction had to be applied to cause redness and even some degree of inflammation. It was important not to draw the tractor towards the affected area. Frontal headaches were cured

[3] Noted for his electrical experiments, American visiting Europe.
[4] Inventor of or rather advocate of the guillotine, and a strong upholder of capital punishment.
[5] Noted for his chemical experiments; he was guillotined during the Revolution.

by drawing from the forehead over the head, then down the back of the neck, and so downwards. The Medical Society was sceptical and soon after the patent had been taken out he had to resign.

Perkins died prematurely of yellow fever, but his son, a Yale Master of Arts, sold the tractors in England and wrote a work on the subject.[6] A work on the subject was also issued by physicians in Copenhagen. J. Haygarth of Bath, however, claimed that wooden tractors painted to look like the genuine article, produced the same results.

Several eminent physicians have maintained that magnets do influence the human body. This was the view of J. Elliotson (1791–1868), J. B. Luys (1828–1897) and J. Charcot (1825–1893). They were all shown, by visitors or assistants substituting imaginary objects for real magnets, that the same results could be obtained by suggestion.[7]

Charcot was soon convinced that magnets were not necessary for the production of mesmeric phenomena, nevertheless he continued to regard the effects as due to physical causes, the nature of which was admittedly not fully known. Moreover he regarded these phenomena as identical with hysteria, and he pointed out that the mesmerised person, like the hysterical one, often goes into a state of lethargy, or falls into a cataleptic trance, and even into a condition of sleep-walking (somnambulism). This view has been abandoned by later investigators, since the aforesaid conditions are not the only ones, or even the chief ones, found in the mesmeric condition.

It need hardly be necessary to remind the reader, at any rate if he is old enough to remember the early years of the present century, that there was formerly quite a trade in magnetic appliances for curing every kind of human ill. Such advertisements are rarer than they used to be, but at one time there was a considerable market in magnetic belts, magnetic vests and even magnetic rings.

In the early days of electricity it too was regarded as a sort of magical power. Dr. James Graham (1745–1794) had at one time a so-called Temple of Health in London (first in the Adelphi and later in Pall Mall). Therein was a wonderful bed, charged with electricity, perfumed with vapours and illuminated by coloured lights. Married pairs were allowed to sleep therein (for a huge

[6] B. J. Perkins: *The Influence of Metallic Tractors on the Human Body*, London, 1798, also later edition.
[7] Or so the stories tell, yet these yarns bear a suspicious resemblance to one another, and also to the supposed de-bunking of Blondlot's N-rays.

fee) with the object of begetting beautiful and intelligent offspring. Whether the beauty and intelligence were the result of the electricity, the odours, or the coloured lights is not clear.

Hypnotism. The first break with the physical idea of mesmerism is due to the Abbé de Faria (1755–1819). After spending some time in India Faria returned to France and practised medicine in several Paris hospitals. He denied the existence of a magnetic fluid and said that the so-called magnetic sleep and other phenomena of a mesmeric nature were not due to the operator, but depended on some change in the subject. Towards the end of his life he defended this view in a book.[8]

Another early worker was the Marquis de Puységur (1751–1825) who practised mesmeric healing gratuitously on his estate at Bugancy, France. He is generally credited with discovering mesmeric somnambulism, and believed that in this condition his patients developed clairvoyance, telepathy and other occult powers. De Puységur was the first to draw attention to what is now termed *post-hypnotic amnesia,* the ability to forget about what happens during mesmeric treatment. He was also claimed to be the first to discover artificial somnambulism, *i.e.* sleep-walking state induced by hypnosis. He even suggested that telepathy and clairvoyance could be developed during magnetic sleep.

The mesmeric trance (now called *hypnotic catalepsy*) during which rigidity of muscles can be developed to an extraordinary degree was discovered and investigated by Pététin of Lyons in 1787. A person in this condition may be laid flat, resting only on the back of the head and the ankles, for a long period.

Another French occultist who was interested in mesmerism, and who also had a hand in starting the movement now called spiritualism, was Baron du Potet (1796–1881) who came to England and gave instructions to others.

Among those influenced by Du Potet was John Elliotson (1791–1868). He was a professor at University College Hospital, but when he began to use mesmerism he was forced to resign. He founded a mesmeric hospital in 1849. He believed in clairvoyance and phrenology, and sought to combine these with mesmerism. He was the founder and president of the Phrenological Society and wrote about phrenology in his book on physiology.

J. Braid (1795–1860) a Scottish surgeon practising in Manchester was an outstanding investigator of mesmeric phenomena, who

[8] *De la Cause du Sommeil lucide,* Paris, 1819.

proved Faria's contention that everything depends on the subject's nervous condition. He used, for example, pressure, slight strain and bright light to obtain the right state. He coined the term *neuryp-notism*, which he afterwards abbreviated to *hypnotism*. Elliotson and Braid performed a number of surgical operations under hyp-notic anaesthesia. Other surgeons also used it. The first to do this was probably J. C. A. Récamier (1774–1852) in 1821. It must be remembered this was before the days of chloroform and other anaesthetics. When these came into use hypnosis became unneces-sary, and went out of use, as being difficult and uncertain, except in some cases of childbirth where it was sometimes used ("twilight sleep") from the belief that chemical anaesthetics might be bad for the child. Hypnotic anaesthesia has lately been revived to some extent, but has several obvious disadvantages.

J. Esdaile (1808–1859) a medical officer of the East India Com-pany used hypnotic anaesthesia for surgical purposes in India. He had a small hospital at Calcutta where this method was adopted, and the work went on for some time. In 1836 C. Poyen lectured on mesmerism in the U.S.A., introducing it widely in that country.

J. Milne Bramwell (*b.* 1852) a leading English hypnotist drew attention to the fact that, under hypnosis, a subject may be able to notice stimuli which are too weak to affect him when not under this influence (*hyperaesthetic perception*).

Suggestion. A. A. Liébeault (1823–1904) a physician who began practising at Nancy, France, in 1864, became the leader of what was known as the Nancy School, in opposition to the Salpêtrière School of Charcot. Whilst the latter maintained the physical theory, Liébeault was convinced that hypnosis was due to mental factors. He introduced the term *suggestion*, defining it as the transmission by words or gestures of ideas to the mind of the subject. It is true that he assumed that the latter was in the sleeping condition, but to get the patient into this state of rest it was soon realised that ideas also play a part. This view soon became widely accepted. It does not explain how ideas affect physiological processes, or why the ideas are accepted, but it does express the view that ideas, not physical forces, are what are transmitted in hypnotic phenomena. The modern view, that ideas can be unconscious, has contributed to the success of the theory of suggestion.

H. Bernheim (1837–1919) a professor in the University of Nancy, strongly supported Liébeault, and himself hypnotised a vast number of subjects. He was the leader of the Nancy School.

H. E. Beaunis (1830–1921) a physiologist and psychologist, who established at the Sorbonne the first French laboratory of experimental psychology was another famous follower of Liébeault.

J. R. L. Delboeuf (1831–1896) a philosopher and psychologist in Belgium worked on hypnotism, and was remarkable for making blisters and burns disappear by suggestion.

A. H. Forel (1848–1931) psychiatrist and entomologist was a well-known hypnotist in Switzerland. He found he could regulate the monthly periodicity of the human female by suggestion.

In Germany eminent hypnotists included : R. P. H. Heidenhain (1834–1897), Professor of Physiology in the University of Breslau;[9] W. T. Preyer (1841–1897), Professor in the University of Jena, known for his work on child psychology and A. Moll (b. 1862) psychiatrist and writer on sex and the occult, whose textbook on hypnotism is well-known.

Auto-suggestion. Émile Coué (1857–1926) was a French pharmacist who met Liébeault in 1885 and began to practise hypnotic suggestion. He gradually became convinced that all suggestion is *auto-suggestion.* This would explain, he maintained, why different subjects and different operators vary in their susceptibility to one another. He started a campaign to teach people to use auto-suggestion for their own welfare, as well as for helping others. In all this work, he claimed, it is not the will of the subject, but his own imagination, which is responsible for obtaining the effects. To influence the imagination Coué used parrot-like repetitions. His teaching spread widely and the Neo-Nancy School, for training, was established in 1910. Later the Coué-Orton Institute was founded in London.

[9] Father of the noted histologist, whose haematoxylin stain is well known to biologists.

CHAPTER XXXII

PALMISTRY

Bodily Form and Fate. The two oldest studies, purporting to elicit a relation between mind and body are *palmistry* which attempts to read character and fate on the palm of the hand, and *physiognomy* which judges from the face. The latter does not degenerate into fortune telling so frequently as the former, which is rather notorious in this respect.

Palmistry. Palmistry was practised in very early times. It was certainly known in India and in classical Greece. Aristotle has many references to the hand and its supposed significance. There is also the story, related by E. Heron-Allen,[1] that Aristotle, whilst investigating archaeological remains in Egypt, discovered a book on palmistry upon an altar dedicated to Hermes in that country. It was written in Arabic in letters of gold, and Aristotle presented it to his patron, Alexander the Great. Later it was translated into Latin by Hispanus, and an extremely early manuscript of the translation was found by Heron-Allen in the British Museum.

The same author quotes Juvenal and Quintilian, the latter referring to the gesture-language of the deaf and dumb.

The branch of palmistry purporting to predict the future is called *cheiromancy.* It goes in a long list of other forms of divination, all of which are condemned by the Catholic Church because prediction of the future invalidates man's free will. Of course more cautious palmists may say that the hand only indicates tendencies,[2] but many are not so particular as to specify this.

It was probably in the Middle Ages that palmistry assumed its modern form. Apart from divination it is divided into two branches of study. The first of these is *cheirognomy.* This deals with the shape of the hand and the character of the fingers, their relative size, etc. The second branch of study, *cheirosophy,*[3] deals with the

[1] *A Manual of Cheirosophy,* 8th ed., London, 1896.
[2] Heron-Allen, *loc. cit.*
[3] Heron-Allen, however, makes cheirosophy synonymous with palmistry, and divides it into cheirognomy and chiromancy, the latter of which is our

lines on the hand, and the spaces between them, on the occult principle of analogy.

Solistry. The ancient Chinese used the foot as well as the hand for their determinations of character and destiny. Many of their conclusions were probably just, as they dealt with the rank and profession. They used lines and marks, such as we use in palmistry, but in addition could distinguish specifically oriental symbols, such as the tortoise, bird, trees, flowers, books, scissors and pieces of embroidery.

Graphology. P. Aldorisio invented *graphology* in Naples in 1611. It is the science of reading character from handwriting. This is one of the subjects that has developed considerably in recent years. There is no doubt that handwriting is useful in medical diagnosis, as diseases may affect the muscular control of the hand.

Aldorisio in the same year and place also brought out another new science that has never been followed up. It was called *gelato-scopy* and consisted in a kind of divination from laughter, the chief classification of the different kinds of laughs being based on the vowel sounds. Surely some of our psychologists ought to follow this up! Both graphology and gelatoscopy were regarded by their author as parts of natural science.

---

cheirosophy. Edward Heron-Allen (1861–1943) wrote also on the barnacle myth and was known as a naturalist, specialising in Foraminifera.

CHAPTER XXXIII

THEOSOPHY AND OCCULT SCIENCE

Theosophy. This word means divine wisdom, or according to Mme. Blavatsky the wisdom of the gods. It was not uncommonly used by mediaeval theologians, was particularly applied to the teachings of Boehme, and was also used for the system of Swedenborg. It thus applied to an esoteric approach to higher or inner worlds and the unseen generally. It will be remembered that an early Swedenborgian society was termed *theosophical.*

But today the term *theosophy* is usually applied, in a more specific way, to the belief or teachings promulgated by the Theosophical Society founded by H. S. Olcott and Helena P. Blavatsky in the United States in 1875, and which is now a world-wide organisation.

Colonel Olcott (1832–1907) was an eminent agriculturalist and prominent barrister who took an interest in the occult in early life. He was the first president of the society and wrote on psychic research and Buddhism. He met Mme. Blavatsky in 1874.

Helena P. Blavatsky (1831–1891) was a Russian of princely family. At the age of seventeen she married General N. V. Blavatsky who was then in his forties. She soon left him, and travelled in Egypt, India and Tibet. She was interested for a time in spirit phenomena. She is believed to have met certain adepts, afterwards called the Masters, and thereafter was guided by their instructions. She went to America and, after founding the Society with Colonel Olcott, the two of them went to India, where the headquarters of the Society were eventually established, at first in Bombay, moving to Adyar, near Madras, in 1882, which is still the centre. In 1877 Mme. Blavatsky first published her *Isis Unveiled,* an attempt to show that the ancient mythology of many peoples contains the basic principles of a rational religion. More important still, in 1888 two volumes of her great work: *The Secret Doctrine* appeared. After her death a third volume was added. Finally a still more complete edition was produced by her followers. The work is a commentary on *The Stanzas of Dzyan* said to be from *The Mani Koumboum,* the sacred scriptures of the Dzungarians, who inhabited the Dzungarian mountains in the north of Tibet. The commentary expounds the successive manifestations of the Supreme Being in a series of worlds and the successive periods of beings in such worlds, and shows how man evolves in a succession of incarnations, ending up in the bliss of Nirvana. *The Secret Doctrine* is an enormous work of great erudition, touching upon many points of religion, philosophy and science in a manner that, when it was published, was altogether novel to Western civilization. Even now it is a puzzle to serious commentators although it has come in for attack from several. Madame Blavatsky also produced psychic phenomena, which were adversely reported upon by the Society for Psychical Research. She was a crowned Princess of the Ancient and Primitive Rite of Adoption.

After the death of Mme. Blavatsky, and the resignation of the first president, there was a dispute as to whom the authentic messages of the Masters were coming. One large section numbering three quarters of the Society broke away, under the leadership of W. Q. Judge (1851–1896), who was succeeded by Katherine A. Tingley (1847–1929). This organisation, long called *The Universal Brotherhood* established its headquarters at Point Loma, California. There were several other schisms. What became the main society expanded greatly and spread into many countries. By 1938 there were no less than 43 national societies, all branches of the main organisation. Some of these disappeared during the Second World War.

Modern Theosophy owes much to the labours of Annie Besant (1847–1933) and C. W. Leadbeater (1847–1934). They modified certain crudities in Mme. Blavatsky's teaching. They also founded various organisations, based on theosophy, the best known being (i) Co-Masonry, which was supposed to be a purified rite, but which admits men and women to the same degree unlike ancient masonry, and (ii) the Liberal Catholic Church, which maintains the sacraments, but does not insist on dogma and (iii) the Order of the Star in the East which was intended to herald the coming of a new Messiah. These have not been popular with many theosophists, but they are not officially part of the Theosophical Society. Annie Besant was second president of the Society and Leadbeater presiding bishop of the Liberal Catholic Church.

The objects of the Theosophical Society are to form a nucleus for universal brotherhood of man without distinction of race or creed, to encourage the study of comparative religion, philosophy and science, and to investigate the unexplained laws of nature and

the powers latent in man. No member of the Society is compelled
to accept the teachings, but a general body of belief is held by most
and available to all ready to accept it.

Anthroposophy. Rudolf Steiner, Ph.D., Vienna (1861–1925), a great
commentator on Goethe, and an exponent and upholder of Goethe's
scientific views, became associated with the theosophists in 1902
and was later a leading figure in the German section of the Society.
He preferred to describe the universe and man in German terms,
rather than in the Sanskrit, so much used by most theosophical
authors. When in 1912 Leadbeater was putting forward a young
Indian as World Teacher, a matter that caused a great sensation
at the time, Steiner withdrew from the Society and founded the
Anthroposophische Bund, now a widespread movement, represented
in England by the Anthroposophical Society. Steiner was an inde-
fatigible worker. He not only concocted a view of the cosmos and
man, with its own terminology, and different in detail from the
theosophical, but tried to combine with Christianity, reviving some
old heresies and inventing some new ones of his own. He encouraged some of his followers in establishing a new religious
sect, called the Christian Community (*Christliche Gemeinschaft*),
which bore the same relation to the Anthroposophical Society as
did the Liberal Catholic Church to the Theosophical Society. He
wrote on a great many subjects. He evolved a new form of architecture, which was exemplified in a huge wooden building at
Dornach in Switzerland, burnt down in 1922.[1] He invented a bio-
dynamic system of agriculture, a new form of medicine, produced
new ideas in education, industry, natural science and politics.
Special schools, works, laboratories, clinics and farms, worked on
these new ideas, were established by his followers. *Eurhythmy*[2] was
a new art invented by Steiner; it was based on the connection of
bodily movement with mental and emotional states. He also produced mystery plays.

Numerology. We have seen, in the ancient branch of kabalistic
science called Gematria, that the letters of the Hebrew alphabet
corresponded with numbers, and were used to signify the same. Now
the idea was, in quite early times, extended to the Greek and
Latin alphabets, and as the Latin is the alphabet used in most
European countries, and those that are exceptions (Russia, Greece)

[1] Rebuilt in concrete 1925–1928.
[2] Not to be confused with the *eurhyhmics* of Jaques-Dalcroze.

use the Greek, it means that any word in a European language can be converted into a number. Now numbers are symbolical and what they signify is supposed to be connected with each name. Thus from your own name you can get a number. If the number is above ten some numerologists will add up the digits composing it.

It would be too large a task to enumerate the symbolism, even of the first twelve numbers in any detail. In fact it would require a book in itself.

The Development of Man. We now come to two purveyors of the marvellous who lived for a considerable time in Russia. G. I. Gurdjieff (1867–1949) was a carpet dealer and originally, in all probability, an Armenian. Little is known of his birth or early life, but he acquired a considerable fortune through trade in the East, and is supposed to have visited Tibet, Turkestan, Persia and other Eastern countries. At the time of the Russian Revolution he was teaching occultism in Russia. Later he was in the United States and finally set up a centre at Fontainebleau, near Paris. He taught a peculiar cosmic system, but his main idea was that human beings are not fully conscious. He devised activities, involving close contact with nature and dancing combined with concentrated bodily control, in order to bring his pupils to a more highly conscious state and a more advanced development. The majority of human beings are, he thought, more than half asleep all their days, and it is impossible for them to attain the higher harmonious condition, which is reached only by his successful pupils. Towards the end of his life his great work began publication. It was called *All and Everything* and the first series aims to destroy beliefs and views rooted for centuries in the human race. Appropriately enough it has, as one of its titles, *Beelzebub's Tales to His Grandson* and takes the form of a conversation taking place on a space ship travelling through the cosmos. This appeared in English in London, 1950.

The other Russian was P. D. Ouspensky (1878–1947). He was with Gurdjieff for a long time in Russia, but eventually broke away from his group for personal reasons. He thought highly of Gurdjieff's teachings. Ouspensky has written works on philosophy. The first was an attempt to rewrite philosophy. It will be remembered that Aristotle wrote great classics of logic called the *Organon*. Much later Francis Bacon wrote *Novum Organum* in which he revised Aristotle's idea and introduced the inductive method of interpreting nature. So Ouspensky called his work *Tertium*

Organum in which he uses the fourth and higher dimensions to complete the description of the Universe. Later he wrote *A New Model of the Universe* and *In Search of the Miraculous*. He holds a peculiar idea of immortality, according to which, when a person dies, he passes backward in time and becomes another person. Two persons can change places. In this way a single life may be really repeated by more than one individual. It need hardly be said that this queer idea has no grounds in any sacred tradition. His ideas of matter also have no relation whatsoever to scientific chemistry.

J. G. Bennett, a contemporary English writer has made known the views of these two Russians, but has lately become involved in a movement called *Subud,* which is repudiated by some of the other followers of Gurdjieff and Ouspensky. Alice Bailey, a prominent theosophist, and Gurdjieff both predicted an important teacher was to come in the future. Gurdjieff once told Bennett to look for such a teacher in the East Indies. Now in 1901 Muhammed Subuh was born in Java, and he, in his twenty-fourth year had a wonderful experience. A ball of light, brighter than the sun appeared, and entered into his body through the crown of his head. Thereafter he became aware of certain spiritual changes, and was able to pass on to others this ability to change. The process is called *the latihan.* Anyone who received this spiritual power from Subuh, could be delegated to pass it on to others. Bennett and others invited Subuh to Europe, and a group was formed. Their symbol consists of seven concentric circles, marked by seven equidistant radial lines. Bennett believes that the latihan opens up the higher centres of man, a process that Gurdjieff was trying to effect by more laborious means.

INDEX

f after a number denotes a footnote

Mantras, 149
Mareth, R. R., 23 and f
Marqués-Riviére, 67
Martinism, 291
Mass, The Black, xxvii, 240–257
Mathers, MacGregor, 287
Mathers, S. L. Macgregor, 258
Maunder, E. W., 21 f
Mead, G. R. S., 119 f
Megalithic Temples, 33
Meganthropus, 15
Melancthon, P., 297
Memphis and Mizraim, Rite of, 283–285
Menhirs, 32
Merlin, 34, 168
Mesmerism and Hypnotism, 303–309
Mesolithic culture, 19, 20
Meteorites, 38, 39
Metallotherapy, 305
Minoan Civilisation, 113
Minos I, 115
Monuments of Egypt, 47, 48
Moses, 77
Mosheim, J. H., 216 f
Mother, The Great, 18
Mummy, 43
Murray, A. Margaret, 246 f

Napoleon, 265
Narwhal, 25
Neolithic culture, 19
Newton, Isaac, Sir, 264
Nostradamus, 260
Numerology, 314
Nymphs and Satyrs, 118–119

Occultism, What is?, 14
Od, Odyle or Odic Force, 299–300
Odin, 126
Ogham alphabet, 101
Ogres, 15
Olympians, 114
Olympic Games, 113
Olympus and the Satyrs, xv, 113–125
Oracles, 115–117
Oracles (Tibetan), 152
Ouspensky, P. D., 315
Oxford, A. W., 81 f

Pagoda, 139
Pa-Kwa, 137, 138
Palaeanthropus, 16
Palaeolithic Culture, 15
Palladium, 39
Palladium, Order of the, 278
Palmistry, xxxii, 310–311
Paracelsus, 208, 209
Patanjali, B. S., 60
Peet, T. E., 32 f, 33 f

Peladan, Sar, 225
Penates, 119
Pepper, J. H., 159 f
Phallic Worship, 57
Pharaoh, 41
Pipe, 25
Pistis Sophia, 98
Pithecanthropus, 15
Plotinus, 123
Ponape, 36
Pontifices, 154
Pope Joan, 156
Popes, 157
Popol Vuh, 52
Precession of the Equinox, 21
Preuss, K. Th., 23 and f
Proclus, 125
Prostitution, Sacred, 56–57
Psychometry, 301
Ptolemy, 21
Pyramids of Egypt, v, 41–48
Pyramids of the New World, vi, 49–54
Pythagoras, 120
Pythagoreans, 119

Radiesthesia, 295–297
Randolph, P. B., 224
Regardie, I., 84 f
Reincarnate Lamas, 150, 151
Relics, 140, 155
Renaissance Astrologers, 189–193
Rite des Elus Coëns, 290
Roheim, G., 23 and f, 24
Rome and Byzantium, xix, 154–159
Rosary, 26
Rose-Croix, 223–4
Rosicrucian Manifestoes, 217–220
Rosy Cross, The, xxv, 216–225
Russian Court, Magic at the, 268–273

Sabbat, 245
Sacrifices, 53
Saint Martin, L. C. de, 291
Saintyres, P., 161 f
St. Germain, Comte de, 280
Sastri, H. K., 59
Sceptre, 24
Scotus, Duns, 186
Seabrook, W. B., 27 and f
Serpent, 58
Serpent Worship, 89
Sex Magic, 66–67
Shamanism, 28, 29
Shepherd Kings, 42
Shinto, 140, 141
Shipton, Mother, 260
Sinanthropus, 15
Sinistrari, L. M., 249